THE LAW AND ETHICS OF THE PHARMACEUTICAL INDUSTRY

Biography

Prof M.N.Graham Dukes is a physician and international lawyer, holding both Netherlands and British nationality. He is Professor of Drug Policy Studies at the University of Oslo, Norway, and Emeritus Professor of Drug Policy at the University of Groningen, The Netherlands.

From 1958 to 1972 he was engaged in research in the Pharmaceutical Industry, latterly as Research Manager of a multinational company. From 1972 to 1982 he was Medical Director of the Netherlands Commission for the Evaluation of Medicines, and from 1982 to 1993 head of the Pharmaceutical Programme of the World Health Organization (Europe) at Copenhagen, Denmark. Within WHO he initiated and managed as a research project *The European Studies of Drug Regulation*. Since 1993, alongside his university duties, he has worked as consultant on drug policies for the World Bank, the World Health Organization and various bilateral donor organizations, serving in many countries to develop and implement drug policies and legislation; in the legal field he has assisted in numerous cases in Europe, the U.S. and Japan involving drug-induced injury.

His publications include the Editorship of the international reference work *Meyler's Side Effects of the Drugs* (since 1975) and the complementary *Side Effects of Drugs Annual* which he founded in 1977. He also wrote *The Effects of Drug Regulation* (WHO, 1987) and was lead author of *Responsibility for Drug-Induced Injury* (1990, 1998) and *Drugs and Money* (WHO, 2003). He is also Editor of the *International Journal of Risk and Safety in Medicine*. He has published some 250 scientific papers on research, policy, law and economics in the field of medicines.

The Law and Ethics of the Pharmaceutical Industry

By

Graham Dukes
MD MA LLM

Professor Emeritus of Drug Policy Studies
University of Groningen
Lecturer in International Drug Policy
University of Oslo

ELSEVIER

Amsterdam – Boston – Heidelberg – London – New York – Oxford
Paris – San Diego – San Francisco – Singapore – Sydney – Tokyo

ELSEVIER B.V.
Radarweg 29
P.O. Box 211, 1000 AE Amsterdam
The Netherlands

ELSEVIER Inc.
525 B Street, Suite 1900
San Diego, CA 92101-4495
USA

ELSEVIER Ltd
The Boulevard, Langford Lane
Kidlington, Oxford OX5 1GB
UK

ELSEVIER Ltd
84 Theobalds Road
London WC1X 8RR
UK

First edition 2006

British Library Cataloguing in Publication Data
A catalogue record is available from the British Library.

Library of Congress Cataloging-in-Publication Data
Dukes, M.N.G. (Maurice Nelson Graham)
 The law and ethics of the pharmaceutical industry/Graham Dukes.–1st ed.
   p.   cm.
 Includes bibliographical references and index.
 ISBN: 0-444-51868-1 (alk. paper)
 1. Drugs–Law and legislation. 2. Pharmaceutical industry–Moral and ethical aspects.
 3. Pharmaceutical industry–Standards.   I. Title.

K3636.D853 2005 2006
174.2'951–dc22   2005052580
ISBN: 0-444-51868-1/978-0-444-51868-2

∞ The paper used in this publication meets the requirements of ANSI/NISO Z39.48-1992 (Permanence of Paper).
Printed in The Netherlands.

Preface

Any sector of society has both its written and unwritten rules of behaviour, which develop and change as time goes by. That applies to science, manufacturing and commerce as it does to any other area of human activity. The rules may be universally agreed and widely respected, or they may be controversial and applied only in part or only by some of those concerned. At their best, however, they are analogous to the rules of play in a game, setting procedures and standards to which the participants should adhere. They serve on the one hand to ensure that the activities of a sector can proceed logically and smoothly in the common interest, each participant knowing the steps by which he can proceed and the standards to which he is supposed to conform and can reasonably expect others to conform as well. The rules of behaviour will also serve to ensure fair play; they will not protect any party from risks inherent in the field in which he engages (such as those of commercial failure, financial loss or genuine scientific error) but they should prevent misunderstandings, and provide some protection against deceit or hidden dangers; they may also help to safeguard a party from the worst consequences of its own errors.

Many rules of proper behaviour tend to emerge and develop progressively in the light of experience, at first in a quite informal manner. They may reflect what is widely perceived as common decency or an "ethical" standard in one's dealings with others; perhaps more often they reflect practices which are found to be convenient and helpful for all concerned and are at the same time acceptable for other sectors of society. At a later phase, once the rules have been widely accepted and applied, they may be consolidated into written codes or even confirmed officially in laws, regulations and international agreements. Exceptionally, such official measures may have to be imposed on a sector where standards and rules have failed to emerge spontaneously or are not respected sufficiently to safeguard the interests of society; it is however, well known that legal measures are most likely to succeed where there is already broad acceptance of their principles.

Where the rules applicable to trade and industry are concerned, the business of developing, making and selling pharmaceuticals merits special consideration. It is a prominent and constantly expanding sector of commerce, but also one which is immensely powerful and influential in the entire process of health care. Above all, because of the nature of the products with which it is concerned, it is one with an unequalled potential to do good or harm in entire populations. Such power and influence bring with them social and moral duties; genuine respect for the pharmaceutical industry's achievements is today balanced by concern and criticism regarding its more questionable activities and practices, particularly in matters where commercial interests and the broad public interest do not run parallel.

The nature of pharmaceuticals has changed several times in the course of history and it continues to evolve, but some of the best and worst characteristics of the field have remained very similar over long periods. When William Withering in the eighteenth century developed extracts of the foxglove as a treatment for disorders of the heart, he set standards of practice to which any modern pharmaceutical corporation might be considered to be bound. Beginning with meticulous observation and analysis of certain practices in folk medicine he developed a hypothesis which he proceeded to study and confirm by careful experimentation; he found a means of assuring and maintaining the quality of the remedy which emerged from his work; and he communicated his findings and advice in a responsible manner to the medical world at large. Conversely, the charlatans who at the same time were selling supposed remedies for phthisis on the streets of London represented a tradition of commercialized quackery which, to the detriment of society, had long existed and which has persisted in some measure, on the periphery of society, ever since.

The rules of behaviour that may be considered to apply to today's pharmaceutical industry have emerged over a very long period and the process goes on. Even the immensely detailed standards for quality, safety and efficacy laid down in drug law and regulation during the second half of the twentieth century have their limitations as tools for ensuring that the public interest is well served. In particular, national and regional regulatory agencies are heavily dependent on industrial data for their decision-making, their standards and competence vary, and even the existing network of agencies does not cover the entire world. What is more there are many other areas of law and regulation affecting the industry, concerning for example the pricing of medicines, the conduct of clinical studies, the health protection of workers and concern for the environment. In some fields it is indeed hardly possible to maintain standards through regulation. In seeking to ensure, for example that research to develop new medicines is sufficiently attuned to real public and medical needs, public policy will have to operate by means other than the creation or imposition of written law.

There are also useful sources of standards other than official rules. One can look to the codes of practice developed within the walls of industry itself, principles laid down by judges in the course of litigation, and many thoughtful proposals advanced by others which can point to an emergent consensus. One should also examine some of those standards which have long been basic to the practice of medicine and pharmacy and which by analogy are applicable to an industry that has assumed a major role in health care. In addition one must study legal and other rules which have developed in related fields, such as those concerning employment in chemical plants, the humane treatment of laboratory animals, or the labelling of food products. On the way one will need to look carefully at some current sources of disagreement on what has been or should be attained and at some obstacles to reform. Above all one must seek to determine which unwritten rules may be distilled from the day-to-day practice of individual companies and to what extent these would appear to be constructive, realistic and more broadly attainable. In all these matters one must strive to be objective, seeking a balance between those valid interests which may not be fully compatible with one another and avoiding those biases which may have been created or encouraged by the subtle machinery of lobbying and persuasion.

This book does not represent an attempt to create *de novo* any universally applicable set of rules; rather it brings together those which are largely in use already, either because they have been formulated explicitly or because they are recognized and applied instinctively by so many who work in the field. In some areas – notably that of drug regulation – the written rules run already to many hundreds of pages, and it would be pointless to repeat them in detail here; it is more important to examine the principles that underlie them and the extent to which the rules are consistent and effective. As far as day-to-day work in the field goes, a long series of interviews (as well as less formal conversations) with those who work inside the pharmaceutical industry or in close contact with it, have been very informative. By examining the matters on which a broad consensus exists at one level or another, or at least seems to be dawning, one can identify the norms which are largely in use and on which a formal agreement seems to be necessary and attainable. In some areas where science is undergoing marked change, as in biotechnology, entirely new ethical questions are coming to the fore and need to be answered at least provisionally if the law is to keep pace with life. Rules should be there to lubricate progress and not to stifle it. Good law and sensible regulation are needed, in the interests of the pharmaceutical industry itself as well as those of patients and populations across the world.

Graham Dukes
Oslo, Norway, August 2005

Table of Contents

Acknowledgements

In compiling this book I have been encouraged and supported by many experts and critics both within and outside the pharmaceutical industry and trade. My conversations with them have been frank and open, and I respect the fact that the views and facts made known to me have often been presented and documented confidentially. In a field where controversy is rife, often reflecting the fact that reliable information is hidden, or at least hard to come by, this willingness to talk behind closed doors has been of immense value.

The literature relevant to the various aspects of this theme is vast; a selection of the most helpful material will be found in the list of references. I would particularly like to mention here just three authors. Two decades ago, Dr John Braithwaite of the University of Canberra provided an important impetus to the study of these issues, both in the course of conversation and through his books on corporate practices; his *Corporate Crime in the Pharmaceutical Industry* threw important light on some of the less desirable ventures of the industry down to 1984 and helped me in identifying initially some of the areas in which reform and rethinking already seemed to be in progress. Similarly, I owe a transatlantic debt to the work of Norman Bowie of the Center for the Study of Values of the University of Delaware; a philosopher's thinking on matters of business ethics provides a most valuable structure for analysing and tackling the challenges of an entire sector. Judith Richter's excellent volume *Holding Corporations Accountable*, though it centres on the transnational corporations supplying breast milk substitutes, is a modern classic on the governance and control of commercial firms operating in the field of health. Many other writers from whom (and sources from which) I have benefited are listed among the references. I owe a special word of thanks and admiration to Ellen 't Hoen and all my other friends in that splendid organization Médécins sans Frontières who are doing so much to ensure that the world of medicine – and of medicines – becomes a better and fairer place.

Particularly where issues of drug injury are concerned, certain short sections of this book were originally derived in part from the complementary volume *Responsibility for Drug Induced Injury* (Second Edition, IOS Press, Amsterdam, 1998) and I owe a debt of gratitude to my co-authors of that volume, Prof. Mark Mildred (England) and Prof. Barbara Swartz (USA). A number of passages which I contributed in 2003–4 to the report of the Working Group on Access to Drugs of the United Nations Millennium Project have also found their way in amended form into this text, and I would like to acknowledge the input which I received in this way during debates in that Group.

    Finally, I must express my gratitude to many whose work has been fundamental in the practical preparation of this volume. The original concept for the book in its present form grew out of meetings with Ms Joke Jaarsma of Elsevier whose enthusiasm and support for my published work in the field of medicines over a period of nearly 30 years has been a constant source of inspiration and encouragement. Ms Joke Zwetsloot, also of Elsevier, has been forthcoming with patient guidance and assistance throughout the preparation of this book. And all the time my family has put up with me, but has also been a fertile source of ideas, information and original thoughts; thank you, everyone.

Graham Dukes

List of Boxes, Figures and Tables

PART A:
THE DEFINITION OF STANDARDS

Chapter 1

The Pharmaceutical Industry and Its Products

1.1. The Concept of a Pharmaceutical Product

The pharmaceutical industry is essentially one which supplies the community with what are known technically as "pharmaceutical products". The latter have for different purposes been defined in different ways, but for any broad discussion some of the existing definitions are likely to prove too narrow and too static.

In the broadest possible sense a pharmaceutical product, known in everyday usage simply as a "medicine" (or less accurately as a "drug") can be defined as *a substance or a complex of substances which is administered to man or to animals in order to prevent, diagnose, alleviate or cure a disease, to relieve a symptom, or to modify bodily function in some way*.

Traditionally, for many centuries, pharmaceuticals largely comprised herbs or their derivatives or extracts, and less commonly materials of animal or mineral origin (Mann 1984). At the present day most of them are largely based on substances created in the laboratory or mixtures of such substances, only a few being obtained from the plant or animal world. In the foreseeable future, however, a fair part of the market may well be accounted for by substances or tissues prepared by genetic engineering, i.e. by a modification of biological processes in living organisms. Techniques currently in development, such as the introduction into the human system of modified genes, may further change concepts as to what constitutes a pharmaceutical product, but they will still fall under the broad definition given above; most of the questions which they raise are likely to be very similar to those raised by the currently more familiar type of medicine. The same will undoubtedly hold good for new and as yet inconceivable approaches to medical treatment emerging in the future; so long as there are both exploratory and industrial elements involved in their development, manufacture or sale, they will raise familiar issues: Do they work? Are they safe? Are we getting to hear the truth about them? And couldn't they be rather cheaper?

The definition of a pharmaceutical product used here, like some of those to be found in national law, is also sufficiently broad to include blood products, sera and vaccines, as well as products meant for veterinary use. It could also be considered to extend to some products used to prevent or treat diseases of plant crops ("phytopharmaceuticals") because at some point they may enter the human system in the form of residues. Some of these groups of products have customarily been dealt with under separate legislation, but that is mainly because rather different types of expertise may be required to deal with them, or because they fall administratively under different government agencies; the legal and ethical issues relating to them are not basically different to those arising when one considers medicines of the most familiar type administered to man.

There will always be borderline products which may or may not be regarded and dealt with as pharmaceuticals. Is a vitamin supplement a food or a medicine? An ordinary food or a cosmetic may in some instances be on the borderline, especially when it contains substances which have a biological effect or when it is claimed commercially to have some medicinal value. There have been debates as to whether pharmaceutical laws should apply to "street drugs" such as marihuana, or even to tobacco or alcohol, at least for certain purposes (see Section 9.9.9). Contraceptives can, on the other hand, reasonably be regarded as being intended to "modify bodily function" and thus as falling under the definition of pharmaceuticals, at least if they are "administered" rather than being used externally (as with condoms and other purely mechanical devices). Finally, there are still divergences in national practice as to whether or not the starting materials for making a pharmaceutical product should fall under the same ethical and legal rules as do finished products ready for use. All these issues arise daily and decisions often have to be taken *ad hoc* on individual products.

A minor problem is that of nomenclature, at least in English. The term "pharmaceutical product" or simply "pharmaceutical" is administratively and legally clear in any language but it is not in popular use. In the United States such a product is often termed a "drug", but that term is confusing since it is also used for illegal substances sold on the street as stimulants or hallucinogens, or for controlled substances falling under special international conventions because of their addictive or other potentially dangerous properties. In Britain and most other English-speaking countries, the term "medicine" has come to be preferred and it has also been adopted in recent years by the World Health Organization and other international bodies. Corresponding terms are to be found in most other major languages; in French the term "médicament" corresponds to the English "medicine"; German refers to an "artzneimittel" (literally a medical agent), Dutch to a "geneesmiddel" (a curative agent) and the Scandinavian languages to a "legemiddel" (a treating agent). All these terms are clear, especially since in each language separate words have come into use for products used in complementary or alternative therapy which to a greater or lesser extent (and rightly or wrongly) fall outside the formal rules governing pharmaceutical products.

1.2.   The Development of the Pharmaceutical Industry

Throughout much of history, both in Europe and other parts of the world, knowledge as to the preparation and use of remedies was traditional and slow to change. Most of the plants and other sources from which medicines were compounded were familiar and available everywhere in the countryside. Many plants, for example, contain atropine-like substances, widely used in traditional medicine as sedatives, anti-diarrhoeal agents or mydriatics and even put to use as hallucinogens, widely distributed in the plant world. Knowledge of the use of plants in medicine thus resided largely with ordinary country people, who could gather their materials and make their remedies in the home, although "healers", apothecaries, physicians and members of religious orders often had a particular (and sometimes secret) knowledge of particular plants and treatments. In so far as one could speak of a pharmaceutical industry it was largely a home or cottage activity.

Progressive urbanization, from the late middle ages onwards, was one important stimulus to the development of a specialized industry and trade in medicinal products. Much of the population lost its direct contact with the land and with the world of plants and became dependent on the makers and sellers of remedies. Among them were mere charlatans and pedlars, seeking a rapid reward from the sale of remedies which they knew were worthless. On the other hand, there were the apothecaries who became increasingly recognizable as a profession specializing in the making and dispensing of drugs according to established recognized standards. To some extent, indeed, apothecaries banded together to establish an embryonic industry. In England, the Worshipful Society of Apothecaries of London was established by Royal Charter on December 6, 1617 (Copeman 1967); by 1623, the Society had established a laboratory for the production of galenical and vegetable substances. In 1671, the Society found it necessary to equip in addition a chemical laboratory to produce and test the remedies of chemical (generally mineral) origin which were by then coming into favour and which could in this way be supplied at reasonable cost and to an acceptable standard to the retail apothecary. The step from such activities to the establishment of a true pharmaceutical industry was a small one. In the eighteenth century, The Society of Apothecaries acquired a monopoly for the supply of medicines to the Army, the Navy, the Crown Colonies and the East India Company, maintaining its own herb gardens for the purpose (Copeman 1967). It was the experience gained in such work that led a number of apothecaries to establish their own pharmaceutical manufacturing operations, some of which survive to the present day (Mann 1984).

Such developments, which had their parallels in a great many other countries, continued throughout the eighteenth and nineteenth centuries. In Europe, the era of inorganic remedies (based largely on arsenic, mercury and lead, which had been in use in medicine in some other cultures for a much longer period) provided what proved to be largely a false – and toxic – trail, but almost at the same time, the discovery of smallpox vaccination by Jenner and his underestimated contemporaries (Dukes 1987) opened up a dramatically new approach to the prevention of virus-borne diseases. William Withering's systematic development of digitalis from a secret folk remedy to a reliable medicine provided a further route to innovation in medical treatment. Working in a similar way, Magendie in France was able to assimilate morphine, veratrine, brucine, emetine, quinine and strychnine into the practice of orthodox medicine (Magendie 1822). All these substances, once they had been defined in this way and provided with published descriptions of their mode of preparation, lent themselves to extraction and standardization on an industrial scale.

The most decisive breakthrough of the nineteenth century was, however, the realization that the synthetic organic compounds which were now emerging in increasing numbers from the laboratory could have promising and sometimes dramatic applications in medicine. Justus von Leibig discovered both chloral and chloroform in 1831 (von Leibig 1832) though it was typical of the rapid developments of the period that others appear to have made the same discovery at about the same time (Mann 1984). Paraldehyde was introduced as a narcotic in 1884 (Cervello 1884), and the antipyretic agent antipyrine appeared in that same year, the latter opening up the era of the non-narcotic painstillers (Filehne 1884). Four years later, sulphonal was introduced as a soporific (Kast 1888) which was to pave the way to the barbiturate sedatives. Two other mileposts were passed in the early twentieth century. One was the demonstration of the antisyphilitic effect of arsphenamine by Ehrlich's group in 1909, which initiated an era of anti-infective chemotherapy (Ehrlich and Hata 1910); the other, 20 years later, was the demonstration of the antibiotic potency of penicillium cultures by Fleming in 1929, which heralded the antibiotic era (Fleming 1929).

All these and similar developments, together with the aftermath of the industrial revolution in Europe and North America, reflected the emergence and rapid growth of an active research-based pharmaceutical industry in the late nineteenth and twentieth centuries. The German dye industry, which was in the forefront of organic synthesis by the latter years of the nineteenth century, and the "drug houses" founded by apothecaries and pharmacists in Great Britain and the USA, formed nuclei around which the pharmaceutical industry as it currently exists was able to develop.

The further development of this industry in the twentieth century has largely parallelled that of other enterprises exploiting technology in the public interest. Like those other industries it was particularly stimulated by the technological spin-off from the Second World War, the economic boom of three decades which followed and the rapid development of science, industry and the consumer economy in some hitherto underdeveloped parts of the world. It benefited however, more substantially than any other industry, from a vigorous public demand for its products. The constant call for new and better means of treating and alleviating disease, and the willingness to pay large sums of money in return has made the pharmaceutical field an attractive one for investment and development; despite the uncertainties involved in much of the research which has to be undertaken, the rewards have often been very substantial. The pharmaceutical industry has become, and remains even during periods of recession and in spite of the controls imposed upon it, one of the most profitable sectors of commerce. It sometimes experiences substantial setbacks but these tend to be short-lived and to be confined to certain firms; in the long run, it is only likely to grow by adjusting its course so as to seize the successive opportunities which the health market has always provided and will no doubt continue to deliver.

1.3. The Unique Nature of the Pharmaceutical Field and the Need for Rules

For a long period, the lawmakers saw no particular reason to interfere with the new industry. Pharmaceutical regulation had existed for many centuries but had primarily been concerned with the exercise of the pharmacist's profession and the practice of retail pharmacy, and not with individual medicines. The authorities were alerted from time to time to the malpractices of the charlatans and nostrum-makers (see Section 9.3) but without taking action to counter them. Some acknowledgement of the need for control of the medicines field was shown in the United States with the passage of the pure Food and Drugs Law of 1906 which prohibited "adulterated or misbranded" foods or drugs from interstate commerce. The law did not, however, provide any satisfactory means of determining whether a drug was misbranded in the sense of making undocumented claims, and it soon became clear that the courts were not prepared to regard false statements about a drug made by its manufacturer as "misbranding". The Act also failed to grant the new Agency which it created the authority to ban unsafe drugs. Not until 1912 did the Congress redefine "misbranding" to include false or fraudulent claims. In Britain some regulatory control over the sale of "poisons" was introduced during the nineteenth century, but even after this was strengthened in the Pharmacy and Poisons Act of 1908 there was still no limitation on the provision of dangerous drugs or poisons provided they had been prescribed by a physician, and the pharmacist remained authorized to sell such products to persons with whom he was familiar. Not until the Defence of the Realm (Consolidation) Regulations of 1917 gave the British Government extraordinary powers during the First World War were measures taken relating to specific medicines regarded as dangerous; the sale of barbitone, morphine, cocaine and similar drugs was thereby restricted to patients for whom a physician had prescribed them. The occurrence during the War of severe adverse effects to the new antisyphilitic (neo-)arsphenamine pointed to the fact that barbitone was not the only new synthetic drug to create problems and it led to a Government enquiry but it was to be a further generation before a more generalized approach to the new pharmaceuticals was adopted in Britain or most other countries (see Section 3.5).

Since rules of behaviour have been found to be necessary within any type of business (see Chapter 2) and within the health sector and professions (Chapter 3) it is not surprising that when legislatures did finally turn to examine the pharmaceutical industry such a broad regulatory approach was adopted. Because within this industry various types of activity interact, intersect and need to be taken into account, differing interests need to be weighed against one another and some novel ethical problems and conflicts of interest can arise. In particular, while the health interest and the business interest often run parallel, they can also diverge and conflict with one another. Such conflicts have been thrown into particularly vivid profile by a series of drug-induced disasters in the twentieth century; they have been illustrated and defined in greater detail in the many thousands of cases in which patients have brought successful litigation against pharmaceutical manufacturers for alleged fault resulting in injury; many of the rules necessary to avoid or contain these conflicts have progressively been laid down in the relevant laws and regulations. When the notion of risk is emphasized however, it is well to recall that the history of the borderland between medicine and pharmaceutical commerce has been one of harmony than that of disharmony; fearful things have happened, but they are the exceptions that prove the rule, the beacons pointing to the reefs that must but also can be avoided.

The most fundamental conflict which can arise is likely to be that between the immediate commercial objective (i.e. the need to earn money and reward investors) and the primary health interest (i.e. the need to provide medicines that can maintain or restore health). An ideal pharmaceutical product would be one which in well-defined conditions reliably maintained health or either alleviated or cured disease, which introduced no new risks of any significance, and which could be made accessible and affordable to all who needed it. Very few new drugs attain that ideal in all respects. There is therefore a constant temptation to extract additional income from a drug by astute presentation (which stresses its merits and lays little weight in its shortcomings) and by opportunistic pricing. To some extent the argument commonly advanced by the industry that marketing encourages the physician to choose the best treatment for his patient is valid; the doctor is stimulated to look for interesting and significant advances in treatment and to let his patients benefit from them. Price regulation at its most constructive is designed to encourage this process. The market will, however, only function in this way if the physician receives reliable information as to the merits and possible risks of each of the drugs between which he is expected to choose. For this reason a great deal of drug regulation as it exists at the present day is concerned with the dependability of information and the reliability of the science on which it is based. The lawmaker's concern is that, if these things cannot be reasonably assured, the choice of a patient's treatment may be all too readily be determined by commercial pressures rather than by the actual merits and risks of the available forms of treatment (see Chapter 5).

The need in this field for clear rules, whether purely ethical or imposed by law, is however also a direct consequence of the fact, already touched on in the introduction to this volume, that medicines have such an extraordinary potential to do great good on the one hand, yet also to inflict serious harm on the other. In many instances extreme care is needed to ensure that a truly promising drug is developed, studied and used in such a way that it is as beneficial as it can be without proving disproportionately noxious. Repeatedly, promising drugs have made only a brief contribution to health care or none at all because at some stage they were not wisely handled by their originators or by the authorities; in such instances both medical treatment and business interests stand to lose.

1.4.   The Various Roles of the Pharmaceutical Industry Today

From its original function purely as a manufacturer and provider of medicines, the pharmaceutical industry has diversified into a wide range of associated activities. It has come to function among other things as an innovator, a provider of information and even education, a major employer and a significant player in the world economy. It is not the function of this volume to consider whether it should ideally engage in all these fields, though some current criticisms of its activities in these areas must be noted. The present starting point is the recognition that the pharmaceutical industry has entered these and other areas, and the need to consider which rules apply or should apply to its activities when it does so, in order to ensure that the outcome is compatible with the interests of the patient and of the public at large. These issues are considered in Chapters 5–8.

1.5.   Types of Industrial Firms Engaged in the Pharmaceutical Field

The firms which currently make up the pharmaceutical industry fall broadly into two groups. The one has its preferred basis in the creation and development of entirely new drugs which can enjoy a long period of patent protection; the other is engaged mainly in the production of "generic" versions of drugs which are unprotected by patent, either because they date from a much earlier era or because the patents taken out on them by their originator firms have now expired. Both types of undertaking firms can be considered to be bound morally and legally to similar standards but in some respects they must be considered separately because their range of activities differs. Some corporations within the industry are active in both areas and many also have ancillary activities, for example in wholesaling and distribution or in the manufacture of foods, breast milk substitutes or medical devices.

1.5.1. Research-based companies

The "research-based" or "science-based" sector of the pharmaceutical industry is the dominant supplier of medicines to industrialized countries. Almost all of the firms in this sector are based in these countries, a high proportion of them having acquired transnational dimensions. The sector has played only a minor role in most developing countries, especially those at middle and lower levels of development, where it has confined itself very largely to the sale of its products through local agents to relatively affluent urban populations (see Chapter 8). Because of their prominence in the western world and their emphatic corporate public relations, the research-based companies are commonly but mistakenly regarded as comprising the virtual totality of the "the industry", others often being overlooked in discussion.

The principal characteristic of these companies is their involvement in innovational programmes concentrating on the creation, identification, development and marketing of entirely new medicines. Much of this creative work is undertaken in-house, but it is striking that a high proportion of the basic discoveries involved prove in fact to have been made within tax-funded academic and institutional centres; in such cases, the pharmaceutical company acquires the rights to the essential discovery and then develops it further (e.g. through toxicological and clinical studies) to make it ripe for marketing.

The drugs emerging from this process are sold under brand names at premium prices; since the firm will in all cases have taken out patents to the invention, as a rule relating to the active substance (but also to the processes involved in its manufacture) it will generally be protected from direct competition by imitators for a period of some 20 years. During this time the price can be maintained at whatever level its originator has chosen to set, unless a subsequent product proves more attractive.

The research-based pharmaceutical industry is, as already noted, highly profitable and has for many years been the most consistently successful of all major business sectors. In many of the countries within which they operate, corporations in this sector exercise major social and political influence, particularly because of their record in attracting investment, creating employment and building exports. In part, the standards to which they are obliged to adhere are well defined in drug laws and regulations, dealing primarily with the quality, safety and efficacy of individual products. Though they are by no means faultless, these regulatory systems function reasonably well, at least in countries where the necessary infrastructure exists. In other matters, however, recent years have seen wide criticism of the research-based sector of industry and its performance, raising a series of ethical issues going well beyond those of quality, safety and efficacy. Critics, many governments among them, have called for or devised more extensive or effective powers to tackle a series of issues, in particular:

a. High prices: adherence to the commercial policy of charging whatever price the market will bear has allegedly rendered innovative drugs inaccessible to much of the world's poor population throughout the period of patent protection, and has imposed a considerable burden even on the health systems of more affluent societies (Chapter 7).

b. Reliance by some innovative firms on legal or other means to extend the protection of their intellectual property beyond the normal period of patent validity so as to delay further the onset of low-priced competition (see Section 2.2.4).

c. Excessive pressure by companies on regulatory agencies and health services so as to shift policies and decisions in a direction favourable to themselves (Section 3.5.4).

d. Allegedly disproportionate use of earnings for promotion, administration and profit as compared with research (Chapters 5 and 7).

e. Undue pressure on the medical profession and the community generally, geared to the widespread use of items which are unduly expensive, commonly replaceable and not always necessary (Chapter 5).

f. Inappropriate direction of research, with a heavy emphasis on diseases common in affluent populations, with little innovation relevant to the needs of minority groups or poor countries (Chapter 9).

g. Misinformation and use of selected data in order to gain competitive advantage (Section 3.5, Chapter 5).

Much recent activity in the field of law and regulation has been directed to examining and tackling these problems.

1.5.2.   *"Generic" manufacturers*

With the progressive expiry of patents, many of the innovative medicines developed during the late twentieth century have become accessible to any firm wishing to manufacture them; such a firm also has access to the many older medicinal substances which remain in use. The bulk of the 330 medicines listed by the World Health Organization as "essential" for ordinary needs (WHO 2003b) are free of patent protection. The "generic" pharmaceutical industry, as it is usually termed, concentrates on the manufacture of these products, commonly providing them at a much lower price than that at which they were originally marketed (MSH 2005). Pure generic manufacturers are not as a rule transnationals, but they may be based in any part of the world and have their manufacturing operations in low-cost countries from which they export widely; some are now owned by science-based transnationals. Their low costs are attributable only in part to the fact that these firms incur few costs for research and development; they reflect much more the fact that unit profits are kept low, that these firms do not as a rule engage in extensive advertising or promotion for their products, and that production is largely extent undertaken in parts of the world where overhead costs are modest as compared with those in the west.

These generalizations apart, one must note that one "generic" company may be very different from another. Major suppliers in this area are as regards the level of staffing, facilities and the quality of their products no different from orginator companies. The best firms in this field are of high repute and internationally accepted, attaining fully recognized standards of "good manufacturing practice" (Chapter 4). A minority are based in industrialized countries and a number actually choose to provide their products with brand names.

A special group of firms in this field comprises *manufacturers in countries at a low level of development,* some operating under state control to serve national supply requirements. They tend to specialize in the manufacture of generic products for profit but often operate with some form of state subsidy (e.g. acceptance of somewhat higher prices than would be tolerated from a foreign supplier). Very few generic manufacturers based in countries at a low level of development in the third world undertake the basic synthesis of the active components in their products; these are generally imported in bulk (e.g. from chemical plants in China) and the final manufacturer is engaged only in the production of the end-formulation (tablets, capsules, injections etc.), quality control and packaging.

Like the "research-based" sector, the generic industry has is critics. There are indeed a proportion of less reputable companies within this field, especially those based in countries where national regulatory and inspection systems function poorly. Importing countries therefore find it necessary to protect themselves from the products of this disreputable minority through their own drug regulatory procedures, critical procurement and in some fields through international initiatives for the certification of suppliers.

An East African country Y imported low cost pharmaceuticals from a manufacturer in India. When the national quality control laboratory reported quality defects in a number of the products, an expert group was sent to India to examine the source. It was found that the firm with which the orders had been placed possessed only office facilities and a small packaging unit. The drugs themselves were obtained from a variable number of small manufacturing operations with no quality control routines and sometimes very primitive facilities. (Interview 14)

One should however also recognize that the research-based industry has commonly sought to undermine trust in the quality of the drugs emanating from any or all of its generic competitors, seeding the perception that all generic products are "cheap imitations" and by their very nature unreliable. Particularly in the United States the research-based companies appear to have been highly influential at largely excluding "generic" supplies from the public health system, while in many countries individual purchasers are found to pay considerably higher prices than necessary to obtain medicines in their branded versions in the generally mistaken belief that these are superior in some way to their generic equivalents.

1.6. The Reputation of the Pharmaceutical Industry

For a long period, the pharmaceutical industry, and more particularly its science-based wing, has devoted a very substantial effort to building up its image with governments, health professionals and the public. Successful public relations, alongside well-documented successes in creating new "breakthrough" medicines and spectacular commercial achievements as reflected in profits and export figures, have generally created a very positive view of the industry. Running counter to this is the influence on external opinion of high drug prices or of incidental drug disasters (reflected in the sudden withdrawal of new medicines, litigation for drug-induced injury or "revelations" regarding suppression of information). At the time of writing, negative criticism based on very recent events has come to dominate the scene. Writing in America in July 2004, Marcia Angell commented that:

Over the last two decades the pharmaceutical industry has moved very far from its original high purpose of discovering and producing useful new drugs. Now primarily a marketing machine to sell drugs of dubious benefit, this industry uses its wealth and power to co-opt every institution that might stand in its way, including the US Congress, the FDA, academic medical centers, and the medical profession itself. . . . This is an industry that in some ways is like the Wizard of Oz – still full of bluster but now exposed as something far different from its image. Instead of being an engine of innovation, it is a vast marketing machine. Instead of being a free market success story, it lives off government-funded research and monopoly rights. . . . But big pharma is extravagantly rewarded for its relatively modest functions. We get nowhere near our money's worth. The United States can no longer afford it in its present form. . . . Clearly, the pharmaceutical industry is due for fundamental reform. . . . (Angell 2004b)

In Britain, a Parliamentary Select Committee, after hearing numerous expert witnesses representing many shades of opinion, advanced in April 2005 detailed criticisms of the present situation and numerous proposals for reform, involving both the industry itself and the government institutions charged with controlling its activities or liasing with it. Almost simultaneously with the Angell paper, and prior to the events concerning the adverse effects of the cox-2 inhibitors later in 2004, opinion polls on both sides of the Atlantic were showing a decline in the industry's reputation:

> . . . no industry has fallen as hard or as fast as the pharmaceutical industry, which currently shares the bottom ranks with tobacco, oil, and managed care. Some 57 per cent of poll respondents said that drug prices are "unreasonably high" and only 13 per cent described pharmaceutical companies as "generally honest and trustworthy" (NYTimes 2004)

With critical views of this nature, many supported by documentation, coming from government committees, experts and the public, and with the cost of drugs now being a major source of concern for the health community, it seems clear that legislators and regulators will be under much pressure to bring about reform of the pharmaceutical industry and of the environment within which it operates. In considering the factual evidence one must at this point seek to identify to what extent criticism of the pharmaceutical sector is justified and what form a reworking of law, regulation and ethical standards might be expected to take.

Chapter 2

Sources of Standards for Business and Industry Generally

2.1. Grounds for Defining and Respecting Business Standards

In order to examine systematically the legal, ethical and other standards that apply to the pharmaceutical industry, it is helpful to consider in the first place the standards that are supposed to apply in business generally or in various other manufacturing sectors. These have all been well studied; many of them apply literally to the pharmaceutical industry, while others impinge on it indirectly. This chapter will briefly consider the general standards of business and their origins, while Chapter 3 will examine other relevant sources of standards including those derived by analogy from the health professions.

2.1.1. General

In any form of business enterprise, as noted in the Preface, certain rules exist to govern the behaviour of the institution and those who work in it. The rules are not always clear and they are not consistently respected, but their existence is evident and the need for some sort of standard is almost universally acknowledged. The majority of the rules are not specific to a particular type of business; they are fundamental in any enterprise because without them the business cannot operate consistently or harmoniously or play a constructive and acceptable role in serving society. These general rules concern the way in which the business operates, both internally and in its environment. Other rules, underlying and complementing these product standards, are activity-related, e.g. specific to the manufacture of goods of a particular type; it is obviously improper (but also unwise) to produce an unsafe bicycle, a glue that adheres only for a short time or a newspaper that does not attempt to tell the truth.

Because business cannot operate successfully without them, many such rules tend to grow up instinctively in the course of time, reflecting practical necessity on the one hand or what is perceived as common human decency on the other. These are what may be described as "ethical" rules (see Section 2.1.3). As time goes by they are increasingly complemented by more formal rules which are adopted by the corporation (sometimes at its own initiative, at other times reluctantly in response to outside pressure), or which have simply been imposed by authority in the form of laws and regulations. Such formal rule-making will often, in effect, standardize and formalize internal norms that already exist, but that have proved to be too variable or too vague, or that have been insufficiently respected and therefore need to be restated. On other occasions, the rules have to be created outside the sector and imposed on it, for example when the needs of society, or the risks which it faces, may have developed so acutely or become apparent so rapidly (e.g. as a result of a disaster) that there is no opportunity to await the informal development of standards within the business community. Ideally, however, such externally conceived standards will at least be formulated in consultation with business so that all reasonable interests are so far as possible taken into account, leading to rules that are realistic and can be adopted willingly or even gladly.

However fast and far the law or regulation on a particular matter may have developed, they do not render a sense of ethics superfluous. While the laws of the land (and rules established in international consultation) are supposed to represent the standard of behaviour to which all citizens should adhere, they do so only within certain limits. One limit is that imposed by the generality of the law, which will never foresee any situation or provide a detailed answer to every question. Another limitation is that imposed by progressive social change; standards of acceptable behaviour change as society moves ahead, and it may be a matter of years before the written law catches up with these changes; the interpretation of the law by the judges constantly clarifies and to some extent modifies and extends the law's scope, but even this process cannot entirely keep pace with shifting and developing ideas; the law will often only incorporate new standards after they have crystallized out through a period of uncertainty. In any real situation, there will be numerous daily opportunities to take behavioural decisions, whether consciously or instinctively; many of those will be taken in conformity with the spirit of the law, whether or not its letter is clear on the matter; and that will happen because at every time and in every place there is likely to be some widely shared belief as to what constitutes proper behaviour; that belief is the essence of ethics and the mirror of the law. Sometimes it may be derived from the belief that a certain pattern of behaviour will have the best consequences for all concerned (the "goal-based" approach), on other occasions from a sense of obligation to society generally, for example as expressed in the Ten Commandments (the "duty-based" approach) and on other occasions it will arise from the feeling that one must act to respect certain rights of others (the "rights-based" ethic) (Dworkin 1977, Botros 1992, Foster 2003).

The need for ethical rules in business, irrespective of whether they are part of the written law or not, has come to concern a wide public and the mass media, for example where issues arise relating to environmental pollution, drug toxicity or "insider trading"; most of the population is after all confronted in some way with the acts, omissions and errors of big business, and therefore with consequences such as these. The content of the rules that are intended to keep business running both smoothly and safely may occupy policy makers, economists, sociologists and lawyers, but the essential basis on which they rest is very much the branch of applied philosophy often called "occupational ethics."

2.1.2. *A basis in human rights*

Of the various possible roots of personal ethics, a respect for the rights of other parties is the most concrete and helpful when one is concerned with the field of pharmaceuticals or of health in general. In some respects, the need to protect the rights of one human against the acts or faults of another has of course been recognized for centuries in civil law; the laws of tort and contract perform precisely that role in specific circumstances. What has essentially changed in the last half century is that the broad notion of positively defined "human rights" and the need to guarantee and defend those rights throughout society has been recognized as a basic principle on which many other measures rest. That realization reflected the perils of a modern society in which the weak might find themselves in the shadow of the immensely strong; that stronger party might comprise an autocratic government or equally well a massive commercial enterprise mainly concerned only with its own financial goals and ambitions. Globally, the first true milestone to be reached was the adoption of the Universal Declaration of Human Rights in 1948 by the Member States of the United Nations (UDHR 1948, Art 25(1)); the Declaration was predicated on principles of non-discrimination, civil and political rights and social and economic rights. It was believed that these rights were to be enjoyed by all individual human beings as well as by any group of society. The rights were not seen to be "gifts" to be withdrawn, withheld or granted at will; they were most certainly not viewed as a matter with which governments alone should be concerned.

One of the most basic human rights is that to health. The earliest global statement on human rights and health is to be found in the Constitution of the World Health Organization (WHO 1946). This includes the following relevant passage:

> The States parties to this Constitution declare, in conformity with the Charter of the United Nations that . . . the enjoyment of the highest attainable standard of health is one of the fundamental rights of every human being . . .

Thereafter, the right to health was recognized in a series of other global instruments. The Universal Declaration of Human Rights (UN 1948) itself affirmed that "everyone has a right to a standard of living adequate for the health of himself and his family, including . . . medical care . . .", while the International Covenant on Economic, Social and Cultural Rights and other international and regional treaties recognized in one way or another "the right of everyone to the highest attainable standard of physical and mental health" (ICESCR 1966). The right to health care facilities, goods and services mentioned in the Covenant includes a right to appropriate treatment of prevalent diseases, preferably at community level, introducing in that way the issue of access to medicines and other supplies. Several complementary initiatives were taken in the years that followed. The United Nations at an early stage conducted negotiations to develop a Code of Conduct for Transnational Corporations, but they were abandoned in 1992 under pressure from some major member states (Paul and Garred 2000). Since 2000, however it has again worked on drafts of a human rights code of conduct for companies (UNCHR 2000; see also Section 2.9), while others have further honed the concept of human rights as it applies to the health field as a whole (Mann *et al.* 1994).

Spokesmen for the World Health Organization (Hogerzeil undated) have very specifically noted that access to essential medicines is a necessary component of the fulfilment of the right to health. Mukherjee, in reviewing the current approach of WHO, has spoken of the need to provide treatment to patients because they have a human right to it, rather than because, as is the present reality in many parts of the world, they are able to pay (Mukherjee 2004). The most important facet of human rights where medicines are concerned is thus that they should be within reach of the people who need them; neither distance nor lack of money should be a barrier; that is a very practical expression of what has become recognized to a human right of access to health care. "Where medicines are concerned" means that scientific programmes should be designed to create those medicines which are needed, and that where they exist they must be distributed and supplied in such a way that they are accessible and afford-able (Millennium 2005).

Unavoidably, there are two practical reservations inherent in declara-tions of concrete rights such as these. The first is that, although in law the existence of a right for one person creates a duty for others, there is no spe-cific statement as to *who* should assume that duty. It is evident that, if there is for example a duty dawning in international law to create new medicines for neglected diseases someone has to set about doing it, and one is bound to wonder who these various writers and spokesmen had in mind. Viewed against the background of the immediate post-war period, it seems clear that all the relevant duties were to be allotted to the states parties to the Convention or the Declaration; a state may indeed sometimes be the most appropriate party to create a drug-distribution system within its borders, but states have not shown particular ability in drug research or development. When one views the various moves coming into motion at the present day, one sees that this effort to create drugs for neglected diseases is slowly being assumed by various broad and novel coalitions comprising states, institutes, voluntary organizations (such as Médécins sans Frontières) and multina-tional firms (see Chapter 8). This had not been foreseen in 1948, but it may be the most realistic approach to turning a right into a reality.

The other reservation inherent in these various expressions of duty is that one cannot expect everything to be attainable at once. The Covenant itself acknowledges that there will be limits on implementing rights because of the shortage of resources, and priorities will have to be set. Forty years after the Covenant, one can see the international community moving in the right direction, with the UN Millennium Project sketching the various means by which access to medicines can be attained in the developing world within a specified time.

Naturally, one may consider that in the world of medicines other human rights also come into play; there is a rights basis for healthy condi-tions of employment in drug manufacturing (Section 2.2.5) and perhaps also for the innovator to enjoy the fruits of his invention (Section 2.2.4), which may entail according him patent protection for his useful new medicine.

The original debates during the presentation of the Universal Declaration of Human Rights in the United Nations were much concerned with the risks presented to individuals by the acts of an unjust government authority, but as already noted the intended and actual application of the Declaration was broader. Both this Declaration itself and other international instruments which followed were solely concerned with the individual whose rights could be under threat, and not with the party from which the threat might come. With the very great influence which business in all its forms has in recent decades come to exercise over the lives of populations and over global development, the preservation of human rights has necessarily become very much a concern with respect to the activities of the commercial sector, and especially of transnational corporations, many of which are considerably more powerful in financial terms than are some developing countries (Section 2.9). Viewed in this way, one may in some situations see a pharmaceutical company as presenting certain potential threats to the individual from which society must protect him, yet as other moments as a deliverer of care, ensuring that the individual right to health is assured.

The notion that a company should be overtly concerned about these issues of human rights, and must adjust its policies and acts accordingly, has been widely aired in the business community; entire congresses, university departments and volumes of print have been devoted to it; despite this, the consequences have not always been accepted with a good grace, or at all, and some have remained sceptical (see Mathiason 2002). This could be a consequence of poor perception when matters are presented in abstract terms, a problem considered below. The practical day-to-day consequences for a modern corporation of standards stated to be derived from "human rights" and presented in a solemn UN Declaration two generations ago may be regarded in some circles as being much less significant than, for example the repercussions of a new national regulation on maternity leave for female employees. In reality, the two merely represent different stages in the emergence and the introduction into society of specific rules for which recognition of human rights provides the foundation.

2.1.3.   *The notion of business ethics*

(i) Ethics in daily practice?   It is not entirely easy to move from considering ethics and human rights to discussing the concerns about what constitutes decent behaviour for an individual or a company in day-to-day life. The concept of human rights and the need to respect and maintain them does not in any case, unless interpreted very broadly indeed, provide a complete basis for everyday ethics in business. The very notion of "ethics" is one which many an ordinary individual without a scholastic trait may find it hard to define, and when it is set alongside a discussion of human rights he may find the relevance of these things to his work inside a corporation even more difficult to comprehend and interpret. One can however reduce these things to concrete and recognizable terms, and one must do so if they are to have any practical effect.

(ii) Individual and company standards One of the welcome shifts of emphasis in the social scene of our own time is the greater interest which many people now take – whether they are in business or the professions or some other walk of life – in the broader significance of their own daily work for the society around them. From one day to another, the individual's acts and the decisions which he takes are indeed directed to the immediate goals which his immediate environment places before him. Most of the time that is all that will concern him. But there are broader questions – and sometimes it is good and necessary for the individual to put them. These immediate goals: are they right and proper goals to keep the world moving along as it should? By achieving them, large or small, shall we make the world a better place in some modest way? Or just the reverse? And when they conflict somehow with one another which way should one turn? What is the decent thing to do?

These are issues for the individual, but one can put similar questions as regards the behaviour of a corporation or an entire business sector. Following a period of accelerating liberalization, business is in our time strikingly pleased with itself. By and large, it makes a great deal of money and the wind is almost constantly blowing in its direction. Yet outside business, in this equally significant world where there are educators and professionals and plain citizens in all walks of life, but where there is often no great insight into stocks or shares, business is sometimes often looked at askance. What is it doing and why? What motivates the men with the narrow briefcases and the thousands in the offices around them? And when a Enron collapses or the billions come tumbling down, as they do from time to time, the question is put: Has it not become all too smug and self-centred? Is business working for the world, or the world working for business?

If one takes a party political view, one may pass simple judgement on capitalist business one way or the other; it is inspiring or it is loathsome, and no two ways about it; but ethicists and philosophers have no such ready answers to these questions or even to the simpler questions which a thinking person in business may put to himself when he finds time to sit and consider his role. A role is composed of goals, some near at hand and some further away, with rights and duties lining the road to those goals and a complex of rules, principles and practices pointing the way. Yet all the way there are decisions to be taken and it is the totality of those decisions on which one will ultimately be judged and – in looking back – on which the individual may judge himself. What good have I been doing? The question of ethics can be written as simply as that.

(iii) The purpose of business   Such issues are rather less problematical in those walks of life where a professional credo defines achievement in terms closely linked to doing good and earns society's gratitude almost without question. One doctor or teacher may be rather more competent than another doctor or teacher, but both will spend their lives doing good almost by definition, the one by healing and the other by teaching, and the usefulness of their work will not be questioned. For anyone going his daily round in the complex environment of business and industry it may be less straightforward. Certainly, in faithfully following out his task description the good manager keeps the wheels of business turning; he provides people with gainful employment, supplies good products to the nation, pays his contractors on time. Yet as it achieves all these things, a business still has a wide margin within which it can serve society better than it strictly need, or less well than it could. It may search for ways of contaminating the environment rather less seriously than before, while all the time supplying better mousetraps; or at the opposite extreme it may scrounge on its pensions fund, and penny-pinch on production costs by bringing in supplies from the dismal sweat-shops of Asia. Many a business is in fact, when one penetrates to the facts, found to be in engaging both in decent and less decent practices at the same time. Yet however ethical or unethical its behaviour, this behaviour does not originate from any disembodied company personality; ultimately it can be traced back to the people who make up the corporation – or perhaps to a relatively small number of them who are influential enough and who care – or who perhaps fail to care sufficiently.

In attempting to decide what constitutes decent behaviour on the part of a business – or of a given individual within that business – we have various starting points, only a few of which have yet been touched on. The Philosophers may offer us the *deontological* approach – the examination of all those agreements, contracts, rules, laws and obligations that bear on a matter; that is necessary though incomplete and it will not provide answers where the one obligation runs counter to the other. There is also the *utilitarian* approach, involving an examination of the consequences of alternative courses of action, but here too the choice is likely to be far from black and white. Either approach can derive a great deal from examining precedents, good and bad. What one must try to identify, both for the business or sector as a whole and for the individual, is an approach which, as Norman Bowie puts it, is "consistent with the nature and function of the business enterprise itself and with universal moral norms" (Bowie at p. 12) – in so far as one can identify the latter.

Why, to put Bowie's approach into an even simpler form, does a commercial company exist? Even when trying to answer that basic question one will encounter some individuals who take such a dogmatic approach as to put a broad consensus quite out of reach.

(iv) The Friedman dogma   Two classic examples of business dogmas may be briefly considered here. One is derived from the work of the American economists Milton Friedman and Theodore Levitt. In their view, the function of the corporation is quite simply to maximize profits for the shareholders. In the most extreme interpretation of that view, nothing else is of even comparable importance, and arguments as to the social duty of a business, or even its duty to the client, must be set aside unless in performing those duties there is direct benefit to the shareholders.

> In America, that view came to the fore in classic form before the Supreme Court of Michigan more than 80 years ago.[1] Having becoming a very successful manufacturer of motor-cars, Henry Ford had in a given year decided to reduce the prices of his cars. The immediate effect of this would be to reduce dividends. Certain stockholders duly brought a case against him, demanding a restoration of the level of payouts. As the judge put it in his summing up: "The record, and especially the testimony of Mr Ford, convinces that he has to some extent the attitude towards shareholders of one who has disposed and distributed to them large gains and that they should be content to take what he chooses to give. His testimony creates the impression, also, that he thinks the Ford Motor Company has made too much money, has had too large profits, and that although large profits might still be earned, a sharing of them with the public by reducing the price of the output of the company ought to be undertaken. . . . There should be no confusion (of which there is evidence) of the duties which Mr Ford conceives that he and the stockholders owe to the general public and the duties which in law he and his co-directors owe to protesting minority stockholders. A business corporation is organised and carried on primarily for the profit of the stockholders. The powers of the directors are to be employed for that end. The discretion of directors is to be exercised in the choice of means to attain that end and does not extend to a change in the end itself, to the reduction of profits or to the non-distribution of profits among stockholders in order to devote them to other purposes."

That view was not long maintained in its full rigour; it was clear to many that a business needed to serve many interests, and indeed that in some respects the stockholders would in the long run benefit if those other interests were in the short term respected. In the United States however it

---

[1] Dodge v Ford Motor Company (S. Ct Mich. 1919) 204 Mich. 459.

was not until after the Second World War that a court moved even slightly towards that view.

> In the *A.P. Smith* case in 1953,[2] the court permitted the firm in question to make charitable donations to Princeton University. It based its decision however on the view that the donations concerned could assist the University in increasing its output of graduates of whom the company could in the future have need.

Although since the *Smith* decision corporations have become increasingly active in philanthropy one must note with Bowie that, formally speaking, the judgement itself provided only a basis for donations which, given in the short term, could ultimately serve the interests of the firm and thus benefit the stockholders. Only gradually has the broad view emerged that corporations, as major elements in society, do have a true social duty to perform, distinct from the evident duty which they owe to their investors. In a sense the US Courts, in their slow acceptance of the view that companies owed society a duty, were already out of touch with developments in society. Both in tort law and in specific legislation (such as that relating to car manufacturing from the early twentieth century onwards, or in laying down particular duties for the drug industry from 1928 in Norway, 1935 in Sweden and 1938 in the USA itself), the community had long accepted that a company had other important duties in society than to reward its stockholders. One might add that, particularly in the last two decades, stockholders themselves have begun to express their concern on social issues, sometimes exerting vigorous pressure on the firms in which they invest to pay greater attention to environmental or other common interests: in Britain, corporate reporting now includes an obligation to provide extensive information on a firm's social activities (SIF 2004). The view has also come prominently to the fore that in the affairs of a company various "stakeholders" must play a role, including the staff and the company's contacts and clients; in this view the investors no longer hold an exclusive right to benefit or to interfere, although there is an evident duty on the company's part to maintain and progressively enhance the value of their property.

The social duties of a modern business can be and have been viewed from numerous other angles. Simply by virtue of being an active member of modern society, a company has numerous constraints on what it can do, no matter how powerful it may be; the term "corporate social responsibility" is now widely used, though not always in the same sense. Panyarachun (1998)

---

[2] A.P. Smith Manufacturing Company v. Barlow 1953.

has argued in simple terms to a business audience that there is a clear need at the present day to restrict to some degree, in the interests of what he terms "morality", the strict economic application of the principle of the "survival of the fittest" – in this case a situation in which a national interest or that of a population group or individual can be overridden by the interests of a corporation, simply because the latter is financially more powerful. He traces modern thinking on business morality back to the 1970s when for the first time the view began to be challenged that in the conduct of business and of the economy in general, economic value must take precedence over all other values. In the new thinking, the drive for value, profit and growth would be intermeshed with considerations of stability and social duty, and with both the input and the competing interests of a large series of stakeholders. The latter would include investors, employees, customers, communities and the environment, while hovering over the whole there would be the issue of human rights. Policies to serve all these various ends would have to be transparent, and there would have to be full accountability, through one channel or another, to the community at large.

(v) Loyalty to the company Another dogma, and one which when pressed to extremes can impede the performance of an individual's social duties when he is employed by a corporation, is that of loyalty to the firm. As a basic principle, underpinning effective leadership and promoting a team spirit, it need not be questioned, but when the principle becomes a rigid and narrowly defined standard it can obstruct progress. The difficulties arise when one seeks to consider the degree to which the individual within the corporation can and should take independent initiatives, which are not specifically required in his task description and are not merely a matter of carrying out to the letter instructions received from Executive Management. Much of the effectiveness of a firm relies on the internal atmosphere, the team spirit, and the knowledge that sensible and constructive things will be done all the time without always awaiting specific instructions.

> When I joined this big drug firm in the early 'seventies to help with Human Resource Management, I was handed several large files of "Management Circulars" – instructions on procedures and suchlike – which had been issued frequently from the time the company was set up forty years earlier. I was asked to pull them together, update them and codify them into a procedural manual so that everyone knew how to behave within the company. I remember labouring on it for weeks and finally being invited to present it at a Board meeting. The Managing Director, who was nearly due for retirement, was a wise man, much respected by the staff, and he fingered through several pages of what had become a respectable volume. Then he said: "Mr X, this is a tremendous job and you have done it very logically. But the right place for it, I think, is in the Managing Director's cupboard,

safely locked away. You have provided an instruction and a procedure for anything, an exception for nothing and encouragement for no-one. Put this out and I am not sure that anyone will dare to take any initiatives any more. They will simply put on blinkers and obey management unthinkingly. Don't you agree that this volume is rather like a set of prison regulations?" (Interview 12)

The dogma of company loyalty can thus readily mutate into one of unquestioning obedience and the belief that it is better to keep one's mouth shut. It is particularly in this situation that a company with an autocratic management style may run into social conflict through its attempting to carry out policies that reflect an insensitivity to thinking in the world outside. The staff and employees of a large company are likely to represent a cross section of society in which individual beliefs and ideals are represented; they are an excellent test panel and from which feedback on any matter can be either solicited or awaited. If that process is allowed to operate, a course of action proposed by management and proceeding through purely internal review may at the same time be adjusted, amended and improved by purely internal feedback from those who are dealing with it, but who also have a broad view of the world in which it is to be implemented, and some of the problems which it may face.

The company which we were advising had projected a major pharmaceutical–chemical development in one of the border states north of India. The environment hurdles were a great deal lower than in India itself and this seemed to mean that the original technical investment could be substantially less – the whole emissions purification plant could for example be delayed for n estimated five years. Purely economically it made sense, and the firm's own technical people felt that the principal waste materials could be sealed and dumped in what was a pretty empty region. What really turned things around was when they appointed a recruitment management for the proposed plant; he had been backpacking in the country and he seemed to know it backwards – it was he who, quite unasked, dropped on us the story of a big nature reserve, orientated to tourists, as well as the environment – that was due to be set up by the King, working with another Ministry – which was intended to save a threatened animal population and secure a future for a depressed area and an underprivileged racial minority. People had been dreaming of it for years, and for all sorts of reasons we were going to ruin it completely; but because we had walked in with tens of millions in our pocket they had kept quiet about it, afraid that we might withdraw our investment. It cost us something to move our whole project two hundred miles to the north, but people in the company warmed to the idea and we did it. (Interview 35, translated)

In a corporation which has found the right balance, there will in other words be a constant creative input at all levels of the staff but also a spontaneous corrective influence from the same quarter. This process may be one of the best means of ensuring that the firm remains in tune with society.

The doctrine of loyalty can also prove problematical if it stands in the way of what is sometime termed internal whistle blowing. A staff member who encounters some serious form of malpractice within the firm – involving, for example the acceptance of bribes or kickbacks from suppliers – should be in a position to report it in a confidential manner without prejudice to his own position. Many companies have internal procedures that are intended to render this possible, recognising that such malpractice can be injurious to the firm itself as well as to others. The issue is touched on further in Sections 2.7 and 2.8.

(vi) Distance from society   A very real problem of day-to-day personal ethics in the industrial situation is that of distance – both in terms of topography and of organization. A small merchant, trading in a traditional village, has a direct relationship to his customer. Aspects of that relationship – whether expressed in terms of decency, morality, honesty or ethics, will deter him from selling her an unclean beefsteak, installing in her kitchen a device that could well explode or overcharging her for work in her garden. Where one is dealing with a modern industrial product, the ultimate home purchaser is several commercial links – and perhaps many thousands of miles – removed from the commercial manager who releases it onto the wholesale market. The manager will obey regulations and follow written procedures, but he will not have the face of the future user in mind. The user is even more remotely removed from the worker on the factory floor who has screwed the product together. Where medicines and the pharmaceutical industry are concerned, the chain is even longer and less direct than with most other goods. As will be noted in other sections, the end-user will in the case of a prescription drug not even choose it himself or herself and may even (where the package is relabelled in the pharmacy) be unaware of its origin. The commercial director, for his part, may well regard all matters relating to the efficacy or safety of the product as having been dealt with by his research colleges or the national regulatory authorities. In such a situation, one cannot argue that the traditional interpersonal relationships provide a foundation for ethical behaviour. The staff of the pharmaceutical company are in all likelihood decent and caring in their dealings with one another, but where the acts and omissions of the corporation as a whole are concerned they can only sense that the responsibility lies elsewhere and it may be very difficult to determine where that point is located. In one of the most tragic of drug disasters, when thalidomide led to the birth of thousands of malformed children, a thorough study of the events failed to detect any individual who felt a sense of guilt, despite the fact that the tragedy could have

been prevented or at least arrested at the start (Sjöström and Nilsson 1972). Individual recollections confirm the picture:

> I joined the G. Company only in 1979, ten years after the thalidomide events, and some years after the various law cases had been closed. Various books had come out examining the events of that period. Once I got to know people well enough to talk about thalidomide it struck me how many of the long-term staff were absolutely defensive of the firm. They had seen all the published allegations about negligence and indifference and even cover-ups, but they felt it was all due to the firm's bad luck– it could have happened to any drug company, they said – no-one whom they knew was to blame for those problems. . . . As to the victims, well people just said they were "out there" somewhere and one only read about them . . . (Interview 35)

(vii) The attitude of management   The response of the business community as a whole to the move for "social responsibility" in business, and to the pressures in this direction from governments, the public, the media and others, has been distinct, though variable and often hesitant. Some firms have shown themselves more anxious to engage in image-building than in true reform – a serious temptation since there is an entire profession devoted to building images on command. There is still no wide consensus among businesses as to how much regulation can be accepted on behalf of the common good, or what degree of self-discipline can be adopted without a firm jeopardizing its need to grow and to function efficiently. Some standards for the social accountability of business in various fields have been developed at meetings and under the auspices of international agencies, though it is often unclear what their influence is. Ultimately, real change seems most likely to come where many individuals within a business realize that that there is a need for such change, and that many forms of business will be better for it. The pharmaceutical industry is not the only one in which fundamental changes in behaviour are likely to be required and can to prove beneficial to the community as a whole. As Panyarachun (1998) has put it:

> Ethics and business are not adversaries. In the long run, they need each other. The market cannot be sustained by economic value alone. It requires a set of ethical standards to make the market not a place of exploitation, but of mutual gain. In the midst of change and pressure for more corporate responsibility, and the search for an appropriate and balanced role of business, it has been said that "the task is rather like rebuilding a ship while it's still at sea."

In Section 2.8, the question will be considered whether it is useful to lay down specific standards in a formal code of ethics for a pharmaceutical concern.

2.2. Laws and Regulations Relating to Business and Industry Generally

Not only do the laws and regulations relevant to business practice date back for many centuries, but it is striking that many of their basic purposes and principles have remain unchanged over that time though they have become massively institutionalized. While the details of business law naturally differ from one legal system to another, some elements which these systems have in common need to be briefly considered here because of their relevance to the field of pharmaceuticals and to ethical principles. As noted above, provisions of the law have in many cases confirmed what were earlier only ethical rules of behaviour, but this does not necessarily turn them into pillars of stone. After legal rules have been put in place, there always room for their interpretation; a sense of ethics may do much to determine whether they are interpreted in a minimalist manner or fully in the spirit of the legislator and in line with the needs and expectations of the community.

2.2.1. Contract and sale of goods

Laws regulating contracts and the sale of goods are at the heart of business; their essential purpose is to establish a routine for honest dealing, in which, to cite the French Civil Code "one or several persons bind themselves, in favour of one or several other persons, to give, or to do, or not to do, something" (CC 1101). In the most common of all types of contract, that for the sale of goods, one party agrees to provide the goods as specified and the other to make a specified payment which he regards as fair and reasonable having regard to the nature and quality of the goods to be purchased. The seller may or may not provide specific warranties as to the product; in a formal sale by contract a general warranty is likely to be included, for example to the effect that:

> ... the Seller warrants that the goods are of satisfactory quality and that they comply with any specific description or specification supplied by the Seller to the Buyer in writing ...

In addition there may be implied warranties, which are defined differently in various legal systems. Fundamental however is that the purchaser too has a duty. In his own interest, he must have considered the goods and agreed on the price to be paid for them in the light of their nature, quality and their suitability for the purpose for which they are to be used. The law assumes that he will do this, and will do so critically, before committing himself to the purchase, a principle reflected in the legal adage *caveat emptor* – let the buyer beware. He will in the most ideal case be able to form a view on these matters by physically examining the goods, but to some degree he is likely to have relied on statements made by the seller. Having obtained and used the goods, he may still conclude that they did not correspond to his expectations. Should that reflect the fact that he has been misled he may be able to seek recompense at law from the seller. In all other instances he may however be obliged to conclude that his own judgement has been incorrect.

In the circumstances of modern business, the laws relating to individual contracts of sale commonly play only a secondary role when disputes and issues of duty arise. French Law, and a number of other systems analogous to it, has always construed a contractual relationship between the original supplier and the ultimate buyer, however many intermediaries there may be; other legal systems have not done so. With the ultimate consumer of a product several stages removed from the original supplier and with specific legislation dealing with product liability (Section 2.2.2) and the supply of particular types of product, such as medicines (Section 3.5), other rules are more in evidence and the buyer's ability to protect himself directly is weakened. A cautious mother looking for apples in the market will still examine them one by one before purchasing. The buyer of a complex industrial product, such as a television set, will be much more dependent for his protection on expert advice and on the terms of whatever written guarantee may be offered by the seller. The situation with respect to pharmaceuticals is in several respects even more complex. The ultimate user of a prescribed medicine will obviously be heavily dependent on the doctor who ordained that he should use it, but the process does not end there. Even the prescriber is unlikely to have formed his own view at first hand on the merits of the medicine though he may have used it to some extent and with success in other patients; he will however rely primarily on the information provided in reference books or compendia and on statements approved by the regulatory authorities; to a considerable extent he is also likely to have been influenced by printed advertising and the visits of the company's detailman. Even after the drug has been administered neither the physician nor the patient will generally be able to assess whether it has served its purpose or not; many illnesses are self-healing irrespective of treatment, and even the most effective medicine cannot be expected to work in every case.

It is not quite true to say that the *caveat emptor* principle does not hold good in such a complicated chain of events; rather it operates in an unusual manner, with the patient relying, directly or indirectly, on a series of persons or authorities whom he has understood he can safely trust. Their involvement provides him with as much assurance as he can reasonably expect that the medicine which he purchases will be reasonably suitable for the purpose for which it is intended – reasonably, that is, bearing in mind that a drug will not always be effective or well tolerated in every patient who takes it (Chapter 4). *Caveat emptor* also applies very clearly at various other points in the chain, for example when a pharmaceutical manufacturer buys his starting materials in bulk from a chemical supplier; here the laws relating to contracts of sale (and not uncommonly the rules of private international law as the goods cross national boundaries) all come into play. The cautious purchaser will in such a situation require and analyse samples before the contract is concluded, and when the goods arrive he will analyse each batch again to make sure that it corresponds to the sample. Such issues are however not specific to this particular industry and they need not be further discussed here.

2.2.2.   The law of tort and non-contractual liability

The law of tort, dealing with conflicts between parties who have no contract with one another but where the one nevertheless claims that the other has done him an injury, has found extraordinary application where medicines are concerned and particularly in instances of drug-induced injury. The patient who considers that he has been injured by a pharmaceutical product that was prescribed for him finds himself at the end of a long chain of possible causation. It may have been incorrectly dispensed by his physician, wrongly dispensed by the pharmacist or pharmacy assistant, carelessly administered by a hospital nurse or improperly stored by a wholesaler or importer; any of these intermediaries may be to blame. However, it is also possible that the drug presented from the start certain inherent risks that had not been recognized or revealed by the firm that developed it, that a particular production batch of it was incorrectly made, that the batch was contaminated during packaging or that the instructions for use were misleading.

In all these latter cases, a claim is likely to be brought against the manufacturer. Courts have for many years allowed claims to be brought by the ultimate user of a defective product against the manufacturer with whom he has no direct contractual link:

In the legendary Scottish/English case of Donoghue v. Stevenson of 1932, a woman had consumed (but had not purchased and hence had no contractual rights) a bottle of ginger beer which, apparently because of a fault during production or packaging, contained the decomposed remains of a snail. She claimed that she had in consequence been poisoned, and she sued the manufacturer in negligence. In that case, the judge, Lord Atkin, laid down the test for the duty to take reasonable care thus:

> "The rule that you are to love your neighbour becomes in law: You must not injure your neighbour; and the lawyer's question: Who is my neighbour? receives a restricted reply. You must take reasonable care to avoid acts or omissions which you can reasonably foresee will be likely to injure your neighbour. Who then in law is my neighbour? The answer seems to me – persons who are so closely and directly affected by my act that I ought reasonably to have them in contemplation when I am directing my mind to the acts or omissions which are called into question."

The judgement not only applied tort law to a situation in which there was no vestige of a contract, but also provided an extremely wide definition of the scope of the manufacturer's duty to the ultimate user of his product – his "neighbour". During the years that followed, numerous cases were brought by patients against pharmaceutical manufacturers under this form of tort law, commonly on grounds of negligence which had led to the injury of an individual user. The cases in which liability and negligence were established related variously to manufacturing defects, failure to provide appropriate instructions or warnings or (even after the emergence of modern regulatory systems) the sale of a medicine which could not reasonably be considered to be demonstrably efficacious or safe. Such litigation has set out many aspects of the duty which the manufacturer can be said to owe to the end-user of his product. Where the product itself is concerned, there is an evident duty to respect current legally defined standards of efficacy, quality and safety, even where the national regulatory agency has failed to take action or has even wrongfully approved a product that does not meet these standards; many thousands of older products marketed around the world still await official assessment in some countries, a failure on the part of the authorities which cannot be regarded as constituting implied approval of their continued marketing. Similarly, a manufacturer has a clear duty in general commercial law to provide truthful and adequate information on his packaging and the accompanying directions folder, irrespective of whether the drug regulatory agency has insisted on this under medicine legislation or not (Section 3.5.4).

Particularly in Europe, the nature of cases brought by consumers against manufacturers has changed to some extent since the passage of the European Union's Product Liability Directive of 1985, discussed below, and the corresponding standards in use elsewhere. However, the scope of the duty and the identity of the ultimate user to whom a duty is owed could hardly be described more comprehensively than in Lord Atkin's words as cited above. However distant and anonymous, he is still the manufacturer's "neighbour".

2.2.3.   Consumer protection legislation

As already pointed out, the traditional legal measures to protect the end-user of a product against the faults of its producer, where this proves necessary, are not ideally adapted to the complex situation existing in the modern field of pharmaceuticals. Neither the simple principles of the law of contract are fully applicable, nor is the law of negligence in tort. In the last two decades, however, new measures have been devised to provide adequate protection for consumers in any field of trade, and they have to some extent been tested by the Courts in cases where injury is alleged to have been done by medicines.

The European Union led the way with its Product Liability Directive of 1985; this was subsequently enacted into closely similar laws in the member states; the United Kingdom's Consumer Protection Act of 1987 (DTI 1987) may be taken as an example. The operative principle here is that *a product will be considered defective if it is not as safe as persons in general are entitled to expect.* A standard formulated in this manner is obviously subject to a great deal of interpretation by sellers as well as buyers, and the question for either party will clearly be how expectations arise in any particular field and what those expectations actually were in a given case. Views on such an issue might differ strongly and one can see much room for the application of ethical principles.

For a start it is necessary to be clear what, in the case of medicines, the public patient's "expectations" are and how they are likely to arise. In a society where, prior to marketing, a medicinal product has to pass the threshold guarded by a regulatory agency, with its criteria of quality, safety, efficacy and truth, it would be simple to argue that one's expectations as a patient will simply be that in practice the drug can be expected to deliver what the approved data sheet and package insert have promised. Since however none of these criteria are absolute, the question still arises as to what degree of efficacy or safety the end-user is entitled to expect, and at what point he can characterize the product as "defective" in the sense of the Product Liability Directive. In a landmark decision in London's High Court in 2001,[3] relating to a product used in hepatitis, Mr Justice Burton distinguished two types of

---

[3] AA and others vs. The National Blood Authority and Others. Case 458. Judgement of 26 March 2001 by Mr Justice Burton.

problem arising with a product. Where a product was manufactured according to a specified production standard, a particular batch which failed to meet that standard (e.g. because it was contaminated with glass splinters, or for that matter a dead snail) would be regarded as "non-standard" and hence "defective" according to the Directive. However, where a product as normally produced had some recognized adverse effects (e.g. liver toxicity) it would nevertheless be a "standard product" and hence not defective in the view of the Directive. That case still left open the question as to whether a typical end-user might not have derived legitimate expectations regarding a product from some other standard. That specific issue arose before the English High Court in 2002 with respect to oral contraceptives[4]:

> From about 1960 onwards a number of firms had marketed oral contraceptives, Because they were highly effective, they were welcomed despite the fact that the original products of this type ("first generation") proved capable in a proportion of users of causing thromboembolic complications, i.e. blood clots, which were sometimes fatal, Some years later a "second generation" of oral contraceptives was marketed with which the risk of such complications was much reduced; these products became very widely used throughout the world. Since the patents on these product were due to expire, three firms took the initiative prior to 1990 to market products comprising a so-called "third generation" of oral contraceptives. These met regulatory criteria for efficacy and safety, but within a number of years evidence appeared that the incidence of thromboembolism had again risen. No evidence was produced that the third generation offered any particular benefit, such as might have outweighed an added risk.

> Proceedings were brought against the three firms on behalf of a number of British women who had suffered thromboembolism, in some instances fatal, while taking the new products. It was argued before the court that women as a whole had come to regard the second generation oral contraceptives as comprising a reasonably acceptable standard and that subsequent products falling below this standard should be regarded as "defective." While the deliberations of the Court appeared to accept this as an acceptable point of view, it had been agreed with the parties in advance that, in view of the uncertainties of clinical statistics, the existence of a sufficiently increased risk to render the third generation products "defective" in the eyes of the law could only be regarded as proven if it was shown that the thromboembolic risk had at least been doubled. The final judgement was that, according to the best evidence available, the risk had probably been increased but by a lesser amount (apparently some 70%) and the action therefore failed.

---

[4] Queen's Bench Division: High Court (London): XYZ and others (Claimants) versus (1) Schering Health Care Limited, (2) Organon Laboratories Limited and (3) John Wyeth and Brother Limited. Judgement by the Hon. Mr Justice Mackay. London, 29 July 2002. Case No. 0002638. Neutral Citation No; (2002) EWHC 1420 (QB).

In the light of these two cases – and more are due to follow them – it seems correct to conclude that the expectations of the public with respect to a drug will be clearly influenced by the standards set by closely similar products which had been widely regarded by the public as acceptable at an earlier date; if the degree of safety (or, presumably, quality or efficacy) is less, the product will be considered "defective" under Consumer Protection Legislation.

The latter case is a striking instance of a situation in which a clear ethical standard might be said to exist, but where the operation of the law in its support was impeded by the shortcomings of statistical methodology. The marketing for purely commercial reasons of a new generation of these pharmaceuticals that fell somewhat below the safety standards set by their predecessors, yet offered no counterbalancing advantages, raises troubling ethical considerations.

Taken alongside principles laid down during earlier litigation in tort and in various legal debates and papers, the European Product Liability Directive certainly provides further guidance as to the standards which pharmaceutical firms need to maintain towards the ultimate users of their products in terms of safety. In particular, a product should possess the degree of safety such as "persons generally" are entitled to expect; this approach provides a reasonably objective means of determining whether or not a defect is present, and it does so without referring to the expectations of a particular litigant or a particular producer.

It is also fairly clear that when deciding whether a product is defective a Court will take into account all relevant circumstances, several of which the manufacturer has within his control, namely the manner in which the product has been marketed and any instructions or warnings provided alongside it.

On various other issues, several of them relevant to medicines, the Directive still needs to be further interpreted by the Courts. The view has for example been authoritatively advanced that under the Directive a product will not be considered defective simply because a safer version is subsequently put on the market. That may be an understandable approach, but it is also arguable that the arrival of a safer alternative could raise the public's expectations and create at some moment an ethical obligation to withdraw the earlier product as carrying an unnecessary and avoidable degree of risk (see Section 4.2).

In addition, some of the defences provided under the Directive can and undoubtedly will be interpreted in rather particular ways where medicines are concerned. The "development risks defence", more generously allowed in English law than elsewhere in the European member states, permits a firm to demonstrate in its defence that, at the time it supplied the product, the state of scientific and technical knowledge was not such that it might have been expected to discover the defect. When this defence comes to be considered in a Court case involving a medicinal product one will have to bear in mind the now very evident principle that a drug manufacturer continues to bear scientific responsibility for his product throughout its life, with a commensurate duty to update his knowledge and research at all times (see Section 3.5.6).

2.2.4. *Intellectual property; trademarks, patents and data exclusivity*

(i) *Property and human rights*   In considering above the various social roles which a firm must be considered to have taken upon itself (Section 2.1), the need was stressed to find a fair balance between the self-interest of a corporation and its investors on the one hand and the interests of the remaining parties (notably society as a whole) on the other. Sometimes the means which a corporation uses to defend and advance its own interests will seem fair to itself but very unfair to the outside world. In such matters both ethical and legal questions arise, and in the pharmaceuticals sector some violent disputes erupt. A fictitious but typical type of case is outlined here:

> A science-based pharmaceutical company X develops a unique drug for the cure of a fatal disease D; the disease occurs world-wide and claims some 40,000 victims yearly, many of them among indigent populations in East Africa. X takes out patents on the drug in as many countries as possible to protect it from imitation by others. Claiming high research costs and low expected turnover, X sets a price of $5000 per patient for a complete cure. This puts it out of the reach of most poor patients, though an international charity pays for the treatment of 1500 patients a year. A Pakistani firm (P) then ignores the patents and markets a cheap copy of the drug, selling for only $ 50 per course of treatment. To protect its profits, the X corporation takes legal action against P and forces the latter to withdraw from the market. According to a church charity the loss of the low-cost drug will now result in the deaths of some 30,000 patients a year from disease D.

Variants on this episode might present a situation in which X is willing to licence the drug to P but demands a prohibitively high licence fee, or where the dispute relates purely to the improper use of X's registered trade made. In either case a purely commercial interest has come into conflict with one of health and human rights. There will be a need to find a solution in the courts or through some form of ethically based mediation, for example through the International Red Cross.

Trademarks and patents are ancient and respectable means of protecting from imitation or theft the commercial property of a business and the intellectual achievements of an inventor. As has been the case for centuries, controversies relate to the extent to which a piece of intellectual and commercial property can and should in fairness to the originator be protected without unduly limiting the rights of others to benefit from it and without injuring third parties. Less familiar disputes have arisen around secondary tools which originators in the medicines field have devised to extend the protection which they enjoy *(see sections (v) and (vi) below).*

(ii) Trademarks and counterfeiting Registered Trademarks, widely protected throughout the world in the form of names or symbols associated with particular medicines or their manufacturers, have become an essential tool of the trade in "speciality" medicines – the original versions of new drugs marketed by their originators. While a drug substance will, early in its existence, acquire an "international non-proprietary name" allocated by the World Health Organization, it is in fact likely to become best known under the registered "speciality name" chosen by its original manufacturer and protected as a trademark. Menutil, the simple and readily remembered trade name of an appetite depressant, clearly has advantages both for businessmen, prescribers and patients as compared with its international non-proprietary name (diethylpropion) let alone its full chemical designation (α-diethylaminopropiophenone). One encounters little opposition in principle to the existence of trade names, which can enjoy an extraordinarily long and some respects useful life. Both legal and ethical disputes nevertheless arise in this field.

The most straightforward of these relate to blatant infringements. A secondary firm may produce a *counterfeit* of the original drug, labelling it with the protected name and symbol, for distribution in markets where there is little chance of control or prosecution. In a variant of this practice, subtle changes are made in the presentation of the name or symbol, perhaps sufficient to evade prosecution yet too subtle to be noticed by the typical prescriber or user; if the Burroughs Wellcome product Septrim, bearing the firm's symbol of a unicorn, is counterfeited as Sepptrim bearing the emblem of a horse, the difference may be overlooked at the point of sale, and in a small market the loss suffered by the trademark owner may be insufficient to risk costly and slow litigation. Offences such as these are in some parts of the world common, particularly since the "speciality" version of a product may, even after expiry of a patent on the active component or manufacturing method, well command a higher price than a generic version sold under the international non-proprietary name or a new and unfamiliar brand. The fact that medicines combine high monetary value with low volume and weight makes them a particularly attractive commodity for fraud, and they move readily across national frontiers.

While as regards their composition counterfeit products are in some cases close copies of the originals, many are medically valueless and some are dangerous. The trade in these fraudulent products thus represents a persistent threat to health and runs counter to both pharmaceutical and commercial law, but it naturally also contravenes the principles of good business practice. The subcontinent with some thousands of drug producers of greater or lesser repute or notoriety is regarded as a major source of illegal products, a situation which may be alleviated as the newest provisions of Indian patent law (MSF 2005) come into effect (see Section 2.2.4).

The suppression of this trade is a matter in which the interests of public health and those of the *bona fide* trade and industry run almost entirely parallel. The problems of counterfeiting are only likely to be solved as national pharmaceutical inspectorates and trademark authorities around the world become more effective and legal procedures more efficient. However, any *bona fide* firm operating in a developing country (or any other area where counterfeit or substandard drugs circulate) can be considered to have a duty to work with the authorities, including police and customs offers, to suppress this abuse of the market.

The counterside of the trademark situation relates to the extent to which the prestige attaching to an original trademark is often heavily exploited by the originator firm as a means of maintaining a high price even after expiry of the patent. The suggestion is sometimes deliberately imparted that the low-cost generic equivalents, which appear entirely legally at this time (Chapter 11), are no more than discreditable counterfeits that pose risks to health. There can be no reasonable justification for creating and maintaining costly confusion of this type in the minds of professionals and patients and in ethics there is every reason to avoid it.

(iii) Patent law   Particularly within recent years, patent practices in the pharmaceutical field have been challenged, and accusations of unethical policies have often been directed not at small and obscure firms but at multinational corporations or at the research-based industry as a whole. Although some have argued in the course of the years that there should be no patents at all on medicines (Gandhi 1981), the basic principle is not as a rule questioned since they provide a stimulus to research. The principle dispute centres here around the degree and duration of the

protection which is reasonable in the pharmaceutical field, and around some of the methods which the research-based industry has used to prolong its monopoly on new drugs. Particularly in low-income countries, the maintenance of monopoly pricing through patenting is criticized as essentially depriving poor populations of affordable up-to-date treatment. In order to assess what may be considered proper practice, one needs to consider the conflicting points of view.

The duration of patent protection on an invention has varied from place to place and from time to time but in recent decades it has generally been standardized at 20 years. In many manufacturing areas, this award of what is in effect a 20-year monopoly to the innovator proves to be acceptable to all parties. These are areas characterized by intense competition and rapid innovation, in which the market life of a product is often a decade or less; during that period the innovating company can secure a generous return on its development investment by charging prices which the public is often eager to pay for the latest product. There is no doubt whatsoever that the situation as regards pharmaceuticals is somewhat different. Where a new medicinal drug bears sufficient promise in preliminary studies to be awarded a patent, this is secured as early as possible so as to be ensured of protection. At this stage, however, much work remains before the product is ripe for marketing; lengthy clinical trials and toxicity studies have yet to be performed and an extensive file assessed by national regulatory authorities before a marketing licence can be obtained. The consequence of this is that by the time an innovative new drug becomes available to patients, a considerable part of its patent life – sometimes as much as half of the 20-year period – may have expired. Within the period that remains, sales of the drug have to earn back the costs of research (including losses on failed projects) and make an adequate contribution to profits and overheads before the patent expires and generic versions of the product are launched by low-price generic competitors. The view of industry itself is that in such a situation one is obliged to charge whatever price is necessary and obtainable, and that there is justification for seeking to extend protection further by whatever means are available. Critics of the industry on the other hand point to the fact that the resulting prices of new drugs, calculated to provide what they view as grossly excessive profits, put them entirely out of reach of many who need them, and that the means used to extend the period of protection represent misuse of provisions not intended for this purpose. Experience with new drugs for the treatment of AIDS and HIV infection is cited as demonstrating the consequences of this situation in public health terms (Dyer 2004);

entire populations of AIDS sufferers, particularly in Africa, have become heavily reliant on low-cost drugs which can only continue in production if a solution is found to patent problems. The situation will be considered fully in Chapter 7 from the point of view of drug pricing.

(iv) The TRIPS agreement   Towards the end of the twentieth century, the process of patent protection across the world was still, from the point of view of any innovator hoping to reach a global market, very unsatisfactory. Patents were issued only at the national level, but many countries had imperfect patent systems and some none at all. Innovative industries in various fields therefore pressed governments over the course of several decades to correct this situation, which was portrayed as a serious obstacle to innovation and economic development. With the establishment of the World Trade Organization, which in 1995 replaced the earlier General Agreement on Trade and Tariffs (GATT), the basis was laid for global agreement on the issue and it was under the auspices of these organizations that negotiations were conducted. The TRIPS Agreement (the Agreement on Trade-Related Aspects of Intellectual Property Rights) ultimately came into being in 1994 (TRIPS 1994, RFSTE 2001, Drahos and Braithwaite 2002). In essence, the agreement created a world-wide network of national patent bureaux; defective systems were to be reformed and new bureaux created where there were none.

It was evident that the Agreement, concluded between governments but with massive industrial backing, would face much opposition from some developing countries that had benefited from the defects of the old situation in terms of opportunities both to manufacture and to purchase low-cost copies of products which evaded the patent barrier. That situation was prominent in the pharmaceutical field where countries in Africa, South America, Asia and elsewhere were heavily dependent on generic drugs, the prices of which were generally a mere fraction of those supplied by originator companies. India, where several thousand drug manufacturing plants operated, largely outside the patent field, was an especially active supplier of low-cost pharmaceuticals to much of Africa and other developing regions. Activists had for their part pressed the TRIPS negotiators to recognize the risks to health if these low-cost medicines ceased to be available, and some Governments had also shown comprehension of the dangers. The result was that the TRIPS agreement indeed made certain provisions to soften the effects of what threatened to be an all too drastic and abrupt change in the situation, though it was at the outset entirely unclear what significance these measures could have. In November 1998, the World Health Organization's Executive Board, alluding to the possible risks to the supply of low-cost medicines to poor populations, unanimously urged WHO's member states:

> . . . to ensure that public health rather than commercial interests have primacy in pharmaceutical and health policies and to review their options under the Agreement on Trade Related Aspects of Intellectual Property Rights (TRIPS) to safeguard access to essential drugs. (as cited by Zaveri 2001)

Ultimately, the health and pharmaceutical aspects of TRIPS were re-examined and clarified at a WTO Ministerial Conference, held in 2001 in Doha, Qatar, which adopted a "Declaration on TRIPS and Public Health". This affirmed the right of national governments to take measures to protect public health and it gave its blessing to broad use of the various flexibilities and exceptions built into the agreement ('t Hoen 2000) While not legally binding, the Doha Declaration was seen by critics of TRIPS as an important step ahead. As of 2005, the principal exceptions and flexibilities to the TRIPS regime as they are currently understood can be briefly summarized as follows:

(i) The requirements set for countries to introduce fully compliant patent legislation have been adjusted to take account of their varying situation. Since the adoption of the Doha Declaration, the thirty member states still at a low level of development (LDC's) will not be considered obliged to grant product patents for pharmaceuticals, provide protection of undisclosed test data or enforce patents that have already been granted, until at least 2016 (Provisions of Sections 5 and 7 and of Part II of the TRIPS Agreement).

(ii) Article 30 of the TRIPS agreement provides that "Members may provide limited exceptions to the exclusive right conferred by a patent, provided that such exceptions do not unreasonably prejudice the legitimate interests of the patent of the patent owner, taking account of the legitimate interests of third parties". An example of such an exception is the so-called Bolar clause that allows for fast introduction of a generic after the patent term by permitting technical preparation for registration of the same drug from an alternative source before the patent has expired.

(iii) Article 31 of TRIPS provides, under certain conditions, for compulsory licensing and government use of a patent. A "compulsory license" is an authorization by the government to itself or to a third party to use the patent without the permission of the patent holder. Most or all countries – developed and developing – have traditionally allowed the government to make use of patented inventions for public purposes with less bureaucratic obstacles than apply to the private sector. Before issuing a compulsory licence, the government must generally have attempted to obtain a voluntary licence on reasonable terms; this will not necessarily apply in the event of "a national emergency or other circumstances of extreme urgency or in cases of non-commercial use." Countries are given considerable freedom to interpret these various provisions. "Public non-commercial use" can, for example, be regarded as covering procurement or production of health care products for use in the public sector. In practice, this means that a procurement authority in a country can start the purchase of generic versions of needed medicines without prior negotiations with the patent holder.

> An important limitation on the original use of Article 31 f was that the type of use which it permitted "shall be authorised predominantly for the supply of the domestic market". This would prevent a government taking these special measures in order to assist another country, for example an African state without its own production facilities. The problem was not solved at Doha and was referred back to the TRIPS Council which in August 2003 aged that a special waived under Article was needed to deal with it. The European Union has at the time of writing proposed a solution to this problem for exports from its own member states (EC 2005) and individual exporting countries are doing the same (DFID 2005)

Many other questions will certainly arise as TRIPS comes fully into effect, and it is likely that there will be further negotiations and disputes before certain issues relating to medicines are settled. The pharmaceutical patent exemption for countries at the lowest level of development has been criticized by some siding with science-based industry (Gillespie-White 2001), but others have seen it as a major step to protect the interests of developing countries (Correa 2002); the generic component of industry has welcomed it though pointing to the problems which remain.

One current source of concern from the public health point of view is the current development in various parts of the world of Free Trade Agreements, certain clauses in which prohibit the participating countries from making use of the compulsory licensing provisions in the TRIPS Agreement (MSF 2004). Developing countries and poor populations will for a long time to come remain heavily dependent for their medicinal supplies on older generic items, supplemented by whatever low cost supplies of newer drugs can be made available either by use of TRIPS exceptions or in other ways.

(v) The "evergreening" of patents   Alongside the debate around the TRIPS agreement, controversy has arisen regarding the various attempts made by the research-based industry to extend patent protection beyond its normal limit. One technique involves the so-called "evergreening" of patents. Towards the end of the period of validity of a patent, the originator firm may seek to enhance the original product in some way so

that either a new patent is issued or an extension granted (NIHCM 2000, MSF 2003a). Where the modification itself constitutes a significant innovation, of importance in health terms, this could be considered a valid step. Critics however argue that such modifications generally provide only marginal benefit in terms of usefulness, efficacy or safety, and that the modified product is unlikely to replace the original except to the extent that prescribers are induced to move to it by techniques of commercial persuasion. The entire issue has now been taken up by activist organizations and it is likely that an acrimonious debate on supplementary patents in this field is to be expected; a welcome element in the new Indian Patent Law of March 2005 is that the possibility of "evergreening" has been restricted so that only new and significant innovations can qualify for supplementary protection (MSF 2005).

(vi) Claims of data exclusivity   As the patent on a medicinal product approaches its expiry date, one additional means which the originator company may still seek to use to obtain continuing protection is to claim "data exclusivity" for its research findings. Unless these findings have in the meantime been published in the medical and pharmaceutical journals, they are only within the firm's own archives or in the confidential files of the national regulatory agencies which originally required the data in order to assess and approve the product for marketing. Companies have therefore argued that these files remain confidential to the agencies concerned and cannot be used for any purpose. Taken literally, this would mean that even after expiry of the patent, an agency would not be permitted to use its knowledge of the scientific information in these files in order to assess and approve a generic equivalent from a secondary manufacturer; the latter would hence be obliged to repeat all the human and animal studies in order to secure a licence. This could mean that the price of the generic equivalent would be greatly increased, or that the originator firm would retain its monopoly for a further period.

From the early years of regulatory law, the principle had indeed been accepted that certain data in an agency's files should be treated as confidential. The original reason for this provision was simply to protect a firm's commercial secrets from being viewed by potential competitors. The Netherlands Law on Medicaments of 1958, one of the first truly modern pharmaceutical laws to be passed, decreed that:

> The members and secretary of the Board (for the Evaluation of Medicines) are obliged to regard as confidential all information regarding the composition or preparation of marketed medicines which becomes known to them by virtue of their tasks . . . (Art 29 (1), WOG 1958)

There was at first some uncertainty regarding the exact scope of such confidentiality rules; the "composition" of a medicine could not literally be regarded as secret, since it was to be listed on the package, at least as regards the active components; the term "preparation" could however relate to all stages of manufacturing, whether patented or not. Over a very short period it became clear that the Board would indeed regard the entire contents of the regulatory file as comprising company secrets, and that all those Civil Servants who were members or servants of the Board would similarly be bound to secrecy by virtue of their professional oath. This principle has since been applied, in one form or another, in the practice of many other major regulatory authorities; second applicants without original data have been allowed to succeed only where the original product has become so widely recognized that an "abridged application" can be drawn up on the basis of published literature.

From the early days of comprehensive regulation, however, it was clear that in the public interest some limits might on occasion need to be imposed on the confidentiality principle. It was conceivable, for example that in connection with some important issue of public policy certain materials relating to a drug might need to be disclosed to third parties; when in 1959/60 the thalidomide disaster occurred, though it did not reach The Netherlands, an example was at hand of such a situation. The law however made no provision for any such disclosure, and some participants to early discussions on the matter considered that these data must be regarded as "property", over which the originator must retain complete control; at most, in their view, the owner might be requested to release the data voluntarily. Others proposed a compromise; in issuing a licence for a drug, an agency might in their view impose a condition that data could be released in particular circumstances; here too, however, one would be departing from the original intention of the legislator.

It is clear that, during the period which followed those early debates, many agencies did use data from their files in order to assess equivalent generic products submitted at a later date and have continued to do so. The issue is however clearly not settled. With the current and impending expiry of many important patents, science-based firms are now increasingly taking up once more their original view that "generic firms" seeking to market their own versions of these drugs have no right to rely at any time on the scientific work submitted to obtain the original registration. It is also evident that the European Community, where in 1965 the basic Directive 65/65 initiated drug-regulatory activities in Europe, has over the years shown considerable support for the innovative role played by science-based firms, and the promise of similar innovation from the more recently arrived biotechnology industry. It has therefore favoured the view that some degree of protection of the data deposited with regulatory authorities is "advisable". It has also considered that patent procedures alone might provide insufficient protection, for example where new uses had been developed for an older substance or for an entirely unpatentable natural material.

It is not known how the Commission came to regard this approach as "advisable," but it is clear that the research-based industry had pressed heavily for a move in this direction, whereas parties concerned with the pricing of products to the public and to health systems have contested the Commission's view. One argument which appears to have played a role with the Commission was that, at the time, there were no patents on pharmaceuticals in Spain or Portugal (Correa 2002 at p. 9, Watal 2000). When in 1986 revised legislation was enacted under Council Directive 87/21/EEC, note was taken of the Commission's position, although it was not precisely followed. Article 4.8 of Directive 65/65/EEC was amended to provide three possibilities for submitting an abridged application: the original provider of the test data could consent to "follow-on" registration being granted on the base of the original data; the follow-on registration could be based (where appropriate) on the published scientific literature; or it could be decided that the new product was "essentially similar" to a product already registered, and which had been registered for six years or more; a period of 10 years would apply where "high-technology medicinal products" (87/21/EEC) were concerned or where a member state considered that the 10-year period was required in the interests of public health. The period was not to be extended beyond 6 years if this would carry protection beyond the validity of the patent unless the new item were to be used for a new indication, documented by new evidence.

Most of the larger Member States, with substantial levels of manufacturing, in fact chose the 10-year option. However, the Community also ruled that the period from which the maximum period of protection was to run began for all countries with the first registration granted within the Community. The situation created in this way went some way towards meeting the managers of the science-based industry's wishes, although it was clear that they would have preferred long-term or permanent retention of their exclusive rights to their data. The issue has been tested in court in the United Kingdom:

> In Britain, Smith Kline & French Laboratories Ltd ("SKF") took legal action to prevent the authorities from allowing others to use their data even after expiry of the ten year period. The case revolved around cimetidine which had been marketed

in 1976 and enjoyed a patent dating from 1972 that was now to be protected by patent for 20 years, i.e. until 1992, though with allowance for licensing to other parties after 1988. In 1987, SKF sought to restrain the agency from registering generic versions of the drug on the basis of SKF data. The court of first instance granted a restraining order but this was overturned in the House of Lords,[5] thus finding against SKF. In their view:

"It is essential for the licensing authority to compare the applications of the first and subsequent applicants in order to satisfy themselves that both products are similar, safe, effective and reliable. The licensing authority cannot discharge its duty to safeguard the health of the nation and its duty to act fairly and equally between the applicants without having recourse to all the information available to the licensing authority, confidential or otherwise . . . "

Although it is perhaps true to say that there is some considerable debate as to whether or not the sort of activity contemplated by the legislation amounts to "making use" of the data, the Lords were clear in any case as to the resulting regime. If a pharmaceutical company wants to market a new medicinal product in the UK, it has to comply with mechanisms created under the legislation, which allow (only) a limited period of exclusivity. If they do not like this, then, in the view of the Lords, they need not apply to market their medicine in the UK. The House of Lords indeed went on to suggest that use of regulatory procedures to obtain protection from imitation amounted to misuse of the system. The ultimate consequence was, therefore, that the generics producers involved in the case were allowed to rely for their application on the evidence originally submitted by SKF in order to obtain a product licence for Tagamet.

The notion that it would be inhumane, in the interests of data protection, to demand repetition of experiments on animals was not raised, but it may be noted that in the United Kingdom this issue has been brought up in connection with regulatory practice in the field of agricultural chemicals; in that field, repetition of studies in "vertebrate animals" has been expressly excluded. The parties are "encouraged" to come to an agreement (with compensation) on the sharing of data and can even be obliged to do so (Garratt 2005).

An interesting compromise on this issue is to be found in the area of "orphan drugs", i.e. medicines developed to treat rare conditions or serve a market that is unlikely to provide a fair return on investment (Chapter 7). In order to encourage research in such fields, the European Union introduced

---

[5] *R v. Licensing Authority ex p Smith Kline* (H.L.) [1990] 1 A.C. 64.

in 2000 an accentuated degree of data protection for such "orphan drugs" (Regulation 141/2000). Where a drug has been licensed under this connotation no "similar" product can be registered for that indication for a period of 10 years, subject to a number of conditions. The 10-year period of exclusivity may however:

> ". . . be reduced to six years if, at the end of the fifth year, it is established, in respect of the medicinal product concerned, that the criteria laid down in Article 3 are no longer met, *inter alia*, where it is shown on the basis of available evidence that the product is sufficiently profitable not to justify maintenance of market exclusivity . . ."

A number of drugs have been registered under this provision, but it is at present too early to determine its ultimate effects either in terms of innovation or exclusivity.

In the United States, practice regarding data exclusivity has varied both within the field of medicines and beyond. The research-based pharmaceutical industry had argued for protection unlimited in time, and from 1962 onwards the Food and Drug Administration had indeed insisted that generic applications submit original data. Subsequently, a learned review (McGarity and Shapiro 1980) pointed out that practice had been inconsistent; in various health-related fields, including medicines, originator firms had successfully restrained the relevant government agencies from using the research data held in their fields as a basis for approving copies of their products, which they had claimed were "trade secrets". Nevertheless, data on the testing of antibiotics and additives were fully disclosed; and in certain fields chemical test results were being disclosed for use by competitors subject to payment of compensation. Where the regulation of pesticides and toxic substances was concerned, Congress had indeed intervened to rule that health and safety data are not proprietary. MacGarity *et al.* themselves pleaded for a consistent approach, stressing the public interest in a greater accessibility of data. As far as medicines were concerned, the authors considered that:

> ". . . It would be desirable if the pharmaceutical industry, to eliminate the social waste and possible human injury associated with duplicative testing, would join the FDA in devising an acceptable solution"

As in Britain, the issue reached the Courts; in the area of agricultural chemicals the relevant legislation (FIFRA) allowed a second applicant to rely on the originator's regulatory data, and when the Monsanto Company claimed that this amounted to "improper taking of property" its claim was rejected. Ultimately, in the field of medicines, the matter was taken up in the Drug Price Competition and Patent Term Restoration Act (the "Hatch-Waxman Act") of 1984, which allowed a period of up to five years of data exclusivity before a secondary application could be filed. This compromise provision was welcomed by the generic industry but regarded by research-based firms as a defeat; however, it was accepted by the latter with relatively good grace since at the same time American patent protection was being extended.

The 1992 North American Free Trade Agreement (NAFTA), strongly influenced by the USA, also provides for 5 years of data exclusivity (Trade Secrets, Article 1711), but with a potentially important exception:

> (5). . . . the Party shall protect against disclosure of the data . . . except where the disclosure is necessary to protect the public or unless steps are taken to ensure that the data is protected against unfair commercial use . . .

Outside the USA and the European Union, the issue of data exclusivity only came into focus in negotiations under the auspices of the World Trade Organization for what ultimately became the TRIPS Agreement of 1995 (see above). After an acrimonious debate, the final text of TRIPS, strongly influenced by the USA and the European Community, included a clause 39.3, which rendered exclusivity of regulatory data compulsory, though with some significant reservations:

> Members, when requiring, as a condition of approving the marketing of pharmaceutical or agricultural chemical products which utilise new chemical entities, the submission of undisclosed test or other data, the origination of which involves a considerable effort, shall protect such data against unfair commercial use. In addition, Members shall protect such data against disclosure, except where necessary to protect the public, or unless steps are taken to ensure that the data are protected against unfair commercial use.

There has been much debate on the proper interpretation of the clause and its exceptions. The concept of *"unfair commercial use"* as contrasted with "fair" commercial use is unclear, no fixed period of exclusivity is specified, there is no mention of compensation, and it is uncertain what measures will be regarded as being "necessary to protect the public". It is even uncertain whether the internal mobilization of data held by an agency in order to assess a second application constitutes improper "use" under the article or not. With such uncertainties, it is not surprising that, 5 years after the TRIPS agreement was concluded, Switzerland, and Australia were still found to be breach of their obligations to provide data exclusivity, as was Canada. It would appear that so long as the data are protected against unfair commercial use, by whatever means, member states will be free to disclose the data.

Like some other aspects of TRIPS, Article 39.3 has given rise to a massive debate which is far from concluded (Gorlin 1999, 2000). There is good reason to believe that countries will continue to interpret this clause in their own particular way. Japan, for the present, is likely to maintain its principle of issuing no second marketing license to a drug for the first 6 years, so that its acceptability in practice can be further assessed, after which an extensive report will be issued by the agency – this in itself constituting in the view of some observers a breach of Article 39.3. Research-based firms, and governments following their views, will continue to challenge the fact that the Article provides no fixed period of data exclusivity.

In much of the world, the principle of data exclusivity is now being accepted (Abbott 2004). Moves in this direction took place in New Zealand in 1994 and in Australia in 1998. In Turkey the European Federation of Pharmaceutical Industries and Associations (EFPIA) was the prime mover in ensuring that the European Commission demanded action in this respect, including rigid conformity with Article 39.3 of TRIPS. In November 2004 EFPIA, alongside the USA, was similarly active in public criticism of Israel for failure to provide data exclusivity. In the meantime, the United States is active in promoting new regional Free Trade Agreements, which adopt its own views on data exclusivity for pharmaceuticals. Present trends indicate that data exclusivity will be adopted almost universally within the foreseeable future, but it is also necessary to realize that there is also an active counter-movement, viewing these developments as potentially dangerous in that they stifle true competition and seriously weaken the situation of poorer countries where drugs are already largely out of reach for financial reasons; in that view, the scientific data which underlie the introduction of a new medicine are a "public good" to which there should be as much access as possible. It is understandable that the pressure exerted on behalf of the research-based industry almost exclusively represents self-interest; but it is questionable whether, at least among the governments of industrialized countries, one is not approaching a moment when a broader world view of the matter will be taken.

As in so many other respects, the deep differences of opinion unfortunately reflect the lack of any hard data on the extent to which this form of data protection is necessary in order to protect industrial innovation and ensure fair but not excessive commercial returns on an original drug. Such hard data are very unlikely to emerge and the future is likely to involve a series of compromises between various points of view. However, if such compromises are to be reasonably fair to all parties, general agreement on various matters is still needed.

- One starting point for compromise would be a clearer definition of the situations in which the patent system is likely to provide entirely inadequate protection for a significant invention, and in which society should therefore be prepared to offer an alternative involving some degree of data exclusivity.
- Another starting point could be agreement on fair financial compensation of the originator company, where the public interest justifies the use of its data to benefit a second licensee.
- Where data exclusivity exists, agreement is needed on the point in time at which preparations can start for introduction of a secondary version of a product. Under TRIPS, the so-called "Bolar provision" allows a secondary manufacturer to undertake his technical preparations for introduction in advance of the data when a patent is due to expire; in like manner, one might well consider allowing regulatory assessment of a secondary drug to take place in advance.
- Again, bearing in mind the fact that a significant medical innovation may merit a significant reward, one might better define the concept of "novelty". In this connection, the European Court of Justice has provided a helpful ruling to the British courts on the extent to which new indications, formulations and dosages should be regarded as sufficiently innovative to benefit from their own new periods of data exclusivity.[6] A similar approach is needed for all products, some of which are truly innovative in health care while others are from the public health point of view novel only in a limited sense (e.g. new chemical structure).
- Another point of departure could involve early release of data to a licensee who is proposing to market the drug in question only in countries at a low level of development.
- Finally, where a period of data exclusivity is to be allowed it would seem equitable to calculate it from a starting date which is as close as possible that when the original product came into

---

[6] *R v. The Licensing Authority established by the Medicines Act 1968, ex p. Generics (U.K.) Limited, R v. The Licensing Authority established by the Medicines Act 1968, ex p. The Wellcome Foundation Limited, R v. The Licensing Authority established by the Medicines Act 1968, ex p. Glaxo Operations U.K. Limited and Others, ('Generics')*, Case C-368/96 [1999] 2 C.M.L.R. 181.

being, rather than that of any later event; there is some judicial support for this approach.[7]

Any or all of these approaches could form the basis for finding a fair balance between the reasonable needs of the innovator company on the one hand and the fair demands of the community on the other.

(vii) The ethics of data protection The principle of protecting intellectual property to a reasonable but not exaggerated extent has always been widely accepted and an attempt is now being made to implement it globally. Where medicines are concerned one is however faced with two opposing points of view, each claiming to represent the true interests of society. The one attributes much of the therapeutic advance of the last fifty years to the assurance of adequate returns provided by patents and threatens a collapse of innovation if data are not protected. The other point of view sees no such cause and effect relationship and foresees a world-wide health tragedy if low-cost drugs are banished because innovative knowledge has been locked away. Lawmakers, faced with opposing views and challenges to the evidence, tend to end up with texts which can be interpreted in various ways and compromises that serve neither approach satisfactorily. That is the point which has now been reached as regards the protection of medicinal innovation.

The practical reality is that most innovation in this field has been funded and brought about by scientific institutes and commercial firms within a small number of prosperous industrialized countries. For the foreseeable future both the funding and the innovation appear likely to come from these same countries and it is in that part of the world that firm protection of data is most needed and is most likely to be enforced. Much of the developing world will, again for the foreseeable future, be heavily dependent on that process and will be able to contribute little to it, but will be greatly aided by having a degree of freedom to develop low-cost generic substitutes within its own borders. There is some reason to think that present trends will lead towards a solution of this type, with society benefiting both from western-based innovation on the one hand and south-based manufacturing enterprise on the other. The laws and regulations may not evolve greatly through further polemic discussion, but important developments could well result from actual events in the field. Emerging threats of new epidemics could well lead to bold use of the exceptions allowed under the TRIPS Agreement and the Doha declaration, while

---

[7] *Monsanto/Searle v. Galen & Asta ('Tramadol')* [1996] 3 C.M.L.R. 402.

individual conflicts resulting in litigation could well lead judges in their wisdom to demand hard evidence and to enunciate the principles which the world needs but which seem unlikely to flow from negotiations alone.

2.2.5.   Social and employment law

As in any other sector of business, pharmaceutical companies are bound by a complex of laws and regulations determining the relationship between the employer and employee and the conditions under which work is performed. As an almost consistently thriving business sector, the pharmaceutical industry has little need to cut corners as an employer. As in other sectors of trade, however, instances are reported of firms obtaining supplies from "sweat-shops" where conditions leave everything to be desired; in fact the need to produce medicines under well-controlled, hygienic and sometimes even sterile conditions largely rules out such practices, though they exist in small borderline firms on the Indian sub-continent and elsewhere. It seems likely that effective efforts to counter the trade in counterfeit medicines, which appear to have similar sources, will do something to eliminate this disreputable trade.

More specific to employment in the pharmaceutical industry is the question of safety at work. Both in research, quality control and manufacturing there is a risk of exposure to potent substances which can exert biological effects in minimal doses. In most or all industrialized countries there is national legislation, not specific to the pharmaceutical industry, providing adequate protection against physical risk in the course of employment, with rigorous inspection. The only deficiency of such inspection is that it can be insufficiently alert to the emergence of new risks, e.g. due to entirely new types of chemical compound. As with environmental risks (see Section 2.2.6), the company staff involved may be best placed to anticipate or detect such problems at an early stage.

In a highly competitive, secretive but also litigious industry, various forms of internal malpractice have from time to time occurred, and situations have arisen in which too much has been expected of an employee. As late as 1965, a number of pharmaceutical firms maintained internal wards for clinical pharmacology where new drugs could be tested on volunteers found among the staff. In such a situation, the extent to which an individual sensed that he was under a degree of pressure to volunteer for such studies was rightfully questioned:

> We had a pharmacologist, Dr WW, who was rather proud of the fact that he was commonly the first to take a jab of a new drug, just to see what it did to him. It

was no secret that he used to taunt some of the new recruits to the lab – technicians and so on – about being nervous of following his example, and some fell for it and volunteered, thinking it might be good for getting promotion. Most of us steered clear of it, and I think the general feeling was that this sort of thing should be farmed out to a hospital. Finally some pointed questions got asked and the company closed the ward down. (Interview 9)

The practice was virtually abandoned after the media, particularly in the United States, drew attention to the use of what were called "human guinea pigs" in company laboratories. However remote the possibility of this happening at the present day, it could be advisable for pharmaceutical companies, when recruiting staff, to include a clause in their contracts of service explicitly excluding their involvement as research subjects.

Bowie cites other examples of entirely different situations where improper pressure can be exerted on an employee:

Examples come immediately to mind of executives being asked to lie about product quality, delivery dates or estimated costs of future prices. Employees sometimes are asked to carry out negative racist, sexist, ageist or ecological policies or processes when they have value commitments that contradict such policies or processes . . . (Bowie 1982 at p. 14)

Again there is nothing in this type of malpractice that is specific to the pharmaceutical industry, but the particular dangers, in a field as delicate as that of pharmacology and public health, are evident. Braithwaite, in his classic 1984 study of *Corporate Crime in the Pharmaceutical Industry* cites numerous examples of corporate malpractice involving groups of employees, some of whom had been directly instructed to engage in offences ranging from bribery to experimental fraud. To cite a single published example, involving the toxic anti-cholesterol drug MER/29:

Mrs Beulah Jordan had quit Merrell . . . after being dissatisfied at the integrity of the scientific work undertaken by the company . . . Crucial MER/29 testing had been done on monkeys. Mrs Jordan's attention was drawn to the deteriorating condition of her "pet" laboratory monkey . . . According to Mrs Jordan the monkey 'got very mean, there was a loss of weight . . . in our opinion this monkey was sick due to a reaction from this drug.' Mrs Jordan reported this to her supervisor, "Dr" William King (it was later discovered that he had not yet been awarded his medical degree), who in turn informed Merrell's director of biological sciences, Dr Evert van Maanen. Dr van Maanen . . . then decided to throw out the sick male drug monkey . . . and substitute another control monkey in his place which had never been on MER/29. After this decision, Dr van Maanen called Mrs Jordan into his office and instructed her to make this substitution in working up the weight charts. . . . Mrs Jordan resented being asked to ...render a false report, and refused to sign her charts. Dr King ordered her to never mention the substitution. She was told this was

the way the company wanted it and to forget it. She was told that this order had
come from higher up and there was nothing she could do about it but obey the order
and do as the "higher-ups" wanted." (Braithwaite 1984 at p. 61, citing Rice 1999)

Instances such as this, not common but unhappily not unique, illustrate the need for effective ethical concepts within a pharmaceutical company; whether written or otherwise, they form an essential complement to
the provisions of law and regulation. The question of formal codes of
ethics is considered in Section 2.9.

2.2.6.   *Environmental law*

Environmental protection is one of the fields in which, because of
the rapid development of social concepts but also of technical advances,
there has been considerable growth of law and regulation, sometimes well
in advance of ethical norms cherished within institutions or held by individuals. The environmental rules applicable to the pharmaceutical industry differ from those generally applicable to the chemical and allied
industries primarily in the stringency of their standards. The fact, noted
above, that substances used or produced in the drug sector may be so
potent as to exert biological effects in minuscule doses is cardinal. The
oestrogen present in an oral contraceptive is intended to be active in the
body in a dose which may be as low as 20 μg; extraordinary precautions
are therefore required to prevent active quantities entering the atmosphere
or water drainage systems as factory effluent, or escaping from the housing used for experimental animals.

With regulations in force and thorough inspection of operations at
regular intervals in many countries, the principal duty of the corporation
in a field such as this will be to ensure strict adhesion to the existing law
and regulations. Manufacturing is however now also carried out on a considerable scale in developing countries in which environmental provisions
may be less complete or are less consistently applied; the firms concerned
include both manufacturers native to those countries and those established
as daughter companies of multinationals; native firms in particular tend to
be small and to lack the resources to undertake adequate pollution management, while local populations may claim that it receives low priority.
Activist groups have become alert to evidence of continuing environmental abuses under these conditions:

Various reports from India in recent years have described situations encountered
in the rural areas of Andhra state, west of Hyderabad, where some 40% of India's

pharmaceutical production is concentrated, much of it in the form of active ingredients for export. In one particular part of the region the local population have over
a period taken legal action against certain of the local firms for what is described
as long-term and massive pollution of agricultural ground and drinking water with
toxic waste. Evidence presented to the courts was to the effect that many chemicals were dumped in the neighbourhood without any attempt to seal or neutralise
them. One or more of the firms have recently merged into larger groups which
have invested heavily in pollution control, but the area has remained damaged in
the long term by past pollution. (GNN 2005)

There is abundant evidence to the effect that conditions such as these
are most likely where there is a result of popular protest, but also where
there is a growth within management of an ethically based sense of
responsibility for the environment.

In the industrialized countries in the meantime the emergence of
unusual environmental risks as a result of entirely new production technologies is by no means a theoretical issue. Measures taken in recent
decades have been attuned almost entirely to chemical pollution, but these
may be inappropriate to control other threats:

Early in 2004 serious concerns arose among consumer and environmental organisations in California regarding preparations to create a genetically engineered
rice crop which would serve to produce pharmaceutical substances. The latter
would include artificial versions of the human milk proteins lactoferrin, lysozyme
and alpha-1-antitrypsin. An inter-agency group cited a series of scientific studies
pointing to possible risks if these substances were to enter the environment and
contaminate the food supply, a likely consequence of the cultivation of the modified rice. Other adverse consequences could include creation of hardier weeds,
damage to non-target insects and disruption of soil ecology. A similar venture was
due to be undertaken in South Africa by a European-based company. (OCA 1984)

The lesson to be derived from such developments extends well
beyond the specific problems which may arise with biotechnological production of drugs. Other equally revolutionary methods which cannot as yet
be envisaged are certain to emerge, and staff members with specialized
knowledge of the field may well be the first to recognize them in good
time. It is particularly at the senior staff level that one will need to remain
watchful for possible new forms of environmental contamination to which
an external inspectorate should be alerted and of which it may not otherwise become aware sufficiently soon.

A final example of possible environmental risks arising in the pharmaceutical sector concerns the development of particular forms of drug
administration that could pollute the environment. The use of freons in

medical aerosols was for a time viewed as a formulation technique which was likely to become highly popular because of its convenience under difficult conditions. Both regulation (reflecting the adverse effect of freons on the ozone layer) and popular pressure have led to its virtual abandonment.

2.2.7. *Company law and reporting obligations*

Although most of the reporting obligations imposed on companies by law are not specific to any particular sector of commerce, it does appear likely at the time of writing that supplementary obligations will come to be laid on the pharmaceutical industry where society demands greater insight into certain of its practices (HOC 2005). In the United States, data submitted under Company Law to the Securities and Exchange Commission have been widely cited when considering the social accountability of major pharmaceutical companies, notably as regards prices, earnings and the expenditure on research as compared with that on promotion (see Chapters 4–6). Environmental reporting is now becoming a widespread obligation, and increased transparency on a range of socially important issues is now being recommended in Great Britain. The current financial reporting obligations in Britain relating to the content of the Operating and Financial Review are outlined below:

> Publicly quoted companies are required to produce within their annual report and accounts an Operating and Financial Review which will include information concerning:
>
> > the development and performance of the company's business and its subsidiaries and the position at year's end;
> >
> > the main trends and factors likely to affect the group's development, performance and position in the future;
> >
> > the group's business objectives and strategies, available resources, principal risks and uncertainties, and its capital structure, treasury and dividend policies, objectives and liquidity;
> >
> > the group's customers, suppliers, lenders, employees, and environmental, social and community issues relating to the group.
>
> Large and medium sized unquoted companies are similarly required to produce an expanded version of the "fair review" currently included in the directors' report. This will include a business review containing much of the same information required of quoted companies but without the information about the future. (Companies Act 1985)

In the pharmaceutical field, peculiar difficulties can attach to providing information on future financial trends even in the reasonably short term. Provided the bulk of a firm's business relates to the sale of well-established medical products for which there is likely to be a continuing and reasonable need in the foreseeable future, developments can be anticipated as in other sectors; areas of growth, stagnation or decline can reasonably be delineated, and the consequences of external influences such as trends in the national economy or the expiry of important patents can to some extent be foreseen. This is much less the case where entirely new and supposedly innovative products are to be marketed; even at the last moment, markets may be blocked by negative regulatory decisions or unforeseen adverse effects. Where the innovation has been the subject of hyperbolic publicity, the effects on turnover and even on the future of the company as a whole may be dramatic. The remarkable change of fortune as regards the corporations which had marketed cox-2 inhibitors during the 1990s is typical (Boseley 2004, Edwards 2005); presented over a period of years as the latest pharmaceutical breakthrough, some have been withdrawn because of their adverse effects while others have proved undistinguished as compared with products developed a generation earlier. This would not be the first time that a once-promising innovation has proved hollow on more than one front betraying the interests of both the financial sector and of society at large.

2.3.   Competitive and Financial Pressures

The manufacturer of any product on a competitive market is expected, permitted and indeed obliged to meet the demands of that market by meeting the needs and expectations of the consumer. The fact that there is competition will provide the primary impetus to the manufacturer, purely out of self-interest, to attain these standards and thereby to serve society well. In such matters, sound ethics and good business practice might be expected to run closely parallel to meet the community's needs. That they do not always do so can be a consequence of marketing techniques, capable as they can be of ensuring that it is not necessarily the most worthy product that wins the day but surely the most heavily promoted. Here again one faces a phenomenon entirely familiar from other areas of business, yet raising particular risks where health and disease are concerned. The manipulation of desire can in such a field be remarkably simple because of the difficulty that the typical patient experiences in judging the merits of a drug, even once after he has experienced its effects. The mere fact that many conditions and symptoms are self-limiting, and the existence of the ever-present placebo effect means that patients may all too readily come to place their trust in an entirely ineffective medicine and even use it continuously or repeatedly over a long period. It has sometimes been argued, only partly in jest, that there is an ethically defensible case for marketing a placebo since it will satisfy the patient's desire to take a medicine but without exposing him to any risk; the "bottle of pink water", prescribed at one time to satisfy the malingering patient, was not essentially different. It would however prove difficult to devise an ethically acceptable marketing and labelling strategy for such a product.

2.4. Political Influences

Political and financial contacts between governments and the large pharmaceutical corporations are intensive in both directions. Governments have traditionally provided vigorous support to major exporting industries among which pharmaceutical manufacturers are prominent. In the reverse direction, the pharmaceutical industry has in some countries become a major financial supporter of political parties likely to be able and willing to support its interests, but also active in pressing its views upon them through intensive lobbying. The western pharmaceutical industry was extremely aggressive in pressuring governments to conclude the TRIPS agreement of 1994 (Section 2.2.4). At the national level, political lobbying has nowhere become more intensive than in the United States and the United Kingdom:

> In 2002 the American Pharmaceutical Industry was reported to be employing 675 lobbyists at a total cost of $91 million. (Public Citizen 2003)

> "Big Pharma in this country uses its muscle in quite a clever way. . . . They've got the Government conned. . . . No one ever challenges them. The government buys into the scenario that Big Pharma has to be handled with kid gloves. . . ." (Warwick Smith, British Generic Manufacturers' Association. Robinson 2001 at pp. 182–183)

> Between 1997 and 1999, two British pharmaceutical transnationals alone spent a total of $ 17.4 million dollars on lobbyists in the USA, and one of these devoted more than $1 mln – to supporting the Republican Party in a national election. (Oxfam 2001)

> "PhRMA [The Pharmaceutical Research and Manufacturers of America], this lobby, has a death grip on Congress." (Senator RJ. Durbin (D-Ill), quoted by Pear 2003)

Lobbying has become so much a phenomenon of western society that it has come to be accepted as a normal means ensuring that the various voices in society are heard when controversial measures are debated in political circles. The ethical questions which arise in this connection necessarily relate to the fact that it is largely a covert influence, and that it is unlikely to be balanced by equally emphatic representations of any alternative view, e.g. that conveyed by the consumer movement, by specialized activist organizations or even by the generic industry. It is sometimes said that there is no objection in ethics to blowing one's own trumpet, but something of a risk does arise if it is intended to drown out the other instruments and indeed succeeds in doing so. The duty here lies primarily with politicians and administrators, to ensure that records of lobbying activities and expenses are kept and made public, and that the points of view which a politician agrees to consider do at least represent a cross section of what society appears to be thinking.

Finally, it could be argued that when an industry or certain of its member companies acquire a major influence in the state and the community, this creates a particular obligation of openness, balance and honesty to which it should consider itself held. Britain's Parliamentary Select Committee suggested in April 2005 that much more transparency be required of the industry in various fields and others have done the same. Just as with lobbying, one might hope for transparency whenever substantial donations are being made to political causes, to education or in other quarters (Angell 2004 at p. xviii). If these things are being done with honest intentions then there is no reason why they should not be laid on the table for all to see.

2.5. The Influence of Litigation

The growth of litigation involving pharmaceutical companies has, particularly in the United States, increased to the point where the costs involved can have a substantial effect on the well-being and good name even of a large corporation and its shareholders. The cost of legal services to a pharmaceutical company is not usually known, since it is a component of the firm's "administrative costs" and is not separately specified but it is certainly extraordinarily high. Alongside the costs of lawyers are the costs incurring in losing civil and criminal cases, such as those concerned with drug-induced injury. Even the burden imposed by problems associated with a single drug can continue for many years.

In late 2004, the Wyeth company of Madison, Delaware, suffered a fourth-quarter overall loss after taking a charge of $ 21.11 billion in connection with continuing litigation relating to the dietary product Fen-phen which had been withdrawn from the market as early as 1997 after inducing heart disorders which apparently included cardiac valve injury. (Angell 2004)

A decade earlier, the Upjohn company was reported to have settled more than two hundred cases arising from serious side effects of its sleeping remedy triazolam, the risks of which it had failed to notify to the authorities after they had been identified in research subjects; one such case alone was reported to have been settled for more than $ 10 million. (Unpublished)

All such incidents could however pale before the prospect which was reported to be facing Merck Inc., one of the largest western pharmaceutical companies, late in 2004. According to an editorial in The Lancet:

..... the licensing of Vioxx and its continued use in the face of unambiguous evidence of harm have been public health catastrophes. This controversy will not end with the drug's withdrawal. Merck's likely litigation bill is put at between $10bln and $15bln. The company has seen its revenues and its capitalisation slashed. It has been financially disabled and its reputation lies in ruins. It is not at all clear that Merck will survive this growing scandal.. (Horton 2004)

Whatever the outcome of this particular case, it is clear that the costs of major litigation can have a drastic effect on the fortunes of even the largest corporations.

There are however other situations in which the rights and wrongs are less clear and sometimes intermingled. Many and probably most pharmaceutical corporations in the United States are engaged in widespread litigation on multiple fronts with the public health authorities. To cite random examples quoted by Angell (2004):

"Charges have been both criminal and civil. Often they are related to defrauding Medicare and Medicaid by billing for inflated prices, or encouraging providers to do so ...... Bayer, for example was fined $257 billion for helping Kaiser Permanente, the giant health maintenance organization, relabel the antibiotic Cipro (in great demand after the anthrax scare) to hide the fact that the government was paying more for it than the HMO. But defrauding the government by rigging prices and offering kickbacks is not the only charge companies are facing. Others involve anticompetitive practices, which the Federal Trade Commission has been aggressively investigating for several years. ...... Numerous lawsuits have been filed to recover money spent on high-priced brand-name drugs while generics were improperly kept off the market. ...... Between 2000 and 2003, according to Michael Loucks, chief of the Health Care Fraud Unit in the U.S. Attorney's Office for the District of Massachusetts, eight companies paid out a total of $2.2 billion in fines and settlements. Four of those companies ... pleaded guilty to criminal charges." (Angell at pp. 230–233)

Whether in such cases a fault is either proven or alleged, much can be done to limit these ruinous burdens by maintaining ethical standards – for example in the reporting of research findings. So far, when one examines the Court records, there is too much reason to believe that unethical and even criminal practices can pay off handsomely:

> Loucks, citing a sum of $ 885 million paid by TAP Pharmaceuticals in civil cases or in criminal fines in cases involving Medicaid, pointed out that during a similar period the firm had received $ 2.7 billion in revenues from Medicaid, so that it still came out well ahead. (Loucks 2003)

As to the personal burden which prosecutions might imposed on individual staff members, Braithwaite claimed to have encountered two American executives who by internal agreement held the position of "vice president responsible for going to jail" (Braithwaite 1984 at p. 308). Again this points to a strategy in which civil or criminal penalties of various types are coolly anticipated and even budgeted for as a component of policy.

To an appreciable extent, litigation involving the pharmaceutical industry is undertaken by the industry itself as a means of asserting its rights and exploiting every means of expanding its income. To cite Angell once more for a single example:

> . . . drug companies are constantly in litigation (or threatening it) to extend marketing rights on their blockbuster drugs. Manipulating the law to extend marketing rights more than pays for itself, of course. In fact it is one of the most lucrative things Big Pharma can do. . . . (Angell 2004 at p. 120).

An overall view was provided by a lawyer who had served with a health management organization in the USA:

> My main recollection of our hundreds of meetings with the drugs people during those years was the way that, on almost any matter, they sailed in with their lawyers in tow. We often had the feeling that we weren't there to talk as reasonable people with each other, but to be told what to do, have our noses rubbed in the legal texts and precedents, be threatened with what would happen if we didn't go along with them, dragged before the judge on the slightest pretext. A lot of it was sabre-rattling, naturally, but you were pulled into it all the same. We worked with other parties – hospitals, doctors, government departments – as good neighbours, but it wasn't often like that with the industry. They had the feeling they were in charge, that they could beat us down and wear us out if they only went on long enough, and pretty often they did, even when we brought our own lawyers in. It wasn't nice, and it cost everyone a mint of money. Dealing with pharma just left a thoroughly nasty taste in the mouth. (Interview 40)

Litigation brought by or against the drug industry has become a vastly expensive burden on society, ultimately reflected in the high costs of drugs. It is however in addition, deservedly or otherwise, a drain on a company's reputation. While litigation first reached these dimensions in the United States, it has now become prominent in many countries. Much of it could be avoided by ethical behaviour on the part of industry itself in many of the areas dealt with in this study, ranging from honest research and truthful promotion to fair competition and open dealings with public institutions. So long as those standards are not more widely attained, it will be difficult to consider the pharmaceutical industry a fully mature and respected player in society.

2.6. Public Relations and the Public Image

To anyone at the centre of a large corporation, the public at large is sometimes seen as distant and often as passive. The matter has been touched on before in relation to personal ethics (Section 2.1.3); the personal confrontation which once existed between the maker and the user of a product is no longer there – there are many hedges between them. Within the company, the least inspiring view of the public is that it is a remote entity to be supplied through a long pipeline with goods and information, in return for payment through the same route. When it serves the corporation's purposes the public may also to some degree need to be manipulated and provided with slogans and images to ensure that the process of supply and payment continues and perhaps expands. In that view, the public does not have a great influence on the corporation; the latter lives in a world populated by itself, its stockholders, its business colleagues and competitors, and with access to the professions and politicians who are important to it.

A much more enlightened and modern view credits the public – or a large cross-section of it – with a fairly intelligent view of the corporation, the sector and business as a whole. It appreciates that it has there an audience which is critical of medicinal products, which wants information and openness rather than slogans and images and which has learned to be less trusting of Mammon than it once was. Among that audience are a large number of voters and a surprising proportion of small investors, either holding stock themselves or represented through investment funds and pension schemes. It is therefore recognized as being of importance to maintain and promote the firm's credibility with the public.

However, as Vance Packard found in his book "The Image", more than 50 years ago, the creation and culture of a carefully sculpted image of a firm or product in the public mind became in the course of the twentieth century a science of its own. An image was to be devised and designed by an advertising agency, commonly in the form of a slogan accompanied by suggestive symbols and subtle twists in typography. What is questionable is the extent to which the public in course of time has remained susceptible to such superficial forms of persuasion, particularly when specific aspects of a company's actual performance, favourable or otherwise, come much more strongly to the fore in the media.

> The company I have in mind, which hadn't managed to produce anything at all worthwhile though its own research, nevertheless chose as its slogan at a given moment "Meeting the calls of modern health" and variants on the theme. People may have noticed it, but they must have noticed much more what the headlines were saying. The firm had marketed one disastrous drug that killed people after they hid the incriminating data; they had taken a licence on thalidomide just before the scandal broke about its effects in pregnancy; and three of its directors ended up in jail because of fraudulent public advertising. After that I don't know that the slogan did them much good. (Interview 20)

It is often the question whether criticism in the media is not too harsh. Merck Inc. by contrast, as one of the largest corporations in the field, had built an enviable reputation built on considerable successes in research, but also on an important philanthropic programme providing donations of a much-needed drug for river-blindness in West Africa; unhappily it was in 2004 to face very extensive adverse publicity following its withdrawal of the anti-rheumatic drug Vioxx, discussed elsewhere.

It is perhaps significant that efforts to bolster reputations in the public mind have been more successful and enduring when linked to the genuine achievements of a particular firm than when attempting to portray the virtues of an entire industry; a single scandal can all too readily impinge on the reputation of all concerned.

If there is an ethical lesson to be drawn from all this it may be that a pharmaceutical company can best cultivate trust and credibility by its recognizable creditable deeds over a long period. Individual drugs may rise and fall, but ongoing good works are accepted as evidence that a firm in this field is genuinely committed to science, health and the public good. In their day, the reputations of both Wellcome and CIBA benefited from the work of the Philanthropic Foundations bearing their name, while Merck became permanently associated with the long-term publication of its prestigious Merck Index and Merck Manual. It may be that more managers in this field should take to heart the adage advanced by Alsop, on expert on corporate reputations, that the best way to acquire and retain a good reputation in business is to deserve it (Alsop 2004). As to the creation of images, to quote the same author once more:

> Your Golden Rule should be to tell it straight, You may even end up creating goodwill and fortifying your reputation. (Alsop 2004)

2.7.   The Location of the Company Conscience

Ethical – or decent, or moral – behaviour, by whatever name it goes, is for any individual a question of conscience. While conformity with law and regulation can be externally controlled and assured, it is the individual himself or herself who must listen to the "still small voice" that calls for proper behaviour according to whatever standards he or she has assimilated. The personality of a corporation is however separate and distinct from that of its members, however much or little they may contribute to it, and there must be some identifiable means of at least alerting the corporation from time to time when it strays from what may be regarded as the strait and narrow path, and perhaps also of calling it to order.

If the corporation has a formal and well-assimilated formal code of ethics (Section 2.8) that may provide some degree of guidance on proper behaviour, though there will always be some problematical situations which even the most comprehensive code has failed to anticipate. Even a written code formulated with the best of intentions and displayed in the entrance hall or the President's office will not itself ensure conformity. Whistle-blowing by conscious staff members where errors loom may be valuable, but that may in turn itself create tensions between those having divergent views. Ideally, therefore, a company should identify some means of creating an identifiable and effective company "conscience", and many pharmaceutical companies have claimed to do so, though in a very variable manner.

> You could very well say that I was the conscience of this firm X; when they disagreed in the management on what was acceptable, they came to me at the Faculty and asked me to advise them, and they accepted my judgement, and I got a little annual payment for making myself available. I remember ruling against some experiments in young women, and censoring some draft advertisements, and I got them to take some old rubbish off the market. Being outside the company and fairly well known I had some authority and kept them out of some scrapes, but I didn't have the chance to go around the labs nosing into things as I really ought to have done, and they did sometimes get into trouble for things I knew nothing about (Interview 12)

> I was the Medical Director and I was supposed to make sure the advertising was right and proper. Still, sometimes they "forgot" to show me ads I wasn't likely to appreciate. And once when I'd turned down a text about some drug for what they called hypotension they waited until I was on holiday and then got it signed off by

my predecessor who was retired and senile. When it suited them, they talked about me being their medical censor, but it wasn't the way it should have been. (Interview 4, translated)

Yes, I think the firm had fixed it pretty well. Dr Y. had just retired but he wanted to go on helping and they gave him a *laissez-passer* to drop in wherever and whenever he liked and check on meetings, documents, protocols, anything he wanted to. He was discreet about what he found, but he had authority and we all felt he did a lot of good, both keeping up standards and making sure we didn't do anything reckless. (Interview 15)

Not a real conscience on two legs, but the firm did have these Standards Committees in the departments who had to sign off all sorts of things and were pretty critical. They knew the law and they had a fairly good idea as to what was over the edge as regards taking risks, like hurting animals without good cause. And there was a Medical Committee who always wanted to know what the drummers were telling the doctors, and if they were giving them presents. (Interview 31)

There may be no ideal solution to the issue of a "company conscience" since much will depend on the company and the extent to which management itself feels it can assume this role. From the above examples and from the literature on this issue – mainly relating to other industrial sectors – some principles do seem to emerge. While certain tasks may need to be in the hands of specialized committees (e.g. dealing with animal experiments), there is much to be said for appointing an ethics adviser with a broad knowledge of the corporation's work and the rules likely to be applicable to it, whether technical or commercial. The adviser should have sufficient seniority and reputation to earn and maintain respect and the authority both to carry out investigations and to make presentations to senior management when needed. He might well be supported by a lawyer (since legal and ethical issues can overlap) and by an interdisciplinary advisory committee which he could consult on marginal issues and which could propose formal rules where needed. The adviser might be the appropriate point of resource for whistle-blowers, capable of dealing with their concerns in strict confidence. Finally, since ethical standards within a firm need to be fostered and maintained, the adviser should ensure that they are developed, taught and understood.

A final point in this connection is that when a pharmaceutical corporation breaches the law, a court may hold an individual employee personally liable for the offence. The principle has often been applied in the United States but an English case may be cited here:

In a case brought by the Department of Health and Social Security, Roussel Laboratories were accused of issuing an advertisement for their drug Surgam (tiaprofenic acid) which "was misleading in that the claims for gastric protection and selective prostaglandin inhibition were not justified or substantiated by clinical or other appropriate trials or studies", and of claiming in the absence of adequate evidence that "Surgam was safer and had fewer or less incidence of side effects than indomethacin in the treatment of arthritis." The medical director of the company, Dr. Christopher Good, was accused of consenting and conniving at the issue of these claims. With respect to four of the five advertisements in question, Roussel Laboratories and Dr Good were found guilty and substantial fines and costs were imposed. In passing sentence the judge said that he did not consider these to be trivial offences, and expressed the hope that the pharmaceutical industry would pay great attention to its advertising in the future. The sentence was upheld on appeal.[8]

2.8.   Company and Industry Codes of Behaviour

2.8.1.   *Types of codes*

Most company "codes of behaviour" (sometimes termed codes of conduct or ethics) are readily accessed; some are published or can be found on the internet; they are not dark secrets, and indeed companies tend to exhibit them with some pride. One can therefore readily form a view of the form which they take and the purpose they are intended to serve. The general conclusion which one is bound to draw after surveying a number of these codes is that they are extraordinarily variable as regards their purpose, their form and their content. Some can be considered good and useful; a few hardly arise above the level of status symbols.

It would be invidious to compare individual named codes, but two contrasting models are presented here. Box 2.A presents a code based on a number of actual examples found within pharmaceutical firms of varying size in the United Kingdom or the United States. The emphasis on this type of code is on business operation and on adherence both to the law and to certain internal rules. Box 2.B is entirely different; it is largely theoretical and has been constructed to reflect certain principles of ethics considered in the present volume and to suggest how these should be respected in the practice of a pharmaceutical company and its staff. Neither of these models is perfect. Any corporation developing a code of its own might need to assimilate certain elements from each of them, as well as issues peculiar to the company itself.

---

[8] Central Criminal Court (1986); *Queen v. Roussel Laboratories and Christopher Saxty Good*. Judgement by Capstick J., December 19th.

CODE OF BUSINESS CONDUCT AND ETHICS
TO EVERY EMPLOYEE

Eksampel Pharmaceuticals, Inc. (the "Corporation") is firmly committed to carrying on its business in accordance with all relevant laws, edicts and regulations and in keeping with the highest standards of business ethics. This Code of Business Conduct and Ethics (the "Code") reflects the business practices and principles of behavior underlying this commitment. Management requires that each officer, director, and permanent or temporary employee worldwide will read, understand, sign and display the Code in his or her place of work and abide by it in the performance of his or her daily tasks.

The Code is designed to represent essential guiding principles for Corporate officers, directors, and employees; it must not be considered in any sense to replace, eliminate or modify any additional obligations set forth in applicable Company personnel policies or other agreements or rules established within the Corporation.

Staff who want clarification on issues related to any aspect of the Code should contact the Vice President of Personnel or the Head of the Legal Department.

I. Compliance With Laws, Rules, And Regulations

You are required yourself to comply with the laws, rules, and regulations that govern the conduct of our business and to report immediately promptly any suspected violations of (or suspected intentions to violate) these standards.

II. Conflicts Of Interest

All officers, directors, and employees have an obligation to conduct business in a manner that avoids actual or potential conflicts of interest. Such a conflict of interest occurs when you are or might be in a position to influence an Eksampel business decision that could result in personal loss or gain for yourself or your relative, friend, or acquaintance. Such loss or gain may result not only in cases where you own, control or have influence in a firm with which Eksampel does business, but also when you receive or are promised or led to anticipate any kickback, bribe, substantial gift or favour as a result of any transaction or business dealings involving Eksampel. No presumption of guilt is created by the mere existence of a relationship with outside firms, but the existence of any such relationships must be notified at all times to the Vice President of Personnel and the Head of the Legal Department.

III. Protecting Confidential Information

If you possess, create, have access to or light incidentally upon any confidential business information or scientific or trade secret within Eksampel

---

Box 2.A   Eksampel Pharmaceuticals Inc. (Theoretical Example)

Pharmaceuticals, you shall have a lifelong obligation not to divulge it to any party within or beyond the company except when you have explicit permission and authority to do so. Such information may relate to budgets, experiments and clinical experiences, collaborative relationships, complaints or official reprimands received, compensation data, computer processes, programs and/or codes, customer lists, financial information, legal proceedings, labor relations strategy, marketing strategies, patent applications, pending projects and/or proposals, proprietary research or production processes, employee directories and/or phone lists, research strategies, activities or findings, scientific data and/or formulae, unpublished scientific manuscripts, slide shows, etc, scientific prototypes, technological data or technological prototypes or any other material such as may be considered by Management to be confidential or worthy of protection.

Great care should be taken not to discuss Eksampel's confidential information in public areas such as lavatories, hallways, the cafeteria, parking areas, sports fields etc.

If you expose, lose, divulge or improperly use such material you will be subject to severe sanctions, as specified in this Code.

IV.   Business Ethics

Eksampel's business success and reputation are built upon the honest dealing and ethical conduct of all officers, directors, and employees. Our reputation requires careful observance of the spirit and letter of all applicable laws and regulations, as well as a scrupulous regard for the highest standards of conduct and of corporate and personal integrity. Eksampel's success depends upon the trust of our customers, collaborators, employees, shareholders, contractors, and suppliers, and that trust shall be preserved.

Eksampel's policy is to conduct business in accordance with the letter, spirit, and intent of all relevant laws, regulations, and Company policies, whether or not known to you, and to refrain from any illegal, immoral, dishonest, unbecoming or unethical conduct.

In general, the use of good judgement, based on high ethical standards, should be sufficient for you to determine which acts are acceptable and proper and which are not.

V.   Maintenance Of Corporate Books, Records, Documents, And Accounts

The integrity of our records and of public disclosure , as well as the management of our company, depend on the validity and completeness of the

Box 2.A   Continued

information supporting the entries to our books of account and technical records. The intentional or negligent entry of false or misleading data, or the omission of required data, whether relating to financial, scientific or commercial matters, is strictly prohibited. Our records serve as a basis for managing our business and are important in meeting our obligations to stakeholders. If you suspect any departure or intended departure from these standards it is your duty to report such to the Head of the Legal Department.

VI.   Quality Of Public Disclosures

The Company has a responsibility to ensure that our reports and documents filed with or submitted to the Securities and Exchange Commission (the "SEC") conform with the relevant law; the monitoring of such disclosure and interpretation of the law lie with a Disclosure Committee consisting of designated officers of the Company. It is not your duty or privilege to seek to influence such disclosure or to interpret the relevant provisions of the law.

VII.   Compliance With Code Of Ethics

Any violation on your part of this Code or any part of it will be visited with severe sanctions, which may include permanent exclusion from employment. Civil and/or criminal proceedings may be taken against you whether or not you have enjoyed any gain or benefit through such violation.

If you know of or suspect a violation or intended violation of any aspect of this code, you must immediately report such information to the Vice President for Personnel and Human Resources, copying such information to your superior officer. The Company will endeavor to keep all such reports confidential, including your identity, except where such confidentiality might be injurious to the Company.

VIII   Waivers/amendments of the Code of Ethics

Any waivers of the provisions in this Code of Ethics may only be granted by the Board of Directors, or by a Committee designated by the Board of Directors, and only when such waiver is granted to a particular individual under specified conditions and is deemed to be fully in the interests of the Company's business.

IX   No Rights Created

This Code of Ethics is not intended to and does not create any rights in or for any employee, customer/client, supplier, competitor, shareholder, or any other person or legal entity whatsoever.

Box 2.A   Continued

Guiding principles

1. Pharmalong is a company created and managed to develop, produce and supply medicines for the benefit of the community.

2. The community's call is for medicines of good quality which serve real needs and which are efficacious and safe in use; they must be readily available and affordable and the information provided with them must be truthful and complete.

3. Pharmalong's ability to serve the community rests on the input of its investors, the achievements of its entire staff and the competence and vision of its management ; all these deserve a fair reward.

Business ethics and law

4. As a company, Pharmalong is part of a business community which includes its suppliers, clients and competitors. It will seek to deal with all of these fairly and honestly.

5. From time to time, Pharmalong may encounter reasons to adjust its activities, to assume new tasks or to leave some fields of work to others. Any such changes may be adopted provided they do not impair the company's ability to serve the community well.

6. Many of the principles of operation in the pharmaceutical field or in business generally have been laid down in national or international law, or set out in codes or agreements by which Pharmalong must consider itself bound. In all aspects of its work, Pharmalong will strive not only to respect these standards in full but also to surpass them when possible and to act at all times in the spirit in which they were enacted.

7. As a corporate member of society, Pharmalong will accept the duties imposed by good citizenship and good neighbourliness. As a player in the health sector, Pharmalong will within its own field of work contribute wherever possible to the promotion, maintenance and restoration of health.

8. Where there is reason to do so, supplementary Codes of Ethics may be drawn up, in the spirit of this present Code, to provide guidance in particular fields of activity.

Staff and Management

9. The management, appointed and acting in accordance with the Articles of Association, shall be responsible for the ensuring that the Company as a whole respects the principles laid down in this Code of

Box 2.B   A Model Ethical Code for a Pharmaceutical Company "PHARMALONG"

> Ethics. Management will also make proposals and seek consensus and input from the staff on the further development and strengthening of this Code where that from time to time may prove advisable.
>
> 10. The staff of Pharmalong, in performing the duties laid down in their individual terms of employment, will at all times be encouraged to devise and propose ways in which the Company can best serve the principles laid down in this Code of Ethics, to the ultimate benefit of the community as a whole.

Box 2.B   Continued

Alongside an overall code for an entire company (or an even more generally formulated code intended to serve for the industry as a whole), one might well consider formulating specific codes for particular fields, such as advertising (Chapter 5), animal studies (Section 12.1), (Chapter 5) or even particular forms of social study such as marketing research. The more specific such codes become, however, the more likely they are to comprise a set of operating instructions rather than a guide to proper and ethically based behaviour.

2.8.2.   Style and content of codes

If a pharmaceutical company (or an industry association) considers it useful either to adopt a formal ethical code or at least to debate the principles which might underlie such a code, the two models presented above might well be compared and contrasted. Each has a certain number of elements which are relevant to some aspect of company behaviour, but the approaches adopted are very different.

The "Eksampel" text is essentially a set of instructions imposed upon employees, an extension of their contact of service. The emphasis is upon law, rules and company procedures, on the need for strict obedience to these rules, and upon the fearsome sanctions which await the transgressor. It demands obedience without sparking a positive desire to be loyal. While terms such as "ethics" and "honesty" are mentioned in passing, the suggestion is that the law, the regulations and the company rules are the backbone of appropriate behaviour by which one will be judged; beyond that, the employee is told, his own sense of what constitutes acceptable behaviour should suffice. The general style of the Eksampel Code does not elicit interest, let alone invite the reader to find out more about the positive ethical principles which he should strive to assimilate. In all matters, the Code is stern and attuned almost entirely to the company's financial success. No doubt because of bad experience in the past, the firm has a particular fear of pillow talk, conversations in the canteen and conflicts of loyalty. The employee is ordered to report even the slightest evidence of betrayal of the company by others, but it does not provide him with any firm assurance that his confidentiality will be respected. The Directors are free to waive the Code when it suits what they conceive to be the Company's interests. And at no point in the Code is there any mention of health or of the interests of the community. In essence this document is not a code of ethics or even of conduct, but a set of strict regulations, supplementing the employee's contractual obligations. As to the manner in which it is presented, one is unavoidably reminded of the comparison cited earlier in this volume to a prison ordinance; it is not inspiring.

The Farmalong Code (Box 2.B) concentrates heavily on issues of ethics and decency, and the need for these as the Company strives to serve the public interest, while at the same time making its way successfully in business. In this model, human rights are not specifically mentioned, perhaps wisely since even in this context they may appear somewhat distant and theoretical to some readers; however, the entire concept is built around those services to the community which a pharmaceutical company might be expected to provide if human rights in health are to be respected. The text is not written as a document which is legally binding on any person or institution, but primarily as an aid to interpretation and understanding, and it is sufficiently concrete to serve as a general means of assessing a staff member's attitude and performance. It is sympathetic and persuasive, reminiscent in that respect of the well-known model Code of Ethics for Canadian Business developed at the University of Ottawa (HRREC 2004). It addresses the reader as a welcome new member of a team who has high ambitions and a proper sense of duty to the whole community. It makes appropriate reference to the need to respect the letter and spirit of both national and international law, but it encourages the reader to collaborate in building the firm's own ethical tradition, with fairness and honesty as key concepts in its approach.

2.8.3. *The usefulness of codes*

The long debate of recent years on the usefulness of codes, whether for individual companies or entire sectors of business, has not produced dramatic results. "One study cited by Amnesty International and Pax Christi International in 1998 found little difference in behaviour between companies with and without voluntary codes of conduct . . ." (Paul and Garred 2000). As Paul and Garred conclude:

> These codes are often vague statements of principle that cannot provide reliable guidelines for behaviour in concrete situations. They do not generally include complaint procedures, nor any basis for legal claims or redress....Codes are often neither transparent nor accountable, with their enforcement (or non-enforcement) an internal corporate concern or the responsibility of small monitoring bodies subject to corporate pressure in cooptation . . . (Paul and Garred 2000)

Neither of the model codes for a pharmaceutical company presented above is ideal but they suggest some approaches. The first model, with some amendments to its unfortunate phrasing, could provide materials for internal rules and contracts of service, and for teaching at internal seminars. The sympathetic and encouraging style of the second model, with its accent on combining service to the community with healthy business, appears more likely to arouse interest among staff in the whole question of decency and honesty in this sector. Such a text might embroider the company's image for the shareholder community or for the world in general, but within the company it will require to be backed up concrete measures. An attempt to locate a recognisable "Company conscience" (see Section 2.7) will be helpful in building an ethical tradition, as will training and discussion sessions. A "Code of Conduct" currently maintained by GSK in Britain sensibly notes that:

> Senior management should be a role-model for these standards by visibly demonstrating support and by regularly encouraging adherence by managers. Managers should ensure all their employees receive guidance, training and communication on ethical behaviour and legal compliance relevant to their duties for the Company. (GSK 2001)

Any code to be adopted should indeed be presented as applying not merely to employees but to the corporation as a whole, including its directors and management; one might also recruit support from its investors, many of whom today show interest in the social responsibilities of the firms to which they supply capital. Above all, a code should seek to promote a sense of ownership and commitment on the part of all those concerned.

The question whether, in the light of these examples, a true code of ethics is likely to have an effect on a company's practice may depend very much on the company environment within which it is to be introduced.

Where there is already a strong sense of loyalty and trust and a measure of idealism, the broad discussion and acceptance of a code could catalyse further positive development. If ethical behaviour is to become rooted within a company, the concepts which are to be nurtured need to be understood but they can be relatively simple. They are not matters of deep legal philosophy. The GSK Code, in its closing paragraph, lays the issue before its staff in very elementary terms indeed:

> When in doubt as to the correct action to take, ask the following question. "Would I feel comfortable in explaining this action to my family or close friends or seeing my action reported on the front page of the local newspaper?" The Company is best served when each employee's answer to this question is an unqualified "Yes". (GSK 2001, Article 4.4)

2.9. Transnational Corporations and Influences

The history of pharmaceutical policies and standards is very largely one of individual governments finding ways of dealing with individual companies. In more recent times however, as governments have come to work together, so too there has been a concentration in industry across national borders. Much of the pharmaceutical industry is now composed of transnational corporations, operating in a situation of rapidly increasing globalization. The complexity of these corporations, and the influence which they exert at many levels, markedly affects the extent to which firm policies truly serving the public interest can be planned and then put into effect.

Apart from the global role of the transnationals themselves there is the complementary influence of organizations representing groups of companies of varying size which devise joint declarations of policy and on occasion act together. In the medicines field the International Federation of Pharmaceutical Manufacturers Associations (IFPMA) is the largest of these, but the Organization representing the European research-based industries (the European Federation of Pharmaceutical Industries and Associations, EFPIA) has similar characteristics, as does the global body representing the self-medication industry (the World Self-Medication Industry, WSMI).

Transnational (or multinational) corporations are not of recent origin – companies such as Shell and Unilever, each based both in Britain and The Netherlands, provide a century-old example – but the number, size and importance of transnational enterprises have increased very greatly during recent decades. The world's 500 largest industrial corporations control at the present day 25 per cent of the world's economic output; the leading 300 transnationals, excluding financial institutions, own some 25 per cent of the world's productive assets. United Nations statistics from 2001 show that the largest transnational pharmaceutical corporations in terms of turnover at that time were Aventis (France) with some 91,000 employees, Hoffmann-LaRoche (Switzerland) with some 64,000, Bayer (Germany) with 117,000 (in both pharmaceuticals and chemicals) and GSK (United Kingdom) with a staff of approximately 107,000 (UNCTAD 2005). In 2003, the six largest pharmaceutical producers had total annual revenues ranging from $ 18.8 billion (AstraZeneca) to $ 39.6 billion (Pfizer) with annual growth rates of up to 24 per cent.

The dominant characteristic of the transnational firms in the pharmaceutical field is their sheer power. Even within an industrialized society they can exert a major effect on health, economics and political processes, while in a developing country their resources as a rule vastly exceed those of the national authorities or of any other authoritative body within the country. They have an unequalled ability to transfer and mobilize resources, to create wealth and to promote development, and for such reasons they are generally welcomed into the third world, often on their own conditions. Problematical for society and law, on the other hand, is that a transnational corporation can readily evade those national controls or policies which it regards as hindersome. A government seeking to impose taxes or environmental rules, or even to place restrictions on a particular product or activity, may find itself faced with the real threat that the corporation will in that case transfer some or all of its activities to a foreign subsidiary operating under a more understanding regime. The prospect of the ensuing disruption of employment and exports may well cause the authorities to compromise or to withdraw contested measures entirely. Transnational firms also exert a strong influence on both governmental and intergovernmental organizations, being called into consultation with them and undertaking lobbying both in their individual and joint interests. A former regional officer of the World Health Organization recalls a typical scene:

> When I was with the Minister of Health to advise on pulling together drug policies in Sub-Saharan Africa he asked me to go with him to the Minister of Trade, who was due to have a meeting with this vast pharmaceutical and chemical company X from the States. They turned up with their top brass in the company jet – President, Comptroller and all, to talk about setting up some sort of regional centre here in the capital. You could see from the outset who was in charge, and they knew it. They even knew that my WHO country budget for the entire biennium was ten thousand dollars, and here they were talking in millions and offering to show the Medical College how to train prescribers and fly the Ministers off

to see their New Jersey operation. You could see the people at the Government
table were bowled over – just deeply impressed, and willing to do more or less
anything the company wanted of them. (Interview 6)

Examples cited elsewhere in this volume show how transnational
corporations, working alone or as a group, have had a massive influence
on events ranging from the development of the TRIPS agreement to the
2001 battle over the prices of AIDS drugs in South Africa.

Within a purely national environment, one can see how ethical
standards can be nurtured both within a company and as a result of trends
in society generally, and how ultimately the new standards can find their
confirmation in law. None of those processes is likely to evolve fast, but
progress may be even slower at the transnational level. While a transnational will have certain world-wide business policies, beyond that point
it may in cultural terms be heterogeneous, with a different internal culture from one subsidiary to another; notions as to what society can expect
of it may be very variable. The same applies to the countries and continents where it operates; social beliefs, politics and ways of doing business will differ. In such a situation, a true corporate-wide conviction on
a matter such as the social responsibility of the corporation may be very
slow to develop. Add to that the fact that in each of the countries concerned ideas of law and governance also differ, and it becomes difficult
to see consistent relationships developing and being implemented
between a company and the various societies within which its various
subsidiaries operate.

In theory, transnational business needs to be counterbalanced and
guided by transnational or supranational law. That situation is however only
being approached regionally, notably within the European Community with
its progressive harmonization (and to a degree centralization) of pharmaceutical law and regulation. At a global level, even the imposition of rules
of criminal law is well-nigh impossible (IRENE 2000); the development of
standards can only take the form of recommendations. As at the national
level, there have been attempts to devise "codes". The United Nations,
deeply involved in the experimental development of public–private partnerships, is well aware of the extent to which the pressures exerted on it by
member states can originate from the business sector and has tried hard to
identify standards. Its Economic and Social Council has since 2003 also
been working on the issue of human rights within multinational corporations, though hampered by what it terms "gaps in understanding the nature
and scope of the human rights responsibilities of business" (UN
2003, 2005). The latest report of the relevant Sub-Committee reviews

existing initiatives and standards on corporate social responsibility from a human rights perspective. Since 2000, the "Global Compact" has attempted to bring together the United Nations and major elements of transnational business to develop and implement sound and socially acceptable business principles (Adnan 2000), though its acceptance both in the world of commerce and in activist circles has varied (CEO 2000). While business leaders have welcomed any opportunity to acquire greater influence in the United Nations, there is clearly strong business opposition to any agreement that could lead to the adoption of rules binding on transnational firms. Such developments have, however, at least implemented a debate on some of the rules which may at some date earn a place in global business, including the socially desirable activities to be expected of the pharmaceutical industry. Finally, within the pharmaceutical sector itself there have been international codes intended to cover specific types of activity, notably advertising (see Chapter 5), and these are strengthened by the existence of an implementation mechanism; codes emanating from UN bodies, by contrast, will at most create an obligation for a business to report periodically on its performance.

One counterweight to excessive transnational influence in the pharmaceutical field is the growth of activist movements, in essence seeking to represent the interests of the individual where the normal processes of government do not perform this task adequately. Notable are a number of organizations having both in-country and international units, such as Médecins sans Frontières (Doctors without Borders), based in France, and Health Action International (HAI), operating from The Netherlands. While these were in their early days dismissed by some in the pharmaceutical industry as unacceptably radical, they have gained increasing influence because of their demonstrated honesty, commitment and expertise. Their studies and publications have documented problems and offered solutions, both on general issues and in specific disputes.

Ultimate change in the interests of society must however begin with a willingness within transnational business to recognize its various social duties in the very heterogeneous world in which it has chosen to do business. It may indeed appear difficult to balance the salary needs of Swiss workers against the call for very low drug prices in Northern Uganda or a demand for urgent correction of a pollution risk from the corporation's factory in Brazil, but that is the price of diversity. It is an essential aspect of commerce that every opportunity also brings problems with it; and if a corporation has accepted the complexity of transnational expansion then it is reasonable to expect that management will also be attuned to solving the wider range of problems that come in its wake, including the acceptance of new forms and degrees of social responsibility.

Judith Richter, in a study devoted primarily to the multinational industry manufacturing artificial breast-milk substitutes, has described the effective regulation of transnational corporations as " . . . a critical – and unfinished – task of global democratic governance." Study of the issue, in her words, " . . . highlights important issues for current attempts to establish checks and balances on corporate activities that conflict with fundamental human rights and other social concerns in an increasingly globalised world." (Richter 2001 at pp. 2, 3).

Especially problematical is this rapidly ongoing process of globalization. The term is not exactly defined, but it is a process in which "many chains of political, economic and social activity are becoming international and intercontinental in scope" with "an intensification of levels of interaction and interconnectedness within and between states and societies" (Held 1998 at p. 13). It has both been welcomed and criticized – the criticism relating to the extent to which it may erode national regulation (Paul and Garred 2000 at p. 3) or the overall ability of the state to provide stability and social protection (Stiglitz 2004). The process has co-coincided in turn with (and has been strongly influenced by) one of the periodic swings in social and political beliefs to which society is subject and which, so long as they hold sway, have a powerful influence on the way society functions; the current trend is that to "liberalization". Had globalization coincided with a strengthening of social democracy, it might have been characterized by an accelerated development of international public institutions and governance. As it is, the era has been marked primarily by the rapid development of agreements to promote international trade, industry and the private sector in general. Those involved have conceived these process as being in the broad public interest in that they might be expected to ensure growth of the economy, with a growth in employment, income and consequent well-being. Very little attention has however been paid to the fact, all too well known from national experience, that in certain situations economic and company interests could conflict with other valid interests such as those in the field of health, and that effective checks and balances will be required if harm is not to be done.

In summary, although the ultimate pattern of governance for transnational pharmaceutical corporations cannot be predicted, a number of processes are in motion which may contribute to it:

- The first, undoubtedly, is the further development, both within business and within society in general, of social concepts relating to the role of industry in the community and the acceptance of these ideas in a wider range of countries than hitherto. Publications, education and broad negotiation will ensure that the debate towards consensus continues. Attempts to define sector-wide codes of socially responsible business practices could provide some concrete starting points for debate (HRREC 2004), although the codes themselves may have little effect.

- The second, certainly, is the continued role of activist organizations in providing a counterweight to industry in debate on both general and specific issues. While they will continue to draw attention to weaknesses, they have also by now demonstrated their creative and constructive abilities, and among influential figures in the senior management of the pharmaceutical industry one encounters a distinctly growing measure of respect for their honesty and objectivity in debate.
- A third influence, regrettable but undeniably, emerges from the occurrence from time to time of scandals and malpractices in this field. When these occur it will be important to study and explain them; just as drug disasters catalysed the development of drug regulation a generation ago, so a proper understanding of why some things go wrong within and around the transnational corporations will be more helpful than seeking to deny or excuse them.

The growth of the transnationals in this field of business is likely to continue and perhaps accelerate. Whatever the complexities, there is good reason to see it as a process which, despite its risks, can be turned to advantage in health care and development. That will however only be the case if there is sufficient influence from the side of the community to guide and adjust the process, correct its errors and assimilate it into world health policies.

2.10. "Corporate Social Responsibility" and Government

The term "corporate social responsibility" has been challenged by those who cite examples of its being misused as a mere image-building tool without real significance for the community (Mathiason 2002). The phrase is also used in several quite different ways. A spokesman for the pharmaceutical industry has argued that "the primary societal responsibility of the pharmaceutical industry is to develop new drugs and vaccines" (Bale 2005), while others have laid the accent on manufacturing and supply, or simply on the fact that a company serves the community adequately by engaging in its primary activities (Frost 2005). Many however, choose to speak of "social responsibility" when referring to those ventures which serve society and in which a corporation engages without their being seen as a core part of its firm's business or as intended to promote that business. The term is used here in that sense – as a convenient holdall for bringing together under a single heading the many forms of duty (other than simply rewarding shareholders and stamping out goods to that end) that may be said to have sometimes come to rest on the shoulders of a corporation in modern society and that are sometimes acknowledged and implemented. Those various duties are not homogenous in their content or status. They range from firm obligations imposed on a business by law to tasks which a company has voluntarily taken upon itself, and other duties that are emerging as society learns to formulate better its expectations as to what it can and can demand of a group of people working together constructively as a team.

As corporations grow in some way into that new role, one needs to remain clear as to their relationship to government. In principle, in a democratic world, laws and regulations are made by an elected government, which creates rights and obligations both for the individuals who elected it and for corporate persons. Individuals influence the process by casting their votes. Corporations do not vote, but they can earn respect and rights for themselves through their achievements, and they can strengthen their hand by judicious negotiation and lobbying.

Experiments will be needed before society learns how best to handle an industrial sector where, as is the case with pharmaceuticals, neither law nor corporate management have so far contrived to ensure consistent progress without encountering serious problems. Kofi Annan's Global Compact, touched on above, represents one such experiment. Public-private partnerships represent another such venture, both within countries and internationally. Dr Gro Harlem Brundtland lauded the concept when she introduced the 1990 Earth Summit:

> Partnership is what is needed in today's world, partnership between government and industry, between producers and consumers, between the present and the future. . . . We need to build new coalitions . . . We must continue to move from confrontation . . . . . . through dialogue to co-operation. . . .

All the same, no such partnership had proven its worth when Dr Harlem Brundtland spoke, and the experiments continue. Some such partnerships currently include attempts to develop the pharmaceutical innovation needed for the third world (Chapter 8). Others, at the national level, involve a cautious attempt by government and the pharmaceutical industry to play complementary roles in developing standards for corporate behaviour. In the pharmaceutical sector, the UK Government is preparing a framework to encourage "best practice", gathering illustrative case studies of corporate activity and promoting the publication by companies of their efforts to promote access to medicines in developing countries (DFID 2005). Within the same initiative, pharmaceutical companies are planning to develop broader social involvement in the health sector including the promotion of sustainable financing, support for good governance and programmes to combat poverty, as well as a willingness to share with the governments of developing countries their experience in fields such as logistics, risk containment and supply (DFID 2005). The results of these ventures have to be awaited. None has yet shown that public–private partnerships merit a permanent place in society and recognition in law as an institution within which duties can be filled or rights exercised. At least, however, such developments are a far cry from the *Ford* ruling of 1915, when the view held sway that the only task of a company was to reward its stockholders.

There are still those who express great caution as regards the so-called social role of the pharmaceutical sector (Swoboda 1999) or of industry in general (Jennings 1997, Henderson 2004). Somewhere a balance will no doubt emerge, with the primary functions of a corporation placed at the centre of its activities, and a wide range of other socially desirable and constructive activities recognized as proper tasks to be assumed as and when there is a call for them and its resources allow. A crucial question will be to what extent the parties representing both government and business can succeed in working together where the one has the constitutional task of controlling the other, and where it is constantly obliged, in the process of government, to call the other to order.

Compacts and Partnerships are only two aspects of an effort that has been proceeding now for four decades to find a proper relationship between the interests of society at large and those of the pharmaceutical industry. There is obviously no definitive answer that will hold good for all time. Attitudes will change with oscillations in political thinking, and with the extent to which the industry earns or loses credibility or popular trust in its scientific achievements and with its social behaviour in general. The larger and stronger the pharmaceutical corporations become, the greater the influence they will exert or seek to exert, and the more prone governments will be to encourage and guide them rather than simply dictating to them; yet nothing alters the fact that, as corporate persons, these companies remain subjects of the law.

Chapter 3

Sources of Standards Specific to the Pharmaceutical Industry

3.1. General Considerations

The pharmaceutical industry did not appear overnight. It came into being over many centuries, building on traditions created by others as they served the health needs of the community in their various ways, welding those traditions together and building a new one alongside them. As makers of medicines, the industry inherited much that came from the profession of pharmacy; in its ambition to provide care and instruction for the patient it learnt from the tradition of medicine; it absorbed the learning of chemistry and it brought a dozen newer sciences to fruition. In doing so, it became a new and potent unit of society, which was all the time creating fresh knowledge on the one hand and absorbing new learning on the other, registering achievements and falling into errors, and learning from both experiences.

All these traditions, as well as those of business and industry and the growing concept of human rights in health (see Section 2.1.2 in Chapter 2), were progressively welded together into an industry which acquired a face, a character and a way of working of its own. These things too needed to be defined if the industry was to function as a worthy element of society, capable of enriching it but also willing to heed its needs in order to serve it.

The specific laws, rules and regulations that govern the drug industry at the present day are all of recent origin; they are extensive, and they are still developing. Their scope, though ever broader, is limited to well-defined technical issues. Behind them one can still find the ancient traditions of the professions on the one hand and the unwritten and instinctive rules of ethics on the other, ready to supplement the laws and regulations when new situations emerge, when opinions seem to collide, and when the inevitable question arises: what is the decent thing to do?

3.2.   Standards Originating from Pharmacy Practice

3.2.1.   *A basis in trust*

Because the most central role of the pharmaceutical industry is the compounding and supply of medicines – the traditional role of the apothecary or pharmacist[1] – the standards of behaviour associated with the profession naturally apply in large measure to the industry as well. Drug manufacturing began when individual pharmacists started to make entire batches of drugs in their compounding rooms rather than making up every prescription individually. The industry only gradually became distinct from the profession, and in many parts of the world there are still firms which operate both retail and wholesale pharmacies as well as are engaged in drug manufacturing. The pharmacist of old was in the first place skilled in the taking of herbs to prepare medicines and was believed to have been endowed with that special skill from on high. When King James I of England in 1614 granted a Royal Charter to establish a Society of Apothecaries, it was intended as a means of

> *".......The Lord hath created Medicines out of the Earth: and he that is wise will not abhor them. Of such doth the Apothecary make a confection. He hath given men skill that he might be honoured in his marvellous works; and of his works there are no end . . . with such he doth heal a man and taketh away his pains.*
>
> *There is a time when in the Apothecaries' hands there is good success, for they shall pray to the Lord that he prosper that which they give for curing and relief, and remedies to prolong life . . . . ."*
>
> — *Ecclesiasticus, Chapter XXXVIII*

---

[1] The older term "apothecary" and the more modern term "pharmacist" are here used as equivalents, since in most countries they have a closely similar meaning; the traditional apothecary's shop developed progressively into the modern pharmacy. In some countries and languages however the older term is used only for the practising retailer ("apoteker" in much of Northern and Central Europe) while the term "pharmacist" is used for the scientifically trained professional who may or may not wish to qualify and work as an "apoteker". In Britain the history of the nomenclature is more complex since the former Apothecaries were assimilated entirely into the medical profession in the eighteenth and nineteenth centuries; their dispensing and retailing tasks passed to the "chemists", who had traditionally dealt in chemical substances. See Copeman W.S.C. (1967): The Worshipful Society of Apothecaries of London: A history 1617–1967. Pergamon Press, Oxford.

distinguishing the skilled men from the unskilled, since ". . . very many Empiricks and unskillful and ignorant men do abide in the City of London, which are not well instructed in the Art or Mystery of Apothecaries, but do make and compound many unwholesome, hurtful, dangerous and corrupt medicines and the same do sell . . . to the great peril and daily hazard of the lives of the King's subjects." The King's principal reason to grant the petition, distinguishing the apothecaries from the grocers and other tradesmen, was that their "mysteries" – their special skills and learning – set them apart from all others.

Both before and after that time, the principle was established that the people must be able to depend on the pharmacist or apothecary to perform his tasks in a manner on which they could rely utterly, having insufficient knowledge of their own to judge the medicines which he supplied. Pharmacy standards were and are therefore rooted in the need to create and preserve trust. As in any other profession, the individual consulting the practitioner had to be able to place complete faith in the services, goods or advice that he received. The principle of trust, and of the pharmacist's strict duty to the community and the patient, has been reflected in charters, laws and codes governing the profession in every age:

> Considering the patient-pharmacist relationship as a covenant means that a pharmacist has moral obligations in response to the gift of trust received from society. In return for this gift, a pharmacist promises to help individuals . . . and to maintain their trust. . . Code of Ethics, American Pharmaceutical Association (APA 1994)

> The primary concern of the pharmacist must be the health and wellbeing of both clients and the community. Code of conduct, Pharmaceutical Society of Australia (PSA 1998).

> Pharmaceutical practitioners enjoy a special trust and authority. . . . (College of Pharmacy, University of Texas). (UT 1998)

Standards of practice in the pharmaceutical profession have been most extensively codified in national legislation, particularly from the nineteenth century onwards. They are however also formulated in codes of practice adopted, with or without some mechanism for their enforcement or some type or form of official sanction, by professional associations. In Britain, the 1992 edition of the Royal Pharmaceutical Society's Code of Ethics (Box 3.A) provides an excellent example which has been emulated in simplified form elsewhere, particularly in countries of the Commonwealth. Though it runs in its full version to some 40 printed pages, it is essentially built around nine basic principles, cited in Box 3.A; the remainder of the document comprises the many detailed obligations which flow from the adoption of the nine principles.

Although the seventh and eighth of these principles (and many of the detailed obligations to be found in the full code) are so formulated that they bear specifically on the situation of community pharmacy, the remainder are expressed in broad terms and may be considered to be widely applicable.

PRINCIPLES

1. A pharmacist's prime concern must be for the welfare of both the patient and other members of the public.

2. A pharmacist must uphold the honour and dignity of the profession and not engage in any activity which may bring the profession into disrepute

3. A pharmacist must at all times have regard to the laws and regulations applicable to pharmaceutical practice and maintan a high standard of professional conduct. A pharmacist must avoid any act or omission which would impair confidence in the pharmaceutical profession. When a pharmaceutical service is provided, a pharmacist must ensure that it is efficient.

4. A pharmacist must respect the confidentiality of information acquired in the course of professional practice relating to a patient and the patient's family. Such information may not be disclosed to anyone without the consent of the patient or appropriate guardian unless the interest of the patient or the public requires such disclosure.

5. A pharmacist must keep abreast of the progress of pharmaceutical knowledge in order to maintain a high standard of professional competence relative to his sphere of activity.

6. A pharmacist must neither agree to practice under any conditions which compromise professional independence or judgement nor impose such conditions on other pharmacists.

7. A pharmacist or pharmacy owner should, in the public interest, provide information about available professional services. Publicity must not claim or imply any superiority over the professional service provided by other pharmacists or pharmacies, must be dignified and must not bring the profession into disrepute.

8. A pharmacist offering services directly to the public must do so in premises which reflect the professional character of pharmacy

9. A pharmacist must at all time endeavour to cooperate with professional colleagues and members of other health professions so that patients and the public may benefit.

Box 3.A Royal Pharmaceutical Society (United Kingdom) Principles (From: Code of Ethics, 1992)

3.2.2. *Professional pharmacy in industry*

While definitions of the pharmacist's duties have as a rule reflected primarily the duty of the independent community pharmacist serving the patient directly, modern codes have made clear the fact that he assumes a lifetime commitment so long as he exercises his profession, and that he remains bound to his duty even when he is working for another. As is the case with the physician who holds a position in the pharmaceutical industry (see Section 3.3), the industrial pharmacist is held in law to be exercising his profession (and therefore bound to his professional obligations) when he performs an industrial task. A quality defect in an industrially prepared medicine cannot merely be regarded as a fault of the manufacturer as a legal person, but will also be held to reflect on the individual who bore the ultimate responsibility for the process within which the fault occurred. Laws differ in their designation of the exact positions which must be held by a pharmacist. In France, exceptionally, the Public Health Section of the Civil Code long ago incorporated the rule that a pharmaceutical company must either be the property of a pharmacist, or that a pharmacist must sit on its Board to perform certain broad tasks prescribed by law. As a rule, his role has been more circumscribed:

> A Decree under the Netherlands Medicines Act of 1958, from which so many other European statutes were derived, ordained that: "The preparation of a packaged medicine by a manufacturer must take place under supervision of a pharmacist, who can be deemed to perform this function in consequence of his qualification to exercise the profession of pharmacy" though the decree did provide for exceptions where another well-qualified and experienced person was available. By 1975, the European Community's Directive 75/319 required that the manufacturer must employ a "qualified person" for this purpose (EIGP 2005), and when the Directive was taken as the basis for revision of the United Kingdom legislation it was decided that this person might be a pharmacist or a suitably qualified chemist or biologist.

At present, whatever the national law, any pharmaceutical firm operating in industrialized countries or exporting its products is likely to employ a pharmacist at the most senior level in the production process, generally with the overall responsibility for the division or at least as head of the unit responsible for quality control. In such a position, he will in fact be performing a task in the community closely similar to that of the traditional community or hospital pharmacist. Trust in him to perform this task competently will effectively remain as firm as it has ever been; whatever role he plays in production he should be considered as having a professional obligation not merely to carry out instructions conscientiously but also to ensure that to the best of his ability he maintains and enhances standards in a manner which he regards as desirable and necessary for the sake of the user.

Pharmacists have also progressively assumed a range of other tasks in industry beyond production and quality control, being involved in matters ranging from the editing and approval of drug information or the study of adverse reactions to the training of detailmen or the proper disposal of waste goods. In such matters, the pharmacist will still encounter standards laid down for him in the codes governing his profession. A breach of these standards may not contravene any law or even an internal company rule, yet it may well run foul of a professional code and justify disciplinary action. A pharmacist accepting employment under general or specific conditions that render it impossible to act according to the dictates of his professional conscience may similarly be in breach:

> *On employment and conditions of service:* "A pharmacist must neither agree to practise under conditions which compromise his professional independence, judgement or integrity. . ." (PSA 1998, Principle 5)
> *On drug approval and adverse reactions:* "A pharmacist must not. . . . sell or supply any medicinal product where there is reason to doubt its safety, quality or efficacy or where there is clear, new evidence that demonstrates or places doubt on previously established product safety or where a product may impose a hazard to the patient's health or condition." (PSA, para 1.2)
> *On sales and supply:* "A pharmacist must exercise professional judgement to prevent the supply of products likely to constitute an unacceptable hazard to health. . . ." (PSA 1998 at 1.3)
> *On waste disposal:* "A pharmacist must ensure that all reasonable care is taken when disposing of medicinal products and chemicals." (PSA at 1.4)
> *On provision of information to home or export markets:* "A pharmacist has a duty to tell the truth, to act with conviction of conscience, and to avoid discriminatory practices and behaviour". (CPBC 2005 at para 2)

However he practices, the pharmacist has a well-recognized duty to maintain his standard of knowledge throughout his career:

> . . . there must be an established *minimum standard of knowledge* for practitioners, and . . . there must be agreement amongst them about *standards of behaviour* in their professional work. (Appelbe 1993 at p. 225)

No less a standard can be held to apply to the pharmacist employed by the pharmaceutical industry of the twenty-first century. In the oldest tradition of pharmacy, when knowledge of medicinal materials and substances was traditional and developed only slowly, the pharmacist learned his profession through apprenticeship; in the course of the nineteenth century professional training was instituted at many universities and colleges. That training has now in an increasing number of institutions been supplemented with post-graduate teaching in a number of directions, one of them being industrial pharmacy, since basic training in pharmacy does not provide an adequate basis for the wider and demanding pharmaceutical responsibilities which industrial employment brings with it. Beyond that, however, the ongoing development of knowledge, drugs and techniques will demand throughout his career in industry changes in working methods on the one hand or in the information which he conveys to the outside world on the other. However important the literature, much of the knowledge he needs will relate to current findings and developments and will be acquired in his daily work in the professional team of which he forms part; in an important sense, the tradition of apprenticeship has returned:

> A pharmacist has a duty to maintain knowledge and abilities as new medications, devices and technologies become available and as health information advances (APA 1994)

This could be regarded as imposing a duty on the industrial pharmacist to ensure of his own accord that his knowledge and skills are updated but also a duty on the corporation employing him to provide him at least with the opportunity to learn continuously.

The European Industrial Pharmacists Group has published both a general Code of Practice for Industrial Pharmacists (EIGP 2005) as well as a number of specialized codes; these are attuned primarily to the needs of those working as "Qualified Persons" (in the terminology of the European Directives) in this field throughout Europe; the code is concerned mainly with technical and not with ethical issues.

3.2.3. *Allocation of general pharmaceutical responsibilities*

It is clearly in the first place up to a pharmaceutical firm to decide on the specific tasks which a pharmacist will be called upon to perform in its service, according to its particular needs. The question arises, however, whether every company should not employ a Chief Pharmacist having broad responsibilities for the maintenance of pharmaceutical standards throughout the company. Surprisingly enough this is not to date universal practice. While it is common to have a Medical Director with tasks in every division of the company, most industrial pharmacists are appointed to specific fields of work, and even where the title of "Chief Pharmacist" exists the responsibilities sometimes cover only issues of production and quality. A pharmacist working in any other division (for example, drug information) may therefore be relatively isolated from his professional colleagues in other sections and unable to fall back on a senior member of his profession for support when the need arises.

An important role which a true Chief Pharmacist could play would comprise the ability to tackle new and unanticipated situations within his professional ärea. An example concerns the field of general environmental pollution with pharmaceuticals and their metabolites, an issue which has arisen only recently:

> A growing body of scientists are turning their attention to projects which assess the impact that pharmaceuticals, because of their wide dissemination, could be having on the environment. General effluent analysed by Italian researchers has been found to contain 26 pharmaceutical agents. While pharmaceuticals are designed specifically to have biological effects, evidence of the damage which they might do to living organisms is largely lacking or contested. In 2004 the European Commission established three scientific projects to investigate the issue; it was anticipated that the pharmaceutical industry would be invited to contribute to the work. (Scrip 2004, p. 6)

3.2.4.   *Trade interests vs. professional interests*

Throughout its existence, much of the pharmaceutical profession has been confronted with the question as to how its professional and its commercial role can be exercised alongside one another without standards being compromised:

> . . . there is undoubtedly a difference between the trading outlook and the professional outlook. The tradesman, however honest, is principally concerned with the profitability of his business. His main object is to achieve as large a financial return as possible. He holds his customers to be the best judges of what they want and he seeks to satisfy their demands. . . . The professional man working in his special field of knowledge where his advice is crucial must be the judge of what is best for his client and customer. If he does this according to the standards of his profession, then the advice he gives must, at times, be to the practitioner's own financial disadvantage. . . . (Appelbe 1993 at p. 229)

These problems arise most clearly in retail pharmacy, where a pharmacist who also owns his business will regularly be faced with situations in which he has to chose himself between financial gain and professional propriety. Where, as in many western countries, a pharmacy may be owned by a firm or a commercial proprietor, there can be a greater or lesser conflict

between the financial interests of the owner and the desire of the professional manager whom he employs to serve his clients in a manner befitting
their needs and interests. There is a direct parallel here with the situation in
a pharmaceutical firm where the need to serve ambitious commercial goals
may on some occasions raise the temptation to compromise with one's professional principles:

> The firm has always been pretty genuine in its dealings, and so long as I was in
> quality control I don't recall a single moment when my judgement was ignored; if
> I wasn't willing to sign off a batch then I didn't do it and it went into the waste
> channel. I did run into sticky moments when I moved to the subsidiary in Rio,
> where I was the only scientific person backing up the management and sales staff
> because now and again I saw things happening around me that I'd rather not have
> seen. That advertisement I remember, that had the detailmen sniggering – it wasn't
> truthful and the drug should have been pulled from the market years ago – but it
> wasn't my responsibility. Still I did make some noises here and there and finally
> people agreed that we should drop that campaign. You can't always put your foot
> down – you have to persuade people to rethink things – and then you can do some
> good. (Interview 45)

The crucial point is that when a pharmacist is appointed to an industrial firm, he is chosen because he is able to bring his professional knowledge and thinking into the corporation, and not merely because he has a
decorative title; in one way or another he brings with him a duty to ensure
that the ethics of his profession are respected and standards maintained:

> If you ask me whether it was always easy then the answer is no, nor am I going to
> pretend that when you jump on your pharmaceutical high horse you are always
> going to get your way. You are a member of the firm's team and you have to live
> with that, but that doesn't mean simply giving you professional blessing to every-
> thing that happens. Sometimes you may shake your head at something you can't
> avoid, but you have to make an effort to put it to rights and not just let them roll
> over you. The great thing is that by remaining as firm as you can you soon get
> plenty of right-thinking people going along with you. (Interview 17, translated).

Where a pharmacist has left independent professional employment
to join the staff of a pharmaceutical company the principles set out in his
professional oaths and codes may no longer be legally binding on him, but
there can be no doubt that unless he explicitly abandons his profession
(for example, to take up a purely commercial function without further use
of his title or qualifications) he is still morally bound by them. An example would relate to the pharmacist who takes up an industrial position in
which he replies by letter on the company's behalf to queries from
professionals or the public. If he makes use of his title or qualifications in

signing such letters the recipient is entitled to believe that the text reflects his professional judgement on the matter at hand, or at least a company view which the writer does not find to be at odds with his professional beliefs.

Viewed from another angle: by engaging in the preparation and supply of drugs, and in recruiting professional pharmacists to participate in that task, a pharmaceutical company may be considered to have bound itself to respect the principles of the pharmacist's Code of Ethics.

To summarize the ways in which the above six principles of the Royal Pharmaceutical Society's Code can be said to govern the situation:

(1)   "Prime concern" for the welfare of the patient and public will necessarily mean that this concern must override commercial interests where the two conflict.

(2), (6) The need to avoid bringing the profession into disrepute, and thereby weakening one of the pillars of health care, means that a pharmaceutical company should allow its pharmaceutical staff to exercise its best professional judgement in all matters, avoiding any duress which might lead them into compromise or submission.

(3)   In interpreting the laws and regulations incumbent on industry, for example, as regards product quality and drug information, a firm should involve its professional staff and respect their views on the matter.

(4)   When handling confidential information with respect to patients and their families – for example, in the conduct and evaluation of clinical studies – a firm must treat this information with the same respect for private life which a retail pharmacist will be expected to exercise.

(5)   If a pharmacist is to function as such within a pharmaceutical company he must be given a sufficient opportunity to maintain and extend his professional knowledge – for example through access to literature and attendance at meetings and courses.

On various of these issues, the professional role of the pharmacist overlaps with and complements that of the industrial physician (see the Section below).

3.3.   Standards Originating from Medical Law and Ethics

3.3.1.   *Primary duty to the patient*

The standards of duty incumbent on the practising doctor have been defined on many occasions, both in general and specific terms. Like the pharmacist, the medical man carries those duties with him when he joins an industry, and by extrapolation they become part of the industry's own obligations to the community. The broadest view of medical duties in society is that with which every treatise on medical ethics opens:

> Doctors are expected to behave with honour and probity towards patients, other doctors and the rest of society. The doctor's primary responsibility is to patients, and their best interests must be put above all other considerations. (BMA 1988)

That principle alone creates a basis for a series of ethical rules applicable to the practice of the industry. They range from a duty to investigate and ensure the reasonable efficacy, safety and quality of a drug to an obligation to provide sufficient information and guidance on its properties and appropriate use. The duty to put the patient's interest "above all other considerations" is directly relevant when the temptation arises – as it will in any commercial undertaking – to cut corners and manipulate facts in the interest of profit.

3.3.2.   *Current medical expertise*

Of the various duties of a physician which relate to the choice and application of therapy, the most fundamental is the obligation to acquire and maintain sufficient competence to perform his tasks satisfactorily. The duty is long recognized, but it is of vital importance for a physician in the industrial situation; *firstly*, he is likely to be at the cutting edge of research and therefore faced to a greater extent than the practising physician with a constant flow of new facts, but also of new hypotheses and theories which have yet to be tested or confirmed. *Secondly*, the physician in industry is inevitably surrounded with partial views which have developed within the team of which he forms part, and which he constantly needs to test against the flow of opinion in the medical and scientific world outside, and on which he may need to exercise strong influence if standards are to be maintained. Like the pharmacist (see Section 3.2.2 above) he must be presumed to have been appointed to his post because of his ability to provide professional input and judgement and not merely to embellish the company's policies with a professional flourish.

3.3.3.   The duty of care

A pharmaceutical firm does not care for the individual patient in the sense of choosing or supervising his treatment, but the tools, information and guidance which it provides to practising physicians underlie an important part of the care which those practitioners provide. That guidance is largely given in general terms (for example, in data sheets and directions folders) but physicians do repeatedly turn to the medical department of a drug company to seek advice on matters relating to treatment and will ordinarily receive a fully documented answer based on (but also interpreting) the current literature to which the company is likely to have more ready access than a physician in an isolated practice. Like the company pharmacist in an analogous situation (see Section 3.2.2) the physician who provides that advice in his medical capacity has a professional obligation to provide it to the best of his ability, uninfluenced by company preferences; where he cannot provide a well-founded answer, for example because of his lack of contact with the patient, he should make this clear.

On occasion the Courts have not hesitated to hold a medical staff member personally (or jointly and severally) responsible for a fault made by the company where this clearly lay within his area of medical responsibility. A misstatement, after all, can injure or kill as surely as a careless injection:

> The case of Dr Christopher Good of Roussel Laboratories was summarised in Chapter 2. At the time it was considered by outside critics that the judgement could have a salutory effect on the maintenance of advertising standards, but in subsequent discussions it was notable that pharmaceutical physicians and scientific staff within other companies tended to come to the defence of the accused. It was argued variously that the evidence as to the drug's properties was ambiguous, that a degree of commercial licence was permissible, and that it was unreasonable to hold a medical director liable for what were essentially acts of commercial management. A physician in Dr Good's situation could and should in their view seek to guide commercial management in an ethically acceptable direction but could not be held responsible for the outcome in individual situations. (Interviews 8, 21 and 33)

It may be noticed in the above connection that Section 124(1) of the United Kingdom's Medicines Act explicitly makes the medical director of a company responsible for the content of each advertisement. Company physicians have also been charged in Germany and the US for company offences, particularly concerned with the withholding of safety information. Two classic instances related to drug tragedies in which failings on the part of the medical staff played a direct role:

> Following the "thalidomide" tragedy in the Federal Republic of Germany, a prosecution for involuntary manslaughter was indeed brought against nine individual members of the staff of the Grünenthal Company including physicians. The case was however allowed to lapse after two years, perhaps as part of the general settlement agreed upon with the company[2]

> Criminal proceedings were successfully instituted against Dr William Shedden, a senior employee of Eli Lilly in the United States for delays in the submission of adverse reaction reports on benoxaprofen (Oraflex) to the FDA; a $15,000 fine was imposed.

3.3.4. Confidentiality

While it is well recognized that the doctor has a duty to maintain strict confidentiality regarding his professional encounters, the meaning and limitations of that duty are not well defined. There must obviously be exceptions, provided for in the patient's best interests, but they are not specified in the classic texts. The Hippocratic oath (which is in most matters too far removed from modern medicine to be useful) comes a little closer to the issue of confidentiality but it remains vague:

> Whatever, in connection with my professional practice. . . . I see or hear, in the life of men, which ought not to be spoken of abroad, I will not divulge, as reckoning that all such should be kept secret. . . . (Hippocratic Oath, as cited by Arras 1989 at p. 4)

The practising physician has a close knowledge of his patient and of the latter's medical history and circumstances, and the trust which he enjoys to regard this knowledge as strictly confidential must be virtually absolute with a few narrow exceptions to serve the patient's best interests. Under most normal conditions, the physician within industry will not find

---

[2] See opposed interpretations by Braithwaite J. (1984) *op. cit.* at p. 73 and Klijn K. (1982): Produktaansprakelijkheid en de farmaceutische industrie. (Product Liability and the Pharmaceutical Industry) Reported in *Pharm. Weekbl., 117*, 144–145 at pp. 145–146 (*in Dutch*).

himself in this situation, but industry maintains close contacts with practitioners on many fronts and in the field the rules are not always interpreted so strictly:

> One might as well realize that, with photocopying machines around, patient information gets everywhere. As a medical adviser to the home sales unit I have a desk full of paper every morning from GP's wanting my advice on how to deal with some case or other, and plenty of them come with xeroxed patient cards and a scribbled note – what am I supposed to do? I may not want to know that Lady G's debutante daughter has had a couple of abortions but now I do. . . . (Interview 8)

There is obviously a place in every medical department for a paper shredder to dispose of unwanted confidences, but also for a special filing system for those confidences that for the moment may need to be retained.

Much closer contact to patients can arise in some other situations, notably where the firm sponsors a clinical study (see Section 9.2) and a company physician is appointed to monitor it and to assist the independent investigator in reporting on it. Despite the strict division of tasks and responsibilities between the monitor and the investigator, with the latter handling the care and treatment of the trial subjects, it would not be realistic to assume that under normal ward conditions, the monitor can perform his task adequately without knowing the identity of the trial subjects or having sight of their files. Some of these facts, with the identity of the patient concealed by coding, will be necessary for the record and analysis of the study, but thereafter the identifying data must pass no further or enter the company's archives; even towards his own superior and employer, the staff physician has a professional duty to remain silent – again with a narrow scope for discretion in the patient's interests:

> A company physician M was designated as monitor of a clinical trial to be carried out by the investigator D in a local hospital. During the study, which concerned a Phase I investigation of a new sedative, one of the four patients developed an abdominal crisis with tachycardia and hypertension. The investigator D found no explanation and refused to continue the study, regarding the drug as potentially dangerous. When the monitor M reported the findings within the company, his medical director B raised the possibility that the trial subject might be suffering from an undiagnosed acute porphyria in which case this type of drug would have been regarded in advance as contraindicated; he felt that in the patient's interests the investigator should be alerted to this possibility. The investigator initially declined further contact with the firm on the matter which he regarded only as an

issue between himself and his patient, but confirmed at a later date that the trial subject, a recent immigrant from the Mediterranean Region, had now suffered a second attack after exposure to alcohol, and that a diagnosis of acute porphyria had been confirmed. He thanked B for his professional advice. (Interview 2)

3.3.5. *Allocation of general medical responsibility*

As in the case of the industrial pharmacist, it is up to a pharmaceutical company to provide a task description for the physician entering its service, primarily according to its specific needs. However, when one examines some of the legal and ethical problems which arise repeatedly in the practice of the pharmaceutical industry, one encounters all too frequently events that one must regard as representing breaches of medical duty or ethics. It is generally far from clear whether in such a case the company has acted contrary to the wishes of its medical staff or the latter have simply not been consulted. Interviews within companies point to some surprising limitations in the competence accorded to medical staff in the day-to-day operation of a firm. While every well-established firm has a Medical Director, and it is clear enough that clinical studies should always be designed and managed under the authority of a competent company physician, one commonly finds that physicians are not directly involved in the final editing and release of clinical reports for regulatory purposes, in the final instruction of detailmen before the launch of a new product, or in the definitive design and text of advertisements. Faults in these areas occur repeatedly; they create unnecessary risk and do collateral damage to the industry's reputation.

A simple example of a situation where a medical staff member should have an opportunity to intervene in commercial decisions could concern the withdrawal from the market of products which are commercially unattractive, yet for certain patients remain essential. (Scrip 2004a at p. 7) At the very least an assurance should be found that patients will have access to an identical or closely similar product from another source.

Examples of misleading advertising are unfortunately legion, with both official and self-regulatory bodies frequently requiring the withdrawal of promotional materials that are medically indefensible. Two contrasting examples from 2004 may suffice:

A promotional leaflet had been issued for an angiotensin II antagonist; the product had documented side effects which were listed in the approved Summary of Product Characteristics, yet the leaflet used the term "placebo-like tolerability" and made an unproven claim that the product was superior to others. The FDA required withdrawal of the material as being misleading. (Scrip 2004c at p. 2)

In 2004, the Warner-Lambert company[3] agreed to plead guilty and pay more than $430 million to resolve criminal and civil charges related to illegal and fraudulent promotion of unapproved ("off-label") uses of Neurontin (gabapentin) in the U.S.A. The drug had been approved by the FDA only as adjunctive therapy for partial seizures in epileptics. According to an Associate Attorney General, the firm had promoted the drug for treating bipolar disorder, ALM, attention deficit disorder, migraine, seizures from drug and alcohol withdrawal, restless legs syndrome and various other pain disorders and as a first-line monotherapy treatment for epilepsy. Illegal marketing tactics included false or misleading statements to health professionals regarding Neurontin's efficacy and its approved indications, lavish weekends and trips for doctors who prescribed Neurontin, and use of "medical liaisons" who represented themselves. often falsely, as scientific experts in a particular disease (Scrip 2004a at p. 4)

Yet another example of a situation where a physician having a broad medical-professional view might be in a position to improve standards relates to the performance of clinical experimental studies which have no genuinely scientific purpose. Elsewhere in this volume the type of pseudo-scientific "promotional" study is considered that in fact serves only to accustom a physician to the use of a new drug. Another example concerns the type of study that is sometimes deliberately designed to produce misleading data, e.g. the performance of a comparative investigation against a drug that is likely to deliver an inferior result. The British House of Commons Select Committee that investigated the industry in 2004–2005 raised the matter in the light of an instance reported to it by a witness:

It is claimed that many clinical trials are designed to fit desired outcomes or, worse, primarily for marketing purposes, rather than the advance of health care or scientific understanding. Dr Richard Nicholson, editor of the Bulletin of Medical Ethics, told us: A clinical trial was proposed to my ethics committee some years ago of Vioxx versus naproxen and we wondered to ourselves why on earth Merck want to compare this with naproxen. They did not give us the details initially and then when we asked and asked, we finally found out that they had already carried out major trials against the two major anti-inflammatory drugs . . . and found absolutely no advantage of their drug. They were hoping that by comparing it to naproxen, which had just five per cent of the market, they would be able to show an advantage (HOC 2005, para. 180).

---

[3] The offence was committed prior to the acquisition of the Warner–Lambert Company by Pfizer.

Unfortunately these are not the most extreme examples of the failings which one encounters:

> According to reports in a number of medical journals in 2004, the serious risks (including suicidal behaviour) involved in using a particular SSRI antidepressant in children were on the basis of an independent meta-analysis found to outweigh the dubious benefits. The firm had in fact been aware at an early stage of the fact that efficacy had not been adequately demonstrated in this age group, but in an internal consultation had concluded that it would be undesirable to admit this in the information literature since this would "undermine the product's profile." The negative clinical trial results in children were therefore suppressed. An authoritative editorial remarked that the idea of a drug's use being based on "the selective reporting of favourable research" should be "unimaginable" yet that in this case the firm appeared to have sought to "manipulate the results" in its favour. (Editorial 2004; Whittington 2004)

In instances such as the above it is important to determine in retrospect not merely how and where such ill-advised decisions were taken within the firm but what the involvement of the medical staff was; it is understandable that in the commercial sections of a company there will sometimes be transgressions in matters of ethics, but it is indeed "unforgivable", to use the terminology of The Lancet, if it should transpire that it happened with the connivance of the professionals whose task it should be to prevent them.

It might be concluded that in every pharmaceutical company there should be an allocation of general medical responsibility – for example, to a physician who is a member of the Board – to ensure that all issues of medical importance that arise in the course of the firm's work are dealt with in a responsible manner, irrespective of whether or not they fall within the competence of any specific staff member.

3.3.6.　A code of ethics for pharmaceutical physicians?

Beginning in 1970 a number of national groups of physicians practising in the pharmaceutical industry were formed in order to create the basis for a speciality within the medical profession. In a number of centres university-backed training courses have since been implemented and diploma courses instituted. Box 3.B shows a Code of Ethics currently maintained by the American Academy of Pharmaceutical Physicians. Subject to the reservations expressed in Section 2.9 as regards the value of Codes of Ethics in general, the debates that lead to such initiatives are

---

THE AMERICAN ACADEMY OF PHARMACEUTICAL PHYSICIANS CODE OF ETHICS FOR THE PRACTICE OF PHARMACEUTICAL MEDICINE

The AAPP Code of Ethics sets the standard of conduct and behavior for AAPP members responsible for medical considerations in pharmaceutical and medical device research and development, and post-marketing product safety surveillance.

The Code describes the principles that guide ethical decision-making to ensure that the best interests of patients and study participants, as well as their families, doctors, nurses and other health care professionals, are served. The Code seeks to assure safe use of medical products.

The Code establishes a standard for addressing ethical dilemmas in pharmaceutical research and its applications.

Members of the American Academy of Pharmaceutical Physicians (AAPP) accept the fundamental responsibility to:

Give first priority to the well being of participants in research studies and patients who use pharmaceutical products and medical devices.

Ensure that potential risks to clinical study participants are minimized, that these risks are fully evaluated against potential benefits, and that potential risks and benefits are clearly communicated to study participants and their physicians.

Apply sound ethical values and judgment in the design, conduct and analysis of clinical studies, and in the interpretation of results.

Adhere to the principles of good clinical practice and research.

Support the dissemination only of scientifically sound information from clinical trials and other investigations, without regard to study outcomes, for the benefit of medicine and science.

Ensure that all industry-based, medically relevant product information is fair, balanced, accurate, comprehensive and easily accessible, in order that patients and physicians can make well-informed decisions about the use of pharmaceuticals and medical devices.

Strive to understand and respect differences in values across cultures and to appropriately adapt behaviors while maintaining ethical principles.

Foster the education and professional competence of AAPP members, to enable them to uphold ethical principles in the practice of pharmaceutical medicine.

Appropriately question, consult and advise each other regarding medical and ethical concerns, and to seek external opinions, as appropriate, in the best interests of patients and clinical study participants.

Box 3.B A Code of Ethics for Physicians in Industry

helpful in approaching a basic consensus on the principles that should underlie such work, the emphasis often being placed on the conduct of clinical trials and the maintenance of standards in drug information.

When reading papers produced by some pharmaceutical physicians for outside consumption, one encounters a tone of confidence and success (Simpson 2002, Prasad 2003) yet it is all too well known that the conscientious physician in industry does encounter repeated situations of stress and conflict in matters where medicine and commerce intersect (RCPE 2005). There is also an uncomfortable discrepancy between these upbeat papers and the all too frequent reports of transgressions which an effective medical conscience should have been able to prevent. In the case of physicians, just as for pharmacists, the most vital step in the coming years will be to bolster the realization that the health professional within the management of the pharmaceutical industry must be allowed to maintain a sufficiently strong and independent position in which he can ensure that industry remains the servant of the community and not its master.

3.4.   Standards set by Pharmaceutical Legislation and Regulation

3.4.1.   *The evolution of modern drug regulation*

The notion that the community needs to adopt rules to ensure that medicinal products are suitable for their purpose is a very old one. According to the historian Clifford Allbutt, the Roman authorities took action in the time of Galen (AD 131–201):

> About the middle of the second century the materia medica, and the shops of the public pharmacists, were subjected ... to official inspection; first, for the Imperial household and Court, and so afterwards for the public. (Allbutt 1921 at p. 11, as cited by Mann 1984)

However with no systematically acquired knowledge on hand concerning medicines, their preparation and properties, such efforts remained very sporadic. In the fifteenth century, the Viennese authorities enacted strict rules to suppress the practice of "false apothecaries" selling valueless medicines to the public; quackery and other abuses however remained rife everywhere. During the outbreak of bubonic plague in London in the 1660s, many medicines claiming to alleviate or cure the condition were offered for sale. Some, such as those sold by the licensed apothecaries or publicly recommended by the College of Physicians, were formulated with the best of intentions, but others did not rise above the level of charlatanism, a fact which attracted the attention of the satirist Daniel Defoe and others:

> . . . it is incredible and scarce to be imagined, how the posts of houses and corners of streets were plastered over with doctors' bills and papers of ignorant fellows, quacking and tampering in physic, and inviting the people to come to them for remedies, which was generally set off with such flourishes as these, viz.: "Infallible preventive pills against the plague." "Neverfailing preservatives against the infection." "Sovereign cordials against the corruption of the air." "Exact regulations for the conduct of the body in case of an infection." "Anti-pestilential pills." "Incomparable drink against the plague, never found out before." "An universal remedy for the plague." "The only true plague water." "The royal antidote against all kinds of infection"; – and such a number more that I cannot reckon up; and if I could, would fill a book of themselves to set them down. (Defoe 1722)

In the early eighteenth century and again during the nineteenth century, individual writers proposed the setting up of a body to assess medicines before they were marketed. Shortly after 1900 the British Medical Association, inspired by pioneering ventures in Germany and The Netherlands, published two volumes of analyses of commercial drugs intended for home use, largely demonstrating that they were ineffective and that their promotion was misleading (Box 3.C; BMA 1908).

By that time society was essentially facing three essentially separate scenarios where medicines were concerned. In the first and much too obvious place were still the "ignorant fellows, quacking and tampering in physic" whom Defoe had known – the mere charlatans, whose dishonest trade sooner or later had to be suppressed. In the second place there were the serious apothecaries, conscientiously processing herbal and other remedies which had been known for centuries but which in the main had never been evaluated for their medical properties; many nascent pharmaceutical firms were using and mixing the same materials to the best of their ability. In the third place, however, there was an entirely new generation of medicines which had first come to the fore with the growth of synthetic industrial chemistry in the late nineteenth century and now blossomed in the twentieth. Some of the early innovations were beneficial and relatively harmless: "Aspirin" (acetylsalicylic acid), which was developed in Germany in 1899, was reported to have been tested for toxicity only on "two small fishes" but fortunately proved to be remarkably well tolerated in human subjects. Other innovations were less innocent; the organic arsenicals, which were used with some success to counter venereal infections at the time of the first World War, proved in due course to be so toxic that the British Government established a Commission to report on the matter and make recommendations (MRC 1922).

BEECHAM'S COUGH PILLS

These cough pills, sold from a town in Lancashire, cost 1s 11/2d per box, containing 56 pills.

The following extracts are from a circular enclosed with the box:

Persons suffering from Cough and kindred troubles should relieve their minds of the idea that nothing will benefit them unless it be in the form of a lozenge or taken as liquid. Let them try *Beecham's Cough Pills*, and they will never regret it.

The *Cough Pills* do not contain opium; they do not constipate; they do not upset the stomach. On the first symptoms of a Cold or Chill, a timely dose of Beecham's Cough Pills will invariably ward off all dangerous features. For years many families have used no other Winter Medicine. Householders and travellers should avail themselves of this good, safe, and simple remedy for Coughs in general, Asthma, Bronchial Affections, Hoarseness, Shortness of Breath, Tightness and Oppression of the Chest, Wheezing, etc.

The doses may be from three to six pills morning, noon and night.

The pills had an average weight of 1.4 grains. In spite of the statement that they "do not contain opium," analysis showed morphine to be present, together with powdered squill, powdered aniseed, extract of liquorice, and a resinous substance agreeing in character with the resin of ammoniacum. Approximate determination of the proportions of the ingredients is alone possible in such a mixture; the results obtained pointed to the following formula:

Morphine	0.0035	grain
Powdered squill	0.1	,,
Powdered aniseed	0.3	,,
Ammoniacum	0.3	,,
Extract of liquorice	0.4	,,

in one pill

Box 3.C Analysis of Beecham's Cough Pills, 1908 (BMA: Secret Remedies, 1908)

The lack of a recognized methodology to evaluate the merits of drugs, old or new, was now severely felt, but a true clinical science – with drug studies as one of its components – was slowly emerging. In 1921–1992, Frederick Banting and Charles Best in Canada extracted insulin from the pancreas and systematically demonstrated its antidiabetic use, first in experimental dogs and then in human patients. In 1933, Sir Thomas Lewis in London established the basic principles of clinical investigation (Lewis 1933). In 1935, Gerhardt Domagk in Germany published his findings in mice with the synthetic dye prontosil red, which proved

capable of protecting them against experimental infection with strepto-
cocci. In 1939, Sir Lionel Whitby in London and Evans and Gaisford in
Birmingham demonstrated the efficacy in lobar pneumonia of the
prontosil metabolite sulphapyridine, which had been synthesized in
Britain by Messrs. May and Baker as M&B 693. These and other pioneering studies at last began to lay the basis for a systematic approach to medicines, their development and their evaluation.

Not surprisingly it was precisely at this time that, with such tools to
hand, drug regulation began to emerge. The first national drug regulatory
agency in Europe was established in 1928, when Norway created an official body to licence all new medicines entering the market; (Andrew 1995)
Sweden followed the example in 1935. In the United States, certain basic
requirements regarding drugs had been introduced early in the century.
Under the Pure Food and Drug Law of 1906 products that were "adulterated or misbranded or poisonous or deleterious" could not be manufactured, vended or transported, and existing procedures for establishing
quality standards were given legal authority (Congress 1906). A much
strengthened law, with specific safety provisions, was undergoing drafting
by 1933 but its enactment was precipitated by 1938 by a major drug disaster. Elixir of Sulfanilamide, first of the sulphonamides, had been marketed by an American firm as an elixir using an untested but toxic solvent
(diethyleneglycol) and over a hundred people had died as a result. (Nielsen
1986 at p. 3, Wax 1995, Daemmerich 2003). Similarly in France it was a
disaster that led two decades later to a realization of the need to establish
firm rules. The tin compound Stalinon, developed as an oral treatment for
furunculosis, had been inadequately tested for safety, and it was reported
to have led to a hundred deaths and as many instances of serious injury.
(HP1958) The climax of concern and the full realization of the need for
the community to react came however in 1960–61 following yet another
major therapeutic disaster, when the synthetic sleeping remedy thalidomide, developed in Germany and recommended for use in pregnancy,
proved to be capable of inducing serious malformations in the unborn
child. The nature of the adverse event was entirely unanticipated in the
medical world where the view had sometimes been advanced that the
embryo and foetus were largely protected from noxious influences, and it
provided a clear signal that new medicines might have a grave potential to
do harm as well as good, perhaps in an entirely unexpected manner.
(Sjöström 1972, Teff 1976). Elsewhere in Europe, drug laws were enacted
or revised, while in the United States the existing Food and Drug
Administration was endowed with additional powers.

While the major concern at the time was with means of ensuring the safety of new medicines, there was parallel concern regarding their efficacy, the quality of their production and the truthfulness and completeness of the information provided on them. On all these matters, instances had been documented of serious shortcomings, and the progressive rise of clinical pharmacology had shown how necessary it was to examine drugs systematically in human subjects if their effects were to be properly defined. The comprehensive Medicines Act passed in The Netherlands in 1958 therefore made provision for evaluating all these and related matters, both for new products and for drugs already on sale. A Board was to be established to establish more detailed standards and to carry out the necessary evaluations of individual drugs with the support of experts and competent laboratories. (WOG 1958)

In retrospect, it is fair to say that the Netherlands model, alongside the longer experience with functioning evaluation systems in Scandinavia, provided the essential foundations for what were later to become the provisions on control of medicines applicable to all member states of the European Community, provisions which developed rapidly from 1965 onwards. (EG 1965)

Today there is no doubt that official regulation of drugs in some shape or form is a necessity. As an Australian Trade Practices Commission put it in 1992:

> Few consumers have sufficient technical or medical background to make rational and informed choices about therapeutic goods . . . . For this reason, the selling of pharmaceuticals is restricted to protect consumers from possible health risks and deception (TPC 1992)

The argument also holds good for most health professionals; they have become confused by the flow of new drugs and heavily dependent on the industry for the information which is made available on their appropriate use. How well equipped the regulatory systems of the 1960s were to protect society from new risks remains a matter of debate. Neither within the industry nor behind the regulatory table was there a great deal of experience in extrapolating from experimental findings to field expectations; the correlation between animal findings and effects in human subjects was poorly understood. In case of doubt, the golden rule for an agency appeared to be to request more data and the golden rule for a manufacturer to protest, sometimes reasonably and with success. On one occasion, when an Australian regulator requested toxicological studies with a hormonal product lasting 8 and 12 years in dogs and monkeys, the company concerned had to point out that towards the end of these periods the animals would have passed the reproductive period and the prime of life and might be expected to be particularly sensitive to toxic effects. (Walsh 1975)

The belief from 1960 onwards that active drug control was needed cannot be said to have sprung primarily from any mistrust of the pharmaceutical industry, however serious some of the errors or misjudgements made by pharmaceutical companies in the course of the years. As one experienced drug regulator saw the situation in retrospect:

> Of course there were some scoundrels around – you'll meet those in any walk of life – these are the descendants of the quacks of oldentime. But the great bulk of all the people who came to the green baize table for the hearings with our Board over the years were experienced, right-thinking, well-informed people who wanted to do a good job on all sides. The Board's demands caused them plenty of trouble, but they appreciated that we were acting on behalf of all the millions of other people who were going to be taking the drugs we approved, and that we had to be fairly sure in our judgements. In the company labs they had been mothering these drugs for years – they had grown rather fond of them and proud of them, and they appreciated that it was a good thing for us to come in from a distance and take a neutral view. (Interview 3)

The volume of legal and regulatory material governing the pharmaceutical field is today immense; the directives, guidelines and other materials issued by the European Community alone run as of 2004 to five large volumes, and the material emanating from the United States' Food and Drug Administration is of similar extent. Much of that material relates however to matters of technical and procedural detail. The fundamental principles of regulation, and the broad standards which in the public interest it seeks to protect and advance, are relatively straightforward and increasingly homogeneous. Examples of those standards in many specific fields will be considered in later chapters of this book.

3.4.2.   Policy, legislation and regulation

Where the state adopts a comprehensive approach to the pharmaceutical field, it is likely to involve action at three levels:

- A *national drug policy* will set out the overall goal and the ways in which it is intended that it is to be achieved. This is essentially no more than a declaration of intent, but it is immensely helpful both for government itself in building up and maintaining all the tools that it needs, and for any other party – such as the pharmaceutical industry – in understanding what is intended. A very brief statement of a national drug policy was proposed by the World Bank in 1993:

The aim of the National Drug Policy is to ensure that effective and safe medicines of good quality are accessible and affordable to the entire population and that they are rationally used. (World Bank 1993)

However brief, this comprises the six essential elements of policy: efficacy, quality, safety, accessibility, affordability and rational use; each of these brings with it subcomponents – rational use, for example, must involve the necessary standards regarding both professional and public information and education.

It is perhaps surprising that newer and younger countries, building up drug policies *de novo*, have been the most prone to begin with a formal declaration of drug policy, either as an independent declaration or as a component in the law. Western countries have built up their policies on medicines piecemeal and some components are often missing; one cannot, for example, identify "affordability" as a component in any of the elements of law or regulation in the US despite the fact that drug prices in America have become a serious problem for many. A comprehensive list of components which may be found in any fully developed national drug policy is presented in Box 3.D and a recent example of a national drug policy in draft (drawn up in Afghanistan in 2003) in Box 3.E. Although the exact composition of a drug policy does differ somewhat with a country's structure and state of development, it should not be too readily assumed that any elements on the comprehensive list are irrelevant; "Choice of Drugs", for example, indeed relates primarily to the formulation of a National Essential Drugs List for a developing country, but it is equally relevant to the need to specify which drugs are to be available in a pharmacy, at a hospital, or on board ship.

- *Laws* comprises the second level of action. A National Medicines Law formulates the structures and procedures necessary to assess, approve and licence medicines, and deals with some closely related issues (such as advertising, adverse reactions and clinical research). Such a law is sometimes wrongly regarded as the totality of government action but most such national laws are in fact strictly limited to the handling of individual medicines. Laws will also be required (and will generally be enacted separately) to cover the profession of pharmacy, the relevant aspects of medical practice, price control, animal experimentation and other matters. Laws will as a rule have a long life, and can be amended or rescinded only by the Parliament.
- *Regulations,* made under the authority of the law, provide the massively detailed rules which are needed to put the law into operation. The general scope of drug regulation, as it impinges on many parties in society, has been defined elsewhere (Dukes 1997 at pp. 89–100). Regulations are adapted to circumstances as necessary and can as a rule be amended by Ministerial order without referral to the legislature.

Legislative and Regulatory Framework
Legislation and Regulations
Drug Regulatory Authority
Drug Registration and Licensing
Pharmaceutical Quality Assurance
Postmarketing Surveillance
Regulation of Prescription and Distribution
Choice of Drugs
Principles of Drug Selection
Selection Process
Selection Criteria
Use of Essential Drugs Lists
Traditional Medicines
Supply
Local Production
Supply system strategies and alternatives
        Procurement mechanisms
        Distribution and storage
Rational Use of Drugs
Objective Drug Information
Rational Use of Drugs by Health Personnel
Rational Use of Drugs by Consumers
        Promotional Activities
Economic Strategies for Drugs
Role of Government in the Pharmaceutical Market
Measures to encourage competition
Public Drug Financing Mechanisms
(Public financing, user charges, health insurance, external assistance)
Measures to improve efficiency and cost effectiveness
Human Resources Development
Role of Health Professions
Human Resources Development Plan
Education, Training and courses
        National Collaborating Networks
        Motivation and Continuing Education
Monitoring and Evaluation
Responsibilities
Indicators for Monitoring
        Periodic Evaluation
        Research
Operational Research
Drug Research and Development
Technical Collaboration among Countries

Box 3.D Components of a National Drug Policy (Adapted from WHO 1995)

I - DEFINITION AND GOALS

1. There shall be a National Medicines Policy for Afghanistan, which has been adopted by the Ministry of Public Health of the Islamic Transitional Administration.
2. The essential purposes of this Policy shall be to ensure:
    - that all medicines available in the country, whether of domestic or foreign origin, are effective, safe and of good quality, and are fairly priced.
    - That medicines are used in a proper manner, appropriate to the needs of the patient
    - That all reasonably necessary medicines are accessible to patients at all times and in all parts of the country
    - That a patient needing a medicine shall not be deprived of it because of any unreasonable financial barrier
3. The Policy shall be founded on the basis of the best existing practice in the country, while benefiting from experience elsewhere in the region and in the world at large.
4. The Government, acting primarily through the Ministry of Public Health and its partners, will ensure the coordinated introduction and implementation of the Medicines Policy.
5. Alongside official initiatives to implement and advance the policy, the Government will promote the active involvement of all the parties involved, including the health professions, trade and industry and the general public.

II - SUPPLY AND CONTROL OF MEDICINES

In keeping with overall Government policy, the task of manufacturing, importing and distributing medicines will be accorded primarily to the competitive private sector. The State, for its part, will assume responsibility for the maintenance of standards through a process of licensing and inspection.

In order to ensure continuity in the supply of cost-effective medicines to public sector hospitals the State may in the phase of transition, and thereafter exceptionally or in emergency situations, make special arrangements for the public importation or manufacture of medicines or vaccines.

III - EFFICACY, SAFETY AND QUALITY OF MEDICINES

The task of ensuring that medicines are as efficacious and safe as possible, and that the necessary standards of quality are attained, will devolve primarily upon a National Medicines Agency, charged with the evaluation and licensing of individual medicines and medicinal products, and with the Inspectorate of Medicines.

IV - THE PROPER AND APPROPRIATE USE OF MEDICINES

Prescribers, pharmacists and patients all bear responsibility for ensuring that medicines are used in a manner which is consistent with current knowledge and opinion, and which is appropriate to the individual's needs.

Box 3.E The National Medicines Policy of the Islamic Transitional Administration of Afghanistan (Draft 2003)

V - ADVERTISING AND PROMOTION OF MEDICINES

The private sector will be free to advertise and promote its medicines to the health professions and (in the case of a certain limited range of medicines) to the public. The Government will set standards to which such promotion should adhere, and the Inspectorate of Medicines will be charged with ensuring that these standards are maintained.

VI - INFORMATION ON MEDICINES

There shall be a Medicines Information Centre, ensuring the provision of reliable and impartial information on medicines to the health professions and the public. Its activities shall include the compilation and updating of the Afghanistan National Formulary, the publication of a Bulletin on Medicines, the maintenance of a register of adverse effects of medicines, and the provision of information on request to health professionals and others.

VII - ACCESSIBILITY OF MEDICINES

The public and the private sectors should play complementary roles in ensuring that medicines are promptly and readily accessible throughout the country.

VIII - LOWERING OF FINANCIAL BARRIERS

Illness inevitably involves suffering, inconvenience and expense; in ensuring that the burden of illness is so far as possible fairly shared, the community must apportion its resources so as to ensure that individuals are not so unfairly burdened with the costs of medicine that they are unable to undergo adequate treatment.

IX - POLICY DEVELOPMENT: INVOLVEMENT OF THE HEALTH PROFESSIONS AND COMMUNITY

Members of the medical, pharmaceutical, dental, veterinary and nursing professions and other health workers, as well as representatives of the public, will be encouraged to contribute actively to the implementation and continuing development of the Medicines Policy. To this end, an Advisory Council on Medicines Policy will be established to advise the Minister of Public Health; its constitution and task will be defined in regulation.

X - SELECTION OF MEDICINES

With many thousands of medicines existing in the world, and a scarcity of resources to finance them, it will often be necessary to set priorities. To this end the   National Medicines Agency charged with advising the Minister of Health on those medicines which are most necessary or acceptable in particular situations. The selections must be impartial and must be updated from time to time. In particular it will be necessary to maintain:

a. A National list of Essential Medicines, vital to basic health care, which must be prioritized as regards regulatory approval and supply to health services.

b. A List of Free Sale Medicines, i.e. medicines that can be bought and used by any member of the public without prescription to relieve mild symptoms.

c. Medicines which because of their particular risks or specialized mode of use must be subject to special restrictions on their availability.

Box 3.E   Continued

The starting point for all the rules which form part of general drug legislation and regulation is the *public health interest alone*. While in many situations the interest of the manufacturer in introducing a new medicinal product will run entirely parallel to the public health interest, this will not always be the case. There is an implicit assumption, readily confirmed through experience, that on occasion a manufacturer will for commercial reasons wish to maintain or introduce a product which is from the public health point of view defective in terms of its efficacy, safety or quality, and that in such situations, the authorities must be capable of arresting the process until or unless the defect is remedied. The exclusive concern with the public health interest means that a national regulatory body will not and cannot enter into compromises in order to serve some other interest, for example, the desire to maintain employment or to avoid a threatening bankruptcy. In some countries, however, the Government as a whole may have the authority to override decisions of a regulatory agency where it is considered necessary to serve a broader interest by doing so. And in other countries, it is a well-recognized fact that agencies are sometimes pressed and lobbied into action – or inaction – against their better judgement.

3.4.3. Issues of responsibility and liability

In a normal business setting, as considered in Section 2.2, the manufacturer of a consumer product bears a considerable degree of responsibility to the end-user for the safety of his product and may be liable to him if it proves disproportionately injurious. He may also be liable in various respects to other parties, such as the prescriber and pharmacist. From time to time the suggestion has however been advanced that where a national regulatory agency has been created, and issues a marketing licence for a particular drug as being efficacious and safe, it is the agency which assumes both responsibility and liability, exonerating the manufacturer from blame and involvement should adverse consequences ensue:

> Nobody suggests that the regulatory agencies should become protagonists for the pharmaceutical industry, but to the extent that their existence stems from people's wish to have access to drugs that are effective and also safe, they have a residual responsibility for what they wish on the public. If, on some occasions, they and not the manufacturer of a new drug are held to share part of the blame for unexpected side-effects, they should be provided with the funds to pay what the courts consider to be their share (Nature 1983)

Some spokesmen for the pharmaceutical industry have on occasion taken the same point of view:

> . . . the logical conclusion to be drawn . . . is surely that governments should themselves share in the responsibility for compensating any patient who is caused unexpected injury by the use of a marketed pharmaceutical product (Douglas 1984)

Governments have for their part generally denied that an agency which has performed its task normally and conscientiously can be held liable for any injury done by a drug which has been officially licensed:

> It is still the responsibility of the manufacturer to answer for his manufacture, whether there is a scrutiny system or not. By a scrutiny system we provide the public with as much protection as we can, but the responsibility is still upon the manufacturer (Joseph 1972)

The issue has been put to the test in various countries in the course of litigation and the official view has prevailed. To quote a court in The Netherlands:

> In The Netherlands Medicines Act there is nothing indicating that any organ of government or the government itself will, in cases where the pre-registration scrutiny of a drug has a positive result, assume the liability of the applicant for defects in the product which may appear at that time or later.[4]

There seems to be no reasonable doubt today that the existence of a regulatory or licensing agency leaves unchanged the situation of the manufacturer as regards his responsibility for the safety of his product and his liability for any disproportionately injurious defect which may emerge in the course of its use. The agency may naturally in quite different circumstances find itself held liable for the adverse consequences of a drug being present on the market, but that situation will only arise if the agency has acted in a biased manner, corruptly or without due care.[5]

---

[4] Rechtbank Arnhem (1984): Judgement of June 28th in the Halcion case (Named patients v. Upjohn). *Consumentenrecht, 86–87. (In Dutch)* In this case a large number of patients claimed that they had suffered injury from taking the hypnotic Halcion (triazolam) in accordance with the instructions, and took the view that since the Netherlands Board for the Evaluation of Medicines had initially approved the medicine for sale it must bear part of the liability for their injury.

[5] For a more extensive discussion of this topic see Dukes 1998 at pp. 346–352.

3.4.4.   Relationship of the applicant to the regulatory agency

(i)   *The whole truth*   The regulatory agency is the doorkeeper to the pharmaceutical market. The law and regulations which govern the agency, together with any interpretation or guidance which the agency itself may have provided to applicants, determine the duties of the pharmaceutical manufacturer when seeking a licence to market a drug, and when exercising the terms of the licence following approval. Foremost among the initial duties of the applicant is to ensure that the scientific and technical material submitted to the agency is complete, clear, dependable, truthful and objectively presented. The agency is unavoidably heavily dependent upon this material in taking its regulatory decision, since it is likely to have only a limited opportunity to verify independently the facts laid before it.

There are unfortunately many well-documented instances of failure on the part of companies – including corporations with a global reputation – to live up to this standard.

> In the case of the sleeping remedy Halcion (triazolam), developed by the former Upjohn company, evidence was produced from Great Britain, The United States and The Netherlands showing that incriminating material, pointing to the occurrence of severe psychotic reactions in certain early trial subjects, had been omitted from the regulatory file. (Dyer 1991, Abraham 1999)

In other situations the allocation of fault is less simple; both the authorities and the firm may have held material suggestive of risk, and failure to act promptly may have been due to the fact that the firm and the authorities failed to blend their material in good time so as to attain a critical mass of evidence:

> When Vioxx (rofecoxib) was withdrawn worldwide by Merck Inc. in 2004 because of cardiovascular adverse effects it was stated that evidence of these effects had been available to the manufacturer several years earlier but had not been communicated to the regulatory agencies. This was undoubtedly true. However, some information from the field was available early to national adverse reaction reporting systems: as early as 2000 the Netherlands Adverse Reaction Monitoring Centre (Lareb) had presented to a meeting of National Centres a new signal of cardiovascular disorders relating to rofecoxib with a relatively high reporting rate early in treatment and some incidence of fatalities (Edwards 2005 at p. 11)

An experienced regulator, commenting on defects in certain files submitted to an agency, has commented to the present author that, from the regulator's point of view, the manner in which information is edited for submission can be as misleading as failure to submit the information at all:

> Some files submitted to us seemed to have been craftily edited to suggest partic- ular conclusions and to consign unpleasant details to complex tables in appendices where they might readily be overlooked. Nothing was entirely omitted and noth- ing was strictly incorrect, but one had the distinct impression that one was astutely being manipulated. (Interview 21)

(ii) *Conditions of approval*   National laws continue to differ to some extent as regards the type of conditions which the regulator can impose when granting a marketing licence. Basic in all cases is that the licencee must adhere to the technical terms of the approval, e.g. as regarding the disorders for which the product may be recommended, the warnings which must be provided, other aspects of the labelling, or the channels through which the product is permitted to be sold. Some agencies regard it as within their competence to require that supplementary studies be carried out in order to answer open questions; others will delay approval until or unless this work has been performed and the questions answered satisfactorily. Where the law is less than clear regarding such a condition, the agency may have no formal complaint should the firm subsequently fail to perform the work; where there is a good relationship between the agency and the appli- cant a "gentlemen's agreement" may be effective.

Following approval of a drug the regulatory regime is also likely to require or request the company to keep the agency informed on any new information or emergent evidence which could cast a new light upon the product's characteristics, safety profile, quality or efficacy (see also Section 4.1). Most regulatory systems lay a specific obligation on the firm to provide reports of suspected adverse effects of which it becomes aware; there is at least an ethical obligation on the company to carry out this duty conscientiously and promptly, since the agency itself is unlikely to have the capacity to carry out adequate monitoring of all the products which it has approved for marketing. Experience shows that, with an entirely new drug, relevant new experience is mostly likely to emerge within the first 2 years after marketing, though it can occur at any time. Objectivity in reporting is especially necessary, however unwelcome the report may seem:

> In a case that was the subject of litigation against a manufacturer in the USA it emerged that the product was capable of producing permanent derangement of vision, with an onset of symptoms after some 15 months or more of treatment. The defendant claimed that he had received only eleven dubious reports of visual

effects after three years of marketing. On legal discovery of material in the defendant's archives however, 118 relevant reports were found, 107 of which had been
marked "invalid" using an internal classification under which numerous reports
were invalidated for trivial reasons, e.g. "Doctor failed to answer telephone call",
"Patient's age not indicated", or "possible co-medication". An external expert
reclassified the causal link in 60 reports as "likely". Under FDA rules these should
have been reported to the Administration, 18 of them as a matter of urgency.
(Personal notes, plaintiff's witness)

From actual experience it would seem that many firms recognize,
alongside their legal duty to report possible problems arising with marketed drugs, a moral obligation to undertake supplementary studies where
these seem advisable to clarify or confirm the evidence.

(iii) *Conformity and self-discipline* Very similar considerations
apply to a company's advertising and promotion for an approved drug (see
Section 5.2). An agency may have some capacity to monitor the content of
promotion in order to ensure that it is within the terms of the approval
which has been granted, but again its resources are limited. It is also
unlikely to be able to monitor the content of information provided to
physicians by a company's travelling detailmen, certainly where this information is provided orally. In the event of contravention an agency can usually do little more than prohibit the repetition of an advertisement which
has already appeared, or impose a penalty. The company itself will thus
still have the duty to ensure in advance that its advertising and promotion
are in accordance with the claims and conditions approved when the drug
was licensed.

An issue already touched on in Section 2.2.3 is that which arises
when a regulatory agency fails in its duty and a defective product remains
on the market. It is clear that the rise of regulation does not obviate the
need for the industry to maintain adequate standards on its own; conversely it must also be the case that where regulation lets society down the
industry itself must come to its own defence; it will still have to assume
responsibility for quality, safety, efficacy and truth and liability when
these are not adequately ensured.

(iv) *Collaboration or Confrontation?* On many occasions the contact between a pharmaceutical company and a regulatory is positive and
constructive. Although an agency is not likely to commit itself in advance
to accepting a proposed experimental scheme it will often be able to draw
on its broad experience to advise an applicant on a specific issue, e.g. the
most appropriate means of quality control. In the least favourable situation, an agency may find itself exposed to stress and pressures, exerted by

a particular applicant or by the industry as a whole. One of the most insistent forms of pressure has been the attempt by sections of the industry over a long period to secure more rapid assessment of regulatory files. As a general rule many agencies have in the course of time agreed to a basic evaluation period of 120 working days for the initial evaluation of a file. Assuming that an agency is operating efficiently, this is found to allow sufficient time for the scientific assessment of the material relating to a drug of a recognized type; this is however not likely to be the type of product the approval of which can be regarded as urgent from the public health point of view. An unusually innovative product may confront an assessor with novel problems regarding quality control, the relevance of animal studies, the interpretation of clinical findings or other issues, and it may be very undesirable to undertake a rushed assessment. A former FDA official has recalled the reason why thalidomide was not approved in the United States:

> At the time when children in Europe were being described with phocomelia because their mothers had been treated with thalidomide in pregnancy, the NDA for the United States was still on Dr Frances Kelsey's desk in Rockville MD, thank goodness. There were no cases of phocomelia in the file but Dr Kelsey could see that there was something highly unusual about the drug, and she wanted to take a good look. It was a dead simple molecule, but there was something odd with the neurological findings and for that reason she wanted more time and more data; that saved an awful lot of kids in this country from phocomelia. Richardson-Merrell, the Vicks Vaporub people, had been licensed by Grünenthal to take the market in the States and Canada and they wanted that approval quick, so they were furious, making a real nuisance of themselves and putting Frances under a lot of stress, but she stuck to her guns. (Lloyd, interview 1998).

According to Daemmerich, citing Kelsey herself, the company contacted the FDA's Bureau of Medicine 50 times to press for approval:

> At one point, company officials contacted Kelsey's supervisor in an attempt to speed the approval. Two days later, they contacted Kelsey directly "and tried to get me to say I'd agree to pass it in a day". A week later, Kelsey wrote to the firm that she had read reports from Europe describing cases of nerve damage among patients using Thalidomide. When Kelsey accused the company of failing to disclose this data, Merrell's representatives threatened to sue the agency, calling her statement "libelous". Kelsey nonetheless held her ground and repeatedly demanded additional data until the company eventually withdrew its application in March 1962. (Daemmerich at pp. 11–41)

The case is unhappily not unique.

Although laws and regulations do set deadlines for the completion of regulatory assessments, it is clear that these are theoretical and a firm will be unwise to insist that a deadline be met; where the relationship with the firm is good, one will commonly find that less complex files are assessed more rapidly than the law prescribes but that complex issues may take a little longer where the interests of public health so demand.

3.4.5. Old vs. new products

At the time when national regulatory agencies in Western Europe assumed their task, the pharmaceutical market was already a large one. In the Netherlands some 4,000 drug products were on the market and in the United Kingdom more than 30,000; in Germany, where many medicines of purely local significance existed, the total was estimated as being in excess of 100,000. To define and apply the standards which a *new* medicine should meet was relatively straightforward; the law and regulations could for example specify that its efficacy must have been demonstrated beyond reasonable doubt in a certain number of double-blind randomized controlled clinical studies against placebo. It was however clearly impracticable and unnecessary to maintain the same costly and labour-intensive requirement for each of the many thousands of older drugs. For some, efficacy and safety could be fairly considered to have been demonstrated by long acceptance and by positive statements in the scientific literature and authoritative textbooks. For others, such serious doubts existed on all sides that they were quietly withdrawn from the market. Not surprisingly however there was a considerable group of older products with respect to which disagreements arose between manufacturers and regulators, and these have only slowly been resolved; the process is far from complete and in some parts of the world it may continue for many years to come. A practical approach which seems to have been agreed between regulators and manufacturers in many instances is for a "licence of right", limited in time to be granted to these borderline older products, especially where no serious risk is apparent and there is no proven alternative treatment. During the validity of the licence, the manufacturer is then obliged to undertake supplementary work – or identify relevant published literature – to provide an adequate basis for a definitive decision. Such an obligation might be considered as reflecting a more general obligation on a drug manufacturer to update the scientific basis of any product as long as it remains on the market (see Section 4.1); it also runs parallel to the needs imposed by purely commercial considerations (Section 2.3).

3.4.6.   *The global coverage of law and regulation*

The original drug regulatory agencies operated on a purely national basis; as authorized bodies instituted under territorial law it could not have been otherwise, and in view of the fact that there had traditionally been marked differences between countries in the drug market and in concepts regarding the use of medicines a national approach seemed entirely logical. Even by that time however, the pharmaceutical industry increasingly comprised international firms, the principal medicines which they produced were disseminated worldwide and as the dimensions of the pharmaceutical problems to be solved became clear there was every reason to tackle the issue on a multi-country basis. The Nordic Council on Medicines initiated a work-sharing scheme between the agencies of the five countries, while in the Benelux area – Belgium, the Netherlands and Luxemburg – the possibility was created for new drug applications to be handled by a joint Commission acting on behalf of the three countries; the Commission operated from 1974 to 1977. By the 1970s, however, the European Economic Community – initially composed of six states – had realized that if its provisions for the free movement of goods were to apply to medicines the latter must be evaluated and approved for marketing in all these member states in a harmonized manner (EEG 1965). The solution involved measures in three directions. In the first place, while retaining the existing national regulatory agencies, a series of consultative committees were put in place to ensure that there was ongoing collaboration on general and specific issues. Second, an extensive programme of harmonization was undertaken, ensuring that national laws and regulations were to all intents and purposes identical. Third, after a number of experimental approaches to centralization had been considered, a fully centralized procedure for drug approval was created that could progressively over time assume the entire regulatory function for the European Union as a whole; until that time a "decentralized procedure" using the regulatory resources of the member states, would continue to function alongside it (see Section 3.4.7).

Alongside the consolidation of the European Union as a major regulatory unit, a further development was underway. In 1990, the International Conference on Harmonization of Technical Requirements in this field (ICH) was brought into being, intended to ensure the full and parallel development of medicines control in a large part of the industrialized world, comprising the European Community, the United States and Japan. The ICH is now widely, though not universally, viewed as being well on the way to establishing a gold standard in drug regulation which the entire world might well emulate (see however Section 3.4.7). One might also note that from the outset the International Federation of Pharmaceutical Manufacturers Associations provided the Secretariat to the Conference, reflecting the growing conviction within the pharmaceutical industry that it should itself work actively towards the formulation of appropriate rules safeguarding the public health, but at the same time seeking to ensure that such rules were also acceptable from its own point of view. The WHO was granted observer status at the Conference; it has continued to support similar developments in drug regulation in other parts of the world, as have the World Bank and various bilateral donor organizations.

Despite this massive progress, one has to realize that, viewed from a worldwide perspective, the regulation of medicines is still very far from attaining the minimum standards that would be needed if these processes alone were to provide a sufficient guarantee of standards for the world's population. As noted earlier, the largest nucleus of homogeneous regulatory material is that developed by the member states of the European Union, the United States and Japan, working independently or through the ICH, representing a total population of some 825 million and (as of 2004) a total of 27 countries. The total world population is however currently in excess of 6 billion, comprising a total of some 200 countries and territories, and it is in the 85% of the world where regulatory systems are commonly defective that some of the most serious problems in drug supply and drug standards arise. Although according to the WHO a fair proportion of its member states had by 2003 some form of drug law and regulation, only a minority of these attained the standards set by the ICH. As WHO reported at that time:

> Currently about 20% of countries have well developed and operational medicines regulation. Of the rest approximately half have regulation of varying capacity and level of development, and 30% have either no or very limited medicines regulation. The reality is that many low-income countries cannot ensure the safety, efficacy and quality of medicines circulating on their markets. The problems of ineffective regulation transcend national borders and have global implications. Smuggling of medicines is widespread. Even manufacturers who fail to comply with good manufacturing practice (GMP) requirements can still produce medicines for domestic use and for export. Often controls on exported medicines are less stringent than for those used domestically (WHO 2004).

In many developing countries, as studies continue to show, there is not only a lack of comprehensive regulation but also of funding and of competent manpower to implement it. In too many instances, national registration of drugs remains a mere administrative formality, which provides no guarantee that the public will be supplied with effective and safe drugs of good quality, or with reliable information. In other instances there is clear evidence that even the work of technically competent agencies can be and often is undermined by corruption or by political measures which are allowed to override technical decisions.

The most positive conclusion which one can draw is that few national agencies are today obliged to act in isolation as they did two decades ago. Strict provisions regarding the confidentiality of data, insisted upon by industry as a means of preventing leakage of vital information from a company to its competitor, initially prevented national agencies from communicating openly with one another. Although the principle of confidentiality is in some respects still jealously guarded lest the manufacturing secrets of one manufacturer should leak to another via the regulatory offices, it is acknowledged that there must be a considerable sharing of facts and conclusions between agencies if they are to work efficiently, and that industry itself can only benefit if a degree of collaboration and mutual recognition reduces duplication and delay. Many smaller and weaker national agencies, which find themselves unable to undertake full assessments of individual drugs or firms have within the last decade chosen to rely on decisions taken by respected agencies elsewhere. What this means is that the smaller agency may in practice choose to licence a medicinal product for sale only if has already been authorized by one or more major regulatory bodies, e.g. in the United States or within the European Union. Work sharing between agencies, which was pioneered two decades ago in the Nordic countries, is now prominent in other parts of the world. Regional agreements of this type on work sharing are however now established or emergent in the Balkan area, in South-East Africa, the Gulf States, the ASEAN nations and the countries of the Eastern Caribbean. Bilateral aid agencies, the World Bank and the WHO have in the meantime done much to raise and homogenize regulatory standards in the many countries to which they have provided support in developing regulatory activities.

The above considerations do not lead to the conclusion that regulatory standards and decisions should ideally be the same in every country. They are most likely to be closely similar as between countries at a high level of development, with a strong economy and comprehensive health services serving the entire population. Even here however concepts of what is desirable will vary to some extent with tradition, topography, political and social beliefs. These may for example influence the formulation or interpretation of rules relevant to the approval of abortifacients or the release of products for sale without prescription or through non-pharmacy retail outlets. Deliberate deviations from any "ideal" global standard of regulation are much more marked and common in developing countries with a weak economy and defective health services (see also Chapter 8). This situation arises, for example, where a particular drug has in a scientific sense been superseded by a newer product which is more effective, safer or more convenient in use; in a developing country, the older product may still merit regulatory approval where the newer drug is prohibitively expensive or has to be administered under sophisticated conditions which are not available. Similarly, many developing countries with low-cost manufacturing facilities for certain drugs still do not have the economic or human resources to apply current standards of "good manufacturing practice (GMP)". For many drug products, a somewhat lower standard of quality is medically acceptable and will need to be defined and applied if the supply of drugs to the population is to be maintained.

On occasion, multinational research-based companies have shown some comprehension of these difficulties in the developing world, even providing assistance to third-world manufacturers to upgrade their standards. In other instances, self-interest appears to have taken the upper hand, with vigorous lobbying in favour of sophisticated products and demands for the prohibition of low-cost alternatives.

3.4.7. *Criticism of regulatory standards; deregulation*

From an early date, some elements in the pharmaceutical industry have almost consistently criticized the establishment and development of regulatory regimes. In the most extreme view, regulation is largely unnecessary since firms are sufficiently realistic and well meaning to develop and respect adequate standards of their own without bureaucratic or political interference in their business. Drug regulation, or particular facets of it, have also been viewed as a potential threat to the industry and to the drug development process. In 1984 indeed, a senior official of the Italian industry declared that if regulation were to continue in its current form, the pharmaceutical industry might be killed off entirely. (Anon 1984)

The repeated assertion that regulation has stifled innovation was not confirmed in a large European study of innovation undertaken by the Charles River Group for the European Union and published in 2004 (CRA 2004; see also Chapter 7). What does appear to have happened is that the growth and development of regulation over some 45 years has coincided with a number of periods during which innovation has alternately accelerated and slowed, but also with the emergence of some entirely new and serious challenges in therapy (notably HIV/AIDS). There has also been a predictable decline in the total number of new drug introductions by virtue of the fact that fewer borderline products meet newer criteria.

Only on a few fronts has a clear pattern of deregulation been discernible, and on none of these can one entirely foresee the ultimate effects. There can be no doubt that in the early years of regulation, following the shock of thalidomide, some excessive demands were posed; where these have proved superfluous and unnecessarily burdensome they have been quietly dropped. Beyond this, several ongoing trends can be distinguished:

(i) The *first* of these relates to some exceptional situations where there has been a public clamour to provide at least some sort of possible treatment for serious diseases with a high mortality. Especially in the United States, massive pressure by HIV/AIDS activist groups has led to very rapid evaluation of new drugs for these conditions, where the uncertain hope of saving a number of lives has been accepted as outweighing the risk of unknown adverse effects or therapeutic failure. In 1986, following a public protest, the principal AIDS drug (zidovudine) was approved by the FDA in 107 days, and from 1990 onwards a "treatment IND" procedure was introduced under which pharmaceutical companies were permitted to distribute unapproved "investigational new drugs" to patients with life-threatening diseases provided there was some reason to believe that they were effective and would not expose trial participants to significant new risks. A "parallel track" review also allowed FDA officials to grant provisional approval to such drugs while the definitive review was still proceeding. Other measures to meet the AIDS crisis included the simplification of clinical trial requirements and the adoption of "surrogate end points" rather than relying on long-term survival as a measure of efficacy. (FDA 1998, Daemmerich 2003 at pp. 33–35) The entire course of events relating to AIDS can best be considered separately from other forms of deregulation; pressure of public opinion, spearheaded by activist groups, and the need to react in some visible manner to a serious new threat to public health led to the adoption of extraordinary measures rather than to a general revision of approval procedures. Experience with these approaches is however likely to prove helpful in dealing with other health emergencies. Outside the USA, agencies have also sought to expedite the assessment of drugs of potential value in HIV/AIDS but without creating special procedures.

(ii) The *second* change has been a widely noted acceleration in the speed of drug assessments in general over a period of some 20 years. Again the change was most emphatic and most heavily publicized in the USA. This reflected on the one hand the fact the FDA had over a period of time become appreciably slower in assessing drugs than other western agencies, and on the other the fact that pressure to reform the system had become so emphatic. By 1970 America had clearly built up a "drug lag" and researchers such as Lou Lasagna and William Wardell, with firm support from the pharmaceutical industry, publicized the fact emphatically. For a long period, the FDA had been criticized and subjected to repeated Congressional investigations because of its supposed laxity, leading to a constant tightening of regulatory requirements (Schmidt 1974); now it was attacked, sometimes in vicious terms, for its excessive stringency. When Cromie in Britain spoke in 1979 of the "mass murder activities of regulatory authorities" (Cromie 1979) it was a statement which, while misrepresenting the sparse facts on which it was based (WHO/(EURO 1984 at p. 243), could only add fuel to the flames of demands for reform in drug regulation as a whole. While there was certainly a need to re-examine some of its stricter requirements, comparisons of the FDA's assessment rate as a well-structured and cautious agency with the output of the still nascent and inexperienced agencies in much of Europe put the US agency in an undeservedly unfavourable light. Events since then have led to a further relaxation of the FDA's requirements and a weakening of its authority. While it has succeeded in recording ever-higher rates of approval for new drugs, Angell and other critics lean to the conclusion that the US agency is now being paid to work excessively fast – "in its rush, it is demanding less evidence of safety and effectiveness"; (Angell 2004). Her conclusion could be supported by the finding that the number of new medicines withdrawn from the US market because of safety problems has in recent years increased and that the agency has in some instances been much slower than analogous bodies in Europe to remove dangerous drugs from the market. There has also been a distinct change in mentality, with FDA staff viewing themselves as serving to "facilitate" new drug development rather than to represent the public interest.

No final assessment can yet be made of the effects of these changes in and around the FDA, either as regards public health or the long-term interests of the pharmaceutical industry. Neither will be served if regulatory demands fall below the level that is required to ensure that the medicines can in general be regarded as safe and efficacious. The most disturbing aspect of events over a 40-year period in the US is that changes have been based primarily on extreme external pressures and not on a careful evaluation of experience; two decades of massive demands for a greater degree of restriction in the public interest have been followed an equally long period of almost hysterical calls for relaxation. There is a risk that a single drug drama in the near future could result in a further reversal of policy in the direction of greater stringency. A poorly motivated oscillation of policies is hardly likely to serve the real interests of public health or those of the pharmaceutical industry.

(iii) In the *European Union* the trend to deregulation has been brought about less by external pressures than by the internal process of unification. While the "centralized" approval procedure is still of relatively limited influence, the "decentralized" procedure has since its finalization in 1995 come into widespread use as offering an efficient means of attaining common decisions throughout the Union. An industrial applicant hoping to market his product through the latter procedure is required to submit his file, drawn up in accordance with European requirements, to a national agency of his choice (the "Reference Member State") indicating the countries ("Concerned Member States") in which he wishes to obtain a marketing authorization. The Reference Member State performs the initial assessment which is largely determinant for the fate of the application as a whole. From the start, both pharmaceutical companies and national agencies realized that the choice of the right Reference Member State would be crucial. Companies would seek to choose the agency most likely to perform a rapid evaluation, to be most reasonable in its demands and most helpful in carrying the procedure through. National authorities for their part were anxious to win nominations as "Reference Member States" since the very substantial fees set by the Union would now accrue to these agencies only. As critics pointed out, this would readily create a competitive situation in which national agencies might become preoccupied with making their services attractive to industrial applicants rather than with maintaining adequate regulatory standards.

Although the current procedures have now been operative for a decade it remains – as in the case of the USA – impossible to determine whether or not the new system will result (or perhaps already has resulted?) in a decline of standards to unacceptable levels. A series of interviews with regulators and others carried out by Abraham and Lewis (Abraham 2003) found divergent points of view on the matter. Regulatory managers and scientists in industry did not in most cases detect or anticipate any decline in regulatory standards; some perceived a tendency in the

EU as a whole to raise standards. Among National and EU regulatory staff opinions on the issue were almost equally divided.

(iv) *The influence of the ICH* on current and future standards of drug assessment and approval is similarly disputed. In the course of its 15 years of work, the Conference has developed a great many complex guidelines for the scientific work to be submitted by applicants, which in many respects – but not all – reflect the norms established and tested over a long period by agencies in Europe, the United States and Japan; as noted above the work has been undertaken by the regulators of these countries, but with the International Federation of Pharmaceutical Manufacturers' Associations providing the secretariat. One can discern two quite different reactions to these developments. The first is that – in view of the constitution of the Conference – it will always tend to accept the high technical standards which can be implemented by research-based multinational firms and by institutions in Western countries and Japan but exceed what can be attained in the coming years in much of the developing world and by the many secondary manufacturers which serve those countries; these concerns are not issues of deregulation and they are discussed separately in Chapter 8.

The second and entirely different concern is that – behind the general facade of high standards – there is a tendency to erode certain requirements which research-based industry finds oppressive. In an extensive study of the materials, Abraham and Reed (Abraham 2003 at pp. 82–107) have pointed in particular to the shortening of the required period of toxicity testing in non-rodents from 12 months to 9 (ICH 1997 at p. 1) and the proposed simplification of rodent carcinogenicity testing (ICH 1995 at p. 2). They similarly question the proposed abandonment of the requirement that long-term clinical trials in non-serious disorders be preceded by completed rodent carcinogenicity studies, as well as the reduction in the duration of pre-application clinical trials from 12 months to 6. It is striking that in these and other matters the ICH has repeatedly favoured a reduction of standards towards the lowest common level, even when there is evidence pointing to more stringent requirements having demonstrated their benefit in terms of public health. The British House of Commons Select Committee on the Pharmaceutical Industry has very recently urged reconsideration by its national agency of such approaches by the ICH which may not serve the public health interest (HOC 2005 at p. 179). Where such lower standards are indeed implemented it will be important to ensure adequate study of the consequences for patients. Bearing in mind the principles governing the civil and criminal liability of individual employees it should be possible to examine the personal liability of those involved in these measures should they prove detrimental to the health of those using drugs tested only according to the weakened standards.

Conclusions   Over a period of half a century, pressures to intensify, amend or relax the process of drug regulation have waxed and waned, alternated and interacted, and the process is certain to continue. As Dr J. Richard Crout reflected a quarter of a century ago, some time before his resignation from the FDA's Bureau of Drugs:

> There is a positive side to this debate about regulation which has been highly beneficial – that is, it has served to highlight to the public how regulators conduct their business. There is also a growing understanding of the complexity of regulatory decisions. Those with simple solutions are being challenged to think more broadly. On the negative side, however, there is a thoughtless, almost reflex, lashing out against regulation in some circles that is disturbing. While emotional outbursts against the bureaucracy or the government in general are useful in highlighting a problem, they are usually not helpful in articulating a solution to that problem (Crout 1981)

Where requirements for the approval of drugs are concerned there are no absolute rights and wrongs. The most appropriate approach to any drug will depend on the nature of the medicine and its proposed use, yet for the sake of practical operation it is necessary to maintain a series of standard requirements even though these may prove inadequate in one situation and excessive in another. Fortunately, one finds that companies are increasingly prone to consult with regulatory agencies at an earlier stage of development of a drug on the most desirable approach to examining its efficacy and safety, and well equipped and experienced agencies are commonly prove willing to provide advice. It is also good that the pharmaceutical industry has on some occasions not merely argued the case for deregulation but has also undertaken work to provide sound evidence for new and simplified approaches which appear attainable and beneficial for all concerned. What is needed at the present day is a broadly based study of regulatory experiences, such as WHO has called for in the past, so that patterns of regulation can reflect the manner of working that has proved most reliable without being excessively burdensome (WHO/EURO 1985). Without the development of such an approach there is a considerable risk that regulation will be buffeted from one extreme to another by processes which have much to do with emotion and self-interest, less to do with science, and nothing at all to do with law.

3.4.8. The role of the WHO

The WHO has in the 60 years since its establishment performed a major role in promoting consensus between its member states on health issues including pharmaceuticals; it has not attempted (or been invited) to play a supranational role though in some matters its influence in bringing about the enactment of national policies has been substantial. Its Essential Drugs Programme, (see Chapter 8) implemented with limited funding and in spite of considerable opposition, can only be said to have succeeded by virtue of its moral authority.

The Constitution of WHO does in fact render it possible to go somewhat further but political and other obstacles have as a rule preventing it from doing so.

Relevant clauses of the Constitution, drawn up in 1946, authorize the Organization:

2(k) to propose conventions, agreements and regulations, and make recommendations with respect to international health matters and to perform such duties as may be assigned thereby to the Organization and are consistent with its objective;

2(u) to develop, establish and promote international standards with respect to food, biological, pharmaceutical and similar products;

Article 19 reads as follows:

(1) The Health Assembly shall have authority to adopt conventions or agreements with respect to any matter within the competence of the Organization. A two-thirds vote of the Health Assembly shall be required for the adoption of such conventions or agreements which shall come into force for each Member when accepted by it in accordance with its constitutional processes.

Article 20 reads:

Each Member undertakes that it will, within eighteen months after the adoption by the Health Assembly of a convention or agreement, take action relative to the acceptance of such convention or agreement. Each Member shall notify the Director-General of the action taken and if it does not accept such convention or agreement within the time limit, it will furnish a statement of the reasons for non-acceptance. In case of acceptance, each Member agrees to make an annual report to the Director-General in accordance with Chapter XIV.

Article 21 provides that:

The Health Assembly shall have authority to adopt regulations concerning:

(d) standards with respect to the safety, purity and potency of biological, pharmaceutical and similar products moving in international commerce;

(e) advertising and labelling of biological, pharmaceutical and similar products moving in international commerce.

Article 22 notes that:

Such Regulations adopted pursuant to Article 21 shall come into force for all Members after due notice has been given of their adoption by the Health Assembly except for such Members as may notify the Director-General of rejection or reservations within the period stated in the notice.

These provisions of the Constitution have not led to the global pharmaceutical policy and rules which some had anticipated in 1946. For a long period, the basic political division of the world rendered it impossible for the Organization to be used as a trusted forum in which concrete technical measures of this type could be effectively developed; instead such developments came about primarily in firm regional groupings, such as those which arose in Western Europe and which have even acquired a growing measure of supranational authority. It seems obvious however that where the world community approaches agreement on any health issue the consensus might well be appropriately expressed through the Organization, using the procedures in its constitution.

One element that has to be taken into account where WHO's work in the pharmaceutical field is concerned is the marked antagonism which has on many occasions erupted between industrial interests, represented as non-governmental organizations, and groups of health activists:

The long and vexed history of the International Code of Marketing of Breastmilk Substitutes, adopted by the World Health Assembly in 1981, has been extensively documented elsewhere (Richter 2001 at p. 2ff). The Code was adopted at a time when the need for effective external regulation of transnational corporations had become widely recognized and when there was much evidence that the substitutes were an inadequate alternative to maternal milk. Its provisions sought to prevent the promotion of substitutes for breastmilk in a manner which would compete with breastfeeding. Passed in the face of powerful opposition, it was thereafter adopted by the Executive Board of UNICEF as a minimum standard. Nevertheless over the ensuring twenty years the Code was fully assimilated into national law in no more than twenty countries.

The shorter history of the Assembly's Ethical Criteria for Medicinal Drug Promotion, passed in weakened form by the World Health Assembly in 1988 is not dissimilar (Richter 2001 at pp. 92–94). The International Federation of

Pharmaceutical Industry Associations (IFPMA) had been in official relations with WHO as a "Non-Governmental Organization" and the adoption of the Code on Breast Milk Substitutes in 1981 had been viewed as a warning that similar steps might be taken in the pharmaceutical field and would need to be defeated (Peretz 1981). As a precautionary measure the Federation at the time launched its own Code of Pharmaceutical Marketing Practices, arguing that the industry should be given time to implement this, and that WHO insistence on the formulation, implementation and monitoring of an international regulatory Code would waste precious public resources. Consumer, health and development activists were of a different opinion and developed a model regulatory framework as a basis for action by the Organization. WHO was now faced by lobbying on the issue from industry, the citizen action network and governments with divergent interests. The United States, despite its own strict regulatory framework in matters of drug promotion, argued that ". . . the World Health Organization should not be involved in efforts to regulate or control the commercial practices of private industry, even when the products may relate to concerns about health. (Boyer 1986) For this and other reasons the United States withdrew a large proportion of its financial contribution to WHO in 1986 and 1987. The Director General of the Organization, Dr Halfdan Mahler, nevertheless convened a Working Group to develop a Code, and this was adopted, though in weakened form, by the 1988 World Health Assembly.

Despite the many limitations on the scope of WHO's work, much has been achieved. Numerous meetings have attained consensus between expert groups from member states on technical issues relating to drug control and drug policy, and their conclusions have in many cases later been implemented in adapted form in member states or regional organizations. Many of the principles of drug regulation now in use were worked out between experts through WHO's European Studies of Drug Regulation from 1972 onwards (WHO/EURO 1985) and the Organization's International Conferences of Drug Regulatory Authorities; others have been laid down in the long series of books and technical reports from WHO which cover the field and are universally regarded as authoritative. The close contacts established in recent years between the medicines regulatory authorities of many countries, largely at the initiative of WHO, have similarly done much to promote and harmonize the development of legal and regulatory standards within national borders and ensure the training of staff. At the present time, WHO is largely responsible for bringing into being a series of public–private partnerships to assist developing countries with drug supplies, and in certain fields it has established a system of pre-qualified drug suppliers. While effective action at the level of the Assembly (or the corresponding Regional Committees) can still be effectively paralysed by opposition, the Organization's specialized units are extremely active in producing published materials and in providing technical support to policy development within individual member states.

While it may be tempting on many specific matters to regard WHO as being placed outside the main area of action where pharmaceuticals are concerned it may be more realistic to view it as the only truly global auditorium in this matter, an important sounding board on disputed policy issues, and an arena where new issues can be faced and concepts for action developed for implementation elsewhere. Ultimately, it could be the most logical repository for systems that, having grown up elsewhere, have matured to the point where they can enjoy universal acceptance.

3.5.   Self-regulation in the Pharmaceutical Industry

In Sections 2.7, 2.8 and 5.2, various aspects of self-regulation in the industry are discussed. During polemical debates on the subject of pharmaceutical regulation, companies and their associations have frequently declared or implied that, after a period of immaturity and uncertainty, the industry has now come to adulthood, and is largely capable of regulating itself. There is, as noted above, much ongoing pressure to reduce the burden imposed by drug regulation, the implication being that the industry is largely capable itself of ensuring quality, efficacy, safety and the reliability of the information that it supplies. Industry points in particular to existing codes of behaviour and ethics drawn up within companies or for the whole sector, to its voluntary withdrawal of drugs proving to be insufficiently safe, and to its collegial collaboration with major regulatory agencies to establish agreed standards within the ICH. Those critical of industry regard the performance of self-regulation to date as unsatisfactory and suggest that the industry has been dragging its feet both in ethical and certain technical issues. Certainly, it is not difficult to find large numbers of instances of acts and omissions which merit criticism. Breach of well-defined major obligations is less common than in the past; but there is a general and regrettable tendency to neglect ethically clear standards of behaviour or decency, or to put a minimal interpretation on duties. There has been much criticism of the general approach adopted by industry to the pricing of drugs in developing countries (see Chapter 8); excessively raucous advertising, widespread use of kickbacks and other improper incentives are among the other points of much concern. What is more there are still in many parts of the world firms which claim to belong to the sector yet which do not approach the requisite standards; it is from such sources that counterfeit and substandard drugs continue to emerge, as much to the concern of *bona fide* firms as to that of the authorities.

However encouraging it is to see positive achievements and declarations of honest intent, one can only regard the industry as a whole as a sector that still goes along rather grudgingly with some of the standards that society seeks to impose on it, and is still prone to pay lip service to high standards of decency where more is called for. Self-regulation is growing, but appalling things continue to occur, and one would not dare to conclude that the industry is now fully capable of taking care of itself.

PART B:
ACCEPTANCE AND IMPLEMENTATION OF STANDARDS

Chapter 4

Ensuring Quality, Safety and Efficacy

4.1. Pre-marketing and Post-marketing Duties

At the time when modern pharmaceutical law and regulation began to emerge, they were conceived in the belief that serious problems and disappointments with medicines might largely be avoided if enough evidence of quality, safety and efficacy were provided by the manufacturer prior to their introduction. The requirements which were set for approval therefore related to the provision of such evidence, of sufficient quality and delivered in sufficient volume and good time. It was said that, had these requirements been introduced earlier in the century, some past disasters (see Chapter 3) might have been avoided, since the problems could have been predicted, for example, using studies in small rodents.

Certainly, the ability of the early organic arsenicals to damage various organ systems (Salvarsan 1922) might have been foreseen in this way, since they were broadly toxic in all species. The tragedy with diethylene-glycol as a solvent for Elixir of Sulfanilamide (Nielsen 1986, Wax 1995) could similarly have been predicted in animals, as could the toxicity of diiodoethyltin which underlay the Stalinon disaster of 1957 (H.P. 1958). However, when the hypnotic thalidomide induced phocomelia in large numbers of children in 1960–1961 the only early signs of toxicity had pointed in a rather different direction (neurotoxicity). After the tragedy, attempts to recreate the phocomelia-inducing effect using studies in pregnant animals only succeeded after much effort and then only satisfactorily in certain sub-species (Folb 1990 at pp. 1–8); this threw a serious doubt on animal tests as a predictor of unusual effects in humans. The law cannot reasonably impose on industry a duty to perform particular studies unless there is fair reason to believe that they will serve the public interest.

Similar problems arose with the belief that one could draw final conclusions on the efficacy of certain drugs before they were approved for marketing. The broad pattern of efficacy could be established in clinical trials, but once a medicine was used on a much larger scale in the field, surprises could emerge. It became clear, for example, that after a medicine had been marketed on the basis of well-conducted clinical studies and had been used for any length of time, tolerance to it might develop, necessitating an increase in the dose or a move to an alternative drug; when an antibiotic came into widespread use, microbial resistance to it might soon emerge. Efficacy apparently proven in a well-recognized disorder may or may not prove to be attainable in a closely related disorder or in certain subgroups of patients. On occasion, the dose estimated in the initial studies might ultimately prove inadequate:

> From 1969 onwards, clinical studies with ibuprofen concluded that it was effective in rheumatoid arthritis in doses of 400 mg or 600 mg daily, though higher doses were tolerated. (Martindale 1977 at p. 193) Thirty years later, in 1999, commonly cited anti-inflammatory doses were 2000 mg to 2400 mg or more. (Felleskatalog 1999)

During hearings before the passage of the 1962 Kefauver–Harris Amendments to America's Food, Drug and Cosmetic legislation, both scientific and public representatives had stressed the need for legal and medical certainty in drug regulation (Nielsen 1986); the legislation as amended required both efficacy and safety to be proven, the applicant being firmly obliged "to show whether such drug is safe for use under the conditions prescribed, recommended or suggested in the proposed labelling thereof"(Art 355d). The authorities were nevertheless entitled to withdraw their approval if efficacy or safety were subsequently found not to have been established, thus introducing an element of doubt. In the meantime the pioneering legislation in The Netherlands (WOG 1958) had exhibited even greater caution; the efficacy and safety were to be demonstrated "according to the judgement of the reasonable man" and the judgement of the reasonable man could clearly change as time went by. What all this meant was that a firm applying successfully to market a new drug was by no means handed a guarantee of its future and permanent acceptability. The need for continued watchfulness on the part of the company was also apparent from the obligation to maintain records of apparent adverse reactions and report them to the FDA, but also from the requirement that the manufacturer maintain records on other matters relating to the drug, communicating new developments to the agency in the same manner. Provisions such as these, which have subsequently found their way into many other national laws and regulations, mean that the manufacturer or other licensee for a drug today has continuing duties with respect to the drug so long as it remains on the market.

By the time that the process of harmonising drug regulation came into swing across much of the world in 1990, the process of new drug approval had therefore been complemented by procedures to monitor both efficacy and safety throughout the life of a product. The legal duty of the manufacturer to maintain his commitment to the product throughout that period was laid down clearly by the Tokyo District Court in a 1978 judgement dealing with the complications caused by clioquinol:

> When . . . products have already been placed on sale and put into clinical use for humans or animals, documentation and information in medical, pharmaceutical and other related sciences concerning such products, including homologous chemical compounds, should be constantly collected. If, as a result of such activities, there are indications that undesirable side effects exist, a comparative, quantitative study of the reports on the clinical safety of the products available up to that time should be concluded to determine the extent of the suspicions concerning possible side effects. Where such suspicions do exist, the companies are required to establish as soon as possible the existence and extent of the side effects of the said products by conducting animal experiments or studies on the history of drug-related symptoms and by engaging in follow-up research. In addition . . . they are required, as part of the duty to foresee, to notify other pharmaceutical companies that manufacture or sell similar products and to so request information from them on both past and future side effects of the said products so as to obtain a more defined perception of and better foresight regarding such side effects . . . .[1]

Except for the Court's postulate that manufacturers had a duty to report adverse effects to each other, much of the above remains literally valid today.

The life of a drug product, during which new knowledge about it may emerge, may be very long indeed; acetylsalicylic acid (aspirin) was described by Felix Hoffmann on October 10, 1897 and marketed shortly thereafter, becoming one of the most widely used medicines of all time. Yet its probable link to Reye's syndrome, that was seriously affecting several hundred children yearly in America, was not propounded until 1965, and its ability to affect favourably the prognosis for cardiovascular disease was not made credible until the work of Elwood and Cochrane in 1974; there is probably yet more news about aspirin, good or bad, to come.

There may even be at least a moral duty to investigate safety problems further after they have led to the withdrawal of a drug, in the hope of finding explanations which can help to assure future drug safety in the field concerned:

> After the ICI beta-blocker practolol was withdrawn because of fibrotic complications, both the company itself and others undertook much work to determine whether the risk was associated with particular structural characteristics and could be avoided with other beta-blocking agents.

---

[1] *S.M.O.N. Patients v. The State and others* (1978), Judgement, at p. 322 per Kabe J.

All this means that the initial approval of a drug, however demanding the process may be, is in essence only a provisional step; it may need to be modified as time goes on and new knowledge of the product's properties accumulates. For some drugs it may be necessary to require the originator company to undertake intensive monitoring, set up supplementary studies or perform particular tests during treatment. New Zealand was a pioneer in "intensive monitoring", an arrangement by which a limited patient population receiving a drug is followed in great detail so that all events, wanted and unwanted, can be recorded. Now known as "monitored release" it can be required where an agency cannot take a firm decision on the future of an apparently valuable drug without more detailed information from the field. The exact duties differ from one regulatory system to another, but for all drugs, post-marketing surveillance in the form of adverse reaction monitoring and submission of new findings from other sources will be necessary. There are very few drugs about which, at the time of their introduction, there is nothing left to discover.

A concurrent problem is the fact that the standards prescribed by the law – which calls for quality, efficacy and safety – are not as exact as they appear on paper. Standards in medicine or biology are rarely as sharply defined as they can be in pharmacy or any other of the exact sciences. Some aspects of the quality of a drug can be defined in exact mathematical terms, but neither safety nor efficacy can be so rigidly circumscribed. Estimates of each inevitably vary; no drug can be expected to prove effective in 100% of the patients for whom it is prescribed, and no drug is entirely free of adverse reactions. In all three fields therefore one encounters difficulties in interpreting the law when taking decisions on particular drugs, either at the outset of their career or later.

A related problem is the interrelationship of the three basic issues. Initially, some pharmaceutical firms favoured a regulatory system in which quality, safety and efficacy, listed as separate items in the law, would also be assessed as separate matters. It soon became clear that this would not be realistic:

In 1964 the Committee on the Safety of Drugs was established by the British Health Ministers with a small staff. Strictly speaking it was authorized only to assess medicines for their safety, and some manufacturers objected to its assessing efficacy issues as well. The Committee however made it clear that one could not evaluate one without the other; whether or not a particular degree of toxicity was acceptable could depend very much on how effective and important the drug was in medicine.

In the same manner, and much though some applicants objected to comparative evaluation as falling outside the legal criteria for assessment, the acceptability of a medicine would inevitably depend on whether its efficacy/safety balance was at least comparable to that of medicines already available. The classic example cited in debate at the time was that of antimicrobial treatment. In 1930, with no antibiotics available, lobar pneumonia was commonly a fatal disease, and had a drug been created at the time that was capable of saving 30% of lives it would have been a god-send. Once penicillin had appeared a decade later and had proved capable of curing most patients, anything offering a lesser ability to cure would have been rejected out of hand.

> Several striking examples of this phenomenon were seen at the time when regulation was fast developing. Until the late nineteen-fifties, patients requiring diuretics were normally treated with the highly effective organic mercury compounds despite their ability to damage various organ systems, elicit anaphylactic reactions and precipitate cardiac arrest. (Meyler 1960 at pp. 70–71) As soon as the well-tolerated thiazide diuretics became available, the mercury compounds were discarded as obsolete (Dollery 1972 at p. 313). Somewhat similarly, the highly addictive and toxic barbiturates largely lost their place during the same period to the benzodiazepines; (Shepherd 1972 at pp. 51–60; see also section 4.3. below) the dependence-producing potential of the latter became evident only much later (Medawar 1992).

On occasion, manufacturers have successfully defended their products in court precisely on the grounds of their favourable efficacy/safety balance (see Brahams 1990, cited under Section 4.3.6).

In many of the matters noted above, regulatory agencies have for all these reasons engaged in some extensive interpretation of the very general criteria listed in the law, but have as a rule done so in a consistent manner.

4.2. The Manufacturing and Quality Control of Drugs

4.2.1. *The legal concept of quality*

There is an apocryphal story that the prospective purchaser of a Rolls-Royce motor car who enquires as to the power of the engine merely receives the assurance "Quite sufficient, sir."[2] In a sense this is also the

---

[2] This degree of confidentiality is no longer maintained. The 2005 Rolls-Royce Phantom develops 453 bhp.

most satisfactory answer that could be given to a purchaser asking about the quality of a medicine from a reputable supplier. There is no single, simple and universally relevant means of expressing quality or setting a quality threshold. Desmond Laurence's admirable "Dictionary of Pharmacology and Allied Topics" does not define quality beyond ruling that "It is essential that manufactured medicines be of high and consistent quality." (Laurence 1998 at p. 282) Even plain water has various levels of quality: alongside water approved for human consumption (*aqua potabilis, aqua communis*) the pharmacopoeias provide specifications and modes of preparation for both purified water (*aqua purificata*) which is prepared by distillation, reverse osmosis or other suitable methods and then stored in inert airtight containers, and water for injection (*aqua ad injectionem*) which is sterile and free of pyrogens. Physiological saline – plain salt solution – has at least five measures for quality and several standards; one must know its actual concentration, the degree to which that concentration can be allowed to vary, its degree of chemical purity and the permissible degree of contamination with bacteria, viruses or pyrogens. For a finished medicine there will be far more measures of quality and numerous matters on which experts (and regulatory agencies) may disagree regarding the necessary standards, ranging from issues of colour to stability and from disintegration time to bioavailability. If the quality standards are set too low the medicine may be ineffective or dangerous, whereas if too much is demanded the work of making the medicine and checking the quality of every batch may be so laborious as to render it unaffordable. These are not minor matters, since they have both medical and judicial consequences; the law requires in general terms that drugs be of adequate quality and imposes sanctions if they are not; there are detailed and legally established procedures for setting the standards applicable to any individual medicine and testing to these standards; finally one will be obliged to ensure that the medicine attains all those standards throughout its shelf life, and to reject or discard any medicine that fails to do so.

4.2.2.   *Establishment and maintenance of quality standards*

Society maintains a range of complementary and legally instituted procedures to ensure the quality of medicines; standards are set, manufacturing conditions are specified, and quality is checked both at the time of drug approval and beyond.

(i) Pharmacopoeia monographs   A pharmacopoeia, in the usual sense of the term, is a standard work of reference setting quality norms for

the most widely used medicines; the principal matters covered in the technical monograph for each medicine are manufacturing standards, standards for purity, methods of assay and directions for use (with the emphasis usually on directions for handling and processing). Most significant pharmacopoeias are state publications authorized by law;[3] a well-equipped laboratory is likely to have some 30 current pharmacopoeias to hand including three regional or international volumes (the *International*, *European* and *Nordic Pharmacopoeia*). Although in recent years an increasing number of national pharmacopoeias have been assimilated in whole or in part into the regional volumes, a number of newly independent countries are currently preparing to institute national pharmacopoeias of their own, particularly where there is a national (e.g. herbal) medicinal tradition.

The historical role of the pharmacopoeia was to provide the community pharmacist with guidance on the preparation and testing of medicines, including the identification, selection and testing of herbs, the making of extracts and the blending of ingredients. A national pharmacopoeia would therefore strive to list most medicines in regular use, and the differences between national volumes largely reflected differing flora and herbal traditions from place to place. During the twentieth century, in which time medicine has moved largely to the use of single substances (synthetic or extracted from natural materials) the choice of medicines in daily use has become more uniform throughout the world. The various pharmacopoeias have therefore drawn closer together in their selection of monographs and actual content, often sharing complete monographs. The British Pharmacopoeia for 2003 contains, for example, 2,900 monographs, a proportion of which are shared with the European Pharmacopoeia.

For new medicines developed by the pharmaceutical industry the necessary quality standards are created by the originating company and assessed for their acceptability by the Drug Regulatory Authority of each country or region where marketing approval is sought (see below). Only in later years as patents expire and the medicine becomes available for general manufacture is a public pharmacopoeia monograph likely to be issued, often derived from the manufacturer's work and developed in collaboration with him.

Traditional pharmacopoeias provide only standards for basic medicinal substances and not for finished products, but the latter are now

---

[3] The first pharmacopoeia to gain legal recognition was that compiled by Valerius Cordus, issued posthumously at Nuremburg in 1546. The US Pharmacopoeia was founded in 1820 and accorded status in Federal Law under the Drug Import Act of 1848.

increasingly included in many national volumes and are finding their way into the *International Pharmacopoeia* published by WHO. Manufactured products, whether basic substances or finished medicines, that have been produced and tested to the standards listed in a particular Pharmacopoeia are authorized to be labelled as such (e.g. Propranolol Hydrochloride Injection U.S.P.).

The term "Pharmacopoeia" is also used for similar volumes produced for special purposes by health institutions or independently (Herbal Pharmacopoeia, Hospital Pharmacopoeia). *Martindale's Extra Pharmacopoeia* is a medical/pharmaceutical reference book and dictionary with documented information on most of the medicines and medicinal substances in use in the world.

(ii) Good manufacturing practice, licensing and inspection   Although procedures to license and inspect pharmaceutical factories have existed since the nineteenth century, the standards have been much developed since the introduction of the concept of Good Manufacturing Practice (GMP).

The GMP concept arose after 1963 when the United States FDA first introduced detailed regulations setting out the practices to be followed in manufacturing, packaging and storing medicines. From 1968 onwards the World Health Organization adopted the term in a programme to upgrade and harmonise the standards imposed in its member states. Extensive GMP rules have since been developed for the European Union and in the framework of the International Conference on Harmonisation (see Chapter 3). The provisions and the prescribed arrangements for training and inspection are comprehensive. To cite only the European definition of their scope and purpose:

> Good Manufacturing Practice is that part of Quality Assurance which ensures that products are consistently produced and controlled to the quality standards appropriate to their intended use and as required by the Marketing Authorisation or product specification.

Good Manufacturing Practice is concerned with both production and quality control. The basic requirements of GMP are that:

   i.   all manufacturing processes are clearly defined, systematically reviewed in the light of experience and shown to be capable of consistently manufacturing medicinal products of the required quality and complying with their specifications;

   ii. critical steps of manufacturing processes and significant changes to the process are validated;

    iii. all necessary facilities for GMP are provided including:
        a. appropriately qualified and trained personnel;
        b. adequate premises and space;
        c. suitable equipment and services;
        d. correct materials, containers and labels;
        e. approved procedures and instructions;
        f. suitable storage and transport;
    iv. instructions and procedures are written in an instructional form in clear and unambiguous language, specifically applicable to the facilities provided;
    v. operators are trained to carry out procedures correctly;
    vi. records are made, manually and/or by recording instruments, during manufacture which demonstrate that all the steps required by the defined procedures and instructions were in fact taken and that the quantity and quality of the product was as expected. Any significant deviations are fully recorded and investigated;
    vii. records of manufacture including distribution which enable the complete history of a batch to be traced, are retained in a comprehensible and accessible form;
    viii. the distribution (wholesaling) of the products minimises any risk to their quality.

The term GMP is not yet used consistently, since any country may regard its own manufacturing requirements as guaranteeing good practice. Increasingly, however, the term is now only applied to the highest set of standards as adopted in EU, Japan and the USA, and as a rule agreed in ICH. Factories are now in many countries both licensed and inspected according to these GMP standards, drug inspectors having been retrained to certify and control all production units.[4] However, other manufacturing, especially in the developing world, is still carried out to a lesser standard; as noted in Chapter 8 this is commonly all that can be attained where the resources for full GMP are not available, and for many purposes a lesser standard is entirely satisfactory. Universal adoption of ICH standards regarding quality could in that respect be disastrous:

---

[4] Since it is not practical for every country to maintain full inspection teams, much inspection is now performed internationally under the auspices of the Pharmaceutical Inspection Co-operation Scheme (PIC/S); see http://www.picscheme.org. There are also bilateral arrangements for mutual recognition of GMP inspections between countries.

The issue was raised emphatically in July 2003 at a broadly constituted meeting convened by M.S.F. and the Drugs for Neglected Diseases
Initiative in Geneva in July 2003 which concluded that:

> There are substantial fears that some ICH guidelines might have a negative impact
> on access to essential medicines in developing countries. Specifically, new strin-
> gent requirements for raw materials may raise drug prices without offering any
> discernible public health benefit in exchange. Some medicines that are badly
> needed in developing countries may not be granted regulatory approval, since
> risk/benefit calculations are necessarily made differently in non-ICH and ICH
> countries. In addition, the existing governance structure excludes many of the
> stakeholders affected by the process, including developing countries, consumers,
> and health professionals... The motivation behind extending the guidelines
> beyond ICH countries is not clear. Nevertheless, it is notable that the multinational
> pharmaceutical industry – far more than drug regulators – stands to benefit com-
> mercially and strategically from the globalisation of ICH guidelines, and therefore
> has likely been the driving force behind it. For example, higher standards for the
> quality of raw materials and drugs may allow ICH countries to protect themselves
> from lower- priced (generic) imports from other markets that do not hold to ICH
> quality standards, while ensuring continued access to high quality raw materials
> from non-ICH countries for their domestic manufacturers. (MSH 2003)

As a regulator in Central Asia explained in 2004:

> At the moment some two-thirds of our supplies come from factories, here or in
> neighbouring countries, that do not have GMP certification. We are progressively
> closing those that will never learn how to make drugs, but there are some which
> we would simply call "clean, careful and cautious" which we can call on for sim-
> ple antiacid tablets or even benzodiazepine tranquillizers, and one day we will get
> them upgraded. For the moment they are not the sort of factories we will allow to
> supply us with drugs having a narrow efficacy/safety margin, such as digoxin, or
> any form of intravenous injection." (Interview 38)

Many similar countries are now progressively upgrading their production facilities so that a sufficient number of manufacturers attain GMP
within the coming years, while others are obliged to cease operations.

(iii) Drug regulatory procedures   The national (and in some cases
regional) structures for drug regulation considered in Chapter 3 include
provisions to ensure the quality of products registered; as a rule there is an
associated quality control laboratory to examine both the documentation
submitted by the applicant and to analyse samples submitted at the time of
approval or taken subsequently. The Agency is as a rule closely associated
with the national drug inspectorate which can ensure that samples are
taken regularly at all levels of distribution so as to confirm that quality is
maintained. Drugs failing to meet the required standards may be recalled

or particular tainted batches removed from the market, and sanctions may be imposed.

Since a drug regulatory agency is a multidisciplinary body, differences can arise between the pharmaceutical and the medical concepts of quality:

> The medical experts on the Board often pressed the view in borderline cases that the quality standard which we required for a drug should primarily depend upon the therapeutic index or margin of safety; for a product such as penicillin with a very high index a fair degree of variation in product content could be tolerated, whereas for a medicine such as lithium with a very low index the product content would be permitted to vary only within extremely narrow limits. The nature of contaminants would affect the extent to which their presence could be tolerated in the finished product. Some of the pharmacists on the other hand were prone to insist on the highest attainable standard of quality, for example with product content varying only between 99% and 101% of the norm. Discussions tended to end in a compromise in view of evidence adduced by manufacturers as to the expense of maintaining quality at an unnecessarily high level, especially once a drug was out in the field. (Interview 3)

For individual products such debates generally lead to constructive interaction between companies and regulators in order to arrive at standards which are both necessary and attainable.

(iv) Procurement agencies   In those countries – particularly in the developing world – where there is a public drug procurement system this organisation will as a rule itself maintain (or contract with) a quality control laboratory, to examine samples submitted by firms tendering for supply contracts. The need for many of these agencies to procure at low cost and thus from secondary suppliers means that a relatively high proportion of faults may be found:

> When WHO examined the quality control records of experienced procurement systems in five developing countries it was found that, despite a careful pre-selection of eligible suppliers, the proportion of medicines failing to pass the necessary tests ranged from 14 to 29%.

(v) Certification schemes   Since medicines are constantly being tested at numerous institutions throughout the world there is provision for some information on their findings in order to ensure that faults found at one site do not occur at others. The current arrangements are not fully satisfactory, since some agencies hesitate in view of their confidentiality provisions to make their findings widely available, and others cannot be regarded as fully reliable sources of information. Table 4.A provides a summary of the situation.

Table 4.A
Overview of International Certification Arrangements

WHO CERTIFICATION SCHEME (revised 1992, 1995)
Certificate issued by a national drug regulatory agency, generally to a foreign agency or to the manufacturer concerned.
Warrants that a drug has been granted a marketing licence. Confirms that the manufacturer has passed inspection requirements.
Comments: Is only as reliable as the issuing agency. Does not provide batch-specific information. Not verified by WHO

STATEMENT OF LICENSING STATUS (WHO Model 1992)
Certificate issued by a national drug regulatory agency in an exporting country, to an importing country
Warrants only that a particular drug has been granted as national marketing licence
Comments: Is only as reliable as the issuing agency. Does not provide batch-specific information. Not verified by WHO

BATCH CERTIFICATE (WHO Model)
Certificate issued *either* by the manufacturer *or* by the national drug regulatory agency in an exporting country
Confirms that an individual numbered batch has been shown to conform to product specifications.
Comments: Usually requested for antibiotics or where drugs are suspect. Only as reliable as the issuer; easily falsified. Not verified by WHO

FREE SALE CERTIFICATE (non-WHO)
Certificate issued by a national drug regulatory agency in an exporting country
Confirms only that a particular product is on sale nationally
Comments: Does not confirm that the product has been evaluated for efficacy, safety or quality or has been approved.

GMP CERTIFICATE
Certificate issued by a national drug regulatory agency in an exporting country
Declares that a specified plant manufactures pharmaceuticals to "GMP standard"
Comments: Only as reliable as the issuing agency. GMP standards can vary.

ANALYTICAL BATCH CERTIFICATE
Issued by a manufacturer
Copies of analytical tests and results for particular batches of a drug.
Comments: Only as reliable as the issuing manufacturer. Easily falsified. No confirmation of national marketing licence.

(vi) Manufacturer's research   The fact that the above sources of standards lie with official bodies should not obscure the fact that, as mentioned above in (iii), the first well-researched proposals for the setting and testing of quality standards very commonly lie with the original or principal manufacturer of a drug who in his own field may be considerably more experienced than any outside agency in deciding what standards are necessary and realistic.

4.2.3.   Packaging and distribution

The sensitive and potent nature of medicines imposes particular duties on the manufacturer regarding packaging standards and the conditions under which drugs are stored, transported and supplied so long as they remain under his control. Throughout that period it is his responsibility to ensure that they remain in good and usable condition, bearing in mind the conditions to which they are likely to be exposed.

> Glyceryl trinitrate will for example sublimate rapidly unless it is kept in a tightly sealed container. Many antibiotics and vaccines require supply through a refrigerated "cold chain". Glass bottles used for blood or intravenous fluids can develop hair splits allowing infection to enter, while plastic bags may contain toxic "emulsifiers" which leak out into the contents of the bag.

When the manufacturer transfers a medicine by sale or otherwise to another party it is his duty to ensure that it comes into appropriate and authorized hands:

> Each legal system has its own provisions regarding the persons or institutions entitled to handle or trade in medicines, generally limited to licensed importers and wholesalers, pharmacies, health institutions and physicians. Special provisions will apply to certain classes of drugs (e.g. controlled substances, see Chapter 9) and there may be rules regarding transport.

> Manufacturers have on occasion been held liable for negligence where products (stimulants, drugs of dependence, anabolic steroids) were improperly diverted from their stocks into illegal channels.

A manufacturer has no responsibility for the fate of a medicine once he has legally transferred it to another party, but where it becomes necessary to recall a product or a specified batch he should use his best efforts to ensure that it is returned to him. He may also be required or requested by the authorities to issue warnings if particular risks become evident or precautions need to be taken, and in some instances it may be both in his own best interest and that of the public to warn against improper use of his product.

4.2.4. Nature and extent of quality defects

In various parts of the world there is a considerable market in spurious and counterfeit products (see Section 2.2.4), many of these being of extremely poor quality. Setting that issue aside in the present discussion, one can reasonably conclude that quality standards in the legitimate pharmaceutical market are as a whole remarkably satisfactory. Serious defects are in many countries so rare as to be regarded as curiosities:

> Sanders, writing on behalf of the pharmaceutical industry in The Netherlands, pointed to a small number of instances of serious fault reported in the course of some years in that country: in one case, infusion fluids had not been sterile; in a second, a toxic heavy metal was found in vitamin C ampoules; and in a third, digoxin tablets were contaminated with digitoxin. (Sanders 1982)

Major manufacturers have, as noted above, collaborated in the definition of high standards and have themselves respected them, and the progressive concentration of industry in larger units has made it possible to provide the staff and resources needed to maintain proper levels of quality. Where defects have occurred they have generally been attributable to human error. In one calendar year, despite the intensive controls of quality in the US drug market, only 354 drug recalls were ordered by the FDA, many relating only to individual batches (Picariello 2005). An analysis for the year 2000 of the ten principal reasons for such recalls (CDER 2001) showed that these comprised:

- Lack of assurance of sterility in production or testing of sterile drug products
- Deviations from current good manufacturing practices
- Subpotency
- Microbial contamination of non-sterile products
- Chemical contamination
- Penicillin cross-contamination of other products
- Failure of validation of the manufacturing processes or inability to validate it
- Drug product marketed without an approved new or generic application
- Failure of drug to dissolve properly
- Product found to exceed limits set for impurities or degradation.

Detailed data on drug recalls because of quality defects are published promptly on the internet by the authorities in the United States, Britain and a number of other countries. While some agencies have been reticent to follow the example, fearing libel proceedings in the event of error, much wider dissemination of such information could be helpful in eliminating this source of inefficacy and risk.

4.2.5.   Liability for quality defects

While many civil actions are brought against manufacturers for alleged safety defects (see Section 4.3) relatively few are brought for quality defects; the latter are more usually the source of measures taken by the national drug inspectorates, resulting as a rule in the withdrawal of a tainted batch of a drug and occasionally in criminal charges under the medicines legislation.

A prominent civil case, already briefly referred to in Chapter 2, related to an alleged manufacturing defect involving a hepatitis vaccine on sale in Britain:[5] It merits citation in that the defendant manufacturer raised a number of arguments in his defence which could be relevant in other cases though they did not avail him in this instance:

The claimants had been infected with Hepatitis C virus through blood transfusions which had used blood or blood products obtained from infected donors. They brought actions for damages against the defendants, the authorities responsible for the production of blood and blood products. During the period when most of the claimants were infected, the risk of such infection through blood transfusions, though known to the medical profession, was impossible to avoid, either because the virus itself had not yet been discovered or because there was no way of testing for its presence in blood. Accordingly, the claims were brought not in negligence, but under the Consumer Protection Act 1987 which implemented the European Product Liability Directive of 1985 under which a product was defective when it did not provide the safety which a person was entitled to expect, taking all circumstances into account, including the presentation of the product, the use to which it could reasonably be expected that the product would be put and the time when the product was put into circulation. Article 7(e)b of the Act provided the producer with a defence if he could establish that the state of scientific and technical knowledge at the time when he put the product into circulation was not such as to enable 'the existence of the defect' to be discovered. In the trial of the six lead cases, the defendants accepted that a producer's liability under art 6 of the Act was irrespective of fault. They nevertheless contended that, in assessing whether the infected blood was defective, the unavoidability of the risk was a circumstance to be taken into account, and that the

---

[5] A and others v National Blood Authority and another [2001] 3 All ER 289. High Court, Queen's Bench Division, London. Judgement of March 26, 2001 per Burton J.

most that the public was entitled to expect was that all reasonably available precautions had been carried out, not that the blood would be 100% clean. In so contending, the defendants submitted that the infected blood was to be regarded as an inherently risky standard product (i.e. one which performed as the producer intended) rather than a non-standard product (i.e. a product which was deficient or inferior in terms of safety from the standard product, and whose harmful characteristic, not present in the standard product, had caused the material injury or damage). They also relied on the fact that they were obliged to produce blood and had no alternative but to supply it to hospitals and patients, as a service to society. Alternatively, the defendants sought to rely on the art 7(e) defence, contending that an unavoidable risk qualified for protection under it if the producer was unable to discover, by means of accessible information, the defect in a particular product.

Giving judgement, Mr Justice Burton held that:

(1) Avoidability was not one of the circumstances to be taken into account under art 6, even in respect of a harmful characteristic in a standard product. In that provision, 'all circumstances' meant all relevant circumstances. Avoidability was not a relevant circumstance since it fell outside the purpose of the directive, which was intended to eliminate proof of fault or negligence. That was not simply a legal consequence. It was also intended to make it easier for claimants to prove their case, such that not only would a consumer not have to prove that the producer had not taken reasonable steps, or all reasonable steps, to comply with his duty of care, but also that the producer had not taken all legitimately expectable steps either. Even without the full panoply of allegations of negligence, the adoption of tests of avoidability or of legitimately expectable safety precautions would inevitably involve a substantial investigation. If it had been intended that avoidability would be included as a derogation from, or a palliation of, the directive's purpose, it would have been mentioned. It would have been an important circumstance, and it was intended that the most significant circumstances were those listed. In the case of a non-standard product, the circumstances specified in art 6 might obviously be relevant, as well as the circumstances of the supply. However, the primary issue might be whether the public at large accepted the non-standard nature of the product, i.e. whether they accepted that a proportion of the products was defective. That was not the end of the matter, because the question was one of legitimate expectation, and the court might conclude that the expectation of the public was too high or too low. Questions such as warnings and presentations would be in the forefront, but the avoidability of the harmful characteristic, the impractability, cost or difficulty of precautionary measures, and the benefit to society or the utility of the product (except in the context of whether, with full information and proper knowledge, the public had and should have accepted the risk) were not relevant. In the instant case, the infected blood products were non-standard products since they were different from the norm which the producer intended for use by the public. They were defective within art 6 because the public at large was entitled to expect that the blood transfused to them would be free from infection. There had been no warnings and no material publicity. The knowledge of the medical profession, not materially or at all shared with the consumer, was of no relevance. Nor was it material to consider whether any further steps could have been taken to avoid or palliate the risk that the blood would be infected.

(2) The defence in art 7(e) of the directive did not apply where the existence of the generic defect was known or should have been known in the context of accessible information. Once the existence of the defect was known, there was the risk of that defect materialising in any particular product, and it was immaterial that the known risk was unavoidable in the particular product. It would be inconsistent with the purpose of the directive if a producer, in the case of a known risk, continued to supply products simply because, and despite the fact, that he was unable to identify in which of his products that defect would occur or recur, or, more relevantly in a case where the producer was obliged to supply, he continued to supply without accepting the responsibility for any injuries resulting, by insurance or otherwise. Such a conclusion did not mean that non-standard products were incapable of coming within art 7(e). Such products might qualify once, i.e. if the problem which led to an occasional defective product was not known. However, once the problem was known by virtue of accessible information, the non-standard product would no longer qualify for protection under art 7(e). Accordingly, in the instant case, art 7(e) was of no avail to the defendants, and the claimants were therefore entitled to recover against them.

(3) If, contrary to the court's primary conclusion, the issues of avoidability or discoverability of the defect in the particular donation of blood had arisen, precautions to prevent or make a material reduction in the transfer of transmitted infection through infected blood were available and not taken. From 1 March 1989 the blood was defective in all the circumstances and from 1 March 1990 the defect in the donations was discoverable.

(4) The damages recoverable by the claimants could include, dependent upon the facts, provisional or final damages in respect of invasive or debilitating treatments, handicap in respect of employment and insurability, and the provision of gratuitous services.

Alongside this, a single example of a regulatory measure taken in the light of industrial failure as regards quality must be cited here at similar length. It is intended, not in order to cast any aspersions on a particular corporation, but to show how even a well-reputed firm with extensive procedures for quality assurance and control may on occasion fall foul of a watchful agency charged with maintaining strict standards in this demanding field, especially if the firm fails to respond adequately and immediately when the agency expresses concern. It also illustrates the fact that firm measures can and will be taken against a firm merely because the quality standards have been contravened, and not because there was necessarily any risk to patients:

FDA News, March 4th 2005. In a response to ongoing concerns about manufacturing quality, the Food and Drug Administration (FDA) and the Department of Justice today initiated seizures of Paxil CR and Avandamet tablets manufactured by GlaxoSmithKline, Inc. (GSK). Manufacturing practices for the two drugs, approved to treat depression and panic disorder (Paxil CR) and Type II Diabetes (Avandamet), failed to meet the standards laid out by FDA that ensure product safety, strength, quality and purity.

"FDA and the Department of Justice will not allow drug manufacturers to ignore our high public health standards for drug manufacturing," said John M. Taylor, FDA Associate Commissioner for Regulatory Affairs. "Once we discover a company is not following the standards, which were created to ensure safety and quality, we expect them to correct the deficiencies in an expedited manner. American consumers deserve the best health care products on the market today, and companies that are not adhering to these standards cannot assure FDA and American consumers of the quality of their products."

FDA is not aware of any harm to consumers by the products subject to this seizure and it does not believe that these products pose a significant health hazard to consumers. Consequently, FDA urges patients who use these two drugs to continue taking their tablets and to talk with their health care provider about possible alternative products for use until the manufacturing problems have been corrected. FDA has determined that neither product is medically necessary and that alternative products are available for consumer use.

The agency is concerned that GSK's violation of manufacturing standards may have resulted in the production of poor quality drug products that could potentially pose risks to consumers. Among the violations noted during FDA's latest inspection was the finding that the Paxil CR tablets could split apart and patients could receive a portion of the tablets that lacks any active ingredient, or alternatively a portion that contains active ingredient and does not have the intended controlled-release effect. Additionally, FDA found that some Avandamet tablets did not have an accurate dose of rosiglitazone, an active ingredient in this product.

The seizures follow warrants issued by the U.S. District Courts for the District of Puerto Rico and the Eastern District of Tennessee. The seizures were executed today by the U.S. Marshals Service at GSK's Cidra, Puerto Rico manufacturing facility, its Knoxville, Tennessee distribution facility, and a Puerto Rico distribution facility. GSK has voluntarily recalled some of the affected lots of Paxil CR and Avandamet; however, it has failed to recall all affected lots of these products. This failure on the part of GSK resulted in today's seizures by federal authorities.

4.3.   Establishing the Safety of Drugs

4.3.1.   The legal concept of safety

Section 2.2.3 referred to a case in the English High Court regarding thromboembolic injury suffered by women using the third-generation oral contraceptives. That case turned on the question as to whether these products possessed the degree of safety which "persons generally" were under European Product Liability Law entitled to expect, and it was clear that this expectation was in turn based on past experience with the widely used second-generation products. The latter had attained a degree of safety that the community had come to regard as acceptable, as reflected in their widespread use, and "persons generally" had a right to expect that a subsequent product would not be significantly less safe. Safety, as noted in Section 4.1, is not an absolute concept where drugs are concerned since all have adverse effects, and in considering whether a product is acceptably safe one must have some basis for comparison with what already exists, while the degree of risk which may exist must often be weighed against the benefit that the medicine can provide. Many subtle cases are on record and they can give rise to lengthy disputes:

> The analgesic dipyrone (metamizole), introduced early in the twentieth century and very widely used by the public in some parts of the world, was found to induce blood dyscrasias in some patients. Because it was widely used without medical prescription and was especially popular in countries without sophisticated systems for adverse reaction reporting, the incidence of dyscrasis could not be estimated with any accuracy. An "international agranulocytosis study" sponsored by the manufacturer, which suggested that the risk was very low, was both attacked (Offerhaus 1987) and as vigorously defended (Levi and Shapiro 1987). In most industrialised countries the drug was restricted or removed from the market but elsewhere it remained popular. In the critical view the essential reason to reject the drug, irrespective of the statistics, was the fact that other simple analgesics were as effective without exposing the user to these risks at all.

In such cases the manufacturer may be better placed than most to gather and examine the evidence of risk, and withdraw the drug from the market if it is verified. It is equally obvious, however, that where a drug remains highly profitable after a long period he may be hardly motivated to do so, especially as long as statisticians can be recruited who are willing to defend the product. In such an instance, and if there is no public health interest in retaining the drug on the market, unusual forms of pressure may be applied on the part of the health authorities in order to ensure that action is taken:

> An early but illustrative case is that of the disinfectant clioquinol which over a period of more than forty years enjoyed massive and worldwide popularity as an oral remedy and prophylactic for non-specific ("tourist") diarrhoea. Evidence of efficacy with internal use was little more than anecdotal. There was indeed some reason to believe that in long-term use clioquinol might actually induce diarrhoea, thus setting in motion a vicious circle, but the problems were not widely known

and drug regulation was still at an early phase of development. From 1960 onwards however, a neurological condition known as Subacute Myelo-opticoneuropathy (SMON) became frequent in Japan, proceeding to paralysis, blindness and sometimes death. An official enquiry into the cause of the disease led to the discovery of a clioquinol metabolite in the urine of the victims, and a close correlation was subsequently found between use of the drug (which in Japan was unusually heavy) and the occurrence of the disease; cases were also reported in other countries. (Soda 1980, Dukes 1981) The drug was rapidly prohibited or withdrawn in Japan and in many western industrialized countries, but continued to be produced on a large scale for use elsewhere. Ultimately, prolonged pressure by officials of the World Health Organization appears to have led to corporate reassessment of the situation and the manufacture was after a number of years discontinued. (Dunne 1993)

Where a drug is shown, rapidly and convincingly, to bring with it disproportionate risks, a manufacturer will commonly withdraw it without protest and even at his own initiative, believing this to be in the common interest. Serious conflicts between the public and the commercial interest can however arise where the business interests at stake are large and long-standing, and especially where the proof of injury is less than absolute. The legal and other mechanisms which might provide a basis for global public action are still not in place, although much-publicized restrictive actions in one major country or region are often emulated in another.

As discussed in Section 2.2.3, the legal basis for a manufacturer's liability to a user for a defect in his product (including the ability to injure) has to some extent shifted in recent years. Traditionally, he might be found liable in negligence, such as failure to detect the risks associated with his drug, failure to correct them or to warn of them. That is still the case in much of the world. In the European Union, however, he may be found liable if his product does not possess the degree of safety which persons generally are entitled to expect. In either situation it is clear that the manufacturer has a duty to examine the safety of his product and to act according to his findings. Where medicines are concerned that duty is also specifically imposed by drug legislation and has been amply confirmed by the courts.

Periodically, there is discussion as to the legal situation arising when a drug is dispensed for a purpose other than that approved by the regulatory authorities. Use for such a "non-approved indication" is generally regarded as being at the physician's discretion and is not prohibited by drug law. However, if a serious adverse reaction results, the patient will probably not be able to bring a case against the manufacturer alleging that his drug is defective; according to some older American case law, such a departure from the official standards of safe and effective drug use may be held to constitute prima facie evidence of negligence.[6] The issue has been discussed in legal, medical and political circles without being clearly resolved. A relevant question for a Court will clearly be whether occurrence of the injury was attributable to the drug's use in a particular non-approved indication or not. If so, the patient might be able to bring a case against the prescriber rather than the manufacturer of the drug, e.g. if the prescribing was ill-considered. Cautious pharmaceutical firms, for their part, have sometimes distanced themselves, with good reason, from all non-approved uses of their drugs.

> Many major drug manufacturers have furnished prescribers and pharmacists alike with letters of indemnity undertaking to defend against and pay any claims resulting from the use of their drugs. A careful reading of these letters limits the liability of the manufacturer to the approved use of the drug. (Nielsen 1986 at p. 20)

4.3.2. *Physical, social and mental injury*

Before considering further the issue of duty as regards adverse reactions it is helpful to make a distinction between two main manifestations of drug injury since the problems with each have proved to be somewhat different. The most concrete and readily recognized form of drug injury is *physical*. Even though there may be doubt as to causation, the fact of the injury – be it liver damage, gastric perforation or thrombosis – is as a rule incontrovertible. Methods for the detection of adverse reactions are also heavily attuned to detecting physical damage. Where on the other hand a medicine causes some change in *social or mental functioning* or induces some form of *dependence or addition*, this may be more difficult to recognize, especially where the drug has itself been given as a treatment for some mental or behavioural condition. The problem has come strongly to the fore in the last half century, first with the benzodiazepine tranquillizers and more recently with the SSRI antidepressants.

> Medawar and Hardon[7] have briefly summarised a century and a half of problems in this field:
>
> > "Between the 1860s and 1960s, doctors treated mental distress by prescribing alcohol and opium, then morphine, heroin and cocaine. Later came chloral,

---

[6] Mulder v. Parke-Davis & Co., 181 N.W. 2nd 882 (1970).

[7] I am grateful to Charles Medawar and Anita Hardon for much of the material in this subsection.

bromides, barbiturates and many similar drugs. Bar alcohol, each of these drugs was also used to treat addiction – and later found to cause it too." (Medawar 2004 at p. 11).

The barbiturate sedatives were widely used from 1905 until about 1970. As late as 1941, standard medical texts declared that addiction to these drugs probably did not occur (Goodman Gilman 1941), but by 1950 addiction to high doses had been proven and by 1958 "chronic barbiturate addiction" had been demonstrated. In 1957 Hoffmann La Roche introduced the first benzodiazepine tranquillizer, chlor-diazepoxide (Librium) and many benzodiazepines followed either as daytime seda-tives or nighttime hypnotics (Medawar 1992). The belief was widely propagated that these drugs did not produce dependence and they largely replaced the barbitu-rates for this reason. In fact addiction had been demonstrated from 1961 onwards but was dismissed by investigators associated with the company as occurring only with excessive doses or in addiction-prone personalities. By 1973 the Third US District Court of Appeals in Philadelphia, considering a move to have two benzo-diazepines listed as controlled drugs, noted that they produced euphoria, tolerance, withdrawal reactions and paradoxical rage and had a substantial potential for abuse; (Pekkanen 1973) nevertheless, by 1979 benzodiazepine use in Britain alone peaked at 30 million prescriptions yearly. The Roche company long continued, through its associated experts, to deny any significant dependence risk (Marks 1978); the dan-gers however became increasingly clear with the introduction of short-acting ben-zodiazepines where the withdrawal reactions appeared earlier and were more violent. Agitation, amnesia and psychotic reactions, including murderous and sui-cidal behaviour, were documented. There has since been massive litigation against the manufacturers of the benzodiazepines. Though some cases have been side-tracked (notably by the withdrawal of legal aid to 12,000 litigants in Britain) very large sums have been paid out in damages. The injuries concerned were matters which could to a large extent have been recognized, acknowledged, and publicized many years earlier and thereby largely avoided. However, many millions of patients have for much of their lives become accustomed to a tranquillized state in which they are cocooned from worry and stress and concerned about the effects of with-drawing the drugs; so long as their physician is willing to continue to prescribe ben-zodiazepines they have therefore seen no reason to complain.

The history of the SSRI antidepressants, which is still ongoing, is interwoven with that of the benzodiazepines:

It had long been clear that physicians were confused between "anxiety" and "depression", particularly since they could co-exist and the clinical picture varied. During the period of ascendancy of the tranquillizers they had been used for "anx-iety" while depression had been treated mainly with the "tricyclic antidepressants" which were effective but somewhat toxic; both types of drug were often given together. In 1989 the first of a new class of drugs – termed by their makers "selec-tive serotonin reuptake inhibitors" (SSRI) was introduced to treat depression. Fluoxetine (Prozac) was followed by others including paroxetine (Paxil) and ser-traline (Zoloft). There has been criticism both of the literature claiming to prove efficacy and of the hypothesis that depression is linked to serotonin levels. Since it is well known that the majority of cases of true depression recover spontaneously, the true indications for treatment are limited, but sales of the various SSRI inhibitors have attained levels similar to those reach by the benzodiazepines at the peak of their popularity. Popular books, the mass media and some advertising have portrayed the SSRI inhibitors as being suitable for the relief of various forms of unhappiness and worry and have disseminated the notion that these constitute depression; there is also a wide public impression that the products induce a marked form of euphoria ("the happiness pill.") However Medawar (2004) and others have collated the considerable evidence that this type of product in fact induces a serious form of dependence; there have been numerous reports of severe withdrawal reactions and suicides (including children) and as of April 2004 GSK was facing 1500 single multidistrict cases in California alone relating to alleged withdrawal reactions with paroxetine (Paxil). (Scrip 2004c,d).

The above histories illustrate the fact that the study of drug safety is by no means a simple question of collating and reporting unpleasant physical symptoms. The unwanted effects on an individual, especially when they concern states of mind, can be extraordinarily difficult to recognize as such; they may even be mistaken for welcome effects and underlie a demand for the product concerned, a demand that can all too easily be further stimulated.

4.3.3. *Initial evidence of safety*

At the present day the initial evidence as to the degree of safety or risk presented by a new drug is based primarily on the study conducted by or under auspices of the manufacturer prior to its introduction. The principal elements of experimental proof in safety matters of safety, as embodied in present-day regulatory requirements, are briefly summarized in Table 4.B, alongside the types of evidence which may demonstrate efficacy.

At the time when the marketing decision has to be taken, either by the manufacturer or the regulatory agency, the difficulty of extrapolating from the available data to the future patent population is only one of the problems to be faced. One difficulty concerns the scientific dependability of the findings; particularly for the regulatory agency it may be impossible to assess the trustworthiness of an investigator with whom it has no contact, or of the report which has been written on the basis of his work. Another arises because much of the experimental material pertains to animals, and the range of patients to whom the drug has been administered is never fully representative of the patient group who will use it in the field. A third problem is however to decide what degree of risk would be acceptable, even if one could calculate it reliably. For a nasal spray providing mild relief for the

Table 4.B
Elements Contributing to Proof of Efficacy and Safety

Animals	*Human Subjects*

Pharmacology
Action relevant to proposed therapeutic use
Other actions on main systems
Interactions with selected drugs
Pharmacokinetics
	Phase 1: Clinical Pharmacology
	    ○ *20/50 subjects*
	    ○ Healthy volunteers (or patients)
	  • Pharmacokinetics
	  • Pharmacodynamics

Toxicology
Single dose (acute toxicity, various doses)
Repeated dose (from subacute to long-term)
General
  • Subacute, intermediate, long-term
  • Two or more mammalian species
  • Nature of effects at post-mortem
  • Duration proportional to proposed use
  • Human dose level. toxic level,
Intermediate
Special toxicology
  • Mutagenicity
  • Carcinogenicity
  • Reproduction studies
	Phase 2: Clinical Investigation
	    ○ *50–300 subjects*
	    ○ *Patients*
	  • Pharmacokinetics
	  • Pharmacodynamics
	  • Rising dose studies
	(Efficacy/Safety)
	
	Phase 3: Formal Therapeutic Trials
	    ○ *Randomised controlled design*
	    ○ *250–1,000 or more subjects*
	    ○ Patients
	  • Efficacy studies on a large scale
	  • Safety
	  • Comparisons with other drugs
	
	Phase 4: Post-marketing studies
	    ○ 2,000–10,000 or more subjects
	    ○ Patients
	  • Further studies of efficacy and safety
	  • Observations in special groups

Notes:

a. The use of human subjects or animals in studies is only ethically justified if the study serves a serious purpose and is sufficiently well designed and performed to achieve that purpose. General ethical aspects are considered in Sections 9.1 and 9.1

b. For some purposes a study will only be of value if statistically analysed.

c. Long-term recording of clinical observations must be arranged for patients who cannot be included in formal studies but who may incidentally be exposed to the drug (such as pregnant and lactating women, children, patients with serious organic disease)

d. For fixed combinations, the mixture should if possible be tested in special studies against its components

e. Bioequivalence and bioavailability studies may be performed to examine the effect of changes in pharmaceutical formulation or to compare two similar formulations

f. If the drug is likely to be used in special conditions which could affect its performance or introduce risk, it should undergo supplementary testing in these conditions (e.g. tropical climate, genetically distinct population)

common cold, one fatality in ten thousand patients will presumably be unacceptable, whereas for a cytostatic capable of inducing marked remissions in ovarian cancer one fatality in ten may have to be accepted.

> The acceptability of the risks which the sale of a drug entails is dependent on the seriousness of the disease or disorder which it is intended to cure or to combat. The more serious the illness, the greater the risk one is justified in taking. Insomnia is not a serious disorder; a sleeping tablet must not present more than negligible risks.[8]

These non-statistical expressions of risk will also come to the fore again if at a later date the medicine is the subject of product liability claims in court. In most cases the estimate will have to be verbal ("frequent", "rare", "occasional") rather than statistical because nothing more is feasible.

The duty to investigate adverse effects certainly comprises more than mere literal conformity with such official standards, which cannot provide for every possible future situation; it also involves an obligation to perform those studies which seem indicated in view of all that is known as to the characteristics of the product, the purposes for which it is to be used, and the population groups most likely to be treated with it. This will mean for example that:

    a. any indication of risk which is obtained in routine studies should be followed up with specific investigations to confirm or exclude the risk. Once evidence emerged, for example, that beta-blockers could seriously aggravate asthma it became incumbent upon any firm developing or marketing a beta-blocker to quantify this risk for its own product

    b. a drug which is chemically or pharmacologically closely related to one already known to cause a major risk must be carefully evaluated on this score; any new non-steroidal anti-inflammatory drug might, for example, be expected to cause gastric complications, and a new neuroleptic must be expected to cause tardive dyskinesia, until or unless the contrary is proven

    c. a drug which is likely to be used in a particular risk group of the population must be studied in that group. An anti-rheumatic drug

---

[8] Legal commentary on the Netherlands Halcion cases in *Ned. Juristenblad*, 9 February 1990, No. 6; pp. 225–229. (In Dutch).

is for example likely to be used predominantly in the middle-aged and elderly, and it is insufficient to study it in young subjects (WHO/EURO 1988); failure to live up this standard perhaps explained the severe problems with the anti-rheumatic drug benoxaprofen in 1982 (Dukes 1984). Similar special standards will apply if a drug is intended for use in pregnant or lactating women or in children (see Section 4.3.7)

It is clear that if any evidence of fault or negligence is recognized during a clinical trial or subsequently, it will be the sponsor's duty to take whatever action is necessary to protect the participants or to prevent incorrect information from the study being passed on. Exceptionally the error may be such as to play a role in subsequent withdrawal of the drug:

> In March 2001 Johnson & Johnson and Organon voluntarily withdrew the surgical muscular relaxant Raplon (rapacuronium) from the US market. An element in the decision was "… a strong probability that the pharmaceutical company Organon was negligent in the performance of Phase III clinical trials of the drug and post-marketing surveillance. Patients who died or suffered brain damage from surgery in which Raplon was administered from August 1999 until April 2001 or physicians who administered the drug to such patients have a strong scientific and medical basis for complaint against the company". (Drugintel 2001)

4.3.4.   *Adverse reaction monitoring systems*

Up to the time of the thalidomide disaster in 1960–1961 there had been no systematic means of collecting information on adverse effects produced by medicines which had already come into use. Individual practitioners observing unexpected and unwanted effects might report them in a journal letter, and an occasional study might be performed and published of an unwelcome phenomenon, but that was all. Within companies one might find a "complaints register" in which reports of apparent problems of all types were collected, but again unsystematically. From 1964 onwards however a series of countries established national adverse reaction monitoring centres and invited practitioners to report suspected adverse reactions for evaluation. As a rule such a centre would also communicate the reports in outline, without identifying names, to the companies concerned and seek their comments. In the United States the FDA considered it appropriate for physicians to hand their reports to the company's travelling representative and the firms themselves were obliged to pass these reports to the FDA; physicians however also had a right to report to the FDA directly if they so wished, though only a minority did so. The World Health Organization established an International Centre (in Geneva, later in Uppsala, Sweden) where the reports from the national centres could be collated and examined; as of 2004, 55 countries were contributing to the system. The European Union has its own centre (EUDRAVigilance), processing reports from national agencies. More recently, following successful experience in Sweden with direct reporting of adverse reactions by patients, agencies have begun to establish contacts with the public in both directions, both receiving reports and making Drug Analysis Prints publicly available. (Yellowcard 2005)

The legal framework for pharmacovigilance of medicinal products for human use in the Community is given in Council Regulation (EEC) No 2309/93 and Council Directive 2001/83/EC and is based primarily on ICH guidelines. Both the marketing authorisation holder (MAH) and the competent authorities are obliged to maintain pharmacovigilance systems and all relevant information should be shared between them, as well as with other EU and EEA member states. The marketing authorisation holder must ensure that it has an appropriate system of pharmacovigilance in place in order to assure responsibility and liability for its products on the market and to ensure that appropriate action can be taken, when necessary. The marketing authorisation holder should have permanently and continuously at its disposal in the European Economic Area (EEA), a "qualified person" responsible for pharmacovigilance who if not medically qualified should report to, or have access to a medically qualified person. National regulations in some Member States require in addition a nominated individual in that country who has specific legal obligations in respect of pharmacovigilance at a national level. The qualified person is responsible for the establishment and maintenance of a system which ensures that information about all suspected adverse reactions which are reported to the personnel of the marketing authorisation holder, including medical representatives, is collected and collated in order to be accessible at least at one point within the Community for the preparation for competent authorities of the Member States, where the medicinal product is authorised, of the adverse drug reaction (ADR) reports, Periodic Safety Update Reports (PSURs) and company sponsored post-authorisation study reports. Ongoing pharmacovigilance evaluation ensures provision of information requested by the authorities in the countries where the product is marketed, including figures on sales and prescriptions if required. The marketing authorisation holder is responsible for reporting suspected adverse reactions to the authorities of the Member States and the European Agency. For medicinal products authorised through centralised or national procedures, including through mutual recognition, suspected adverse reactions received from health-care professionals should be reported. Spontaneously reported suspected adverse reactions, suspected adverse reactions from post-authorisation studies and those reported in the world-wide literature are included. A reaction is suspected if *either* the reporting health-care professional *or* the marketing authorisation holder believes there is a possible causal relationship between it and the drug in question. Spontaneous reports of suspected adverse drug reactions received from health-care professionals should be reported even if the marketing authorisation holder does not agree with the reporter's assessment of a possible causal association, or if the reporter has not provided a causal assessment. Adverse events which are not suspected of being product related by the health-care professional attending the patient should not be reported unless the marketing authorisation holder has reason to believe that a causal relationship is possible. If the marketing authorisation holder is aware that a health-care professional has reported a reaction to one of its products directly to the authority of a member state, the marketing authorisation holder should still report the reaction, informing the authority that the report is likely to be a duplicate of a previous report. In this situation it is essential for the marketing authorisation holder to provide all the available details including any registration number provided to the reporting health-care professional by the authority, in order to aid identification of the duplicate. Marketing authorisation holders are expected to validate and follow up all serious reactions reported by them to the authorities. All available clinical information relevant to the evaluation of the reaction should be provided.

All expedited reports should be reported immediately and in no case later than 15 calendar days from receipt. The marketing authorisation holder should report, on an expedited basis, all serious suspected adverse reactions, occurring within the European Union and brought to its attention by a health-care professional to the competent authority in the member state in whose territory the incident occurred. For mutually recognised products or products which have been the subject of a referral, these should additionally be reported to the Reference Member State, in accordance with Article 104 of Council Directive 2001/83/EC. The marketing authorisation holder should report, on an expedited basis, all suspected serious unexpected adverse reactions occurring in the territory of a non-EU country and brought to the marketing authorisation holder's attention by a health-care professional in such a way as to be available to the Agency and to all Member States where the medicinal product is authorised. All other ADR reports do not need to be reported on an expedited basis, but should be reported on request or as line listings according to the section on periodic safety update reports, Reports from the worldwide literature in accordance with the provisions of section 1.2.1 are considered to be reports of which the marketing authorisation holder can reasonably be expected to be aware and have knowledge. The marketing authorisation holder is expected to screen the world-wide scientific literature (see section 1.2.2) and report promptly published suspected serious adverse reactions associated with the use of the active substances(s) of its medicinal products, as relevant to the categories identified in Section 1.2.2.1 I. and ii. above. A copy of the relevant published article should be provided in a language acceptable to the member state. The MAH is therefore required to report all serious adverse reactions which have occurred within the EEA to the Member or EFTA State in whose territory the incident occurred and all serious unexpected reactions from outside the EEA to all Member States where the product is authorised and to the Agency. As with other reports from outside the EEA, these reports should be provided electronically to the Agency making use of the data-processing network foreseen in Article 105 of Directive 2001/83/EC.

Reporting forms acceptable to the competent authorities of the Member States, and to the Agency for centrally authorised products, should be used.

In exceptional cases, when a reported ADR impacts significantly on the established safety profile of the product, the marketing authorisation holder should indicate this in the report.

Reports on medicines registered in EU/EFTA member states are accessible to the companies holding marketing authorizations through the EMEA's central computer database Eudra Vigilance.

There has been criticism of an EU provision that a firm having new information on a safety issue need to only inform the national agency where the drug was first assessed for the Union, leaving this agency to inform others. It could be advisable for a firm experiencing a serious problem to inform all agencies at the same time to avoid delay (Tuffs 2001).

Further experience will show to what extent these extensive provisions in the European Union, with the major involvement both of national centres and of industry, will succeed in improving the performance of adverse reaction monitoring without proving excessively burdensome on the parties.

4.3.5.   *Role and duties of industry in ADR monitoring*

Within companies there was for many years a very variable level of activity as regards the monitoring and reporting of adverse reactions; some firms remained with the traditional "complaints register" unless or until a regulatory agency required them to play a more active role. America's FDA was the first to require active industrial participation, to the extent that the majority of field reports arriving from practitioners in the new adverse reaction monitoring system set up by the agency in the mid-1960s (later termed "MedWatch") were expected to be delivered by doctors through company detailmen; in Europe on the other hand most reports from the field were submitted to the national agency directly.

For a long time there was to the outside observer no evident difference in the results delivered by the two systems, though both were characterized by very considerable under-reporting. Both had the fatal weakness that one never knew the degree of under-reporting or the turnover of the drug, so that the frequency of an adverse effect could not be calculated. Both systems produced a useful but very small cross section of the adverse effects actually occurring. Each had some notable achievements in identifying new adverse reactions early, but each clearly missed a great deal. Witnesses in litigation who gained access to company records were able to report in a limited circle to what extent companies had failed to pass on adverse reaction reports to the FDA after discarding a proportion for reasons of varying validity, but this did not become general knowledge.

Only towards the turn of the century and thereafter was the reliability of industry's input into the post-marketing surveillance of adverse reactions seriously questioned. The doubts arose not primarily from the formal monitoring systems but from (initially anecdotal) evidence that major firms had withheld vital negative data on a series of important drugs. To cite a selection of the events which became public knowledge:

In 1959, Messrs Wallace and Tiernan had marketed a tranquillizer (Dornwal) in the U.S. despite warnings from staff experts that it could cause serious and possibly fatal liver damage; the company failed to report the risk to the F.D.A. The firm was subsequently found guilty on criminal charges. (Silverman and Lee 1974)

In 1991-2 a Federal inquiry in the US confirmed earlier evidence that Upjohn had suppressed in its internal archives early data on the ability of its record-selling hypnotic Halcion to induce psychotic reactions. (FDA 1992)

Prior to 2000, as later evidence showed, Warner-Lambert had failed to reveal what it knew about liver toxicity caused by Rezulin, which led to the drug's withdrawal from the market (Chernavsky 2005)

From 1980 onwards, a number of companies had, as noted above, been less than open as regards the risks of their benzodiazepines (Medawar 1992, Revill 2004; see also sub-section 4.3.2. above).

In 2004 it appeared that Merck had delayed by four years the release of its information on the cardiovascular effects of Vioxx (rofecoxib) (Jüni *et al*. 2004, Horton 2004)

In 2004 there was a public call on the FDA for a criminal investigation of AstraZeneca for allegedly delaying the submission of reports of serious reactions to Crestor (rosuvastatin) (HRG 2004)

In 2004, again, the media reported that Lilly had long been aware of the potential of Prozac (fluoxetine) to precipitate suicide (CNN 2005).

Three expert witnesses involved in drug injury litigation and interviewed for the present volume had between 1995 and 2001 the opportunity to examine internal U.S. company records of relevant adverse reaction reports received from physicians; all had observed that a high proportion of these were discarded for trivial reasons and were therefore not submitted to the FDA (Interviews 24, 25, 26).

It is primarily against this background that a serious demand has arisen for a rethinking of the entire system of adverse reaction monitoring and the duties accorded to industry in that system. Were the system inherently strong and capable it might be able to withstand a degree of abuse. An authoritative paper in the JAMA late in 2004, however, set the spontaneous reporting system alongside the other forms of post-marketing surveillance and industry's role in them and found a bleak picture:

The inadequacies of the postmarketing surveillance system (i.e. FDA's MedWatch program with passive collection of spontaneous reports of adverse drug reactions) for ensuring safety are well known and include: reliance on voluntary reporting of adverse events by physicians and other health care professionals; poor quality of submitted reports, often with inadequate documentation and detail; under-reporting of adverse outcomes with capture of only a small fraction of adverse events that actually occur; difficulty in calculating rates of adverse events because of incomplete numerator data on events, together with unreliable denominator data on exposure; limited ability for spontaneous reports to establish causal relationships; and difficulty in determining whether the adverse event resulted from the drug or the disease it was intended to treat.

The major problem with the current system for ensuring the safety of medications is that drug manufacturers are largely responsible for collecting, evaluating, and reporting data from post-marketing studies of their own products. This approach has many inherent problems. For instance, it appears that fewer than half of the post-marketing studies that manufacturers have made commitments to undertake as a condition of approval have been completed and many have not even been initiated. Moreover, despite the mandatory adverse event reporting system for companies subject to the FDA's post-marketing safety reporting regulations, drug manufacturers may be tempted to conceal available data that may signal the possibility of major risks. In some cases, the FDA and drug manufacturers may fail to act on that information and fail to conduct appropriate studies to examine a potential risk rigorously and promptly." (Fontanarosa 2004)

In the same issue of the same Journal, Psaty and co-authors, from their own experience with a major adverse reaction problem leading to withdrawal of a drug, express similar concern. Summarizing the changes in recent years in the U.S. drug regulatory environment aimed at more rapid approval of new drugs, they conclude that that this approach "relied increasingly on the pharmaceutical industry to conduct its own post-marketing safety evaluation." They raise the concern that "a pharmaceutical company's appraisal of suspected ADRs may be influenced by economic considerations," and call for legislation to "mandate and provide adequate support for independent reviews and analysis of post-marketing data." (Psaty *et al.* 2004)

In the light of such concerns and evidence of practice to date, one is bound to ask how dependable the industrial input from some companies into the new European network and central register (EUDRA 2004) can be made. In the US, a thorough re-examination of the process is now being undertaken with a view to improve both its input and its central authority. It could be that the output of that re-examination could be of value in other countries as well, and helpful to the industry in putting its own house in order.

4.3.6.   Safety in overdose

In some cases it can be relevant for a company to demonstrate that a product is relatively safe (i.e. as compared with other drugs) when given in excessive dosage, and this can outweigh certain disadvantages which the drug may possess:

> In 1990 Britain's Licensing Authority took restrictive action against the antide-pressant mianserin because of adverse effects involving the blood. The Organon company challenged the restriction in court since it could be shown that, as com-pared with other antidepressant drugs, mianserin was notably safe in overdose; it was argued that this element should be taken into account when assessing the product's overall safety. Both the Divisional Court and subsequently the Court of Appeal found for the company: the latter considered that under Section 28 of the Medicines Act the Licensing Authority had discretion to make comparisons with other drugs in forming its judgement, and that such comparisons could relate to safety in overdose where this was relevant. (Brahams 1990)

This particular case is exceptional to the extent that antidepressant drugs pose a special problem; many older antidepressants are dangerous in overdose, yet they have to be employed in patients who because of their depression are prone to commit suicide by taking the product in excessive doses; it is not clear that overdose is equally relevant when assessing the overall safety of drugs in other classes.

4.3.7.   Pregnancy, lactation and beyond[9]

Although thalidomide was the most notorious drug disaster involv-ing pregnancy and the unborn child it was not the only one. In the years following, the "hormonal pregnancy tests" in use at the time were accused of disrupting some pregnancies by inducing uterine bleeding despite the presence of a foetus. The anti-nausea combination Bendectin (also known in modified form as Debendox), specifically intended to relieve nausea of

---

[9] For a fuller coverage of the issue of the manufacturer's liability for second-generation injury see Dukes MNG, Mildred M and Swartz B (1998): Responsibility for Drug-Induced Injury, IOS Press, Amsterdam, Berlin and Oxford, at Chapter 12.

pregnancy, was withdrawn on suspicion (probably incorrect) of being a mild teratogen. (Bryan 1980) The most serious of the dramas was that involving diethylstilbestrol (DES) and it illustrates both the medical and legal problems which can surround drug-based teratogenicity: (Noller 1990, Anon. 2003)

Diethylstilbestrol was developed in the United Kingdom prior to 1940 as an effective low-cost oestrogenic hormone. For altruistic reasons the inventor left it unpatented and the drug was therefore soon marketed by many companies. Two U.S. physicians intensively propagated its use in pregnancy for treating threatened abortion or preventing habitual abortion. Few clinical trials were ever performed and the reasons for thinking that it might be useful in pregnancy were mainly theoretical; it is doubtful whether it had any useful effect whatsoever. However, some 12–15 years after the peak of its use had passed it was found that female children of these pregnancies tended to develop vaginal changes when reaching adolescence or adulthood and that these could become cancerous; there was also a high incidence of fertility disturbances among these daughters. Analogous changes were found in some male offspring. The scale of the DES disaster apparently much exceeds that of thalidomide, since the drug was used in many hundreds of thousands of pregnancies, with a particularly high incidence in the U.S.A. and The Netherlands (Buitendijk 1984). Some thousands of cases have been brought to court, most directed against former manufacturers but some against the U.S. FDA. Problems in dealing with liability arise mainly because of the very late manifestation of the injury (making it difficult to prove that the drug was taken) and the multiplicity of former producers. As with the thalidomide case, however, an important element in determining causality is the characteristic nature of the defect. Though the material is not homogeneous and strict statistical analysis of some of the epidemiological data inevitably points to shortcomings, there is overwhelming evidence of a cause-and-effect relationship. There is also increasing evidence that some defects can appear in the third generation, i.e. the grandchildren of the original users (Lynch et al. 1990).

In 1991 claims were prepared by some 100 "DES-granddaughters" in the U.S.A.; they alleged that maternal uterine hyperplasia, cervical stenosis and/or endometriosis caused by their mothers' exposure to DES in foetal life were responsible for their own disorders. The first such claim to be heard, brought by a girl of 9 with cerebral palsy, was rejected by a majority of 6-1 in the New York Court of Appeals in February 1991. The majority judgement was not based on failure to prove causation but on grounds of practicality. To cite Chief Judge Sol Wachtler: "For all we know, the rippling effects of DES exposure may extend for generations. It is our duty to confine liability within manageable limits. Limiting liability to those who ingested the drug or who were exposed to it *in utero* serves this purpose. Judge Hancock, dissenting, considered the conclusion inequitable.[10]

---

[10] *Enright v. Eli Lilly & Co., no. 19*, N.Y. Court of Appeals, February 19th 1991.

The most obvious problem with ensuring safety in this field is that one cannot ethically perform studies in human pregnancy and that no dependable animal model for human teratogenicity has been found. The problems are compounded if the possibility exists of adverse effects in the third or later generations; not only is one without an experimental model, but the problems of proof and of identification of a defendant can be almost insuperable; the defects may be uncharacteristic, and both the drug and the manufacturer may by that time have been largely consigned to history, as was the case with DES.

At the present time, one can do little more than require the manufacturer to gather, wherever possible, reports of any case in which a new drug is – accidentally, negligently or because of a vital indication – administered to a pregnant woman, and record the outcome of the pregnancy. Until or unless certainty is ultimately gained that the drug is harmless in pregnancy, strict warnings must be given. The problems of the third and later generations, should they arise, will hopefully be covered by non-confrontational compensation schemes (see Chapter 12).

Similar considerations arise with respect to the use of drugs in lactation, but it could be valuable to know the extent to which the drug passes into the milk during breast-feeding; animal models would here be relevant, though they might not deliver helpful data on the effect of the medicine on the offspring.

4.3.8.   *Relevance of regulatory approval to civil liability for injury*

For a period, pharmaceutical companies faced with claims for injury caused by their medicines sought to argue that, since their drugs had been approved by a national regulatory authority, they must be considered acceptably safe by a civil court. This view was indeed accepted in 1966 in US litigation regarding injury by MER-29 (triparanol):

> . . . a drug, properly tested, labelled with appropriate warnings and approved by the Food and Drug Administration, and marketed properly under federal regulation, is, as a matter of law, a reasonably safe product. Accordingly, a person claiming to have suffered adverse effects from using such a drug, unless he can prove an impurity or an inadequacy in labeling, may not recover against the seller for breach of warranty . . .[11]

---

[11] Lewis v. Baker, 413 P.2d 400, 404 (Or. 1966) (en banc).

This view has been followed in a number of other American cases in later years[12] but in others judges have exercised their discretion to allow the question of the safety or the benefit/risk ratio of the drug to be reconsidered by the jury as a question of fact. Some defendants have been hesitant to rely on the "prior approval" defence since they have not been entirely open with the FDA – as indeed Merrell itself had not (see Section 2.2.5). Plaintiffs, for their part, have sought evidence that defendants had *not* complied with statute law or FDA regulations, e.g. that the New Drug Application or subsequent data submitted to the FDA had been untruthful or incomplete:

In one American case, an action was brought on behalf of a small girl who had suffered irreversible brain damage as a result of convulsions induced by lidocaine. The Astra company had received earlier reports of such effects but on formal grounds had not passed on information concerning these effects to the F.D.A. as required by regulation. Though the jury concluded that the manufacturer had warned physicians, it found that Astra's failure to report adverse reactions to the F.D.A. was a "substantial factor" in causing the plaintiff's injury. The U.S. Court of Appeals in fact ordered a retrial because the jury had clearly reached a compromise verdict, but the Court fully accepted the argument that if the F.D.A. had been allowed to perform its statutory duty, the risks associated with the drug would have been better understood and more widely appreciated.[13]

As Willig and Ruger have put it: "…failure to follow the law can make an important contribution to a product liability case" (Willis and Ruger 1994), though one should add that the statutory offence has not always been of great relevance to the injury complained of.

Authorities in other countries have pointed out that compliance with statute law and regulations does not exclude a drug manufacturer's liability in civil law, since written law is only one source of a manufacturer's duties. In particular, the general obligation to work according to the current state of the art may create duties which go beyond those officially imposed, especially where the drug licence or the regulations under which it was issued were not of recent date. The latter point was made judicially, though in *obiter dicta*, by the Arnhem District Court in The Netherlands in 1984 in one of the cases relating to alleged injury by the hypnotic drug Halcion:

The fact that Halcion had been registered by The Netherlands Committee for the Evaluation of Medicines and corresponding bodies abroad was regarded as one of

---

[12] Brown v. Superior Court, 245 Cal. Rptr. 412 (1988).

[13] Stanton v. Astra Pharmaceutical Products (1983). US Court of Appeals, 3rd Circ. Nos 82-3364 and 82-3380.

the elements leading its conclusion that the drug was not disproportionately dangerous. On the other hand, in the Court's words, ". . . The control exercised by the government authorities relates to the minimum standards which a pharmaceutical must attain, and not the totality of prudence which is the duty of the party proposing to market the drug. The fact that the Committee for the Evaluation of Medicines had advanced no objections to the text of the introductory folder and the package insert does not therefore mean that the Upjohn company cannot have failed in its duty of care"[14]

In a subsequent judgement on the same matter, the higher Court at Arnhem concluded, despite the fact of registration by the authorities, that the manufacturer had indeed committed a tort against users of the drug by causing it to be registered and marketed without sufficiently warning the users or physicians respectively of the dangerous and unpleasant adverse effects.[15]

In dealing finally with the same matter, the Supreme Court of the Netherlands explicitly stated that registration of a drug by the authorities does not abolish the liability of the manufacturer at civil law.[16]

In England the situation regarding pharmaceuticals is likely to be influenced by several general legal principles derived from case-law involving other sectors. As a general rule of English law, the fact that a defendant has adhered to standards demanded by statute[17] is not decisive in cases where negligence is at issue. The limited pharmaceutical case law seems to show that a court will in a civil case be prone to regard the Licensing Authority's approval of a drug as a preliminary finding of fact which it will be "reluctant to criticize",[18] i.e. it is likely to prove influential in the proceedings, even if it is not determinative.

In summary, despite discrepancies between national systems, evidence that a pharmaceutical company has conformed to its statutory obligations regarding drug registration is likely to have persuasive effect in cases where civil actions for negligence are brought against it, but it will not determine the issue. Conversely, its failure to meet its obligations

---

[14] Rechtbank Arnhem (Court of Arnhem), 28 juni 1984. Reported in *Tijdschr. v. Consumentenr., 1985,* pp. 82–89 and *Tijdschr v. Gezondheidsr. 1985*, pp. 109–114).

[15] Hof Arnhem, 7 July 1987; reported in Tijdschr. Consumentenr., 1987, pp. 272–282 with editorial annotation and in Tijdschr. Gezondheidsr., 1988, pp. 324–329); see also Ten Hoopen M.M. and Rijken G.J., Ned. Juristenbl., 18 February 1988, Nr. 7), pp. 217–224.

[16] Reported in *Ned. Jur. Bl.,* 9 February 1990, afl. 6; pp. 225–229.

[17] *Bux v. Slough Metals Ltd.* [1974] 1 All E.R. 262.

[18] *Smith, Kline and French Laboratories Ltd. v. Licensing Authority*, [1989] 1 All E.R. 578.

under statute or regulation will undoubtedly cause a court to consider carefully whether there is a link between this breach of duty and the injury complained of, and it may discredit the defendant in the view of a jury.

4.4. Establishing the Efficacy of Drugs

4.4.1. The legal concept of efficacy

The law and the regulations require that the manufacturer shall demonstrate the efficacy of his drug; but for all the reasons defined above, the legislator is very reticent about defining what he means by it. The Netherlands lawgiver of 1958,[19] already cited for his common-sense approach, required that a drug should have been shown to have the effect claimed for it "according to the standards of a reasonable man." That comes remarkably close to the thinking of the European Product Liability Directive and the Statutes derived from it which two decades later (Chapter 2) declared that a product should have that decree of safety "which persons generally are entitled to expect."

Continuing in this vein, one might expect the "reasonable man" to hope that a medicine will exert its effect on his illness to a useful extent – either curing him or alleviating his symptoms so that they are much less troublesome, and continuing to be effective for a long time when he uses it according to the instructions. He might also feel entitled to an effect that entirely outweighs whatever adverse effects the product may exert. These are reasonable demands from the user's point of view, yet they have led to difficult exchanges between some industrial applicants and regulatory authorities:

> This applicant came with a non-steroidal anti-inflammatory drug that he wanted to register for use in rheumatoid arthritis. His longest clinical study to demonstrate efficacy was positive, but it had lasted only four weeks. The Chairman pointed out that that rheumatoid arthritis was a chronic condition and that patients would need it much longer; one would need to be sure that in the longer run it remained effective and well-tolerated. The applicant then suggested that as an alternative we register it for the indication "treatment of rheumatoid arthritis for up to four weeks". The Commission considered this unrealistic. (Interview 16)

> We had met this representative before when he presented a new drug for accelerating wound healing; his firm had tested it against an old product XX that was also supposed to heal wounds and they found it just as effective. The trouble was that

---

[19] The late Mr C.J. Goudsmit.

we had no reason to believe that the old drug XX was itself effective so we stressed the need for him to do a trial against a dummy. We never heard any more of it. Then this time he came back with an application for a kale derivative to stop asthma attacks, and proudly showed us that his people had tested it against a dummy, proving that it was more effective. The difficulty this time was the difference was really very slight, and if the drug was effective at all then it was much less effective than the products we already had, like corticoid sprays and betamimetics and cromoglycate, so this time we asked him to produce a comparison with them. He got quite upset and brought a statistician to show that there really was a difference from the dummy, which got us into a discussion on differentiating between statistical significance and clinical significance. In the end they took us to Court, claiming that effectiveness as compared with a dummy was effectiveness in law. Happily, the Court saw sense and upheld us. (Interview 8)

It was a product to relieve intermittent claudication – helping old people who couldn't walk very far without getting pain in their legs. After I had gone through all the statistics with him we agreed that the drug probably increased the mean walking distance for a while from 50 metres to 53 metres. But, said our medical colleagues, that's not enough to be useful to a patient. The man from the firm was a smart cookie; "Well," he said, "what if the poor chap lives 52 metres from the nearest letterbox? (Interview 23).

A product should clearly have the type of *pharmacological* effect and the potency which it is claimed, explicitly or by obvious implication, to possess; a product sold as an antibiotic or a corticosteroid must possess these properties to a clinically significant degree. Similarly, a product must have the *therapeutic* effect claimed for it, i.e. it must be generally effective in the disorders for which its use is recommended. These standards are set specifically by medicines legislation but they also flow from general commercial law (Chapter 2). If a drug does not attain these standards, and a patient can be shown to have suffered injury as a direct result of this fundamental shortcoming of the product (e.g. because of failure to recover from an acute and life-threatening condition), there will be a basis for claiming damages. If, for example, a patient in severe shock is treated with injections of a corticosteroid and his failure to respond can be traced to the fact that the substance in the ampoules administered, though described as a corticosteroid, had little or no such activity, there will be liability.

4.4.2. *Warranties and guarantees*

As noted in Section 4.4.1, efficacy is not an absolute quality and a drug will not produce the desired effect in every patient. A manufacturer cannot therefore be held liable for failure of treatment in an individual patient unless it can be shown to be attributable to total inefficacy of the drug, or unless he has been so reckless as to claim or imply universal efficacy.

> In the past it did happen that guarantees of efficacy were rashly provided. In the nineteenth century a British manufacturer offered the Carbolic Smoke Ball, which emitted aromatic vapours to prevent and relieve upper respiratory congestion; in an advertisement he offered £100 to any individual who, after exposure to the vapours, contracted influenza. A Mr Carlill suffered this experience and claimed the sum to which he was entitled, bringing an action for breach of warranty when the manufacturer refused to pay. The producer argued that there was no contractual relationship between him and the claimant. The Court of Appeal, however, found for the appellant on the ground that an offer had been circulated to the general public which ripened into a contractual relationship when a particular section of the general public had met the conditions attaching to the offer.[20]

Such offers are rare today, but one still encounters them in some parts of the world, though apparently in situations where the risk of the guarantee being taken up is remote:

> In May 2003, the Hong-Kong based firm CK Life Sciences released Vitagain, a drug based on yeast technology that was claimed to strengthen the immune system sufficiently to protect individuals against severe acute respiratory syndrome (SARS). The company chairman issued a declaration that should a client successfully complete the 90-day treatment period and then contract SARS the company would make a compensatory payment from a "health maintenance fund" of 200,000 Hong Kong dollars (US$ 25,641). (PD 2003)

Bona fide firms have on some occasions offered more modest money-back guarantees in the event of failure of treatment:

> In 1994 Merck Inc. offered to refund the cost of treatment with its anti-androgen finasteride for prostatic hyperplasia. The cost would be refunded if the drug failed to improve symptoms within six months or if the patient needed prostatic surgery within two years. A urologist commented that most cases of prostatic hyperplasia indeed reacted well to antiandrogen therapy, though a significant minority failed to improve at all. However, since most patients were only being treated for their symptoms, any subsequent assessment of benefit was bound to be largely subjective. A company spokesman noted that patients "had to comply with treatment at least three quarters of the time for the offer to hold". (BMJ 1994)

There is some advertising for pharmaceutical products which carries with it such emphatic implied promises that an analogous situation could

---

[20] *Carlill v. Carbolic Smoke Ball Co.* (1893), 1 Q.B., 256.

176   *Chapter 4*

on occasion arise [21] and it is common in US litigation for statements of claim to allege that the defendant manufacturer has breached "express and implied warranties of merchantability and fitness for a particular purpose"[22] which can rely heavily upon texts which appear to constitute a warranty. A relevant issue in this connection could be the custom of many manufacturers, noted above, to use extremely emphatic printed advertising texts and visual messages, while approved textual material from the data sheet is appended only in much smaller print. While a strictly formalistic approach would lead to the view that the small print counterbalances the exuberance of the main message, a court might more realistically look to the promises made or implied in those parts of the promotional effort which the physician or patient is most likely (and is indeed intended) to assimilate.[23] It is indeed notable that courts in the United States, where "warranty" plays a more prominent role than elsewhere, have been willing to interpret various forms of promotional text as implying warranties. In the case of vaccines (see Chapter 9) the implied promise of efficacy is particularly strong.

The oral contraceptives constitute a special case, largely because their degree of efficacy is commonly claimed (and correctly assumed) to approach 100%.

> Whether incidental failure of an oral contraceptive to have the desired effect could today in most systems of law result in a successful claim for damages (e.g., for "wrongful birth") seems dubious, though it was a question which greatly exercised the minds of manufacturers of such products when a number of such actions were attempted unsuccessfully in the 1960s. In fact, no manufacturer ever seems to have claimed 100% efficacy for this type of product in so many words, and even though the chance of unwanted pregnancy is with most hormonal contraceptives very small indeed, any physician and patient is today likely to realise that it exists. It is of course clear that if the failure were demonstrably due to a manufacturing defect – e.g., if it could be shown that a manufacturer had in error released a batch of an oral contraceptive in which the active substance was missing – a different situation would arise.

---

[21] See Dommering-Van Rongen L. (1982): *De patient/konsument en de produktaansprakelijkheid (The patient/consumer and product liability)*. Paper presented to the NIA symposium in Product Liability, 18 September. (*In Dutch*)

[22] See for example Reeves v. Geigy Pharmaceutical, Eli Lilly and Gerald B. Moress: Court of Appeals of Utah, November 10th 1988.

[23] Cf. McEwen v. Ortho Pharmaceutical Co. (1975), op. cit.

Firms selling drugs or health products outside the normal regulatory system tend to make extreme claims of efficacy but to complement these with reservations which are likely to exclude claims for liability;

Nebulised "Colloidal Silver", claimed to be effective in treating respiratory disorders, is classified by the U.S. FDA as "not generally recognised as safe and effective". It is nevertheless stated by the manufacturer in promotional material that "results have ranged from excellent to 'near miraculous' ". However the explicit warranty is limited to product quality and "Use and/or results for any application are not guaranteed and no claims are made, other than that to state that "Col-Sil" "Supports and Helps Maintain a Healthy Immune System" as approved by the USFDA." (CS 2005)

Products in the field of "alternative medicine" now frequently issue explicit medical disclaimers:

X is a recent development in the alternative health market, and thus most studies which could be a basis for inference are not double blind controlled studies, but instead anecdotal observations of benefits. As a result, medical claims cannot be asserted until more intensive studies are completed. Our products are believed by the manufacturer to provide significant user satisfaction based on testimonials and anecdotal reports from users. Accordingly, we must by law issue the following disclaimer: The firm does not make or imply any medical claims for products we manufacture. These products are not medicines/medical devices and cannot be relied on to supply medical benefits and are not a substitute for proper medical care. Thirty-day Money Back Guarantee on All Products! (based on Norso 2000)

4.4.3. Efficacy of "old" drugs

Doubts as to the stringency of efficacy requirements commonly arise when a regulatory agency sets out to assess an old drug that has been on the market for generations and has never been tested under modern clinical conditions, yet may have a placebo effect because of its long reputation. Agencies have generally shown some tolerance to such products, assuming that they will at a given moment die a natural death. Section 4.4.5 on "efficacy and compassion" is also in some cases relevant.

A further contested point, noted earlier in this volume, is whether a new drug should only be considered acceptable if it is as effective as (or more effective than) an existing product of the same type, or has some other unique virtue, for example, in terms of safety. For a time, as noted in Section 4.4.1, firms tended to argue that any product that was more active than placebo must be considered acceptable under the law. At the other extreme was the argument that it was undesirable to accept any new drug unless it had clear advantages over those already on the market. In course of time, both extremes have been largely abandoned; as a rule a drug will be considered "effective" in terms of the law if it is clinically and genuinely useful – to an extent that the reasonable man will appreciate.

4.4.4.   Proof of efficacy

The law demands that a drug be efficacious, yet there is very little litigation in which lack of efficacy is alleged; since a drug cannot be guaranteed to have the desired effect in every user this is understandable. On the other hand, regulatory agencies have repeatedly refused or withdrawn licences on the grounds of lack of proven efficacy; between a quarter and a third of applications are withdrawn for this reason, and some of these items appear on the market later as "health products" or "natural products" for which no proof of efficacy is demanded.

The fact, noted above, that field experience may make it necessary to revise one's view of a drug's efficacy (just as is the case with its safety margin) is poorly reflected in the law. As Britain's House of Commons study of the industry has pointed out:

> Drug companies may conduct their own Phase IV studies, comparing the efficacy of their drugs to others, but there is no mandatory requirement for the industry to investigate the long-term effects of their medicines in the community. (HoC 2005 at, para. 63)

This does not appear to presage any coming obligation to conduct Phase IV studies with all drugs; the duties imposed both by current European and American regulations to provide ongoing information to the agencies after marketing are likely to be considered sufficient, with formal post-marketing studies only being required where there is a special reason to carry them out.

The public's belief in the efficacy of drugs in general and in the industry that produces them has wavered and varied. Despite the basic desire of a patient to believe that a medicine will be effective, there has at times been considerable public scepticism regarding the drug trade. For a long period it was engendered by the fact that the most visible and audible makers of drugs were the charlatans whom Daniel Defoe had encountered in the eighteenth century and the British Medical Association so vigorously condemned in the twentieth (Chapter 3). The patient's understanding of illness and of medicines has grown in the course of the years, but the totality of knowledge has grown at the same time, leaving him still very much dependent upon the good faith of others, and all too aware that he can be deceived. Trust in the industry and its products was probably at its highest in the brief era of the wonder drugs between 1940 and 1960 when penicillin, cortisone, poliomyelitis vaccine and the "pill" seemed to change the face of medicine forever. But then came thalidomide and the flimsy promises of the "feminine forever" oestrogens; perhaps not everything was as trustworthy as it had seemed.

Law and regulation function best when they provide judges with firm measures by which to judge real events, and clinical science is not always willing to provide those firm measures. To see Mr Justice May wrestling in London's High Court with a pack of bickering statisticians unable to agree on clinical truth about oral contraceptives and thrombosis leaves one despairing about science but with a sneaking admiration for judicial common sense. And when a prestigious author notes in 2004 that the sponsor of an SSSI inhibitor is perfectly content to deposit it in the therapeutic arena if a mere two out of six trials point to its having some effect, then one can only wish for much judicial – and regulatory – common sense in the coming years.

This is not the place for detailed presentation of the technicalities of clinical-pharmacological proof. They are massively documented and widely agreed. Only when dealing with an individual medicine will one be able to decide precisely which clinical-experimental model and which degree of certainty will suffice if one is to conclude that this medicine is truly effective. Reasonable certainty that a drug is truly effective can only emerge from a complex of studies that have to be considered together; they complement each other and in some instances one may override another; in some situations particular studies may be superfluous, and in others additional work may be required. Table 4.B provides no more than an ultrasummary, for the present purpose, of the elements of proof likely to be needed to satisfy those implementing current legislation and regulation that a drug is effective.

4.4.5. *Publication bias*

A series of workers have examined the question as to whether clinical studies which have been conducted and published under the sponsorship of the pharmaceutical industry show bias in favour of the company product concerned. A systematic review of this work, conducted in 2003 by Lexchin et al. points strongly towards publication bias in sponsored studies:

> ... Studies sponsored by pharmaceutical companies were more likely to have outcomes favouring the sponsor than were studies with other sponsors (odds ratio 4.05; 95% confidence interval 2.98–5.51; 18 comparisons). (Lexchin *et al.* 2003)

Various of those who have examined the matter find documented explanations for publication bias. Companies may select investigators who are known to favour particular drugs or therapies, comparator drugs with a lesser degree of efficacy may be chosen, parameters selected may be those most likely to favour the sponsor's product, and unfavourable studies may be suspended or remain unpublished.

Whatever the explanation in any particular case, the issue is a serious one since the regulatory view on the efficacy (and safety) of medicines is so heavily dependent upon clinical investigations that have been conducted in this way, especially at the outset of a drug's career. A company's obvious duty to conduct and present its work in a balanced manner to the professions and to society generally has hitherto been regarded primarily as an ethical issue, but it is closely linked to its duties in law regarding the submission of evidence to the regulatory authorities. Current moves to ensure that all clinical trials are registered at the outset, (DeAngelis et al. 2005) so that they cannot subsequently disappear from the record, reflects the extent of concern on this matter. To judge from ongoing legal consultations it would seem extremely likely that in the near future the issue of liability for the deliberate distortion of evidence will be increasingly raised with the courts.

4.4.6. *Efficacy and compassion*

An ethical issue which does not yet appear to have reached the courts but is now actively in discussion relates to the situation of drugs which may have only a minimal therapeutic effect yet deserve to be available on compassionate grounds where no more active product exists. The issue has long been in debate in regulatory circles as regards products intended for the relief of symptoms related to senility and atherosclerosis:

> Our Committee faced the problem years ago when we set out to assess an old "grandfather clause" drug, namely dihydroergotoxin, which they also called Hydergine or ergoloid mesylates. It had been sold for years to relieve mental symptoms in the elderly. The serious books didn't mention it and the clinical work was pathetic, but the geriatric homes used it by the cartload. We were all set to

cancel the licence of right until we saw that the FDA in America had registered it. When we talked to Dr Crout, who headed the Bureau of Drugs at the time and was an eminently sensible man he agreed that Hydergine wouldn't pass a real efficacy screen of the usual type, but it wasn't inactive. When people who had been going downhill mentally, and knew it, suddenly found that they could tie their shoelaces again it gave them a boost. That was the sort of thing it seemed to do.
So we registered it, and to my knowledge it's still there. (Interview 5)

Prof. Søren Holm in Wales has raised much the same issue following a preliminary recommendation by Britain's National Institute for Clinical Excellence (NICE) that a number of drugs currently used in Alzheimer's disease are not sufficiently cost-effective to justify their continued use in the National Health Service. He comments:

Alzheimer's Disease is not a nice disease to have for most patients, and caring for someone with Alzheimer's is not easy. It is frightening to literally lose one's mind, and it is a cause of great sorrow to see this happen in a spouse, partner or parent…

…NICE seems to have forgotten one of the central values in health care, the value of compassion. Among the many patient groups that suffer and die, only a few could make a stronger claim on our compassion than those who suffer and die from Alzheimer's. Or, to put it in simpler terms, NICE has forgotten that it is not enough to be effective, one also needs to be compassionate and nice. (Holm 2005)

Compassion should indeed be an element both of medicine and of law.

Chapter 5

The Industry As a Source of Information, Persuasion and Education

5.1.   Need Marketing be Controlled by Law?

Information, education and persuasion are a continuum. The first transmits facts, the second a way of thinking and the third a conviction. All three are major elements in marketing, yet they do not stand alone. Other and subtler forms of marketing can similarly do much to ensure that a medicine is accepted, preferred, or used in a particular manner. Both pharmaceutical law and commercial law attempt to secure some grip on these processes, as do various ethics-based ventures such as those devised by the business sector itself. To understand any of these approaches and the extent to which they are effective, it is helpful to consider at the outset what their purpose is.

Assuming that one is living in a market economy and will continue to do so for the foreseeable future, the starting point will be the belief that competition is desirable, ensuring that society continuously moves ahead, seeking ever better products at an ever better price. In that view, marketing should only be restricted where it threatens to impair a valid public interest, since it is an important lubricant to competition and to the constant process of renewal. Marketing and its various elements can however be used properly or improperly. In any sector, the public sector and the business community are in principle in agreement that improper marketing can result in distortion of competition. As a result of this a product that is not the best or not the most reasonably priced may dominate the field, provided its marketing has been sufficiently astute. The business sector is primarily concerned that this is unfair. The public sector is more concerned that it is wasteful, harmful to the economy and sometimes damaging in other ways. To that extent the sort of control which the pharmaceutical industry would wish to see exerted over marketing and that which is dictated by public interest run parallel. There is however what WHO has described as "an inherent conflict of interest between the legitimate business goals of manufacturers and the social, medical and economic needs of providers and the public to select and use drugs in the most rational way." (WHO/EURO

1993) Alongside much basic agreement on principles, drug advertising is therefore a continuing source of friction on methods and details.

The dominance of marketing over substance may not matter greatly when one is dealing with blue jeans or ball-point pens; the individual who has been induced by marketing to purchase such a product and does not find it to his liking will not purchase it again. Over-emphatic marketing matters rather more in fields related to health, such as the marketing of sugary soft drinks (Allen 1994), high-fat hamburgers (Schlosser 2001) or breast-milk substitutes as an inferior replacement for natural breast feeding (Richter 2001), where a less than optimal product may do harm without the purchaser being aware of it. It matters a great deal in medicines, where considerable harm may be done, such as when a relatively dangerous or addictive drug may come to be widely used, sometimes even for a possibly fictitious disease (Breggin 2001, Medawar and Hardon 2004). In all these latter cases, in contrast to the blue-jeans and the ball-point pens, the public is not in a position to verify the true merits or safety of the product or know its dangers.

5.2. Marketing Codes: from WHO onwards

Many attempts have been made to formulate and implement standards of marketing for medicinal products. That developed by the World Health Organization merits citation in full since it attempts to deal with all aspects of marketing and since, despite its weaknesses, it is for many parts of the world still the only accepted standard. One should however bear in mind its troubled history. (Richter 2001 at pp. 94–95)

> The factual history of the Organization's Ethical Criteria for Medicinal Drug Promotion of 1988 has been recounted in Chapter 3 (Section 3.4.8.). It provides a striking illustration of the extreme and conflicting pressures to which the Organization has been subject when dealing with issues of standards or controls in the field of medicines; however it also portrays the type of conflicts arising at the national level where issues of pharmaceutical marketing are concerned. The original proposal to develop a Code had been raised by the World Health Assembly itself in 1978. Even at that stage however strong divergences of view between member states were emerging. The International Federation of Pharmaceutical Manufacturers Associations, which was strongly opposed to the notion from the outset was in a strong position since it was already in official relations with WHO as a "non-governmental organization", a concept which can embrace commercially orientated bodies as well as those with a primary interest in public health. Consumer orientated activist organizations provided equally outspoken pressure in favour of Code. WHO was ultimately confronted with draft codes from each of these parties. The opposition expressed by the United States proceeded to the point where, for this and other reasons, the US for a time withheld its financial contributions to the Organization.

The outcome could only be a compromise. A study in 1996 was forced to conclude that the criteria had only been used to a limited extent (HAI 1996 at p.3) but they appear to have influenced the contents of new marketing codes developed nationally.

The WHO's Ethical Criteria are reproduced in full, but without appended material, as Table 5.A.

Alongside the WHO code there are many others, often borrowing materials from one another. The latest version of the IFPMA code dates from 1994. The Code of Conduct of the Australian Pharmaceutical Manufacturers Association (APMA 1994) merits examination since it is very fully annotated on points of detail. The Code of Practice for the Pharmaceutical Industry drawn up by the industry association in Britain similarly deserves examination since detailed monthly reports are issued on its interpretation in specific cases by the prescription medicines Code of Practice Authority (CPA 2005).

5.3. Can Marketing be Controlled by Law and Rule Making?

Laws, rules and codes are most effective when their provisions bear on undesirable acts which can be readily recognized, are widely agreed to be improper, and can simply be forbidden, with appropriate sanctions prescribed for transgression. Yet even an apparently crystal clear and universally agreed rule may be challenged in practice:

Thou shalt not kill (Genesis 20, 13)

This is a fundamental commandment, yet here serious controversies arise as to its interpretation, for example as regards the permissibility of abortion or euthanasia and of the withdrawal of life-support systems in the brain-injured.[1] In the field of medicine marketing, even an apparently firmly phrased and basic rule which has been accepted by all parties is likely to build around a number of concepts which can be understood in different ways. In the Australian Pharmaceutical Manufacturers Association's Code of Conduct, the clause most widely applied in dealing with alleged breaches of the Code reads as follows:

False or Misleading Claims: Information, medical claims and graphical representations about products must be current, accurate, balanced and must not mislead either directly, by implication or by omission (APMA 2000, para 1.3)

---

[1] "Thou shalt not kill; but need'st not strive
Officiously to keep alive"
  - A.H. Clough (1819–1861), *The Latest Decalogue*.

Table 5.A
WHO: Criteria for Medicinal Drug Promotion (1988)

Introduction

1. Following the WHO Conference of Experts on the Rational Use of Drugs held in Nairobi in November 1985, WHO prepared a revised drug strategy which was endorsed by the thirty-third World Health Assembly in May 1986 in resolution WHA39.27. This strategy includes, among other components, the establishment of ethical criteria for drug promotion based on the updating and extension of the ethical and scientific criteria established in 1968 by the twenty-first World Health Assembly in resolution WHA21.41. The criteria that follow have been prepared in compliance with the above on the basis of a draft elaborated by an international group of experts.

Objective

2. The main objective of ethical criteria for medicinal drug promotion is to support and encourage the improvement of health care through the rational use of medicinal drugs.

Ethical criteria

3. The interpretation of what is ethical varies in different parts of the world and in different societies. The issue in all societies is what is proper behaviour. Ethical criteria for drug promotion should lay the foundation for proper behaviour concerning the promotion of medicinal drugs, consistent with the search for truthfulness and righteousness. The criteria should thus assist in judging if promotional practices related to medicinal drugs are in keeping with acceptable ethical standards.

Applicability and implementation of criteria

4. These criteria constitute general principles for ethical standards which could be adapted by governments to national circumstances as appropriate to their political, economic, cultural, social, educational, scientific and technical situation, laws and regulations, disease profile, therapeutic traditions and the level of development of their health system. They apply to prescription and non-prescription medicinal drugs ("over-the-counter drugs"). They also apply generally to traditional medicines as appropriate, and to any other product promoted as a medicine. The criteria could be used by people in all walks of life; by governments; the pharmaceutical industry (manufacturers and distributors); the promotion industry (advertising agencies, market research organizations and the like); health personnel involved in the prescription, dispensing, supply and distribution of drugs; universities and other teaching institutions; professional associations; patients' and consumer groups; and the professional and general media (including publishers and editors of medical journals and related publications). All these are encouraged to use the criteria as appropriate to their spheres of competence, activity and responsibility. They are also encouraged to take the criteria into account in developing their own sets of ethical standards in their own field relating to medicinal drug promotion. The criteria do not constitute legal obligations; governments may adopt legislation or other measures based on them as they deem fit. Similarly, other groups may adopt self-regulatory measures based on them. All these bodies should monitor and enforce their standards.

Promotion

6. In this context, "promotion" refers to all informational and persuasive activities by manufacturers and distributors, the effect of which is to induce the prescription, supply, purchase and/or use of medicinal drugs.

7. Active promotion within a country should take place only with respect to drugs legally available in the country. Promotion should be in keeping with national health policies and in compliance with national regulations, as well as with voluntary standards where they exist. All promotion-making claims concerning medicinal drugs should be reliable, accurate, truthful, informative, balanced, up-to-date, capable of substantiation and in good taste. They should not contain misleading or unverifiable statements or omissions likely to induce medically unjustifiable drug use or to give rise to undue risks. The word "safe" should only be used if properly qualified. Comparison of products should be factual, fair and capable of substantiation. Promotional material should not be designed so as to disguise its real nature.

8. Scientific data in the public domain should be made available to prescribers and any other person entitled to receive it, on request, as appropriate to their requirements. Promotion in the form of financial or material benefits should not be offered to or sought by health care practitioners to influence them in the prescription of drugs.

9. Scientific and educational activities should not be deliberately used for promotional purposes.

Advertising

(a) Advertisements in all forms to physicians and health-related professionals

10. The wording and illustrations in advertisements to physicians and related health professionals should be fully consistent with the approved scientific data sheet for the drug concerned or other source of information with similar content. The text should be fully legible.

11. Some countries require that advertisements should contain full product information, as defined by the approved scientific data sheet or similar document, for a given period from the date of first promotion or for the full product life. Advertisements that make a promotional claim should at least contain summary scientific information.

12. The following list, based on the sample drug information sheet contained in the second report of the WHO Expert Committee on the Use of Essential Drugs can serve as an illustration of the type of information that such advertisements should usually contain, among others:

- the name(s) of the active ingredient(s) using either international nonproprietary names (INN) or the approved generic name of the drug;
- the brand name;
- content of active ingredient(s) per dosage form or regimen;
- name of other ingredients known to cause problems;
- approved therapeutic uses;
- dosage form or regimen;
- side-effects and major adverse drug reactions;

(Continued)

Table 5.A   (Continued)

- precautions, contra-indications and warnings;
- major interactions;
- name and address of manufacturer or distributor;
- reference to scientific literature as appropriate.

13. Where advertisements are permitted without claims (reminder advertisements), they ought to include at least the brand name, the international nonproprietary name or approved generic name, the name of each active ingredient, and the name and address of the manufacturer or distributor for the purpose of receiving further information.

(b) Advertisements in all forms to the general public

14. Advertisements to the general public should help people to make rational decisions on the use of drugs determined to be legally available without a prescription. While they should take account of people's legitimate desire for information regarding their health, they should not take undue advantage of people's concern for their health. They should not generally be permitted for prescription drugs or to promote drugs for certain serious conditions that can be treated only by qualified health practitioners, for which certain countries have established lists. To fight drug addiction and dependency, scheduled narcotic and psychotropic drugs should not be advertised to the general public. While health education aimed at children is highly desirable, drug advertisements should not be directed at children. Advertisements may claim that a drug can cure, prevent, or relieve an ailment only if this can be substantiated. They should also indicate, where applicable, appropriate limitations to the use of the drug.

15. When lay language is used, the information should be consistent with the approved scientific data sheet or other legally determined scientific basis for approval. Language which brings about fear or distress should not be used.

16. The following list serves as an illustration of the type of information advertisements to the general public should contain, taking into account the media employed:
    the name(s) of the active ingredients(s) using either international nonproprietary names (INN) or the approved generic name of the drug;
    the brand name;
    major indication(s) for use;
    major precautions, contraindications and warnings;
    name and address of manufacturer or distributor.
    Information on price to the consumer should be accurately and honestly portrayed.

Medical Representatives

17. Medical representatives should have an appropriate educational background. They should be adequately trained. They should possess sufficient medical and technical knowledge and integrity to present information on products and carry out other promotional activities in an accurate and responsible manner. Employers are responsible for the basic and continuing training of their representatives. Such training should include instruction regarding appropriate ethical conduct taking into consideration the WHO criteria. In this context, exposure of medical representatives and trainees to feed-back from the medical and allied professions and from independent members of the public, particularly regarding risks, can be salutary.

18. Medical representatives should make available to prescribers and dispensers complete and unbiased information for each product discussed, such as an approved scientific data sheet or other source of information with similar content.

19. Employers should be responsible for the statements and activities of their medical representatives. Medical representatives should not offer inducements to prescribers and dispensers. Prescribers and dispensers should not solicit such inducements. In order to avoid over-promotion, the main part of the remuneration of medical representatives should not be directly related to the volume of sales they generate.

Free samples of prescription drugs for promotional purposes

20. Free samples of legally available prescription drugs may be provided in modest quantities to prescribers, generally on request.
    Free samples of non-prescription drugs to the general public for promotional purposes

21. Countries vary in their practices regarding the provision of free samples of non-prescription drugs to the general public, some countries permitting it, some not. Also, a distinction has to be made between provision of free drugs by health agencies for the care of certain groups and the provision of free samples to the general public for promotional purposes. The provision of free samples of non-prescription drugs to the general public for promotional purposes is difficult to justify from a health perspective. If this practice is legally permitted in any country, it should be handled with great restraint.

Symposia and other scientific meetings

22. Symposia are useful for disseminating information. The objective scientific content of such meetings should be paramount, and presentations by independent scientists and health professionals are helpful to this end. Their educational value may be enhanced if they are organized by scientific or professional bodies.

23. The fact of sponsorship by a pharmaceutical manufacturer or distributor should clearly be stated in advance, at the meeting and in any proceedings. The latter should accurately reflect the presentations and discussions. Entertainment or other hospitality, and any gifts offered to members of the medical and allied professions, should be secondary to the main purpose of the meeting and should be kept to a modest level.

24. Any support to individual health practitioners to participate in any domestic or international symposia should not be conditional upon any obligation to promote any medicinal product.

Post-marketing scientific studies, surveillance and dissemination of information

25. Post-marketing clinical trials for approved medicinal drugs are important to ensure their rational use. It is recommended that appropriate national health authorities be made aware of any such studies and that relevant scientific and ethical committees confirm the validity of the research. Intercountry and regional cooperation in such studies may be useful. Substantiated information on such studies should be reported to the appropriate national health authorities and disseminated as soon as possible.

26. Post-marketing scientific studies and surveillance should not be misused as a disguised form of promotion.

(Continued)

Table 5.A   (Continued)

27. Substantiated information on hazards associated with medicinal drugs should be reported to the appropriate national health authority as a priority, and should be disseminated internationally as soon as possible.

Packaging and labelling
28. Appropriate information being important to ensure the rational use of drugs, all packaging and labelling material should provide information consistent with that approved by the country's drug regulatory authority. Where one does not exist or is rudimentary, such material should provide information consistent with that approved by the drug regulatory authority of the country from which the drug is imported or other reliable sources of information with similar content. Any wording and illustration on the package and label should conform to the principles of ethical criteria enunciated in this document.
   Information for patients: package inserts, leaflets and booklets
29. Adequate information on the use of medicinal drugs should be made available to patients. Such information should be provided by physicians or pharmacists whenever possible. When package inserts or leaflets are required by governments, manufacturers or distributors should ensure that they reflect only the information that has been approved by the country's drug regulatory authority. If package inserts or leaflets are used for promotional purposes, they should comply with the ethical criteria enunciated in this document. The wording of the package inserts or leaflets, if prepared specifically for patients, should be in lay language on condition that the medical and scientific content is properly reflected.
30. In addition to approved package inserts and leaflets wherever available, the preparation and distribution of booklets and other informational material for patients and consumers should be encouraged as appropriate. Such material should also comply with the ethical criteria enunciated in this document.
   Promotion of exported drugs
31. Ethical criteria for the promotion of exported drugs should be identical with those relating to drugs for domestic use. It is desirable that exporting and importing countries that have not already done so should use the WHO Certification Scheme on the quality of pharmaceutical products moving in International Commerce.

Several of the terms used here can be (and have been) understood in different ways when a dispute arises. More generally phrased clauses in such a Code can be even more difficult to interpret, e.g.:

> **Good Taste:** Promotional material (including graphics and other visual representations) should conform to generally accepted standards of good taste and recognise the professional standing of the recipients. (AAMA 1994, para 1.4)

Such disagreements arise with printed advertising texts, but more considerable problems can arise with more exotic forms of promotion. Promotional managers are by definition creative and inventive, and forms of promotion can be devised which have not been anticipated by the lawmaker and the influence of which is not likely to be fully understood by an assessor or a court:

> We were being quite aggressive in getting this drug YY accepted by the profession, and I don't know that the regulators had any idea what we were up to. We had one symposium for doctors which was all above board and according to the rules, but as detailmen we were transporting the participants forwards and backwards to their hotel in our cars. There was a rather daring folder, quite attractive and readable, pushing the product for an unapproved indication, and we ensured there were some copies lying around in the cars, and most of the doctors got curious, picked them up and took them. If we were asked we simply said it was an "unapproved" text that we were not yet handing out.
> There was also the video we took around when visiting general practitioners – all acceptable, even the nurses who we had given long legs and short skirts – but we also had one or two subliminal messages on the tape that were flashed on the screen and which put across additional messages that got through, though people never remembered seeing them. The advertising code was fine but somehow it was written for the publicity world of ten years ago, and the world had moved on. (Interview 2)

> Regulation will always lag behind the ingenuity of the advertising executives. (Sasisch 1997)

The many existing codes vary as regards their strengths and weaknesses:

The classic *WHO Ethical Criteria* of 1988 are well written and cover a wide range of topics well, but they are so generally phrased that they are difficult to interpret in a concrete instance, apart from the fact that there is no mechanism to enforce them.

The *global industry code maintained by the IFPMA* has a fundamental weakness in its provision that "In all matters of application interpretation and enforcement . . . compliance with national laws, regulations and regulatory decisions and requirements will take precedence." This will mean that, if a weak national regulatory authority has approved a drug on the basis of questionable data, promotion for that drug cannot be questioned.

> The Medical Lobby for Appropriate Marketing (MaLAM), an international network of health professionals, questioned Organon in 1992 about their marketing of adrenochrome for "prevention and treatment of surgical and non-surgical capillary bleeding" in Bangladesh, since the effectiveness of the product was not evident from the world literature. The firm's Medical Director replied that the Bangladeshi health authorities had endorsed this use, and that: "according to our interpretation of the IFPMA Code of Pharmaceutical Marketing Practices a company which has a pharmaceutical product evaluated and registered by an established regulatory

authority can be considered as having provided adequate scientific evidence." (cited by Mansfield 1992).

This defence remains permissible under the 1994 version of the IFPMA code and, as Mintzes comments, it means that the Code cannot provide the minimum standard which in much of the developing world is so necessary. (Mintzes 1998)

Various committees applying *industry-based advertising and marketing codes* clearly do good in maintaining some basic standards of fairness, and they develop continuously in the light of experience. Being based largely on the wish to avoid unfair competition they tend to be strictly applied, and being interpreted by people who have daily first-hand experience of the marketing world their interpretation is well-attuned to practice.

Official promotional rules will continue to be formulated and applied because they provide a legal backing to the control regimen with the possibility of concrete sanctions and even penalties under criminal law for companies and their staff (see Chapter 2) in the event of serious breaches of the rules. The actual role of codes based on legislation will vary with the extent to which voluntary business-based codes are effective. In accordance with the familiar legal principle that the role of law varies inversely with that of other forms of social control (Black 1976), the official and the voluntary codes complement one another. One inevitable shortcoming of official systems is that in the event of a need for repressive action this can only be taken after the promotional effort has been undertaken and perhaps completed, and has already exerted precisely the effect that one would have wished to avoid. A global weakness is that official controls also exist only in a minority of the world's countries and are not always implemented even where they exist (as cited by Mintzes 1998).

Even where national regulations to control promotion are on paper relatively strong, implementation may in some respects be weak. In Canada in 1997, because of reductions in government budgets, the regulatory agency was obliged to delegate control of over-the-counter drug promotion to a private organisation representing the advertising industry (Canada 1997). It has been remarked that "At present, even the United States does not have the capacity to adequately control promotion of the products on its market." (López 1997); at one point a mere thirty assessors at the FDA were available to assess more than thirty thousand advertisements yearly. FDA authors cited by Mintzes in 1998 noted a number of methods used by the pharmaceutical industry to evade the restrictions inherent in the Agency's regulations. To paraphrase them for the present purpose, they comprised:

a. The use of industry-sponsored scientific and educational activities, not regarded as advertising, in order to disseminate messages (see Sections 5.9 and 5.10).
b. Basing claims for products on inadequate scientific evidence. Uncontrolled studies can for example be performed through unqualified groups controlled by advertising or marketing agencies (Petersen 2002) and their "findings" distributed in the form of reprints from non-peer-reviewed journals which publish papers against payment.
c. Use of press releases and materials produced by public relations firms. At the present day it is not unusual for advertising agencies to distribute "news items" in a form ready for use by the lay and professional media; describing new drugs which can be anticipated in the near future, they serve to generate curiosity and lay the basis for future demand.
d. Changing the content of promotional material after it has been approved by the FDA and before it is disseminated; this is strictly speaking a criminal offence, but in view of the limited capacity for inspection it is commonly overlooked; incidental cases that are detected can be excused as "an oversight" and forgiven following due apology.

There are, fortunately, some situations relating to promotion which, while distressing in the juridical-puritanical view, need not be (and usually are not) taken all too seriously. As remarked in another Chapter there is sometimes a reason for compassion, both in medicine and law. Some ancient products continue to enjoy a reputation which does not rest on scientific evidence, but the placebo effect is also as old as the hills and when patients want them they are prone to stay; when however they stay, what can the advertising properly say about them without risking untruth on the one hand or disillusionment on the other? For a new medicine, by contrast, the challenge may be to induce the world to choose it despite the fact that, at the time, its merits relative to older remedies may still be unclear; and if society believes that advertising is desirable, then it must presumably be prepared to allow some degree of poetic licence if it is to attract attention, which is its very purpose.

These marginal topics apart, one cannot consider that in most of the world there truly is at the moment anything approaching an adequate degree of supervision by the community over the process of medicinal promotion. A very few industrialized countries maintain rules or codes and operate systems of scrutiny backed by sanctions; in some of these countries these are also usefully complemented by industry-based systems of control in order to ensure fairness of competition. The global codes have little influence except perhaps as a source of inspiration to those countries now wishing to implement their own. Bearing in mind that much advertising in other sectors around the world functions well and honestly, the present trends in the pharmaceutical sector raise many questions. One has the uneasy sensation that, as Angell argues, the industry has become a marketing organisation rather than one renowned for valuable innovation and high quality production (Angell 2004). In matters of promotion it may have become too sure of itself and in becoming more aggressive and defiant it can run the risk of losing its own credibility with its audience as well as the patience of the authorities and the community as a whole.

A warning sign is the concern expressed by Britain's House of Commons Select Committee in 2005 that the very intensity and dominance of drug promotion may have become a threat to public health:

> The problem is far less to do with any particular activity; rather the volume may distort prescribing practice. At the heart of the problem may be the trend for the industry to become ever more driven by its marketing force. (HOC 2005)

5.4. Basic Information

For the legislator and regulator the simplest issue to tackle is that of the provision of plain factual information. Throughout their existence, the industry and trade supplying packaged medicines have provided information to users, prescribers and dispensers of their products, most basically in the form of texts imprinted on the packaging or in separate package inserts, with a description of the medicine and its proper mode of use. The discreditable examples of the distant past have led to almost uniform agreement that these texts should be objective and not mixed with persuasive material (see Box 5.B and Table 5.C)

With the development of drug regulation and a more scientific industry in the twentieth century the range of information to be provided has become more comprehensive; it now comprises a virtually international

CRIMSON CROSS KIDNEY CURE
This Mixture contains powerful Medicinal Properties for the cure of
Kidney, Bladder, Gravel, and all Urinary Disorders, Dropsy, etc.
Dose: Adults.- One tablespoonful every four hours
Children: One teaspoonful to one dessertspoonful, according to age, every
four hours
The Crimson Cross Kidney Cure may be confidently taken by young and
old alike, in full assurance that, whatever the trouble, a course of the
Crimson Cross Kidney Cure will gently but surely remedy the mischief,
and coax the organs back to a natural and healthy action. Note: Whilst
taking the Cure, it will greatly facilitate the cure if the lower part of the
back and bowels are gently rubbed with Crimson Cross No. 1 Ointment
once a day. The Ointment should be well rubbed in for about five min-
utes, then wiped down with an old rough dry towel, to prevent the linen
from getting greasy.
(Crimson Cross, United Kingdom 1908)

Box 5.B A package insert from 1908

Table 5.C
Information to be Included with Packaging
(according to WHO Ethical Criteria)

Trade Name; international non-proprietary name
Quantitative Composition
List of excipients (quantified if required by law)
Manufacturer and location
Holder of Marketing Authorisation and location
Registration number (if required by law)
Batch number
Approved Indications for use
Pharmacological nature (if required by law)
Dosage scheme(s)
Adverse reactions and interactions
Warnings and Precautions
Stability and expiry date
Symbols (where required by law)

standard, respected by many companies even where no regulations in force.
It is somewhat more extensive than the basic information which, according
to WHO's Ethical Criteria should be appended to advertising texts (Table
5C above).

Current drug regulation has also provided a basis for assessing the acceptability of any such text, in the form of the Summary of Product Characteristics or Data Sheet officially approved by the drug agency at the time marketing approval is granted, subject to later modifications. According to the rules now widely in force, this basic text must appear on or with the packaging, in any factual document disseminated separately (such as a Drug Compendium of Physicians' Desk Reference provided separately to physicians) and as an appendix to any full advertisement. Symbols required by law may include a special emblem indicating that the product is "new" and subject to strict reporting obligations (adverse reactions and interactions) or a sign indicating that the product should not be used by drivers or those operating heavy machinery.

Where a drug has not as yet been allocated an *international non-proprietary name* (a task performed by the World Health Organization), a chemical name will be regarded as acceptable. The *indications for use* should be set out in understandable terms; there is as a rule no obligation to include all indications, and some agencies have given dispensation from listing indications at all where these could cause alarm or distress, e.g. in products used to treat cancers. It is generally recommended that general *dosage schemes* should where appropriate be supplemented by special instructions for particular situations (for example the treatment of the elderly or children). The range of *adverse reactions and interactions* to be included is commonly questioned; a very large number of reports on different unwanted adverse effects may have appeared, and a long list may be confusing or uninformative; a common-sense approach is to list those unwanted effects which are well documented and which are either frequent in occurrence or serious in nature. *Warnings and precautions* should similarly relate to situations of frequent or serious risk and means of avoiding such risk. These latter issues are matters on which the manufacturer or representative may, with a view to his legal liability in the event of injury, wish to provide rather more information than the regulatory agency is anxious to see.

A particular problem arises where too little information can be made available regarding risks in certain common risk situations, such as the use of the product in *pregnant women, during lactation, in the elderly or in young children*, particularly since it may be problematical to conduct studies in these groups (see Chapter 9). While it may appear simpler for a firm in these instances simply to advise against using the product in these groups, noting that adequate information is lacking, various authorities have insisted that since such a product may be used by accident or out of necessity in these groups any data which could be relevant should be listed, e.g. the findings from studies of pregnant animals.

Various proposals have been made in this respect. Some agencies currently suggest that the warnings should be based on a classification of medicines into four groups:

a. Drugs which may be assumed, with a high degree of probability, to have been taken by a large number of pregnant women and women of child-bearing age without any form of definite disturbance in the reproductive process, including an increased frequency of foetal malformations or other harmful effects, having been observed until the present.

b. Drugs which have been taken by only a limited number of pregnant women and women of child-bearing age, without any form of definite disturbance in the reproductive process, including an increased frequency of foetal malformations or other harmful effects on the fetus, having been observed until the present.

c. Drugs which, owing to their pharmacological effects, have caused, or must be suspected of causing, reproduction disturbances that may involve risks to the fetus without their being directly teratogenic.

d. Drugs which in man have caused, or which on grounds of toxicity testing must be suspected of causing, an increased frequency of foetal malformations or other permanent damage. (Sannerstedt et al. (1980)

In a given case it may be extremely difficult to formulate an appropriate statement, and the advice of the drug regulatory agency will be essential.

The information supplied with a product should be *regularly updated*, subject to the approval of the regulatory agency, as new information becomes available. Since there is clearly likely to be delay in the revision of data sheets, national representative offices and distributors should maintain a file of currently existing information which can be made available on request. Important new information on usage or risks should be communicated to prescribers in the form of circulars or through other effective channels. A similar procedure is advisable as regards information on use during breast-feeding.

It is today usual, and in accordance with the rules of the European Union, to supplement the full text with a shorter section providing "Information for the patient" written in lay terms so that it is readily understandable by the average user.

5.5. Persuasion

There is a very considerable difference between advertising which is recognizable as such and the various other forms of persuasion which are commonly used by pharmaceutical companies to promote the sale and use of their products. Some of the latter take such a form that their persuasive role is clear; others are presented more subtly.

5.5.1. Direct textual advertising to health professionals

The most traditional form of advertising directed to the doctor or other health professional is the printed text, distributed in the form either of a brochure or an announcement in a journal. More recently, this type of explicit advertising has extended into new fields, including the use of videos, films, recordings and material available on the internet. From the point of view of law and ethics, explicit advertising is also the least problematical form of promotion, since the advertisement is recognizable as such and the reader is aware of its origin and is free to accept or reject its arguments or to ignore it. It is also relatively simple to lay down a number of principles to which a printed advertisement or its analogies in order media presentations should adhere. In particular its statements and claims should be fully compatible with the texts approved by the regulatory agency. While the advertiser may choose to limit a particular advertisement to a limited theme – for example only one of a series of indications or approved fields of use – essential limitations on use in this field should not be omitted. As noted above, many agencies and firms now consider it necessary to reproduce the full agency approved text for the drug as an appendix to a printed advertisement. Illustrations, slogans and other supportive elements should not present or suggest any contradiction to statements which would be regarded as acceptable in the text. "Reminder advertisements" may however be permitted, which are intended to do little more than remind the reader of the product's name and general nature without an obligation provided warnings, contra-indications or a list of adverse effects.

The only universally agreed set of public rules for medicine advertising to health professionals is still, as noted above, that accepted by the World Health Assembly in 1988, reproduced above as Table 5A. It is virtually encyclopaedic as regards the topics on which standards need to be maintained, the principle problem being its general nature, rendering it difficult to interpret and apply the various clauses in an individual case.

Other Codes and sets of rules tend to be more detailed, with annotations dealing with issues which may be the subject of dispute, Two of the most explicit codes are those of the Australian Pharmaceutical Manufacturers Association, cited under 5.2 and the Association of the British Pharmaceutical Industry, (ABPI 1992)

5.5.2. *Common points of dispute*

Some of the most commonly disputed points in textual advertising are noted below. There is considerable variation in the degree of stringency which agencies or Code Committees apply in assessing advertising material, directed either to the public or to the professions.

(i) *Unapproved indications* Although physicians are generally considered free to prescribe drugs for non-approved indications at their discretion, they may not be promoted. Some offences have been serious, others capable of correction:

> The case of the Warner-Lambert offence[2] regarding the promotion of Neurontin in the U.S. for unapproved indications (see Section 3.3.5.) was particularly blatant since evidence was given that some of these indications had at an earlier date been specifically rejected by the FDA. In many other cases the deviation from approved texts has been more cautious, involving near-synonyms of the approved indication or misleadingly ambiguous descriptions of the uses of a medicine, e.g. in terms of symptoms which could suggest a particular off-label disorder without actually naming it.

> In 2004, Bristol–Meyers Squibb was required by the FDA to publish corrective public advertisements for it lipid-lowering agent Pravachol, following their use of a text which broadened the indications and the description of the patient population for which the drug was indicated. (Scrip 2004b, 2004 at p. 17)

(ii) *Unscientific and inexact claims* Inexact claims unrelated to any verifiable property are often ruled inadmissible, though advertisers may defend them as justifiable generalizations.

> In Britain, the combined oral contraceptive Yasmin was advertised by Schering as a "truly different pill" and "the pill for well-being". The Drugs and Therapeutics Bulletin challenged the claims as misleading since it could identify no concrete advantage over older products of the type. The Code of Practice Authority found in favour of the Bulletin. The Schering company appealed the decision unsuccessfully, but cancelled both the advertisement and a libel action against the Bulletin. (DTB 2003)

---

[2] The offence was committed prior to the acquisition of Warner–Lambert by Pfizer.

(iii) *Comparative claims*   Most codes permit claims of a product's superiority provided it has been proven and the advertisement is not directly derogatory to another medicine. However, disputes may arise when the claim is implied rather than explicit:

> In 2005, the FDA ordered the US Bayer firm and GSK to withdraw a television reminder advertisement for the erectile dysfunction product Levitra; the actress's statement that "Levitra is the best way to experience the difference" was considered to comprise an unsubstantiated claim of superiority over (unnamed) competing products. (PT 2005)

(iv) *Quotations out of context*   Officially approved indications may be wrongfully cited in abbreviated form, omitting limitations. Material from publications is sometimes quoted in part, or figures reproduced without full captions, misrepresenting the author's meaning; outdated publications may be misleadingly cited without mention of their date.

(v) *Misleading illustrations*   Illustrations may imply uses not officially approved, e.g. relief of pain following injuries, use in the elderly.

(vi) *Misleading citations*   Scientific publications must not be quoted or distributed where they point to indications or modes of use which have not been approved by the national regulatory body.

> Firms have challenged attempts to prohibit distribution of such material where it comprises reprints from peer-reviewed journals. In practice, agencies take account of the context in which the material has been distributed. A firm may provide such a paper to a physician who has specifically requested it in connection with his use of a drug for an unapproved indication, but such material should not be distributed spontaneously by a detailman or in the form of a publicity mailing.

(vii) *Distinction of promotional material*   An advertisement or promotional text, e.g. designed to be handed to a practitioner, must not appear to be an independent scientific publication. The exact source of any journal reprint should be indicated.

(viii) *Legibility and placement*   Where approved scientific texts are required to be appended to an advertisement they should be placed immediately alongside or below it and should be in a legible type and style.

> Agencies have challenged the practice of certain journals of placing all such scientific texts together at the back of the journal issue where they are less conscpicuous and less accessible than the advertising texts to which they relate and will not be read in conjunction with it.

(ix) *Pre-marketing advertising*   Advertising or other forms of publicity are not permitted prior to the official approval of a product. This rule should be considered to exclude the publication of "press releases" or similar indicating that a product is about to become available and hence implying that approval is a foregone conclusion.

Although this has been declared to be a formal rule, agencies do not as a rule make efforts to enforce it.

(x) *Testimonials*   Full testimonials or citations, real or fictitious, from professionals or users, should not be used; it should be clear that all statements made in the text originate with the advertiser, except where a scientific publication is cited with full documentation.

An advertisement for a cold rub featured a mother looking at her child and exclaiming "Perhaps it's my fault that she still has a cold?"; the Netherlands Board of Control considered that it used a fictitious quotation, that it implied wrongly that a mother who did not use the product failed in her duty, and suggested incorrectly that the product cured the common cold. (Personal communication, C.H. Kohlinger)

In the US and a number of other countries personal endorsements by political and sporting celebrities of products for erectile dysfunction have remained unchallenged; in FDA practice the rule may have lapsed.

(xi) *Unqualified claims of safety*   While exact statements as to reduction of risk may be accepted, general statements declaring or implying that a product is "safe" or "free of risk" are inadmissible.

In Britain the Medicine and Health Products Regulatory Agency (MHRA) objected to a promotion leaflet for the Novartis angiotensin II antagonist Diovan which used the term "placebo-like tolerability" since side-effects were mentioned in the Summary of Product Characteristics; the claim also suggested that the product was safer than others. (Scrip 2004g at p. 2)

(xii) *Statements creating confusion*   It is not permissible to imply that the merits of a product can be assumed from indirect evidence, e.g. from its source or association with another product.

In 2004 the MHRA in Britain ordered Reckitt Benckiser Health Care to withdraw a television advertisement for its heartburn therapy Gavilast one component of which was the H-2 blocker ranitidine. The advertisement stated that the product was supplied by "the makers of Gaviscon." This could according to the agency create confusion in the public mind since Gaviscon (essentially an antacid) is used by pregnant women, whereas Gavilast with ranitidine must not be so used other than on medical advice. (Scrip 2004g at p. 2)

5.5.3.   *The detailman*

It is recognized in the pharmaceutical industry that the travelling representative (medical visitor, detailman) is for the industry the most effective form of persuasion which it possesses. In 2005, the British House of Commons Select Committee accepted a witness statement that some 8,000 drug company representatives were operating in the United Kingdom alone (HOC 2005 at para. 77). In 2001 in the United States some 88,000 sales representatives were employed to visit doctors and hospitals. (Angell 2004 at p. 126). Representatives both introduce new products and stress the merits of existing ones.

In 1998, Barbara Mintzes (Mintzes 1998) reviewed the few studies available up to that time which authoritatively reviewed the technical performance of company representatives visiting physicians. As she summarized it:

> With data from four countries, the results were remarkably consistent. Sales representatives almost always stated the indications and the drug's brand and generic name, but usually failed to include safety information such as side effects and contraindications and many statements contained inaccuracies. In other words, there was a lack of balance in the information provided, with a greater emphasis on the drugs' benefits and inadequate information on risks.

The results were consistent from work in other countries showing a consistent association between doctors' reliance on the information provided by detailers and inappropriate prescribing. (Lexchin 1997)

Ethical objections which are commonly raised by critics to this form of promotion relate to the extent to which prescribing may be influenced: not merely by objective information provided orally or in the form of materials carried by the detailman, but also by the establishment of personal relationships, gifts or favours made available through these intensive contacts and the ability of the presenter to achieve his sales objective by means other than strictly scientific argument. A part of the medical profession is stated to regard detailing as a useful source of new information: other physicians object to the time occupied by detailing. The regulatory authorities find that they have no fully effective means of ensuring the reliability of the information offered, though requirements may be set as regards the provision of officially approved texts during the interview.

As early as 1968 Part VI of Britain's Medicine's Act embodied broad provisions relating to various forms of promotion including personal representation. The requirement was introduced that:

> . . . no representation likely to promote the use of medicinal products of a particular description referred to in the representation shall be made to a practitioner unless . . . . . . a data sheet relating to medicinal products of the description in question is sent or delivered to the practitioner . . . at the time when the representation is made . . . or has been sent or delivered to him not more than fifteen months . . . before . . . the representation is made . . . (Part VI, para 96(3)).

This requirement has since been emulated and implemented elsewhere. In fact, however, many pharmaceutical firms comply with it by including their current data sheets in a Compendium sent at intervals to all practitioners on behalf of the industry as a whole or a part of it; in that case the detailman will not carry the data sheets with him.

The Australian Code of Conduct similarly requires that whenever a promotional claim is made for a product, either by a representative or in any other manner, it shall be accompanied by the officially approved "product information" (APMA 1994 at para. 3.3). It further states that representatives must use only material which conforms to the general provisions of the code, and that "verbal statements" must similarly be in conformity. The Code requires that medical representatives undergo appropriate training to diploma standard and that a number of rules be respected as regards contact with physicians:

> 4.5. Medical representatives must not employ any deception to gain an interview

> 4.6. Medical representatives should ensure that the frequency, timing and duration of calls, together with the manner in which they are made, are such as not to cause inconvenience. The wishes of an individual doctor, or the arrangements in force at any particular establishment, must be observed by medical representatives.

> 4.7. Medical representatives must not use the telephone to promote products to the medical profession unless the agreement of the doctor has been obtained.

> 4.9. Under no circumstances shall representatives pay a fee in order to gain access to a healthcare professional.

Rules such as these may be regarded simply as norms for the decent conduct of any type of business, but they also represent part of an attempt to establish an acceptable place for the medical representative in the conduct of the medical profession. It is clear that wherever the industry has attempted to establish rules of conduct for its representatives similar rules are emerging.

The fact that regulators do not have any adequate means of monitoring the technical standard or conduct of medical representation means that its acceptability in the long term will be heavily dependent on the one hand on industry rules such as the above and on the other hand on the reception accorded to detailing by the medical profession itself. The view of the individual physician, as noted above, is variable; there have however been attempts on the part of the profession to ensure that this form of promotion plays a genuinely useful rule and that abuses are avoided. Several promising approaches have been developed in The Netherlands:

> From 1985 onwards, as part of a redeveloped course of training for future medical practitioners in Good Prescribing Practice, students at the University of Groningen were trained in critical approaches to drug information, including printed advertising and contacts with medical representatives. Following theoretical teaching, including the use of videos illustrating the detailman's sales techniques, representatives from various firms were invited to present competing products to the class; both parties were subsequently asked to assess and discuss the results of the encounter.

> In some areas and institutions in The Netherlands, physicians and pharmacists have ceased to meet pharmaceutical representatives individually. A detailman is instead invite to meet the group as a whole to make a presentation on a pre-announced topic, followed by joint discussion. Analysis of the results indicates that the standard of detailing is raised significantly. There are fewer interviews, but detailmen are better prepared for their task, and more useful and more reliable prescribing information is provided.

Such ventures on a limited scale appear promising. However it seems clear from various studies of the marketing process, such as the work of Greider in the United States (Greider 2003), that much of the selling undertaken by medical representatives fails to conform to norms such as those to be found in laws or codes of conduct. To cite Marcia Angell's description of the scene in 2004:

> These drug reps or detailers, as they are known, are ubiquitous in the medical world. Usually young, attractive, and extremely ingratiating, they roam the halls of almost every sizeable hospital in the country looking for chances to talk with the medical staff and paving the way with gifts (such as books, golf balls, and tickets to sporting events). In many teaching hospitals, drug reps regularly provide lunches for interns and residents while standing by to chat about their drugs. This "food, flattery, and friendship," as it has been called, (Moynihan 2003) creates a sense of reciprocity in young doctors with long prescribing lives ahead of them. They naturally feel indebted to congenial people who keep giving them gifts. Some teaching hospitals have begun to curb these practices, but not nearly enough of them.

Drug reps are allowed to attend medical conferences, may be invited into operating and procedure rooms, and sometimes are even present when physicians examine patients in clinics or at the bedside. Patients are often allowed to assume the reps are doctors – an assumption that is strengthened when drug reps offer advice about treatment. Take the case of Azucena Sanchez-Scott, reported in *The Boston Globe*. After finishing chemotherapy for breast cancer, she went to see her doctor and found another man in the examining room. The doctor said that the stranger was "observing my work." Only later did she learn he was a drug rep from a Johnson & Johnson subsidiary. She sued the company, which settled out of court. But her experience is not unusual. Drug companies pay doctors several hundred dollars a day to allow sales reps to shadow them as they see patients, a practice called a "preceptorship." One Schering–Plough rep explained that "it's another way to build a relationship with the doctor and hopefully build business." (Angell, 2004 at pp. 126–127)

The rights and wrongs of this personal form of marketing cannot be discussed separately from the promotional process as a whole. To return to the initial section of this Chapter: the reason why public policy occupies itself with the manner in which medicines are sold is, firstly, that money may otherwise be wasted and secondly that harm may be done. As far as the *finance* is concerned: with increasing concern worldwide regarding the costs of health care and medicines, there is much discussion of the fact that so much of the public funding devoted to medicines ends up paying for marketing. Detailing, an unusually expensive means of purveying information, accounts for a substantial part of that sum (perhaps 20% of drug prices at the factory level). As far as *harm* goes, the patient will in the present situation commonly be treated with the drug that is most heavily promoted, but that will not necessarily be the drug that is best for his or her condition. The most optimal form of promotion from the community's point of view is that which puts the recipient in a position to get a clear view of all the facts and in the light of those facts to make the best choice. Law and regulation can do something to get closer to that situation where textual advertising is concerned; they are doing very little and can do very little to ensure that medical detailing serves the community's needs properly; voluntary effort by all parties may perhaps achieve rather more.

Finally: it has on occasion been argued that intensive promotion, including personal representation, may be of particular value in those countries where the health professions otherwise have poor access to medical information resources. It has most certainly played a useful role on occasion, but precisely in those situations questions arise as to whether a developing community can afford this costly means of providing information – financed directly by drug prices – and whether its least desirable influences will not come strongly to the fore among recipients who have had little exposure to competitive selling and little opportunity to built the necessary degree of resistance to it.

5.5.4. *Advertising of prescription items to the public ("D.T.C.")*

Up to about 1990 in industrialized countries, drugs intended for use primarily on medical prescription were promoted only to the medical profession, and to a limited extent to dispensers and other health workers. Advertising of medicines to the public was limited, either by custom or explicit regulation, to items intended for self-medication (see Section 9.3). Subsequently, beginning in the United States and then in New Zealand, a number of major firms began the promotion of prescription drugs to the public, through television, radio, film and the printed media. Initially, the promotion was to some degree masked, reference being made only to an anonymous "new drug", the claimed merits of which were set out, and the reader or viewer was advised to visit a physician in order to seek information or to request a prescription. The name of the firm was supplied. Complemented by explicit advertising to the profession, the approach is been found to have a very marked effect on the prescribing of drugs, and this "Direct to Consumer" (D.T.C.) Promotion has since been the subject of heavy promotional investment. As in other areas, the industry has claimed that the public advertising of innovative drugs comprises a useful form of public education, while some consumer and patient groups object that it serves only a commercial purpose, is costly, and to a dangerous extent transfers the choice of drug therapy from the physician to the much less well informed patient. To an even greater extent than where advertising to the professions is concerned, money flows not to the best and most innovative drugs but to those that are most heavily and subtly promoted.

Shortly after the turn of the century a determined effort was made by industry to gain approval for the introduction of this form of promotion in the countries of the European Union. A proposal to this end was quashed by the European Parliament in October 2002 by a majority of 494 to 42. At the preparatory debates in question, opinion was strongly swayed by the showing of videos and other material from the United States and from New Zealand, much of it being highly specific. The practice also exists in some countries of the former Soviet Union, Latin America and parts of the third world. One cannot predict the future legislative course, but it seems unlikely that in the near future there will be any change in this position.

5.6.   Disease Mongering

A similar subject of much concern to those studying promotional practices is what has been termed "disease mongering" – an attempt to promote the use of particular drugs by emphasising to an indefensible degree their usefulness in circumstances where there may be little sound reason for drug treatment or none at all. The practice takes two principle forms; the first concerns the need for treatment in well-recognized (but not necessarily pathological) states; the other may amount to creation of essentially fictitious diseases. The two approaches are not always readily distinguished. The topic can only be outlined here in the form of a number of examples:

Benzodiazepine tranquillizers and hypnotics: The manner in which these products were publicized from 1960 onwards, leading to dependence on a massive scale, has been outlined in Section 4.3.2 in connection with mental injury. They were recommended for use in a wide range of everyday situations marked by stress, unrest or sleeplessness:

Whatever the indication . . . . Librium (USA, ca. 1960)

It is ten years since Librium became available. Ten anxious years of aggravation and demonstration, Cuba and Vietnam, assassination and devaluation, Biafra and Czechoslovakia. Ten turbulent years in which the world-wide climate of anxiety and aggression has given Librium – with its specific calming action and its remarkable safety margin – a unique and still growing role in helping mankind meet the challenge of a changing world. (Hoffmann-LaRoche, 1970)

"Attention deficit hyperactivity disorder"(ADHD), a condition supposed to occur in children, has been even more violently debated. Particularly in the United States, heavy promotion was primarily responsible for a widespread belief that children experiencing the behavioural traits in question were suffering a mental state demanding treatment with the central stimulant methylphenidate (Ritalin). Promotional measures in support of the wide use of the drug have over a long period included the provision of substantial support to parents' groups representing children with an ADHD diagnosis, advertising to schools and support to the American Psychiatric Association. From 1996 to 2000, prescriptions among American children increased from 1.3 million to some 6 million. There has

208 Chapter 5

been public concern with respect to the drug on several grounds, in the first place because of serious adverse effects, evidence of dependence, induction of suicidal tendencies and increasing misuse. However a substantial group of psychiatric specialists workers have doubted whether ADHD constitutes a genuine mental condition requiring drug treatment, especially since the range of symptoms attributed to the condition is highly variable. In their view the symptoms have behavioural and familial causes which can be corrected and are so dealt with in most other countries. In the United States, a substantial volume of litigation has been brought against the company based on various grounds, including an alleged conspiracy to "invent" ADHD, and lack of research to demonstrate efficacy or long-term safety or to identify a mechanism of action. (Breggin 1998, 2001)

"Social Anxiety Disorder," considered elsewhere in this volume in connection with the SSSI antidepressants (Section 4.3.2) has been described as a fictitious disease, created in order to persuade those who are merely nervous or shy to believe that they are suffering from pathological depression and are in need of drug treatment. (Medawar 2004).

Typical of the examples of direct promotion to the public that has hardened feelings against it outside the USA was a radio advertisement by Wyeth in America for its SNRI antidepressant Effoxor (venlexazine) which was claimed, without substantiation, to be superior to the SSRI agents. In line with the tradition of disease mongering (see below) it began with the passage:

"Hey, how're you feeling these days? OK? Not bad? Come on, is that where you want to be? You know symptoms of depression could be holding you back?"

The FDA ordered Wyeth to withdraw the advertisement in March 2004 on the grounds that it was false and misleading, as well as omitting information on major side effects and contraindications. (Scrip 2004h at p. 12)

Menopausal oestrogen deficiency was initially declared to be an almost universal disorder in post-menopausal women, demanding lifelong oestrogen therapy. The concept was raised in the 1960s by Wilson in America, who associated closely with the former Ayerst company, a producer of equine oestrogens; it was propagated in his book "Feminine Forever" (Wilson 1966). A supposedly altruistic "Wilson Foundation" was established to propagate the notion, and similar publicity tactics were adopted by other oestrogen producers. The use of oestrogens grew rapidly for a generation, with an estimated 51% of menopausal women in the US receiving oestrogens by 1996 (Jolleys and Cleson 1996) but by that time serious doubts were being expressed as to the need for the treatment in all but a minority of women; at the same time serious adverse reactions including endometrial carcinoma were being increasingly documented, with the risks of the treatment apparently exceeding any possible benefits. (Van Hall 1997, Palmlund 1997, Dukes 2004)

It may be doubted whether drug law will succeed in eliminating practices of this type, but experience with litigation suggests that in cases where a disease has been "mongered", misdiagnosis has been encouraged or the incidence of a genuine condition has been grossly exaggerated persons injured in consequence will have a valid cause of action.

5.7.   Financial Incentives

While financial incentives to promote the sale and use of goods are a fundamental feature of a market-based society, there has been a clear reluctance to countenance their use in the field of medicines, where persuasive techniques unrelated to the merits of the product are widely regarded as unacceptable. Within the trade itself quantity discounts and seasonal sales are practised, especially in the area of products for self medication. The accepted norm, even if it is not always respected, is that the use and selection of a prescription medicine in normal society should be determined exclusively by professional assessment of the individual patient's needs.

While promotional techniques within the trade are tolerated, direct incentives to prescribe are not, but in between the two are many other forms of financial manipulation which may or may not be regarded as acceptable, such as support to professional organizations (see 5.10 and 5.11).

Direct incentives to prescribe take various forms; cash bribes may be paid in advance, agreed rewards given on the basis of prescribing records, or mutual arrangements made to defraud the health or insurance system:

In 2001, an Illlinois-based firm marketing an anti-cancer product agreed to a $885 million settlement with federal prosecutors in Boston, who had charged the company with inflating the price of the product and giving "kickbacks" to doctors to encourage them to prescribe it. Federal prosecutors subsequently expanded the investigation, indicting certain employees of the firm as well as doctors who allegedly billed the Medicare system for drugs which they had received as free samples.

In April 2004, eleven employees of a pharmaceutical company were reported to be facing criminal charges in a US district court for allegedly defrauding the US Government of large sums; the charges were *first* that they had conspired to defraud the federal Medicare and Medicaid Programmes by urging doctors to bill them for the free samples which they had received from the company and used to treat patients, *second* that they had provided direct and illegal inducements to doctors (kickbacks) to prescribe a particular drug, and *third* that they had participated in fraudulent drug pricing schemes. Three other employees of the same company had already pleaded guilty. Those now accused argued that the marketing practices in question were common in the drug industry. (Script 2004c at p.16)

In a case brought in the US in 2005, executives of the Serono company were charged with giving financial rewards to doctors in return for prescribing Serostim (rDNA somatropin, i.e. recombinant human growth hormone). As part of the alleged plan, high prescribing physicians were offered an all-expenses-paid-trip with a guest to an International Conference in Cannes, France, in return for writing up to 30 additional prescriptions for Serostim. Each prescription was for a 12-week course of treatment, valued at some $21,000.

Other types of bribe or incentive tend to be considered morally questionable but not directly illegal. Britain's House of Commons Select Committee for example noted a practice whereby a firm might undertake to support a medical charity on condition that a physician involved himself in some way with a drug, e.g. by filling in a questionnaire (HOC 2005 at para 82). Some practices are merely designed to win the physician's sympathy while providing promotional information at the same time; the physician may for example be invited to an attractive dinner or social event where a speaker is invited to describe experiences with a particular product.

Gifts and gratuities not tied to a particular drug, but primarily intended to strengthen the link with the prescriber are common; here there is much discussion as to where the limits of proper practice lie (Kew 2004). The British Medical Journal commented:

Doctors and drug companies must work together, but doctors need not be banqueted, transported in luxury, put up in the best hotels and educated by the drug companies. The result is bias in the decisions made about patient care. (Kew 2004)

Somewhat curiously, when the American Medical Association set out to educate doctors about its ethics guidelines, directing particular against the acceptance of gifts from drug companies, two thirds of the $1 million which the campaign was expected to cost were paid for by the pharmaceutical industry (Okie 2001). However it seems entirely proper that ethical standards in these matters, relating both to the type of incentive regarded as acceptable and the recommended financial limits, should be proposed for each country both by the medical associations and the pharmaceutical industry, perhaps jointly. Existing codes, such as those of the Australian industry (APMA 1994) and WHO (see Table 5.A) suggest some applicable norms. In particular it is usually suggested that gifts linked to brand names should be of token value only, hospitality should be "modest", and that remuneration for services should not be disproportionate to the services rendered.

Finally the issue needs to be settled of financial support by the pharmaceutical industry to medical associations and organizations, either in the form of a general subsidy or payment for particular events, activities or publications. As a rule this is not tied to particular products, though it may clearly be designed to win favour for a firm specialized in a field of interest to the organization concerned (see 5.11). The topic will be further discussed in the closing review in Chapter 12.

5.8. Education

The pharmaceutical industry has often emphasized its role as an educator of health professions or the public. In part it has sought to assume this role by contributing to formal educational programmes either technically or financially, in part by providing materials or programmes of its own. The evident problem which this raises is the likelihood that, since any such contribution is likely to lie within the field of expertise which a firm possesses, it will also be one in which it also has powerful commercial interests. It is too much to expect that these interests will not be reflected in the nature and content of the teaching which it provides or is willing to support. Even where this can be avoided, educational activities will provide the firm with an important means of establishing contact with the current or upcoming professional.

It is probably true to say that at the present time there is something of a cultural gap between countries, and notably between the United States and much of the rest of the western world as regards the acceptable role of commercial (manufacturing and sales) firms in fields such as professional and public education. What is regarded as ethical is in part unavoidably determined by what is feasible. So long as countries with a long tradition of social democracy succeed in maintain adequate resources for all types of education and information the view is likely to pertain that commercial input to these processes is suspect and undesirable. A country with a firm liberal tradition is likely to accept the latter, seeking through the imposition of rules and controls to tackle whatever abuses and problems may result. Public funding for education has in a wide range of countries experienced problems, and with them the growth of a belief that the private sector may be able to supply solutions. Derek Bok, writing of the "commercialization of higher education" (Bok 2003) has noted the increasing breadth of commercial involvement through general and research funding by corporations and the provision of teachers, materials and entire buildings or institutes. Some of these links constitute meaningful forms of collaboration, especially where basic and applied research can be brought together in this way but the involvement of direct teaching at various levels brings with it a real risk that partial interests will come to influence the educational process. The theme goes well beyond the scope of the present study, but it is likely to become more prominent in the near future as government-wide policies need to become attuned to the increasing intermeshing of commerce, education and research.

5.9.   Miscellaneous Forms of Promotion

As in other forms of commerce, explicit advertising of medicines is widely supplemented by various forms of non-explicit advertising to ensure that the name of a firm or a product is repeatedly brought to the attention of those who use it or may influence its sales. The role of small "reminder" advertisements has been noted under Section 5.2.1, but these constitute only one form of supportive promotion. Three of these techniques, all venturing into the borderland of what can be considered ethically permissible, must be touched ion here

(i) *Sponsored papers* Increasingly the medical profession and journals are raising objections to promotion exploiting what appear to be independent sponsored papers in the journals or at congresses but which in fact embody a deliberate promotional message. Some of these papers are indeed the work of independent authors, whose views may genuinely parallel those of a manufacturer (with which he may or may not have financial links). Others however prove to have been heavily influenced or even drafted or financed by a company's promotional department. Closely allied to these are papers produced by physicians or other health workers who have been involved in a firm's research effort but who have agreed that the company shall edit their reports (see Section 4.4.). Critics have noted that over a period of time the number of journal papers favourable to a drug tend to exceed considerably those criticising it in terms of efficacy or safety. This is in large part attributable to the influence exerted by commercial firms on the selection of papers reaching the media and the content of this material. Many of the more reputable journals have now attained a fair balance by requiring authors to provide details of their independence, and of any industrial input prior to assessing or accepting their work. Industrial pressure to secure a favourable spectrum of publications however continues, and it is hard to see that such a practice is in any way beneficial or ethically desirable.

(ii) *Use of patient organizations* While in the United States public opinion on the acceptability of media based "direct to consumer" advertising is divided, there appears to be much greater opposition to other forms of promotion approach to consumers, notably through the recruitment of patient organisations. This has become increasingly common practice and its legal status is dubious:

> A Federal investigation into the sales practices of a company in support of its drug for the treatment of prostatic cancer found documentary evidence that sales representatives had been instructed to seek contacts with organized groups of patients under treatment for this condition. Critics described the approaches as an attempt "to buy goodwill" among patients, which was inexcusable in a setting where many of the latter might be frightened and "easy to take advantage of." The American Cancer Society similarly criticised approaches by sales representatives to patients although it was realised that certain other fields had also used these techniques. In defence of such practices it has been argued by industry and by some practitioners that it is helpful in terms of educating the patients who are to use the product. The executive director of a Prostate Cancer Coalition has stated: "I see it as a business deal. One of the things survivors need most is information, and even if pharmaceutical companies are self-serving and going to make a profit, that information is incredibly helpful" (Cambanis 2002). Andrew Herxheimer in Britain, on the other hand, has sketched some of the risks run by patient organisations which become dependent on industry sources for support, leading them to "misrepresent their agendas." (Herxheimer 2003)

Contact with patient groups is less often undertaken by pharmaceutical companies themselves than by "medical communications agencies" who are specialized in these and other forms of demand creation. Agencies of this type have also been responsible in various countries for campaigns to render the medical or patient world receptive to particular drugs or forms of treatment through developing "key opinion leaders", usually senior physicians, who are commissioned to speak publicly or to medical meetings on topics of importance to particular pharmaceutical companies. As a rule the link between these apparently independent speakers and the companies concerned is not known to the audience; this would appear to constitute a near-breach of the principle – inherent in various codes – that advertising should be recognisable as such.

(iii) *Relationships with other health professions and groups* The principles considered above with respect to the medical profession apply equally strongly to other health professions and groups. Pharmacists, nurses with prescribing rights, medical students and members of various paramedical professions are all the subject of systematic attempts by pharmaceutical companies to cultivate relationships and win favours. Here too there is a need to develop standards which can be agreed and respected by both parties; they are likely to be more effective than an attempt to impose official norms.

5.10. Future Law and Policy

As suggested at various points in this Chapter and elsewhere in this volume, there is now increasing concern in society regarding a number of issues with respect to drugs, especially as regards costs, prices, over-consumption and now also some aspects of marketing; these are interconnected issues. To what extent these will be reflected in policy measures including new forms of law and regulation it is not possible to say, but there is now much pressure to take certain measures to correct some of the less desirable trends which have developed during the last decade. No serious student of the field will seek to cast aside the industry, the advertisers or even the detailman; the need is for firm correction of things which have gone wrong so that all these participants can play a more useful and positive role in society, consistent with the principles of health care, law, drug regulation and ethics. Quite simply, the dependence of the medical profession, and thereby of the pattern of drug utilization in the community, on the manner in which information is presented by the pharmaceutical industry has become a matter of real concern. In some fields, most notably psychiatry, the dependence has in the view of some reputable researchers become alarming, distorting the entire pattern of treatment to a dangerous degree (Breggin 2001, Medawar 2004, Moncrieff et al. 2005). The report of Britain's Select Committee on the Pharmaceutical Industry (HOC 2005) points to an awakening and a political awareness of what is happening. It is hard to see that these matters will remain untouched very much longer by the makers of drug policy.

These issues will be discussed in Chapter 12.

Chapter 6
Pharmaceutical Pricing and Profits

6.1. Pharmaceutical Prices and Controversies

When considering the interaction between the pharmaceutical industry and society at large, it is necessary at many points to pause and consider whether we have sufficient reason to view this industry in a different light from any other. That question needs to be put again when we turn to issues of prices and earnings. In a free market society the prevailing view is that prices should as a rule be determined by supply and demand; there is as a rule no issue of ethics and no need for government interference. All the same, there are in practice many exceptions to that principle. State procurement agencies (for example in the field of defence) have used their leverage to negotiate the prices demanded by their suppliers down to much lower levels than those paid by lesser purchasers. Governments have also interfered in the market where monopoly holders or suppliers of scarce goods have misused their position to price their products out of reach of all but the comfortably rich. All the same, a democratic state will attempt to be reasonable when it does interfere with business; it will seek on the one hand evidence to determine what price appears defensible, bearing in mind the supplier's costs and other commitments; at the same time it will try to assess what value the product can be said to have for the community – in other words what is worth paying.

To a considerable extent, pharmaceuticals do move in a free competitive market, where the purchaser can shop around, seeking the best possible value for his money, and where the supplier sets prices which people are willing to pay, and works as efficiently as possible in order to be able to offer better prices than his competitor.

This ideal picture may be illustrated with an example, in this case analysed purely from the patient's point of view and taking no account of the manufacturer's situation. The "analgesic/anti-inflammatory" family of drugs which relieve pain and inflammation are used in the home as simple headache remedies but also under medical supervision in higher doses for the long-term treatment of conditions such as rheumatoid arthritis.[1] The oldest medicine of this type, still in very wide-spread use, is acetylsalicylic acid (generally known under its original trade name as aspirin). Patents on aspirin have long expired and it is synthesized and processed by many factories across the world. At the present day, a rheumatic patient in Uganda, looking for an aspirin product of guaranteed quality, will per-haps purchase one supplied to pharmacies by the Church-based Joint Medical Stores. (MSH 2004) From the Stores a bag of 1000 tablets of 300 mg each will cost just $1.04, but the price in the retail pharmacy is likely to be doubled, i.e. to $2.08. The retail price thus becomes $0.0021 for each tablet, and assuming a dose for chronic rheumatism as averaging some 50 such tablets weekly the total cost for a week's treatment becomes $0.10, i.e. ten cents of a dollar.

A patient in Britain intending to use aspirin for the same purpose and preferring a low-priced generic product may purchase it from a pharmacy website; he pays about £0.55 for thirty tablets, i.e. the equivalent of US$ 1.37 for the fifty tablets that he needs for a week. Should he prefer a branded product he can obtain fifty plain tablets from a local pharmacy for the equivalent of US$ 2.80, fifty soluble tablets in strip packaging for US$ 3.30 or fifty "caplets" (shaped so that they are easier to swallow) for US$ 3.90, i.e. 39 times the price paid for the same quantity of basic aspirin in Uganda. (P2U Online Pharmacy)

Aspirin remains in widespread use for rheumatoid and other conditions but dur-ing the period 1960–1980 a series of new compounds for these purposes were developed and marketed; the patents subsequently expired. They can have some advantage in that certain patients who experience gastric irritation with aspirin may tolerate these later products better. As of 2005 a Ugandan patient using a typ-ical member of this class, ibuprofen, and allowing once more for the price to be doubled by the pharmacist, would expect to pay the equivalent of 0.6 cents per tablet and (for 50 tablets) would spend in all 30 dollar cents weekly.

His fellow patient in Britain, content with a basic generic ibuprofen, would pay approximately $1.50 for his weekly dose of fifty tablets. He might however prefer alternative forms such as the "spansule" offered by the Goldshield company under the Fenbid name, in which case 50 capsules of equivalent strength would cost him approximately US$ 6.-, i.e 60 times the cost of the basic Ugandan treatment with aspirin.

Late in the 20th century the so-called cox-2 inhibitors were marketed for the same purpose, a prominent member of the group being Celebrex (celecoxib). Some became extremely popular, especially in the United States where they were the subject of intensive television advertising to the public. Still being under patent, celecoxib did not become available through low-cost suppliers in Uganda, but by

---

[1] The figures cited in this illustrative example were taken from publicly available sources but would naturally vary somewhat from time to time and place to place; they may be regarded as typical for this class of products.

2001 the specialty was widely available across the world. In Britain, sixty 100g tablets retailed for £18.34 ($27.50) and provided treatment of rheumatoid arthritis for two weeks, i.e. equivalent to $13.75 weekly or nearly 140 times the price of the basic Ugandan aspirin therapy. The United Kingdom's Committee on Safety of Medicines saw some benefit from the newer treatments to the extent that they would be better tolerated by patients experiencing gastric pain with aspirin; impartial medical authors came to similar conclusions. The new products were not, however, more effective in rheumatism than those a century old, and unlike aspirin the newest generation of products did not provide concurrent protection against cardiovascular disorders. (BNF 2001) Subsequent to 2001, indeed, some drugs in this new class were withdrawn because they presented cardiovascular risks, and similar problems appear to be present to some degree present with others.

The "aspirin" story is intended only to illustrate some issues and conundrums that can arise with drug pricing even in a fairly straightforward situation. Firstly, when stripped off all their overhead costs and exotic presentations, some important medicines can be remarkably cheap to make and financially within reach even of many of the world's poor. Secondly, for a specific type of treatment, an extraordinary range of prices are being charged; a patient who has paid some 140 times the sum that another has laid out may thereby gain some secondary advantages but also run some new risks. Thirdly, as is shown by the example of the cox-2 inhibitors but also of the "caplets", prescribers and patients in industrialized countries can be induced to part with a multiple of the amount they need have paid if they believe this may benefit health or render life a little more comfortable. Fourthly, the reliable and impartial information on the basis of which a proper and critical choice might be made is sometimes available too late (or is presented in too limited a circle) to contribute greatly to the course of events.

The absolute sums in the above example are very small, but they indicate the order of magnitude with which one is dealing. The example is straightforward in that one is dealing with a non-fatal illness and one in which both the doctor and the patient can fairly rapidly determine whether the medicine is relieving the symptoms adequately and is well tolerated, i.e. is providing value for money; if it is not, one can move to another product, perhaps paying a little more. The free market has worked. However, the cost/benefit choice can be much more difficult, as illustrated by an example documented in detail by Dr Jerry Avorn of Boston (Avorn 2004 at pp. 248–257): it is briefly summarized here, and once again examined from the user's angle:

> Patients entering a hospital emergency room with a heart attack have for several decades been treated with an intravenous injection of the enzyme streptokinase. Given promptly it helps to break down the blood clots blocking the coronary arteries,

thereby avoiding damage to the heart muscle and improving the likelihood of survival. Streptokinase costs the hospital some $200 per patient. At a given moment a new product known as tPA (tissue plasminogen activator), developed through recombinant gene technology, becomes available; it has been shown to open the blocked arteries faster and more thoroughly, (GUSTO 1993) but it is not known with any certainty what its ultimate degree of benefit for the patient is; it costs $2000 to treat each patient. In a particular American hospital, which receives a total sum of $4000 from the health care provider for the treatment of a heart attack, the new drug cannot be used unless there is some reasonable certainty that it will be so beneficial as to outweigh the economies that the hospital will be forced to make on other fronts in order to pay for it. The hospital delays a decision, awaiting the outcome of a large comparative study that is being conducted internationally by the tPA manufacturer to compare streptokinase and tPA directly. When the results are published they show that of the patients receiving streptokinase 7.3% die within 30 days, whereas of the patients receiving tPA only 6.3% die within that time; after one year the results still favour tPA. However during the follow-up period strokes occur slightly more often in the tPA group than in those treated with streptokinase and they are more likely to be disabling; there is also a somewhat higher incidence of repeat heart attacks in those receiving tPA. Further study and analysis is then undertaken by the hospital's experts using a computer model and taking all factors including complications into account (Kalish et al. 1995). It leads to the conclusion that use of the newer drug would *on average* extend the active life of a patient by one month; this average would, however, cover a wide range of variation: in reality one patient in a hundred would benefit appreciably but the remaining 99 would experience no difference. The hospital is thus left with a difficult prescribing decision, and one which may need to be taken anew if the prices of streptokinase or tPA are subsequently changed.

These same examples can then be looked at from the manufacturer's point of view. For aspirin and ibuprofen the free market is functioning; prices have become adjusted to the public's willingness or ability to pay. The prices of the cox-2 inhibitors appear to have been several times higher than was justified by their merits as they were ultimately defined, and advertising had to create a market for them that they did not deserve. One must presume, however, that their originators were at the start hoping to deliver something much more beneficial and safer. It would in that case probably have been more ethical to cancel these research projects when it became clear that they would result only in mediocre (and in some instances possibly risky) compounds, instead of seducing society down a wasteful sidetrack, at great expense to all concerned.

The case of tPA is rather different. Without knowing all the facts one must speculate a little: it is not unlikely that one is dealing here with an ambitious and probably costly venture in biotechnology. If that venture is to continue and deliver products capable of saving significantly more lives it could merit support. It is arguable that where such perspectives appear to be dawning, society should do its best to identify them and stretch its resources to the limit to ensure that the work continues, though it is equally evident that this will only be possible in highly selected cases.

All this would suggest that in its own interests, both as regards immediate economies and the long-term development of better drugs, society should approach the issue of drug pricing with much more care and more selectively than it has often done to date. Some of the approaches to drug pricing systems considered later in this chapter show that this is possible.

6.2. The Level of Spending

The amount of money spent on drugs varies greatly from one country to another. In part this reflects differences in consumption levels but also differences in pricing.

> A 1992 study showed that annual expenditure on medicines per head of population at that time ranged from US$412 in Japan to $2 or less in Bangladesh and parts of Subsaharan Africa. At the middle of the range, per capita expenditure was $97 in the United Kingdom and $89 in Norway. (Ballance et al. 1992) At the end of the century these discrepancies had still not been reduced but the absolute levels had risen, e.g. in Britain from $97 to $244 (Bannenberg 2000, OECD 2000, WHO 2000b, d, Scrip 2000).

Medicines cost the National Health Service in England some £7.5 billion every year or some 12% of its total budget, 80% of this being spent on branded (patented) products. In addition £1.8 billion annually is now spent on over-the-counter ("self-medication") medicines (PAGB 2004). The proportion of total health expenditure devoted to drugs is in some countries higher but often disputed because of the manner in which it is calculated; it is however generally much higher in Southern than in Northern Europe, e.g. 26.9% in Portugal versus 9.5% in Denmark (OECD 2000).

Absolute prices of individual drugs vary considerably from country to country, in part under the influence of price control systems:

> In 2000 the Australian Government's Productivity Commission compared manufacturers' supply prices in eight countries for 150 pharmaceuticals. Prices in the U.S.A. were between 80% and 160% higher than in Australia, while prices in Canada, the United Kingdom and Sweden were some 50% higher. Prices in France, Spain and New Zealand were similar to those in Australia. (PCGA 2001)

Finally, the introduction of new and more expensive pharmaceuticals, combined with growth in demand from aging populations, has caused government outlays on pharmaceuticals to increase rapidly in most OECD countries:

> Between 1990 and 1997, a number of OECD countries experienced average annual nominal growth rates in public expenditure on pharmaceuticals of eight per cent or more, including the US (13.5 per cent), Australia (11.4 per cent), Denmark (11.1 per cent), Austria (9.5 per cent), Ireland (9.0 per cent), Japan (8.0 per cent) and the UK (8.0 per cent). (OECD 2000) In Britain, the rate of NHS spending on medicines has risen much faster than the general cost of living. (HOC 2005)

One striking factor in the development of prices has been the arrival of biotechnology products. Though at present used only on a limited scale they introduce a new dimension into price comparisons which could become much more significant in the next decade.

> In the U.S.A. in 2004, Visudyne, a drug for macular degeneration, cost $2,500–4,000 for a course of treatment. Zevalin and Bexxar, each used in non-Hodgkins lymphoma, could cost more than $20,000 per dose. Of a number of drugs available to treat colorectal cancer, Avastin cost $4,400 monthly and Erbitux $10,000 monthly (Warner 2004). These are naturally serious conditions which can justify exceptional expenditure.

Concern both about the absolute level of prices and about price increases have tended, at a time of economic slowdown, to lead to increasingly tense confrontations between Government health agencies and industry regarding the prices of new medicines; even in the United States insurers are commonly either refusing to meet such expenses or introducing stringent assessments to determine which drugs they will fund.

Medicines are generally regarded as costly items, and often as being indefensibly expensive, even in industrialized countries. Critics point to the consistently high level of profit delivered by the science-based pharmaceutical industry, even in periods of economic malaise, question the discrepancy which often exists between the prices demanded and the community's ability to pay, and cite evidence that the prices asked are disproportionate to the costs involved in creating and producing medicines. The industry defends its pricing policies to a large extent on the basis of the costs of research and development, (Teather and Tomlinson 2004) including the work involved in meeting regulatory demands.

6.3. The Manufacturer's Costs

Manufacturing The most obvious question that arises when the retail price of any product is critically assessed is what it cost to produce it.

Where drugs are concerned, that aspect of costing is hardly critical. The figures for manufacturing costs are not published, but the fact that, once developed, medicines are generally remarkably cheap to manufacture, is common knowledge among those who have worked in the industry and is confirmed by the experience of efficient generic producers and of outside observers. (Guilloux and Moon 2000, Carter 2003). WHO itself has calculated that most patented medicines are sold at 20–100 times their "marginal" costs.

> Certain pharmaceuticals are said to have a prohibitively high inherent cost, but that is not proven. The example has been cited of insulin, which even at the best generic prices is still out of reach for the poorest, for whom diabetes remains a fatal disease. Even here, however, it is not clear that, if synthetic human insulin were universally used, the cost would remain at this level.

The manufacturing cost of the newest biotechnological products is entirely unclear, especially where they are still being produced on a very small scale and covering the startup costs of new factories, but the justification for charging $3,750 for a course of treatment with AmBisome in July 2004 (Healy 2004) seems at least questionable, especially when following negotiation the price in Sudan was reduced to $350.

> "You told me just now that a major producer of oral contraceptives has recently offered his product to a developing market at 1% of the U.S. price. I don't know his figures but it would more or less tally with my recollection from my factory days. We had only been in production with our oral contraceptive for a year in the old high dose, and yet the production manager calculated that he was still paying his chemical plant a lot less for the twenty tablets in each bottle than he was paying the glassworks for the bottle itself. The pharmacy price at that time, in the late sixties, was still about twenty dollars for a month's supply." (Interview 33)

Even after making allowance for wholesale and retail margins, these estimates do not tally with the figures to be found in the US Security and Exchange Commission filings (Laing 2001a, see also tabulation in Chapter 7) which set production costs at from 18% to 28% of the manufacturer's revenue, but it is uncertain what secondary costs may have been included under the SEC headings. It is striking how drastically prices can be reduced when special supply contracts are signed, even with health systems in western countries and more especially with donors supplying the third world (see Chapter 8); finally, the costs of generic copies of good quality are far lower than those of the original specialities.

The costs of *research and development*, commonly claimed by the industry to be the main element in drug pricing, are proportionally much less than is asserted (see Chapter 7) and are much outweighed by share buybacks and dividends but also by the sums listed in the SEC reports under "marketing and administration".

> A Bank of America analyst noted in October 2004 that over an 18 month period the nine largest pharmaceutical firms had spent some $56 billion on dividends and buybacks. For Pfizer the total was $22 billion, some 210% of the sum spent on research. Merck returned $7.3 billion, about 143% of research spending. (Teather 2004)

Marketing – primarily advertising – can account for a very high proportion of the manufacturer's total costs. The sums expended are so variable that average figures are meaningless, but in 2000 the total marketing costs of drugs in the US alone probably exceeded US$40 billion. (Goozner 2004 at p. 230)

It is abundantly clear that a high proportion of the money expended by a pharmaceutical manufacturer is not related to activities which will be generally regarded as serving the interest of the community. While industry itself claims for example that advertising and promotion at current levels are essential to maintain a profitable level of demand and production, thus resulting in economies, a manufacturer may clearly find himself in a weak position when the figures are challenged, for example by a health fund seeking an explanation for the price.

6.4. The Ethics of Pricing and Profits

Is it unethical to charge a higher price for a drug than is strictly speaking justified? Experts on business ethics are likely to answer that question differently depending on the environment in which it is put. The notion of setting the price of a product at the highest level that the market will bear and maximalizing profit at all times is widely cherished at a time when many national communities are passing through a strongly liberal phase, yet the resistance which has begun to grow to extreme medicine prices seems to show a trend away from the extreme liberal view. There have been situations in which a medicinal product can be produced only on an uneconomically small scale because there is a shortage of starting materials – that was for a time the case with natural human growth hormone – and in such an instance it will unavoidably be unaffordable for all but a few. It could also apply to the start-up phase in producing a biotechnological preparation. In many other situations, however, the manufacturer has a choice of approaches; financially there may be little difference between selling 1,000 doses at $5,000 each or 20,000 doses at $300 each, and where one is dealing with a uniquely valuable drug it could be argued that there is a moral obligation to proceed as soon as possible to the second alternative and beyond. It is hard to see that the pharmaceutical industry has always respected that principle. The attitude adopted to the supply of AIDS/HIV drugs to the developing world (Chapter 8) until extreme pressure was exerted on the industry was surely reprehensible in the extreme.

A related question concerns profits earned in the pharmaceutical sector. Are excessive profits in this business unethical? Again it is difficult to point to ethical norms which apply or could be applied in this field. The pharmaceutical industry has vigorously maintained the point of view that, as a business which must in competition with others attract and reward capital it cannot in any sense act as a charity. The challenge will be to identify means of defining "fairness" as regards corporate earnings and profits in the health field. It is notable that in its dealings with the industry in Britain, the Government has included an examination of profits alongside that of prices.

> The United Kingdom's Pharmaceutical Price Regulation Scheme restricts the profit which a company is permitted to make on the National Health Service to a maximum of 21% of the capital employed. The actual figures available in 2001 showed a return on capital of 21% of sales through this channel, which is substantially less than the average for British industry as a whole; firms are as a rule required to tender for sales to hospitals, resulting in discounts on the retail price. (ABPI 2001) (Editorial 1997)

It is not impossible that the gradual emergence of non-profit drug development groups in this sector (Chapter 7) will lead to a gradual shift in moral perceptions, bringing them more into line with the concept of duty to the community (Chapter 2).

Finally, it is disappointing to encounter in the legal and general literature so many reports of instances where individual companies or groups of firms have sought improperly to obtain excessive payments from public health systems. The complexity of many price control, insurance and reimbursement arrangements provides numerous opportunities for malpractice that may well be overlooked, but some instances are being challenged at law. A single instance may be quoted:

> In the State of Nevada a suit was filed on behalf of the State, third party payors and several thousand patients against 13 manufacturers, most of them multinationals, challenging their practice of charging for drugs supplied under the Medicaid system at "Average Wholesale Price" (AWP). The complaint alleged that, in many instances, the purported "AWP" reported by the defendant manufacturers bore only a minimal relationship to the prices actually paid by physicians

or pharmacies and was "made up" by corporate pricing committees literally out of "thin air" for the purpose of manipulating pharmaceutical markets and increasing market share.[2] Similar suits were expected in other states.

6.5.   How does Society Control the Prices of Medicines?

When the above question is asked, the first answer, however true, is eminently unsatisfactory from the society's point of view. It is simply the case that, despite considerable concern in the last decade regarding the prices charged for medicines, some countries – with the United States as the foremost among them – do not at the national level formally control drug prices at all. Vigorous opposition by the industry association over many years has prevented any federal form of control being established, the consequence being an unusually high price level as compared with that in other countries; alternative means are now coming into place to keep costs in hand on certain fronts, notably through supply agreements with health providers and measures taken by individual states. It does, however, now appear that when a national government fails to protect the public against excessive price levels the Courts may prove willing to uphold action at a lower level:

> In the U.S.A., where an increasing number of individual states have introduced measures to reduce prescription drug prices for their residents, these have been challenged by industry, but apparently without success. In May 2003 the U.S. Supreme Court rejected a challenge by the nationwide industry association PhRMA to declare unconstitutional a Maine programme that reduces prescription drug prices. The programme was alleged to discriminate against interstate commerce and to be pre-empted by the federal Medicaid law. The Court however recognized the right of states to reject public programmes that may be profitable for certain corporations, but are costly for government.[3]

The industry's mantra is that competition keeps prices in check. Most certainly competition can constrain prices in many commercial markets, but where drugs are concerned direct competition from fully comparable products is markedly inhibited by the ability of the primary manufacturer to obtain protection for his product over a long period of

---

[2] Nevada State District Court. (2002): *Average Wholesale Price Drug Litigation. Plaintiffs vs Abbott Laboratories Inc. and others.* Suit filed January 16, 2002.

[3] *Pharmaceutical Research and Manufacturers of America v. Walsh*, 2003 U.S. LEXIS 4056 (United States Supreme Court, 5/19/03).

time, usually in excess of 20 years; (Section 2.2.4) a low price "generic" copy may therefore only emerge at a moment when the product has largely been superceded by an alternative medicine, claiming yet greater superiority over what has gone before and itself again possessing lengthy patent protection. Full and unrestrained competition between entirely similar products may only be unleashed late in their lives.

In many countries outside the US, a series of mechanisms have been created to ensure that the prices of medicines remain to some extent under the control of the community. Legal provisions establish procedures by which prices may be assessed or negotiated and ordain some of the principles according to which the prices of medicines may be evaluated. (WHO/EURO 2003)

At an earlier phase in the history of drug regulation, the price of a new medicine was in some countries set as an integral part of its evaluation for admission to the market. This had the disadvantage of putting price evaluation in the hands of a body that was primarily constituted to assess scientific rather than economic evidence; it also resulted in delay to the drug approval process. In France, the Government still negotiates the overall price of a new drug before it is permitted on the market. At the present day the two processes are now however in most countries divorced and handled by two different bodies. Price assessment is as a rule the task of a specialized committee of the national health service or the public insurance system and its decisions are applied only to the public supply of drugs, prices in the private sector remaining uncontrolled. Some of the methods which have been used are briefly outlined here, insofar as they relate to manufacturers' prices; complementary means of cost containment are also in use, involving for example control of wholesale and retail margins. However methodical the approaches adopted, all ultimately involve a degree of subjectivity and negotiation between the parties. Manufacturers may find themselves dealing with a public health system purchasing for much of the population or with a series of independent insurers or care organizations, each seeking separate agreement on prices and conditions of supply.

6.5.1.   Calculation of a "fair" supply price

Various attempts have been made to find an objective basis for calculating a price which can be regarded as providing the manufacturer with a "fair" price for his medicine. An ambitious scheme introduced at one time in Italy used a complex mathematical formula based on the various forms of expense incurred by the manufacturer; it did not prove effective in use since the data required were rarely complete and they were as a rule impossible to verify. The same problem arises with various other "cost-plus" systems now in use. As Rietveld *et al.* have pointed out:

> Costs and margins are not independent of company policies; the basic costs of production, research and marketing may vary considerably between companies, Where the company with which one is dealing is a daughter company of a multi-national concern, it can be well-nigh impossible for the outsider to obtain any reliable overview of where and how costs are being incurred and profits taken. Furthermore there is the problem of allocating overhead and research costs to individual products." (Rietveld and Haaijer-Ruskamp 2002)

6.5.2. *Reference pricing* (Huttin 2002)

This method, popular in European countries, assumes that a number of products are therapeutically identical, and that the acceptable price of any new member of the group must be reasonable as compared with the prices charged for the others. A "reference price" is set for the group as a whole, e.g. antirheumatics or beta-blockers, which may comprise pharmaceuticals having an identical or closely similar structure and/or pattern of pharmacological activity. In the Netherlands, groups are constituted on the basis of therapeutic substitution, i.e. any member of the group is regarded as reasonably capable of replacing any other. The government agency concerned then sets a single reference (benchmark) price for the entire reference group; in some systems the reference price is set at the level of the lowest-priced item in the group, while in others it is based on the mean or average price or on international comparisons. Depending on the national procedure, each manufacturer may then be required to charge the reference price or less for his product, or alternatively the manufacturer's preferred prices may be maintained but with the provision that the insurance or reimbursement system will cover no more than the reference price, leaving the patient to pay any excess.

There are variants on the system; the reference may, for example, include only branded specialities with similar components or may be limited to specialities and generic equivalents all having the same component. Whatever the exact rules of such a system it constitutes from the point of view of the authorities a sharp deterrent to high prices. A deficiency of the system, as industry has commonly objected, is its starting assumption that all the drugs in the group are indeed of equal efficacy and usefulness; this approximates to the truth, but it may be unfair to a truly superior newcomer;

it certainly provides little encouragement to any firm to concentrate its research efforts on developing substantially better drugs than those that have gone before.

6.5.3. *Economic evaluation of prices*

This type of regulatory price control seeks to relate the price of a drug to its value to the patient and the community, while making some allowance for the needs of the manufacturer. The impact of the treatment may be measured purely in terms of finance; costs allowed for may then include those associated with follow-up visits to and from physicians, the costs of other pharmaceuticals used (for example, to treat side effects), hospital out-patient visits, diagnostic and therapeutic procedures in hospital, and in-patient stays in hospital associated with the use of the product. Other parameters chosen, depending on the nature of the drug, may include quality of life years gained ("QUALYS"), the estimated gain in working time as a result of treatment, and the overall reduction in mortality. The four main forms of economic evaluation are regarded as comprising:

a. *cost-benefit analysis*, which involves placing an artificial monetary value on such items as health benefits
b. *cost-minimisation analysis*, which compares the costs of two or more therapies with identical outcomes (e.g. cure of an infection)
c. *cost-effectiveness analysis*, used where therapies have the same outcome but the outcome can be achieved to different degrees; this aims to identify the most efficient therapy, i.e. the medicine that minimizes the cost per unit of outcome
d. *cost-utility analysis*, used to compare therapies that have multiple outcomes which may be achieved to different degrees. The quality of life is explicitly quantified and included in this analysis; rather than using a monetary value, outcomes are expressed using a measure of the improvement in health status.

Several countries at the present time request an applicant to supply in advance an economic evaluation of the type needed for assessment, and are willing to discuss in advance the approach which may be most appropriate for a particular type of medicine. Companies have however often found it advantageous to perform such an evaluation voluntarily before entering into price negotiations, even where the method is not formally required by law or regulation; an economic evaluation can also prove helpful if a firm considers that it has reason to apply for an increase in the price of a drug during its market life.

Perhaps the most sophisticated approach to price determination, including economic assessment, is that which has operated for more than 50 years in Australia, where the Pharmaceutical Benefits Scheme was established in 1948/49. The scheme purchases more than 90% of all prescription medicines from the manufacturers at negotiated prices after a thorough evaluation of each drug to determine both its eligibility for the scheme and its anticipated value in medical and economic terms; the medicines are then made available at heavily state-subsidized prices to patients holding prescriptions. The scheme has resulted in low prices to Australian consumers, especially for older drugs, but there has been strong opposition to it by international manufacturers. According to Harvey (Harvey 2001), individual pharmaceutical companies have sued members of the Scheme's Advisory Committee over decisions not to list drugs such as sildenafil (Viagra). Some have successfully lobbied the Federal Health Minister to replace members of the Advisory Committee considered antagonistic to industry; an effort was also made to disrupt full operation of the Scheme under the US–Australian Free-Trade Area Agreement. This complex but transparent and effective approach used in Australia to contain prices is now being widely studied elsewhere, particularly because it appears to work to the benefit of society while providing protection from what might be considered instances of profiteering, and fairly rewarding the manufacturer who has both developed a superior drug and provided sound scientific evidence for this superiority.

6.5.4.   Control of profits and expenses

Where the setting of fair prices for individual drugs raises insuperable difficulties, legislators have sought to achieve cost containment at a higher level, namely by seeking to examine the overall expenditure of a company and to limit the use of funds in particular directions, namely to conduct advertising or to augment profits. Such an external audit is in principle attainable when dealing with a small company, producing and selling only within a particular country. However, as discussed in Section 2.9, a high proportion of major drugs are provided at the present day by multinational or transnational corporations. It is to all intents and purposes impossible to draw up a full and fair overview of the business of such a transnational which may be manufacturing in 20 countries, selling in more than a hundred, and conducting research on several continents. No national pricing agency would in any case have the authority to demand the data or the capability to analyse it, assess it and draw logical conclusions from it as to the admissibility of the firm's profits in a particular market.

What has been achieved is a limited measure of state influence on the budgets of some companies which, while working globally, have a preponderant influence in a particular market. The United Kingdom has for a number of years contrived in this way to contain to some degree the earnings of primarily British manufacturers when they supply medicines to the National Health Service.

6.6. Differential and Equity Pricing

Because incomes, costs of living and the funding of public health systems can differ substantially, even for example between member states of the European Union, the pharmaceutical industry has as a rule maintained differential prices between them, essentially seeking to secure in each market the best price that can be agreed for a drug without risking any substantial loss of sales to a competitor. This is a logical expression of a free international market, and since it apportions the burden of drug costs according to wealth it should operate in a reasonably fair manner to all concerned, though the prices in each market are also affected by price approval systems and other factors. The "parallel import" phenomenon which has emerged as a result of differential pricing is reviewed in Section 6.7.

The term "equity" pricing is best used for the system of extreme price differentials adopted for some developing countries or in certain emergency situations; it is considered separately in Chapter 8.

6.7. Parallel Importation and the Question of Re-importation

Although parallel importation is not a process in which the pharmaceutical industry itself is actively involved, it is a consequence of the industry's use of differential pricing, and the research-based industry has on various occasions sought to limit or prevent it. It has also become the subject of regulation.

The practice first came prominently to the fore in northern Europe in or about 1970; many products manufactured by multinational firms, imported into the Netherlands and elsewhere and registered there by their officially designated agents or subsidiaries, were generally sold in these countries at a considerably higher price than in southern Europe. A number of independent pharmacists and traders therefore sought to develop a profitable business by importing batches of these products from Italy, Spain and other low-cost countries and selling them in the north at prices lower than those charged by the designated agents. They claimed initially that since the products were essentially the same as those already registered under the Medicines Act by the agents, they could be deemed to have been assessed and approved at the national level and could therefore be distributed under the existing medicines licences. The agents promptly sought to prevent import under their licences, objecting that the "parallel" products could well differ as regards packaging texts and sometimes in other respects, and must therefore be the subject of entirely separate assessment and licensing. Having sought guidance within the European Union, the Netherlands Regulatory Agency ruled that the "parallel" products would require a separate form of licence; such a licence could be issued provided there was documentary evidence that the products were essentially identical, and on condition that the packages included appropriate labelling and information material as required under the original licence. The practice of parallel importation has since become widespread, but the pattern of trade varies from time to time according to changes in pricing and inflationary trends.

Official attitudes to parallel trading have varied. From the point of view of health law, the emphasis has consistently been placed on the need for evidence that the originally licensed product and its parallel version are essentially identical in composition and properties, i.e. a requirement similar to that set for generic medicines though generally simpler to meet. National pricing agencies and health services concerned with insurance or reimbursement have on the other hand proved eager to make use of parallel products in the interests of economy.

> Licences for parallel imported products have been refused in those instances where significant differences have been found between the products, e.g. where the content or concentration of the active material differ from those in the licensed form. Marginal differences, such as the use of a different colouring or solvent, have generally been tolerated.

The European Union has favoured parallel importation of medicines as a means of encouraging competition and progressively harmonizing prices within Europe, and its policy has as a rule followed the original line laid down in the Netherlands, both as regards product identity[4] and the need to supply appropriate packaging texts. As regards the identity of the registered and the parallel versions of a product, the European view is liberal: provided there is a documentary assurance that the parallel product

---

[4] *Smith and Nephew* case (C-201/94).

is "sufficiently similar" to that which was the subject of the original licence it can be imported, even if it should prove that it was not manufactured at the same site:

> The European Court of Justice delivered an opinion in April 2004 in a case involving manufacture at different sites.
> The pharmaceutical company Chiesi had a marketing authorisation for Jumex (selegiline) in Italy, while Movergan was selling an identical selegiline-based product under a different name under a marketing licence issued in Germany. The parallel importer Kohlpharma now sought to market Jumex in Germany but benefiting from the licence held by Movergan for its own product. The German Health Authority rejected the application since Jumex and Movergan did not have the same origin. Kohlpharma appealed on the grounds that the two products were not significantly different and that there was no threat to public health by using one rather than the other; the case was ultimately referred to the European Court of Justice for a preliminary ruling. In a non-binding opinion the Court took the view that the application for parallel import of Jumex could validly refer to the licence issued for a product in Germany provided the two proved to be "sufficiently similar."[5]

If this ruling were to be applied to generic drugs as well as to parallel imports it could open up very wide perspectives for intermediate traders.

Case law on the issue of repackaging is still ongoing within the European Union. To date, judicial opinion is that within the European Union parallel importers are allowed to repackage branded goods provided that five conditions are fulfilled:

- The repackaging is objectively necessary in order to enter the market (e.g. because of the language or content of the text).
- The repackaging cannot adversely affect the original condition of the product.
- It is stated on the new packaging by whom the product has been repackaged and manufactured.
- The presentation of the repackaged product is not such as to be liable to damage the reputation of the trademark and its owner.
- The owner of the trademark receives prior notice before the repackaged product is put on sale.

---

[5] Judgement of the ECH, 1st April 2004 (Case C-112/02 - *Kohlpharma GmbH v Bundesrepublik Deutschland*).

Multinational producers have sought in various ways to prevent or discourage parallel importation of their products which would be detrimental to them financially, some such claims being phrased in terms of the public health interest. A recent case in the European Court of Justice, though it can be interpreted in various ways, could suggest that the Commission will reconsider its attitude to multinationals who attempt to counter parallel imports:

> As the price of Adalat, a Bayer product, varied markedly between Spain/France and the United Kingdom, parallel importers were found to be buying supplies in France and Spain for resale in Britain. This deranged Bayer's distribution arrangements and the company therefore decided to reapportion the supplies delivered to their various national wholesalers so that they would meet only estimated local needs and obstruct parallel importation. The European Commission decided that this practice, accepted by Bayer wholesalers, constituted an anti-competitive agreement, which would breach the former Article 85 (now 81) of the EC Treaty, and it was therefore prohibited. On appeal by Bayer the Court of First Instance cancelled the Commission's decision. According to the judgement the Bayer policy was purely unilateral, and while the wholesalers had passively accepted it there was no evidence to suggest that they had positively adhered to it. There had been no contract as understood in Article 81, the company did not ban exports by use of threats or penalties, nor did it establish a system for monitoring the actual destination of the Adalat supplies.[6]

The fact must not be overlooked that the parallel importation of a drug can sometimes be challenged under general provisions of commercial and penal law which are not specifically designed to relate to medicines. In Europe this may be the case as regards goods imported from outside the European Economic Area.

> In Spain, Article 274 of the Penal Code, which came into force on October 1st 2004, prohibits parallel importation of goods of any type with reference to trademark law. If a trademark owner has not agreed to the importation of its products into the European Economic Area (EEA) such importation is deemed illegal and the importer can be fined and gaoled for a period of up to two years. These penalties apply even in the event that the products in question have been bought legally in non-EEA countries.

Re-importation The issue of re-importation has arisen prominently in the United States where pharmaceutical prices are substantially higher than in Canada. Many American residents have therefore had their prescriptions

---

[6] Judgement of the European Court of Justice, January 6th 2004 *(Commission v Bayer, C-2/01, C-3/01).*

filled in Canada, either through personal travel, internet ordering or use of an intermediary, thereby saving 30–50% on the price paid. Where a product of American origin is involved this involves re-importation; where a European or other foreign product is involved the issue is one of parallel import. The practice has been firmly opposed and challenged in law by the US companies concerned, and pressure has been exercised in political circles to seek support for the industry's view, the argument being that, although the goods are of American origin they could have been contaminated during their sojourn in a foreign country. By 2003, drugs to the value of $1.1 billion annually were being brought into the USA in this way, yet the practice remains strictly speaking illegal under a 1987 Congressional decision that drugs shall be imported only by their manufacturers or licence holders.

> A series of multinational firms have attempted to prevent reimportation into the US by imposing restrictive trading measures. GlaxoSmithKline in Britain required Canadian pharmacies, as a condition of receiving shipments, not to sell Glaxo drugs to the United States. Eli Lilly informed their wholesalers that they would be violating their contracts if they supplied Canadian pharmacies that did business with the United States. Other firms took similar steps. (Angell 2004 at pp. 223–224)

> It may be noted that even some persons within American industry have criticised the attempt to prohibit drug purchases from Canada, as "misleading and immoral." To quote one internal critic: "It strikes me as immoral to limit trade to Canada under the guise that it is unsafe, The big safety issue is people not taking drugs - people having heart attacks because they can't afford to stay on cholesterol-lowering medication." (Rost 2004)

Popular protest against these obstructive moves in the US has at the time of writing reached the point where re-importation from Canada seems likely to be legalized in one way or another. There is however likely to be further opposition by the major pharmaceutical companies, arguing in particular at the political level that some drugs imported in this way might prove to be counterfeit or could present unknown health risks. Two laws to allow personal imports from Canada were indeed passed in 2000 and 2003 but have to date remained in a state of suspended animation for this reason (see Angell 2004).

Diversion of supplies   A situation somewhat similar to that of parallel importation applies where a firm has deliberately provided medicines to poor populations at extremely low prices in the framework of humanitarian projects or development aid (see Section 6.5) and these are improperly diverted and resold elsewhere. It is widely considered both in business and in government that this practice is improper and illegal in view of the humanitarian objective of the special pricing; most such supplies have indeed been provided under special contracts according to which diversion is strictly prohibited.

6.8. Future Approaches to Pricing

The current means by which medicine prices are reached in most of the industrialized world effectively involves a series of complementary mechanisms, each of which can be of value in some or all situations. Some have not proven to be realistic, notably those which seek to use internal company data on costs and expenses. Others are somewhat arbitrary, making the price of one drug dependent on the price of others. In many cases some attempt is made to ensure that competition is capable of keeping prices at a reasonable level. A number of countries use multiple mechanisms. Others simply rely on unstructured negotiation with manufacturers, either at the national level or decentralized. There are some striking gaps in the existing systems – failure to control the prices of generic drugs often means that they deliver far less benefit to the community than they should, with the bulk of the rewards going to the intermediate traders involved (LSE 2003). The most promising methods are those, such as used in a particularly ambitious form in Australia, which seek to estimate the monetary value of a medicine to the community; by providing the greatest rewards to the most innovative manufacturers they stimulate progress towards better therapy.

Pricing is one of the situations where it is difficult to build an efficient relationship between a large number of nation-states, each using its own approach, and a relatively small number of transnational firms. The former find themselves in a relatively weak situation, the latter find themselves confused and burdened by the multiplicity of different demands. While the pricing situation differs greatly from one country to another, it could in the future be much more meaningful for groups of countries with a similar developmental and economic situation to deal jointly with suppliers of the principal drugs to find a common approach to the pricing of medicines.

The issue of pricing in developing countries is considered in Chapter 8.

Chapter 7
The Industry as Innovator

7.1. Innovation and Duty

Most considerations of the pharmaceutical research process approach the topic from a *technical* or *managerial* point of view. The *Law* does not determine where or how drug research should be carried out or in what manner it should be funded, except perhaps where it allocates some statutory task in this area to a National Health Institute. Ethics and human rights have usually entered into the debate only in connection with detailed issues such as the conduct of studies in animals (Section 9.1) or human subjects (Section 9.2). The overall situation of research in this sector at the present day does, however, raise a major ethical and policy issue that needs to be examined objectively and without prejudice. An acute controversy has developed, facts have been selected and distorted to support diametrically opposed points of view and it has become unclear to many whether industrial drug research is on the right course for the coming century or not. To understand the issue without acquiring bias, one must go back to some basics.

Law and ethics are both facets of the processes which govern (or should govern) human behaviour, and to examine them one can well begin by considering briefly why the behaviour occurs in the first place. Why is pharmaceutical research in industry carried out, and what determines its nature? There are obviously several answers depending on the level at which the question is put, and all of them may be relevant; in a multidisciplinary organization such as a science-based pharmaceutical corporation, decisions influencing research are being taken continuously, from many sides and at all levels.

At the level of the *individual researcher*, there is often a simple answer as to the starting point for research. It may be that, as a young academic with some post-graduate experience, he is quite simply fascinated by the entire process of discovery, he wants to take part in it and sees an opportunity in industry, but still has a largely open mind as to the direction which it will take. He is aware that, depending on his training, he may, on a given morning, be asked to introduce a 17-beta-methyl group into a steroid molecule, examine the kinetics of such a molecule in rats or turn a bare chemical compound into a dispersible tablet that can be taken by a patient. Making a specific contribution of this type may for him be as satisfying and complete an experience as another individual might find in cutting a diamond or planting a tree. This type of scientist *pur sang* – and he indeed exists – may find that he has no great need to concern himself with the input of his colleagues working in the next building on other aspects of the same project. His personal work ethic is to do his specific job well, write his report, clean his laboratory bench and then prepare for the next set of instructions to come his way. His is the extreme case: the pure scientist, performing good technical work and not over-inclined to look further. He is a pillar of the establishment, but he is not the typical young researcher in the pharmaceutical industry.

In reality, most scientists joining such an organization are both expected and anxious to think more broadly than this; an environment in which chemists, pharmacists, medical doctors and members of a dozen other disciplines work in complementary units alongside each other in any case stimulates a coalescence of thinking. A programme that has apparently failed to deliver the new family of anti-hypertensive drugs that had been envisaged may be slated for cancellation until a thoughtful biochemist notices that some of the new substances have an unusual effect on brain cell cultures and might conceivably play a useful role in atherosclerosis or senility. These things happen, with serendipity and lateral thinking on occasion playing as great a role as straight scientific logic. The new hypothesis may itself ultimately prove unproductive, but it could in turn sow the seed for a related innovation, which the company had never originally intended or expected to produce; yet 5 years later, when a breakthrough treatment for concussion reaches the market and the share prices leap upwards it may prove very difficult to recall precisely how the innovation came about. No personal ethic is involved except the determination to do one's best and the belief of an enlightened research management that innovative ideas need all the space that one can allow them.

If the urge to discover and to think creatively, wherever it may lead, is one factor powering innovation, a second is the determination to plan logical approaches to well-defined goals and to carry them through so long as they hold some promise. Good management alone demands that the bulk of a research programme be built up in this sober manner, without leaving too much space to serendipity. Here it is, however, that commercial, scientific, ethical and financial ideals can soon conflict. It is evident that the greatest financial rewards will be delivered if one can create a "blockbuster" drug;[1] that, however, is likely to demand much time and heavy investment, and when working in this way along the frontiers of science to find something truly novel, one can encounter unforeseen complications (such as side effects or interactions) as well as a fair risk of failure. However tantalising the prospect of breakthroughs may be, there is therefore a constant temptation to devote a substantial proportion of the research budget to devising drugs that are no more than slight variants on existing compounds, but that will probably be simple and quick to develop and are unlikely to deliver unpleasant surprises. The commercial rewards of these "me-too" drugs when they reach the marketplace are likely to be less, but so as a rule are the risks, and there is always the small hope that even among these unexciting compounds, one may find the occasional jewel. That hope is, however, as a rule indeed slim, and the "me-too" drugs are those which are least likely to be viewed as conferring benefit on society. Is it then unethical to produce "me-too" drugs? Some are naturally not deliberately cast in this mould; they are drugs developed with high ambitions which simply did not make the grade. But when one sets out to create a "me-too" by taking an existing product and manipulating the molecule ever so slightly, one is at least keeping the pipeline filled and the factory wheels turning. It is only when the potboilers assume a disproportionate place in the work programme that the ethicist may ask pointed questions.

The ultimate face of a company's research and development (R&D) programme is therefore likely to be largely the resultant of an attempt to balance out these three competing approaches; alongside the daring hunt for blockbusters one will need to find capacity to create some less exciting items and retain sufficient flexibility to profit promptly from incidental, serependitious brainwaves. Even that is not the entire picture. An R&D division will also be expected to deal with some problems arising with older products which may need to be reformulated or upgraded and to evaluate ongoing projects offered on licence or on collaborative terms by other firms or institutions. Against this complicated background, one now needs to consider how well the industry is currently serving the ideal expressed by Harvey Bale (Bale 2005) that "The primary societal responsibility of the pharmaceutical industry is to discover and develop new drugs and vaccines." There could be no clearer expression of the recognition by industry

---

[1] Robinson estimated in 2001 that by 2005 a "blockbuster" drug would be considered to be an item having an annual turnover of some $2.5 billion (Robinson 2001 at p. 14).

that it has a serious duty to the community in this field. The first question will be whether the industry has tried sufficiently hard; the second is to what extent it has succeeded.

7.2.   The Innovation Controversy

Spokesmen for the science-based pharmaceutical industry argue that it has not only assumed a large part of the task of serious pharmaceutical innovation in the modern world but also carried it out successfully over a long period. It justifies the prices charged for new medicines largely on the basis that such prices are needed to fund this research, making due allowance for the large number of projects that fail at one stage or another (Holmer 2002). On the same grounds, it defends the long-term monopolies that it secures on these drugs, to the exclusion of low-cost generic supplies (see Section 2.2.4).

Critics on the other hand allege that, especially in the recent past, and despite its extensive resources, industry has delivered far too little relevant innovation to justify either its position or its prices. This could be due to inefficiency of the research process but also to a failure to direct its research to socially desirable goals. At the same time evidence is advanced to the effect that much of the creativity attributed to the research-based industry lies in fact with academic and other non-commercial institutions. If these things are true, then it is arguable that the entire research situation needs to be overhauled, perhaps drastically.

Both sides of the controversy have been intensively documented, though some of the figures have to be interpreted with caution, and one constantly has to be aware of falling into the error made by some protagonists and antagonists when they select particular statistics in order to make a case.

Britain's Parliamentary Select Committee in its study of the industry found itself faced with contradictory estimates of the proportion of new drugs which could be considered truly innovative, with the figures advanced by industry being much higher than those from other sources. "Over the last decade, there has been a drop in the rate of new molecular entities (NMEs) entering the market. In the USA over the last 10 years or so, the proportion of NMEs offering significant therapeutic advance has varied between 23% and 54% (though other sources suggest that these figures overestimate the extent of useful drug innovation) Dr Richard Nicholson suggested that under 10% of drugs licensed are truly innovative. Drugs and Therapeutics Bulletin noted very few genuine innovations for patients and declining. Many new medicines produce incremental improvements in patient care, the full impact of which may only be demonstrated after use by the NHS for some years . . . ." (HOC 2005 at para 118)

There are in fact various starting points for estimates of the matter. Financial and economic data indicate the level of current expenditure on research. Marketing surveys, regulatory records and sales figures show what drugs are actually reaching the market. They also give some indication of the areas in which there is intensive research activity and conversely of those areas that appear to have been neglected. Finally, one can set the overall output against some of the world's still unfulfilled needs.

7.3.   Statistics and Analyses

7.3.1.   *The real cost of a new drug*

Bearing in mind the widely differing nature of new drugs and the various ways in which they come into being, it is only to be expected that the one will be more expensive to create than the other. Particular attention has been paid to estimates on this score emanating over the years from the Center for the Study of Drug Development at Tufts University in Boston, MA. Founded by Dr. Lou Lasagna at the University of Rochester, NY in the 1960s, and moving to Tufts in 1976, the Center was from the start financed primarily by the research-based industry and saw it as its mission to undertake policy studies that could support the industry case on various contentious issues. During its early period, it produced multiple and influential studies to support the view that the Federal Food and Drug Administration (FDA) was excessively slow and ponderous in its approval of new drugs, greatly raising the costs of development and depriving the American people for long periods of valuable new products. There is no doubt that the Center's work was largely responsible for the relaxation and acceleration of drug approval at the United States FDA during the 20 years that followed. In 1991, the Center released the first of a series of estimates of the costs of R&D in the United States (DiMasi *et al.* 1991). As Goozner summarizes the technique that had been employed, citing the original authors:

> They surveyed industry research-and-development officials to come up with their
> estimate for drug development costs. In the initial study, released in 1991, they
> randomly picked ninety-three new chemical entities under development at a dozen
> big drug companies and asked the firms to report their research-and-development
> expenditures on each stage of development for each molecule. They then divided
> the total expenditures by the number of drugs in the group that eventually gained
> approval from the FDA – thus factoring in the price of failure – to come up with

an average cost per new drug. Their first study pegged the total cost per new drug at $114 million (measured in 1987 dollars).

> They then adjusted that cost for the time needed to secure approval. Economists call this adjustment the opportunity cost of capital. It assumes that the money invested in research and development today, which won't have a payoff for many years down the road, could have been spent on other things or turned back to shareholders as additional profit. The opportunity cost of research-and-development spending increased the final estimate to $231 million per new drug (or $318 million in 2000 after adjusting the price for inflation). (Goozner 2004 at p. 237)

By November 2001, when the Center released an updated study, the average costs of R&D for a new medicine were estimated at $802 million (Tufts 2001), the rapid increase in costs during the decade being attributed to a 12 per cent annual increase in expenses, particularly associated with the long-term study of drugs for chronic and degenerative diseases.

The reliability of the Tufts figures has been extensively questioned by various independent authors and bodies. Goozner has pointed out that in the very extensive public studies carried out by the AIDS division of the National Institute for Allergies and Infectious Diseases, the average costs per participant rose only by 11 per cent over the entire decade (Goozner 2004 at pp. 237–238). In cancer trials sponsored by the National Cancer Institute, the costs were only $750 per patient as compared with $2,500 in apparently comparable studies sponsored by private industry (GAO 1999). Public Citizen/Congress Watch published a detailed critique of the manner in which the Tufts Center had arrived at its figures; their own calculation set the average cost per new drug at no more than $71 million (Public Citizen 2001), an estimate which was in turn firmly rejected by the industry association. Others have pointed out that the latest estimates were based only on a highly selected sample of costly drugs, that the figures make no allowance for tax rebates, and that it was misleading to include the "opportunity costs" (Angell 2004 at pp. 43–46, Goozner 2004 at 231ff.). Angel voices a suspicion ". . . that the real cost per drug is well under $100 million" (Angell *op cit* at p. 46).

7.3.2. *Research expenditure within the company*

The emphasis which the industry has placed on research costs as a justification for the level of drug prices invites a comparison as to the expenditure voluntarily incurred by pharmaceutical firms in other directions. The issue has been touched on in Chapter 6 in connection with price calculations, but some of the original figures may be cited here. The published figures point clearly to the fact that research costs are overshadowed by much greater expenditure on advertising and promotion, as well as by profits and overheads. A fair notion of the expenses incurred by an average pharmaceutical corporation in these various directions is to be found in the data officially lodged with the Securities and Exchange Commission in the USA (cited by Laing 2001a and Henry 2002) (Table 7.A). Figures from other western countries appear to be similar:

Taking the average figures from these 10 major US companies one sees that research expenditure is some 13 per cent while 32 per cent of income is spent on "marketing and administration" and profit averages 16 per cent. One difficulty is naturally that the range of variation is so wide; another is that one does not quite know what is meant by "R&D". Particularly because R&D expenses can qualify for tax deductions, there is a strong tendency in submissions to the authorities to classify as "R&D" various expenses which do not entirely merit the name. As one former comptroller has put it:

> Within the W company we had a certain routine in classifying our costs which tended to shift borderline commercial items and put them under the heading of research. Suppose for example we had spent $100,000 on market research to interview people in various countries, find out what they were using and where there might be a niche for a profitable new product – well, that was going to give us some guidance on which way we wanted our research to go, so we classified it as a research expense though the sales people had initiated the work and carried it out. Then again, once we had a drug licenced and ready to sell, we would give out large numbers of samples to a few hundred doctors and get them to try them out on their patients and report what happened on the forms we gave them; we paid them to do it, because the information might be useful to the detailer and the sales force. Call it sampling and advertising if you like, but it provided information to

Table 7.A
1999 Pharmaceutical Company Data for the 10 Largest U.S. Pharmaceutical Companies

	Revenue (billions)	Cost of Goods (% of revenue)	Market+Admin. (% of revenue)	R&D (% of revenue)	Profits (% of revenue)
Average	17.557	28	32	13	16
Maximum	32,714	54	46	20	27
Minimum	10,003	18	16	6	−9

All data from SEC 10K filings and 1999 company annual reports as cited by Laing (2001a).

the labs so it went down in the accounts as research. That was the way we did it, but I promise you it was the way everybody in the industry was doing it, and one supposes that it looked good on the books. (Interview 4)

One might add that the widespread use of costly "sampling trials" of this type was also recognized – and in the same breath condemned for purely ethical reasons – in a sharp joint editorial in the country's leading medical journals:

Patients participate in clinical trials largely for altruistic reasons – that is to advance the standard of care. In the light of that truth, the use of clinical trials primarily for marketing, in our view, makes a mockery of clinical investigation and is a misuse of a powerful tool. (Davidoff 2001)

Alongside these percentage estimates of costs, one can examine some absolute figures for annual research spending per firm in 2001, as estimated by Moses in 2002 (Figure 7.B); the highest level of R&D expenditure recorded is here 17 per cent.

7.3.3.   Innovation trends over time

The historical evolution of drug research development over half a century or more has been the subject of many thorough studies, which can be summarized only briefly here. It has not been a period of smooth evolution, as is evident from a graph published in 2001 by Achilladelis and Antonakis (Achilladelis 2001) (Figure 7.C).

While such a graph is to some extent misleading, since the nature and quality of the various innovations are at least as significant as their number, some characteristics of the period are apparent.

During some two decades after the Second World War, there was a well-recognized period of intensive innovation, partly based on work which had been undertaken at public expense, and in part in connection with military needs. Industry had exploited these openings and by 1965 entirely new fields of treatment had thereby been opened up and were evolving further. New treatments included a widening range of life-saving antibiotics for infectious diseases, corticosteroids for serious inflammatory conditions and the benzodiazepine tranquillizers for anxiety and insomnia; the antipsychotic agents had released an entire generation of patients from mental institutions, antidepressants come into use, and the antihistamines, anti-inflammatory agents, thiazide diuretics and the oral contraceptives had each opened new perspectives. Within that same decade, however, drug regulations were coming to the fore and slowing

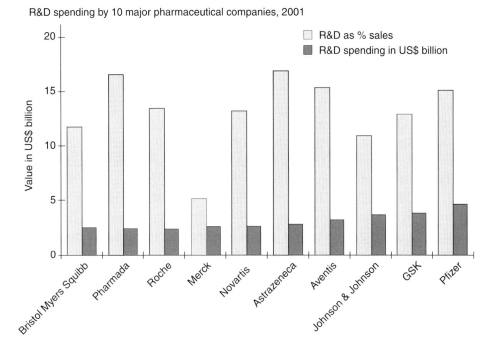

R&D spending by 10 major pharmaceutical companies, 2001

Figure 7.B   Research Spending by Major Companies, 2001 (*Source*: The World Medicines Situation, WHO, 2004).

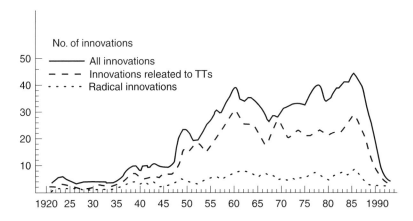

Figure 7.C   Drug Innovation 1920–1990. *Source*: Achilladelis B. and Antonakis N. (2001): The dynamics of technological innovation: the case of the pharmaceutical industry. Res. Policy, 30, 535–538.

innovation to some extent simply by insisting that adequate standards of quality, safety and efficacy were maintained. By 1969, an OECD study was forced to conclude that this innovative wave was, at least in Europe, now almost a spent force, and that the prospects for new breakthroughs in these directions now appeared bleak (OECD 1969). Despite this pessimism, there was in fact within a further 5 years a new crop of discoveries, with the introduction of various classes of enzyme inhibitors, used in conditions ranging from Parkinson's disease to hypertension, while receptor blockers of various types had changed the treatment of peptic ulcer and vascular disorders. A cyclic process nevertheless now appeared to be in motion and a further period of relative inertia ensued. By the last decade of the century some further innovation did come to the fore, but it was not necessarily attuned to the public health interest. A novel series of anti-inflammatory/antirheumatic agents (the cox-2 inhibitors) were, for example, introduced with intensive publicity but these showed no clear therapeutic advantage over the drugs of some decades earlier, little trace of the improved gastric tolerance that had been promised, and they rapidly encountered problems with adverse effects, leading in some cases to withdrawal. In the meantime, however, as WHO has concluded, a new wave of innovation has appeared in other directions, ". . . based on advances in the discovery and application of biotechnology (recombinant deoxyribonucleic acid – DNA – and monoclonal antibody methods) in the production of physiological proteins used in the therapy or diagnosis of many diseases" (WHO 2004.7 at p. 8). Overall there has nevertheless been a sharp downward trend in innovation over the last 10–15 years, and the extent to which the rate of innovation has been influenced by unforeseeable events (as well as some unknown factors) is striking.

7.3.4.   *The spectrum of drugs reaching the market*

The defects of a purely statistical overview of achievements, such as that presented above, can be compensated to some extent by an attempt to determine how relevant to health needs the industry's research output has been over a given period. There are differences of view, but an extensive literature, approaching the issue from various sides, concludes today that the pharmaceutical industry has become a sector more prone to develop drugs promising profit than medicines attuned to major public health needs.

Marcia Angell has cautiously adopted a combined quantitative/qualitative approach to the introduction of new drugs in the United States during the 5 years 1998–2002, the most recent period for which exact figures were available, paying special attention to products which at the time of submission were selected for "priority review" by the Federal FDA because of what was considered at the time (sometimes a little optimistically) to be their potential significance in advancing medicine. To cite her literally:

> Altogether 415 new drugs were approved – an average of 83 per year, Of these 133 (32 per cent) were new molecular entities. The others were variations of old drugs. And of those 133, only 58 were priority review drugs. That averages out to no more than 12 innovative drugs per year, or 14 per cent of the total. Not only is this yield very low, but over those five years it got worse. In both 2001 and 2002, only 7 innovative drugs (that is, new molecular entities with priority review) were approved each year, as compared with 9 in 2000, 19 in 1999 and 16 in 1998. (Angell 2004 at pp. 54–55)

One must be cautious about drawing conclusions as to trends over such a short period, but Angell's analysis at least indicates the meagre overall output and the high proportion of new medicines which contributed very little or nothing to therapeutic progress. Even among those accorded regulatory priority, as Dr Angell herself goes on to point out, the only real breakthroughs during that period related to a small number of drugs which were generally "last-ditch" treatments of value in a tiny group of patients with rare conditions or in whom other drugs had not proved effective. Such medicines have an extremely limited sale and could not have been the intended output of major research programmes. When indeed one examines their history, insofar as it is known, they prove as a rule to have been by-products of research, which had been intended to achieve a much more ambitious goal but which failed in its original purpose. That is naturally of itself an important finding, reminding one that drug research, however well planned, cannot be rigidly steered in a particular direction; it is, however, important to determine what the original intention was, and whether that reflected a genuine ethical commitment by the pharmaceutical industry to tackle the real challenges facing medicine.

Other analyses examine the state of innovation for particular diseases. Lack of progress in innovation for diseases prevalent in developing countries is of particular concern and will be considered separately in Chapter 8, but some of the diseases concerned present global problems. To quote from a report on Tuberculosis by Médécins sans Frontières (MSF 2004):

> . . . Tuberculosis kills roughly two million people every year . . . but at least 4% of all TB patients worldwide are resistant to at least one of the current first-line drugs. Multi-drug resistant (MDR) TB, defined as resistance to at least rifampicin and isoniazid, the two most powerful TB drugs, might be spreading as fast as by 250,000–400,000 new cases each year. Their treatment relies on "second-line" TB drugs that have far lower efficacy and require even longer administration periods (18–24 months) with much higher cost and much higher rates of adverse effects.

The problems with malaria are no less serious. The mainstays of treatment in the past have been chloroquine and sulphadoxine-pyrimethamine, both of which are available at negligible cost. The former is, however, no longer effective against *Plasmodiun falciparum* in most tropical areas, and resistance to the latter is now very widespread. There are certain alternative drugs but their current cost puts them financially out of reach of entire populations (see White 1999 and Attaran 2003). These same problems have been documented extensively by others, sometimes in very unexpected quarters. Early in 2000, America's Central Intelligence Agency produced a National Intelligence Estimate concluding that 20 notorious diseases, including tuberculosis, malaria, denge, cholera and both hepatitis B and C, were rapidly reaching epidemic levels with no sign that they would be arrested (CIA 2000).

One worrying element, when one tries to take a world view, is the extent to which research appears to have occupied itself with what one might almost regard as "frivolous" goals. Following the initial introduction of the "statins", drugs capable of correcting the lipid spectrum in later life and hence reducing the risk of cardiovascular disorders, many firms plunged into the field to develop variants on the theme in order to obtain a share of what was a potentially vast market. By 2004 six such drugs, all slight variants on one another but coming from different science-based firms, had reached the tables of the regulatory authorities; at least one other had already been withdrawn, and seven or more new members of the group, with little to choose between them, were known to be on the way.

An examination of drug withdrawals can also be informative. As Dan Sigelman has noted, not one of the 13 new drugs in various fields withdrawn for safety reasons in the USA over a decade left a therapeutic gap; in some cases more than a dozen usable alternatives remained (Sigelman 2002). A further example relates to the development of drugs for restoring sexual performance, particularly in the elderly; one finds in the patent literature an increasing number of such products emerging from research programmes in a range of countries, pointing to increased innovative activity in that direction. In areas like this, as market reports from industry-orientated journals repeatedly confirm, there is still an overwhelming interest to develop products because of the relative ease and speed with which "me-too" molecules can be created and brought to a market where there is a wide willingness to pay high prices; it is not surprising that, as Robinson puts it, "me-toos and line extensions typically take up around 80 per cent of R&D spending." (Robinson 2001 at p. 12)

The wasteful development of "me-too" drugs on a massive scale is by no means a new phenomenon:

> When Silverman and Lee examined the US market in the early seventies they encountered more than 200 sulphonamides, over 270 antibiotics. 130 antihistamines and nearly 100 major and minor tranquillizers. Most of the newer members of these classes, as they remarked, offered the physician and his patient no significant clinical advantages. (Silverman 1974)

As many of those working on behalf of developing countries have noted, the industry's choice of priority areas for its research amounts in effect to a deliberate decision to emphasize the ills of the affluent, since these are the patients who have the means to purchase new drugs. On occasion, when this is pointed out in debate, the industrial representative points out that all these conditions also exist in the third world, so that the research in question can be said to be tackling universal problems. It is true that hyperlipidaemia and penile erectile dysfunction do exist in the developing world as well as in the west, but they pale into insignificance as compared to the problems presented by still incurable tropical disorders or by infections the causal organisms of which have become resistant to existing drugs.

7.3.5. *The non-industrial role in drug innovation*

The pharmaceutical industry has, as already noted, consistently advanced the argument that it is itself the principle source and motor of innovation. As a vigorously disputed issue, this too needs to be considered dispassionately when the overall picture is considered.

There are indeed a number of examples, largely from the earlier period, of successful innovative approaches which were very largely or completely attributable to industry-based projects. It is generally agreed that Sir James Black, who developed a theory as to the way in which receptors might be blocked, received from the firms with which he worked both the necessary resources and encouragement to develop first the beta-blockers in the 1960s and later the H-2 blockers. However, as Angell points out (Angell *op cit.* at pp. 56–57) many truly innovative drugs in fact stem from publicly supported research. To cite her once more on recent drug innovation in America:

> . . . almost all of that is sponsored by the National Institutes of Health (NIH) and carried out at universities, small biotechnical companies, or the NIH itself . . . Big

pharma began to rely on publicly funded research in 1980 with passage of legislation (which) permitted NIH-funded work to be patented and licensed exclusively to
drug companies in exchange for royalties. And increasingly, that is exactly what big
pharma depends on – licensed drugs, which the drug companies then market and
often patent for additional uses. Sometimes the drugs are completely developed
before they are licensed . . . AZT, the first drug to treat HIV/AIDS, was developed
and clinically tested by researchers at the National Cancer Institute (a part of the
NIH) and Duke University before being licensed to what is now GlaxoSmithKline
. . . (Angell 2004 at pp. 56–57)

There are many other examples of this process of licensing academic
or public work to industry, and public statements on behalf of industry
have confirmed that by 2002 the Pfizer company was earning some 30 per
cent of its revenues from licensed innovations and Merck as much as
35 per cent (Naik 2002). There is naturally nothing reprehensible in a drug
firm's seeking to acquire the rights to promising research from public or
other outside sources, but from the point of view of appropriate innovation
it is evident that the output of this process is in many institutions more
likely to be governed by the choice of interesting academic exercises than
by considerations of public need.

What is regrettable from the ethical point of view is the manner in
which industry spokesmen have sometimes advanced inaccurate statements to bolster their claims regarding research achievement. When, to
take again the same example as cited above, the Chief Executive Office of
Burroughs Wellcome claimed in the media in 1989 that this company had
essentially created AZT therapy for HIV/AIDS, he was strongly rebuffed
on almost every point by the institutional originators of the treatment:

The company specifically did not develop or provide the first application of the
technology for determining whether a drug like AZT can suppress live AIDS virus
in human cells, nor did it develop the technology to determine at what concentration such an effect might be achieved in humans. Moreover it was not first to
administer AZT to a human being with AIDS, nor did it perform the first clinical
pharmacology studies in patients. It also did not perform the immunological and
virological studies necessary to infer that the drug might work, and was therefore
worth pursuing in further studies . . . (Broder 1998)

Bearing in mind that academic and other public research institutions
are generally well not suited to carrying a research project through to the
point where a product is ready for approval and marketing, it is sensible to
look for patterns of collaboration on which basic and early work is often
performed in academia or other public institutions (e.g. military health
research) and handed to industry when a project appears to merit final

development. What one must avoid, however, is a situation in which public institutions become so attuned to industrial needs that the basic and exploratory research at which they excel is replaced by financially attractive work directed to readily accessible commercial objectives. Were that to happen, the present flow of innovation from institutions to corporations could dry up. In addition, it would seem necessary from the point of view of public policy to ensure that the costing of such collaborative work is transparent; it would be wrong if, as has undoubtedly happened on some occasions, the drug prices charged to national health systems and others were to be attuned to supposed industrial research costs when in reality, the costs have been largely met from public funds (Chapter 6).

7.4.　Future Trends and Corrective Measures

7.4.1.　*Should the innovation process change?*

The overall picture of the drug research scene at the present day, viewed either in terms of the quantity or quality of output, is not encouraging. At a time when patents on the breakthrough drugs of the 1980s are fast expiring there are few new drugs emerging to replace them, let alone improve significantly upon them. Failure to find remedies for many major conditions which by their nature should be amenable to drug treatment, especially epidemic infections, is a source of very great concern. There is, however, no single explanation for what is happening to innovation, and in such a complex scene one cannot side entirely either with the optimists or the pessimists. Drug development in the last half century has gone through a series of irregular cycles, during which the lean years and the fat years have alternated without evident reason, and as new approaches emerge (and either succeed or fail) that unpredictable process will continue. Before making predictions one might well look back to the OECD report of 1969 which seemed so sure that the golden years were past. What is becoming evident is however that at the present moment the innovative process needs a thorough reassessment – a brainstorm to determine whether it should not be reinvigorated and redirected. Inevitably one returns again and again to the hypothesis advanced earlier in this chapter, namely that if a body such as the science-based pharmaceutical industry claims to have taken upon itself the duty to provide society with new drugs, and has further claimed massive resources to that end, it has created thereby an obligation to perform that duty to the best of its ability, both in terms of quantity and of quality. Much of the evidence quoted briefly here and extensively documented by others suggests that in recent years it has failed to perform that duty adequately and that even in its policies and planning it may not have taken the duty all too seriously, succumbing too readily to frivolous temptations in somewhat different directions.

There is no sign that such a global reassessment of the innovative machine is taking place within the industry as a whole at the present moment, though it is certainly happening within individual companies. One encounters it also within the United Nations Millennium Project (Millennium 2005), the World Health Organization working in a collaborative study with the European Union (WHO 2004), the MSF-sponsored Drugs for Neglected Diseases Initiative (DfNDi 2005) and many other circles. In the United States it is a central theme in some thoughtful studies by independent writers (Robinson 2001, Hawthorn 2003, Angell 2004, Avorn 2004, Goozner 2004) and the same topic echoes through the work of a parliamentary commission in Britain (HOC 2005) and very many papers in the journals. Nowhere does one encounter any serious desire to alter the fundamental structure of drug innovation, but many of its present weaknesses are identified, notions as to what could be done are being formulated and on various fronts action is already being taken.

Some of the weaknesses have been touched on above; a fundamental challenge is to channel more research effort into areas where society desperately needs more innovation, and to achieve that despite the fact that it can be financially much more attractive for industry to invest in other things, including producing the 17th unneeded statin and expanding direct-to-consumer advertising for potentially popular items. It is all too understandable that such alternatives are chosen; Hawthorn cites Schering-Plough's aggressive campaign to raise sales of its anti-allergy product Claritin in 1998, when a worldwide investment of $136 million in advertising raised sales by 35 per cent to $3.5 billion, representing a massive (60-fold) and rapid return on investment with which no research project is likely to compete (Hawthorn 2003 at p. 160). Corporate ethics in the form of a desire to do good can exert just so much persuasive power to shift such funds into research and influence research choices and no more; commercial managers can hardly be expected to have ethical qualms when their sales campaigns so easily persuade millions to buy tablets which they apparently want and appreciate. At that point, however, one might hope that community and government ethics will take over, recognizing that there are crying needs that are not being fulfilled and that call for public action in one form or another.

If one is going to arrive at a social audit of the entire medicines scene, with the accent on the need for genuine innovation, then there is one starting criterion that must be fulfilled: one must come with the truth and recognize the truth, so far as it is humanly possible to define it. It is a paradox of twenty-first century society that, having arrived at a stage in human evolution where information is so readily and widely available we have also discovered how it can be manipulated cosmetically to suit our convenience, and how we can do that with a clear conscience. The phenomenon of advertising has been considered in this light in Chapter 5. Here one needs to be concerned with the facts that have to be marshalled to make policy. Pharmaceutical and medical scientists themselves do not misrepresent their facts – the very few occasions on which that has been known to happen have led to expressions of shock in the journals, the mass media and the courts, because the strict discipline of science has been betrayed. Yet, any broad public debate on research policy, priority and finance soon encounters a point at which even hard evidence may be set aside if it promises to be inconvenient. Any participant in a vigorous debate may fall into that error, but those who are charged with defending the present state of things seem most ready to sin. Where figures and facts cannot be entirely denied, they are claimed to be irrelevant, capable of misinterpretation, unbalanced, coloured by bias, insignificant or representative. Experts are marshalled to reinterpret statistical data on innovative output so as to ensure that the history is viewed in the most flattering light possible. There are occasions when the stonewallers are absent and consensus is reached, but the consensus which the remainder attain is then easily dismissed as having been reached by an unrepresentative forum. There are industry spokesman who admit publicly to the existence of problems, but so long as their own corporations currently have the wind in their sails they are most ready to suggest that it is other folk who may be in difficulties. Ray Gilmartin, President of Merck, speaking at the Tufts Center late in 2001 when Vioxx was still in the ascendant remarked that:

> If there is any concern, it should be on the part of pharmaceutical companies that are less efficient and that aren't delivering drugs of value to patients. (cited by Angell 2004 at p. 47)

Somehow the discussion has to pass this point, accepting now that pharmaceutical innovation is currently truly facing a serious problem, with grave consequences for society as a whole and for the industry itself. Behind closed doors that consensus often proves rapidly attainable, with honest company executives, research managers and outsiders ready to face the fact that change is called for, and then proceeding to discuss the consequences.

It is perhaps surprising that, with all the obstacles on the road to consensus, so much healthy thinking is now coming to the fore, though from different circles. That may indicate how seriously change is needed. Behind the scenes even some of the stonewallers, having delivered their set pieces, appear to be pleased.

7.4.2. Can industry adapt?

The industry is and has long been very alert to outside influences except where they appear to be purely antagonistic; it responds to incentives, encouragement, scientific innovation and sound ideas whatever their source, and in a sense it is reforming itself all the time. The reshaping of research to accommodate input from biotechnology is a current example. A more classic example, which has been played out over a longer period is the progressive restructuring of mass screening:

> During the post-war growth of industrial drug research between 1950 and 1980 many industrial concerns having pharmaceutical divisions maintained programmes to screen new substances in superficial animal tests for possible biological activity. While it was seen as a distant ideal to synthesize molecules specifically designed to play a particular role in the body, knowledge of molecular biology at the time was too limited to provide a reliable basis for research. Substances originally created as fertilizers, perfumes, solvents or for other purposes therefore underwent a standard battery of simple screening tests in rats or mice. Industrial claims to the effect that, in order to produce a single new drug, many thousands of substances have to be studied date largely from that period. (Robinson 2001 at p. 8, PhRMA 2002 at p. 20) In fact it was very exceptional for mass screening of non-pharmaceutical compounds to produce any findings of value, and the approach was largely abandoned in favour of more tightly directed drug research in areas where existing physiological and pharmacological knowledge provided clues to promising approaches. The successful development of the semi-synthetic penicillins provides an example. Screening was redeveloped in more subtle and sensitive forms.

7.4.3. Is outside action necessary?

The pharmaceutical industry is not waiting for a government or any other body to step in and reform its research activities – indeed it vigorously rejects the notion that any interference is needed. A series of interviews indicate that this is an attitude widely held in the industry; one may be cited here:

> We all know that industry's research is in the doghouse just at this moment. There were a series of worrying things that happened late in the nineties, a number of very critical books came out in the States, and then with the Vioxx story everyone believed that everything was going wrong with our industry; not only were we told that we had no financial future as we were but also that we had never cared about anything but money. None of that is true. Look at the moments when that was said before in our time, and how everything turned out for the best. Not every company will survive, or needs to, but there are leads and projects in plenty, a lot of them in unexpected directions. The more you interfere from the outside, trotting out yesterday's bureaucratic ideas about how things should be organized, the more you will slow down the recovery process. The important thing is to be fair to this industry, and it will be fair to you. (Interview 10, translated)

It is obvious, in view of the experience of recent decades, that entirely new trails can and probably will open up unexpectedly within the next 10 years or less and create fresh opportunities. That is likely to reverse the current decline in achievement in research, at least in terms of numbers of new drugs. The social desirability of whatever emerges may, however, be less than optimal. The manner in which society at times became heavily influenced by the benzodiazepines and the second-generation antidepressants ("the happiness pill") suggests how an irresistibly large market may develop – or be created – around a pharmacological effect that seems to make life more attractive, yet does not enrich it and ultimately creates its own problems. It could be futile and even dangerous for government to try and ordain precisely what research should or should not be doing, but using the tools at its disposal, including approval and pricing procedures, it could well contrive to provide at least some encouragement to researchers in one direction and some gentle discouragement in another.

7.4.4. *The Drugs for Neglected Diseases Initiative*

The *Drugs for Neglected Diseases (DNDi) Initiative*, spearheaded internationally by Médécins sans Frontières, merits special mention as representing one course of action that has been developed with exceptional care and wisdom and – unlike some other projects – is already in being. It also engenders trust because it is motivated by pure idealism, and it recruits the pharmaceutical industry to work with it in a logical manner. MSF has long campaigned for access to more adequate drug therapy in the developing world, and with the DNDi Initiative, it established a positive programme to create some of the treatments which are lacking. The effort is concentrated on the "most neglected diseases", such as sleeping sickness, Chagas disease and leishmaniasis, for which a global drug market is virtually non-existent. Ensuring the development and availability of treatment for these diseases calls for needs-driven drug development, with public responsibility and leadership in both developing and developed countries. Founding partners to date include WHO's Tropical Diseases programme (TDR), the Oswaldo Cruz Foundation in Brazil, the Indian Council of Medical Research, France's Institut Pasteur and the Malaysian Ministry of Health; another Partner is yet to be identified in Africa and there will be patient representation. To use the Initiative's own words, ". . . Acting in the public interest rest, it will bridge the existing R&D gaps in essential drugs for these diseases by initiating and coordinating drug R&D projects in collaboration with the international research community, the public sector, the pharmaceutical industry and other relevant partners" and it will "address unmet needs by taking on projects that others are unable or unwilling to pursue . . .".

While one might see this only as a very small venture, it is in a sense the most significant to have emerged to date, not in the last place because its practical idealism opens doors to collaboration on all sides. Hitherto isolated research institutes in developing countries can complement one another in a broad and well-coordinated programme with clear goals, neutral funding bodies prove willing to contribute resources and pharmaceutical companies are showing themselves ready to make available promising substances which are lying on their shelves but which they have no plans to develop themselves. At a later phase, specific tasks can be funded and subcontracted to these same firms or others. Given inspired management, the DNDi Initiative can not only mobilize precisely the right capacity to fill gaps in particular areas of innovation, but also provide a valuable model for others to emulate, breaking the inertia which has too long characterised this field.

7.4.5. *Governments, communities and donors*

Governments, Communities of Nations and Bilateral Donors are not only charged with service to the community as their primary task; equally significant is that as a rule they have substantial resources to provide that service. Some processes they control directly, through ownership or through regulation; other process they seek to influence in a particular direction for the community's good by making use of those resources, as well as by negotiation and persuasion.

At the national level, government dealings with the pharmaceutical industry have often been inconsistent and fragmented. At one and the same moment, a pharmaceutical firm may find itself pampered by a Ministry of Trade in order to promote exports, denied a licence to import sophisticated Chinese laboratory equipment by the Department of Defence, impeded by plain bureaucracy in the Drug Control Agency when it is about to launch a blockbuster drug and then offered a greenfield site by a local authority to build a new factory in an unsuitable spot. What one can seek to achieve here is an overall understanding of the industry's situation so that these conflicting matters are dealt with in a tolerable manner, serving the public interest while understanding the reasonable needs of business. An excellent example of an overall approach is the thorough examination of the industry undertaken in 2005 by a British Parliamentary Select Committee which sought to examine every aspect of the industry and its function in society, so as to arrive at a reasonably coordinated policy (HOC 2005).

At the international level, an approach to pharmaceutical innovation is now being undertaken by the European Union, with technical support from the World Health Organization:

> The *Priority Medicines for Europe and the World* Project pulls together an entirely different constellation of partners and has a novel motivation. Still in a phase of evolution, the Project was conceived by the European Union in order provide a logical basis for the health activities within the Union's Seventh Programme of Work, due to be carried out from 2007 to 2010. In an initial phase, and in collaboration with the World Health Organization, a study was undertaken of pharmaceutical innovation from a public health perspective, defined as "one that is based on principles of equity, evidence and efficiency". On the basis of this a medicines development agenda is to be developed for support by the European Union and a systematic methodology is to be created. The preliminary work has identified pharmaceutical gaps which affect the citizens of Europe, but marking out in particular those research needs which are also relevant for countries in economic transition and for developing countries. This "commonality of interest" has led to the involvement of WHO. The very considerable funding which the European Union can make available in areas of its choice is not likely to flow directly to industrial activities of the present type, but it could lubricate them in various ways. Preliminary proposals include efforts to reduce regulatory barriers to innovation (see Section 3.5), the use of electronic medical records to provide objective estimates of comparative effectiveness, encouragement of public–private partnerships in selected areas of drug development and the creation of new tools for evaluating innovation.

It is too early to anticipate the repercussions of this venture on the shape and content of future research programmes. Many of the areas identified as demanding more research comprise fields in which the major innovative firms are already heavily engaged, though with considerable duplication of effort. A great deal will depend on the extent to which Community involvement and funding succeeds in rendering new approaches and hitherto neglected fields more attractive both for these firms and for smaller and more specialised firms which might play a greater role than hitherto in drug innovation. This is an ethically motivated venture to the extent that the manner in which the European Union expends its considerable financial resources has always been under close scrutiny, and in this instance a thorough effort is being made to ensure that they serve a concrete public goal in a well-directed manner, serving the health of the population both in Europe and elsewhere.

7.4.6.   *Independent non-profit research centres*

A variant on the DfND Initiative which is emerging in the United States involves independent non-commercial drug research organizations based on philanthropic funding or venture capital, though it remains to be seen how much scientific capacity and capital will be created and maintained in this way. As with the DfND Initiative particular promise could lie in the anticipated ability of these organizations to identify medicines which have been created within large science-based firms to a point in research where their promise appears to merit further work, yet have then been abandoned, probably in most instances for purely commercial reasons or because of other priorities. If this route of development is successful, one might hope that the firms with potentially valuable drugs on the shelf will in the public interest choose to make them ready available to new organizations of this type.

> In the US, One World Health was founded in 2000 by the pharmacologist Victoria Hale who had experience both with the FDA and the generic industry, and was herself aware of drugs which had been abandoned for reasons which apparently had little or nothing to do with any lack of therapeutic promise. For its initial project, a drug falling into this category which appeared valuable in Kala-azar, One World obtained substantial funding from the Bill and Melinda Gates Foundation. The Institute is now developing a product for use in Chagas' Disease, the active component having been produced within a small biotechnology firm which did not have the capacity to carry it development further. (Perlman 2002)

There could well be a place for more organizations of this type, and they appear to be on the way. The "small is beautiful" approach to life attracts workers who would want to feel closer to the goals that they serve in society than they may find possible in a very large and impersonal organization. In various sectors of industry a wave of company mergers spawns a breakaway crop of new specialised centres where projects are carried out on a modest scale, often efficiently and with every opportunity to culture an ethically sound environment. Everything will depend on the quality of management, its ability to maintain broad contacts, and its determination to maintain the idealism which brought it into being.

7.4.7. Official incentives to true innovation

Governments and their agencies, as has been seen in earlier sections, have in the course of the years become deeply involved in mechanisms which have major repercussions for the activities of the pharmaceutical industry – the prime examples being the *drug approval process*, the setting of *prices*, the levying of *taxes* and the granting of *patents*. In each of these matters, its involvement has been differently motivated. Drug regulation and approval systems grew up because experience had shown the need for independent control of the quality, safety and efficacy of drugs and the information provided with them; price approval systems have primarily been introduced to promote the parsimonious use of public funds for national health systems and public insurance bodies; taxes are levied wherever money flows; patents, quite simply, have developed around the desire to protect the inventor from improper use of his invention by others. Although all these forms of government involvement are fundamental in the drug field, none of them is designed to mould the development of the drug market positively in a direction that will serve the public health interest best, yet, all have the potential to do so.

Drug regulation has a fairly creditable record of protecting the community from harm – useless or dangerous drugs and misinformation – yet it has come to maturity in such a way that it hardly reflects the extent to which a new drug serves the real need of society or fails to do so. America's FDA procedures accord a slight degree of priority to drugs which appear to represent progress, but it is a very slim one. One could go a great deal further, using proven techniques to estimate the degree to which a new drug brings something new to health care. Once that estimate has been made, the regulatory process can be adjusted to it using the many variants which are possible under various approval systems. The assessment may be given a much higher or lower priority; a drug can be released generally or restricted to specialists or hospitals; conditions may be attached to distribution or advertising. Much more interference is however possible when it is considered necessary to serve the public interest. A regulatory approach which could well have discouraged excessive investment in "me-too" development was that formerly in use in Norway, where the approval system for many years incorporated a "need paragraph" according to which a product would be registered for sale only if there was a public need for it.

> When Dukes and Lunde examined the market situation of non-steroidal anti-inflammatory drugs in 1980 (Dukes 1981) they found only 7 products of this type on sale in Norway as compared with 11 in Czechoslovakia, 22 in The Netherlands, 27 in Britain, 31 in Germany and 50 in Italy. There was no question of therapeutic deprivation; most Norwegian physicians were in fact using only 5 of the drugs available to them, which provided an entirely adequate choice. In a later study by Enstad (Enstad 1995) it was noted that between 1985 and 1992 between 29% and 47% of all new drug applications in Norway were rejected because of "lack of need."

> Norway was later obliged to abandon its "need paragraph" on entering the European Economic Area since in the European Community the approach had been excluded under strong commercial pressure. As a country with a small population, the restrictive policies of Norway could not be expected to inhibit the degree of "me-too innovation" worldwide, but had it been employed in more countries this approach could well have promoted a shift from "me-too" investment to true innovation.

A "need clause" approach is in fact widely used in the developing world in the form of the "essential drug lists" for public health supply systems discussed in Chapter 8; a parallel concept operates in the form of "hospital formularies" which exist in many countries. However, one would only expect it to play a role in moulding research if it were to be applied to drug approval in major markets.

Avorn has suggested some ways in which even America's drug approval system might develop to reflect genuine public needs where new drugs are concerned:

> The FDA . . . has started to make some tentative steps beyond the YES/NO binary thinking that traditionally guided all its decisions; it needs help in moving much farther in that direction. The agency has to reassess its single-minded reliance on the lowest possible standard.

But, as Avorn notes:

> FDA's enabling legislation states that a drug shall be approved for sale if the agency determines that it is safe and effective. The law makes no mention of "more effective than . . ." or "safer than . . .". The pharmaceutical industry argues that holding FDA . . . to a higher standard would quite literally take an Act of Congress . . .". (Avorn 2004 at p. 380)

Price control mechanisms were considered in Chapter 6. Their ability to enhance the market prospects for truly innovative drugs is considerable, especially if the type of evaluation in use in Australia is employed; Britain's Pharmaceutical Price Regulation Scheme makes at least a gesture in the same direction though in a less methodical manner (HOC 2005 at para 130) and the House of Commons Select Committee has proposed that it be used more actively (HOC 2005 at para 361). As with "need-based" regulatory criteria, however, an appreciate effect on the pattern of innovation is only to be expected if such systems are widely employed; in particular, one would only expect research to be affected if a well-planned control system of this type were to be introduced in the United States.

Taxation systems have in many countries been designed to provide encouragement to innovative activities in industry as a whole, and in the USA the pharmaceutical industry enjoys particular fiscal advantages, yet once again these systems have not been built up in such a way that progressive and truly exploratory innovation is rewarded to a greater extent than "semi-innovative" work. The principles would be the same as those employed in regulation and price control, but would probably need to be employed retroactively so that tax relief is provided once the innovative qualities of a medicine have been tested in practice.

The *patent system*, considered in Chapter 2, is perhaps the most potent of all the mechanisms available to the community to promote innovation, yet in the field of medicines it has not been developed in such a manner that greater protection is enjoyed by those products that confer greater benefits. Angell has noted in particular the manner in which the system has been developed in the United States, strengthening and extending drug monopolies in a manner that blocks competition for long periods (Angell 2004 at pp. 247–250); one might argue that this principle could well be used selectively, once more seeking to provide such additional protection only to those products which are demonstrating clearly in the field that, seen from the patient's point of view, they deserve it.

The distribution of *information* could, in principle, be developed into as powerful a weapon in the community's hands as any other in encouraging the creation of innovative drugs. Many impartial drug bulletins, some published with government support, perform a commendable task in guiding prescribers towards the use of the best medicines rather than those for which the publicity drums have beaten most loudly. Their influence has been shown to be entirely disproportionate to their resources, but as compared with the publicity machine their resources are extremely small.

Such are some of the tools, all of them implements in the hands of elected government, all capable of encouraging the pharmaceutical industry to change course, all rendering the development of truly innovative drugs more attractive and the making of me-too products less so. At the same time there will be a need for greater openness, consultation and trust between governments and industries than there has been in the past; that must mean a process in which government is firm – reasonable and accommodating to business but ever ready to represent the community at large by using the implements of policy where there are needed. The question is only whether the community, through its elected governments, will insist that they be used in the interests of its own health.

7.4.8.   *A total approach to innovation*

It is a truism to say that the community needs all the drug innovation it can get; it is probably also true that the resources available in the world are sufficient to provide much more real progress in this field than is now being delivered.

A number of the tools which exist to improve the situation have been briefly listed above. Others – including philanthropic donations and global efforts coordinated by WHO are discussed in Chapter 8 dealing with the developing world. Yet others exist. One would not wish to forget, for example, the quiet manner in which, both in industry and in academic institutions, work proceeds in some fields where stepwise advances are more readily achieved than dramatic breakthroughs. The pharmaceutical industry has always stressed the merits of incremental progress – with each new drug presenting what may seem to be only as marginal advance over its predecessor, yet representing a further small step in what over a period of time may constitute a significant advance in treatment. Over a period of several decennia that has been the case with the cytostatic drugs used in malignant disease, where a fair advance has been attained in tiny stages, though the available products continue to be relatively toxic. The same mode of progression may ultimately prove to be the case with medicines intended to relieve the effects of atherosclerosis or to slow its course, though here too progress is painfully slow.

In any new development, the role of *academic and state institutions* with research capacity needs to be reconsidered. While they have in fact contributed much to innovation, their contribution has been misunderstood; too often their own achievements have been relabelled as industrial, which is hardly motivating for those concerned. Industry will suffer no harm by acknowledging their role both publicly and in the form of adequate royalties which can make a valuable contribution to the further development of these institutions at times when public funds are thin on the ground. What one should not risk is a trend whereby they become primarily contract research institutions for industry, so dependent on this as a source of finance that their educational task in basic and exploratory research gets neglected; were that to happen, their input of innovation to industry could well dry up.

All the time one is bound to wonder what the effects of entirely new technologies might be. Breakthroughs need not be limited to the traditional type of medicinal treatment; there is no good reason why, for another century, mankind should continue to regard the ingestion of chemical substances as the principal solution to his various ills. Alongside the alternatives which have always been to hand – ranging from psychotherapy to irradiation and implantable devices, entirely new roads to therapy and to the relief of suffering continue to develop. Gene therapy is only one, unthinkable three decades ago. It is entirely possible that an industry which has proved resilient and flexible in the past will adapt rapidly to these and other changes, opening up through its own initiatives better and more economical roads to treatment than those offered by medicines alone. Such developments are also likely to bring with them structural changes. Current developments in biotechnology already suggest that much future innovation will come from small and specialized independent units, whether commercially based or otherwise, capable of developing projects to the point where larger firms can compete for the task of developing them into practical medicinal treatments. By abandoning some of their attempts to undertake basic innovation themselves, the pharmaceutical companies of the twentieth century could reduce their costs and operate with greater efficiency in the twenty-first century. Small units could also take on other tasks, neglected by the mastodons; a small pharmaceutical firm with experience in the antibiotic field, which sees no close prospect of developing a new antibiotic for a particular condition could, if it has sufficient commitment, manage to delay and temporarily overcome threatened microbial resistance by devising novel combinations of existing drugs. These combinations too, however will require proper investigation before they can be accepted and used; effort will be called for and (where the antibiotics concerned come from different manufacturers) collaboration between firms which have hitherto been only competitors.

As was remarked earlier, the "small is beautiful" concept is making headway, in this sector as in others, bringing individuals closer to work situations where they can maintain their ethics, strive for their ideals, and see the rewards of their work close at hand. One is bound to wonder whether "Big Pharma" will need to be quite so elephantine a generation from now.

Chapter 8

The Industry and the Developing World

8.1. Pharmaceuticals in Developing Countries

At the present day, entire populations in developing countries are still faced from year to year with the fact that effective medicines are hardly available to them, or not at all. The problem has a series of causes, the responsibility for which lies with different parties. In most respects however, the underlying obstacle, extending far beyond the pharmaceutical sector, is one of shortage. Consistently, though to variable degrees, developing countries are short of money and education, of skilled people and wealthy institutions. Many lack adequate communication, the means to exploit what resources they have and the ability to attract the business and investment that might bring them prosperity. In some parts of the world all these difficulties are compounded by weakness of the legal system, an unreliable infrastructure and political instability. And in the meantime, laudable development efforts made in one direction are sometimes outweighed by disasters in another; in the field of health, the HIV/AIDS epidemic has proved a catastrophe that was unforeseeable a generation ago.

Where pharmaceuticals are concerned, the figures speak for themselves. The World Health Organization estimates that one third of the world's population lacks access to the most basic medicines, while in the poorest parts of Africa and Asia this figure climbs to one half (WHO 2000a, 2000c, 't Hoen 2002, WHO 2004). The Organization has also estimated that, in Africa and South-East Asia, prompt diagnosis and treatment with appropriate medicines could save some 4 million lives a year (DFID 2003). To view it from a different angle: 15 per cent of the world's population consumes 91 per cent of the world's drugs by value (World Health Report 2003), while every 3 seconds, a child dies of one of the key diseases of poverty, many of which are curable (Amsterdam 1999).

Bearing in mind that medicines are often society's primary instrument for curing and alleviating disease and that (alongside vaccines) they are a prominent tool for its prevention, it is clear that the developing world cannot hope to progress greatly in improving health as long as good and appropriate medicines are in such short supply. A high proportion of deaths in the developing world are due to illnesses which are in principle curable with medicines that currently exist; others might be cured or relieved with drugs that currently seem within the reach of research, given a little more effort and investment in the right direction. Finally, one can point to instances where useful and necessary drugs have disappeared because of lack of commercial interest in their production. In the case of African trypanosomiasis, which leads to some 40,000 deaths annually, the supply of all four applicable medicines had by 1999 either ceased (eflorinthine HCl) or become insecure (sodium suramin, melarsoprol, pentamidine isethionate) (Pécoul 1999).

Over a long period, the international pharmaceutical industry played no role of any significance in the development of Africa or various other parts of the third world. While it vigorously sought growth opportunities in other new markets it found little reason to look to the tropics and certainly no moral grounds for doing so. As a former executive in a multinational recalls:

> Looking back I see a clear contrast between the way the drug business was reacting to the opening up of the former Soviet republics when they broke free in the nineties and what had happened in Africa in the seventies. In the former USSR we indeed hurried in, perhaps almost too hastily, to take part in the development process. You must not however ascribe that to ethics or idealism; we simply wanted to grow as they grew, because that could create a vast market as we went along. The chances looked good because these were mostly industrialised states with a strong workforce, and they simply needed a repair job; our business trainees understood them; we guessed they would soon be looking for western drugs and finding the money to paid for them at decent prices. In places like most parts of Africa we were much less certain. There was a real chance our money would be going down the drain, not into development. With Europe and America taking virtually all we could buy in the seventies we were not going to take big risks in a part of the world that we didn't really understand with diseases that we had no comprehension of. So we did what we had been doing for eighty years, sending our medicines on consignment to agents, hoping to get some money back, and beyond that leaving well alone. (Interview 26)

The result of such experiences has been what the United Kingdom Government has called a "mismatch between pharmaceutical needs in developing countries and the current nature of the global pharmaceutical market" (DFID 2004 at p. 14). The failure of world-class firms to provide a dependable supply of affordable medicines except to a small upper crust in the cities led the public authorities and the missions to set up alternative channels of distribution using alternative suppliers; that in turn rendered the scene even less inviting for the multinationals.

8.2.   The Basis of Duty for Industry

From the 1970's onwards, a series of writers and travellers unleashed a barrage of fury against the multinational industry for its attitude to the developing world. In part it was castigated for its indifference, in part for activities ranging from the sale of anabolic steroids to stimulate the appetite of starving children to the hawking of costly and unnecessary vitamins. The writings were inspired by tragic memories. Diana Melrose in 1982 introduced her *Bitter Pills* with one such story:

> "As the boat drew into the shore we heard a strange sound from the bank. A woman was crying. We found her with a dead baby in her arms and a collection of medicine bottles beside her. She had spent all her money on these expensive drugs….This Bangladeshi woman had never been told what was obvious to the doctor who found her. The baby had become severely dehydrated from diarrhoea. Her death could have been prevented with a simple home-made solution of water, salt and sugar. No amount of medicine could have kept her alive."

The indignation was often met with a denial of responsibility or with counter-accusations of irresponsible criticism. Only gradually, as the century drew to a close, did a debate become possible and a consensus on action slowly begin to emerge.

Although there has been much criticism of the international pharmaceutical industry in connection with the drugs situation in the Third World, any discussion of its performance must be based on a clear view of whatever duties it may reasonably be said to have. In a purely legal sense, a commercial company can only be said to have a duty towards a community in which it has a presence. If Thomas Beecham, making his Pills in Lancashire in the nineteenth century, had chosen to continue his business in the same manner and market in which it began, he would have acquired no duty towards the people of Kenya. Only when a company actively begins to pursue its business within a particular country (whether by manufacturing goods, establishing a distribution system, advertising products to its population or in some analogous way) will it become subject to the laws of that country. The fact that it has sold some of its products to an independent trading house that has proceeded to resell them at its own initiative to a range of countries does not of itself create obligations for the primary manufacturer under the legal systems of those countries. At most he might incur indirect liability if the product were in such a country to prove dangerously defective or falsely labelled; in that case local proceedings might be brought against the intermediary who could then in turn attempt to pursue a claim across national borders against the primary supplier. Such things do happen but not significantly, since the legal route is complex and slow. The manufacturer will only become directly subject to the legal requirements which pertain in the market where his goods are ultimately sold if he has in some way established a presence in that market.

Current discussion of the pharmaceutical industry's performance in (and towards) the Third World concentrates in fact on much broader issues. The realities of the present day comprise a global market in pharmaceuticals in which no more than 500 medicinal substances are of real importance in treatment and in which a much smaller number of international and transnational firms are generally in a position to control their supply and their pricing as well as the development of new and better products. In that situation, the view has emerged that the pharmaceutical industry, having acquired a position of global power and wealth, has thereby also assumed worldwide the moral duties that go with that station. If one accepts that view, then it follows that, to put it briefly, the industry should adhere worldwide to the legal and ethical standards that have now been so widely defined across the world of pharmaceuticals; and it should respect those standards even in those parts of the world where governments and courts are not in a position to proclaim or enforce them.

It was thinking such as this that inspired Oxfam in 2001, shortly after the merger that led to the formation of GSK, to call on the new corporation to set a moral example to the entire industry:

> Oxfam believes that pharmaceutical companies face a major reputation risk if they do not do more to promote access to life-saving drugs in the developing world. This is particularly important at a time of unprecedented scrutiny of the industry's record in this field. The withdrawal of public support could lead the industry to suffer the same problems of staff recruitment and retention suffered by companies charged with complicity in human rights abuses or environmental damage. Perhaps more significantly it carries with it the threat of more stringent government regulation . . .
>
> . . . GSK could assume a critical leadership role by adopting a more supportive approach to public health in its policy towards developing countries, even within the current TRIPS regime. It is both ethically correct and in the company's self interest to ensure that those who own and control medical knowledge use all means at their disposal to stop preventable diseases from killing millions of people every year, particularly if they are using their exclusive marketing position to prevent others from developing the same knowledge. (Oxfam 2001)

A year later, Oxfam joined with two other development agencies – Save the Children and VSO – to examine the activities in the Third World of 11 major pharmaceutical companies; on the basis of their analysis, they developed a standard for assessing the "corporate social responsibility" of drug companies in responding to health problems in developing countries. Their report "Beyond Philanthropy" (Oxfam 2002) offers a series of benchmarks intended to assist investors in assessing the attitude of companies in this field; the benchmarks may also be valuable to companies themselves in designing and reforming their policies and the principles that should guide their activities. The benchmarks relate to company policies and practices in pricing, patents, joint public/private initiatives, research and development and the appropriate use of medicines. Within the 2 years that followed, the industry was considered according to that standard to have made "substantial progress" in reforming its attitude to the Third World.

In seeking to move forward, pharmaceutical companies were also sometimes receiving encouragement from their own shareholders – a considerable shift in thinking from the days of *Dodge v. Ford Motor Company*:

> In September 2004 the Pharmaceutical Shareowners Group, which united fourteen large international institutional investors, completed a study of the policies and plans of seven of the leading drug companies. The study had been sparked in 2001 by the legal action in South Africa in which 30 major firms attempted to prevent the Government from obtaining AIDS from low-cost sources. Alongside the TRIPS Agreement, which appeared certain to maintain high drug prices in much of the world, the case had in the view of shareholders brought about "marked shifts in societal perceptions" about the industry. According to the group: "A view has emerged that pharmaceutical companies have not been playing their part in tackling the public health crises." In so far as senior management had begun to respond to the world's needs, its response had virtually been limited to very tightly defined disease areas in which the industry had been subjected to heavy outside pressure. (Boseley 2004)

At least in their declarations of intent, if not always in their acts, corporate managers have in recent years begun to accept that in their various fields of activity they indeed owe positive duties to developing countries:

> As a leading international pharmaceutical company we can make a real difference to healthcare in the developing world. We believe this is both an ethical imperative and key to business success. Companies that respond sensitively and with commitment by changing their business practices to address such challenges will be the leaders of the future.

A number of basic principles underpin our contribution to improved healthcare in the developing world:

- Sustainability: Our long-term commitment is to make contributions to world health that are sustainable. This applies equally to the research and development we carry out, the preferential pricing arrangements we make and our community based partnerships.
- Appropriateness: We are sensitive to the diversity of countries and regions and the differing needs of populations in terms of existing healthcare infrastructure levels. In all the countries where our products are available, in both the developed and the developing world, we have a duty to do what we can to ensure they are used in a clinically appropriate way. It would be wrong to sell our products in circumstances where they cannot be used with the right clinical supervision or where they are at risk of being misused . . .
- Support for innovation: . . . Patents stimulate and fundamentally support the continued research and development of new and better medicines, including those for diseases prevalent in the developing world . . .
- Partnership: The significant barriers that stand in the way of Access to Healthcare in the developing world must be tackled as a shared responsibility by all sectors of global society. The pharmaceutical industry can play an important role, but it does not have the mandate, expertise or resources to deliver healthcare unilaterally to developing countries. Our activities are undertaken in partnership with organisations that have relevant specialised knowledge, such as governments, international agencies, charities and academic institutions.
- Reporting: . . . We aim to communicate our overall intentions, activities and progress on an annual basis, as well as to provide regular updates on specific programmes and policies . . .
- Sharing responsibilities: . . . We are seeking the establishment of regulatory, legislative and other mechanisms to minimise diversion of preferentially priced products to developed markets, so that patients most in need receive the treatments intended for them and the company generates sufficient revenue to fund future R&D . . . (Extracted from GSK 2004)

One may wince at a few turns of phrase, but in many respects it would be difficult to find a better formulation of the obligations which rest on a multinational pharmaceutical corporation in the Third World and the extent to which these are formally acknowledged by industry itself.

To sum up: Humanitarian considerations alone would suggest that much of society – and certainly all players in the international pharmaceutical field – should be concerned with these problems of the Third World; the situation results in a vast loss of life and much suffering, more particularly among the poor and underprivileged, and it is in blatant contradiction to the fundamental principles of human rights in health considered in Chapter 2. Even if one were to set humanitarian considerations aside; however, the extent of disease across the world can be shown to result in serious damage to the economy and to the functioning of society in the world as a whole. While the consequences of the situation, in terms of permanent invalidism, suffering and large-scale mortality, are felt most immediately in the developing world, the ability of many forms of infectious disease to travel so rapidly means that they represent a threat to all parts of the world. Some of the causes of disease in the developing world may seem so remote that a western pharmaceutical company might consider itself within its rights to set them aside, confining its own activities to those parts of the world with which it was more familiar. In fact, however, any individual or party engaged in drug issues might fairly be regarded as having a moral obligation to contribute at least something to solving the crisis.

8.3.   Industrial Performance in the Third World

In defining proper standards, and in looking ahead to their attainment, it is not productive to dwell at length on the less creditable aspects of drug company performance in the Third World; many authors have done that in detail (see for example Medawar 1979, Silverman 1982, Ahmad 1990, Chetley 1990, Chowdhury 1996) and activist organizations continue to document the record. As Medawar summarized the scene a quarter of a century ago:

> Between them, the drug companies have been accused of virtually every sin that transnational corporations (in the non-extractive industries) are known to be able to commit – short of attempting to overthrow a democratically elected government. In particular, they have been associated with some of the most extortionate cases of overcharging and profiteering; they have been involved in sometimes indecently aggressive marketing activity; and their emphasis on marketing has given them control over technology which, in many developing countries, is virtually complete. On top of this, a significant proportion of their products – probably upward of one third – are authoritatively described as either undesirable or unnecessary, or both. (Medawar 1979 at p. 111)

Entirely in contrast to this are some much-publicized and entirely creditable activities developed in recent years, ranging from long-term drug donations and heavy discounting agreements to participation in WHO-based public–private development partnerships.

> Merck Inc. introduced the antiparasitic and anthelminthic agent ivermectin (Mectizan) into veterinary practice in the U.S.A. prior to 1980. By 1982 there was

evidence that it could be effective in human onchocerciasis (river blindness), a hitherto untreatable condition affecting many millions of patients in the poorest areas of Africa. It was however clear that virtually no patients could afford to buy the drug, and funding from donors or other agencies was unavailable. In 1987, Merck announced that henceforth it would donate "as much Meclizan as necessary, for as long as necessary, to treat river blindness and help bring the disease under control as a public health problem." The programme has continued up to the present in collaboration with international agencies which have helped to create a distribution system.

The Chief Executive Officer of Merck made direct reference to ethical considerations, speaking of "doing the right thing" and remarked in a later interview on ". . . the research people – how disappointed they would be if the drug never reached the people that would benefit . . . (Hawthorne 2003 at pp. 16–17)

Turning back to the other extreme of behaviour one must recall the events of 2001 when 39 major companies lodged a legal case in Capetown against the Government of South Africa to prevent it from importing from India and elsewhere low-cost generic copies of their patented AIDS drugs. The originating companies had already agreed, after tortuous negotiations with WHO and other agencies, to provide considerable discounts on their own AIDS products, but it had become clear to the Government that by using the still cheaper generic copies the available funding could provide treatment to many more sufferers. Legal experts were generally of the opinion that the Government was acting entirely legally under a statute of 1997, and at the last moment the industry group withdrew its case without going to court. While a tactfully worded "settlement" was published it was clear that the industry had capitulated. The attempt which it had made to suppress low-cost treatment for an entire population was regarded worldwide as both tactless and unethical (Hawthorn 2003 at pp. 208–214).

The industry's record in the developing world thus remains a chequered one, even within a single company. The fact is that, while the international industry has taken some major steps towards recognizing and meeting its moral obligations towards the Third World, too little effort has been made to eliminate concurrent malpractices, large or small:

The German company M withdrew an ineffective and potentially dangerous aphrodisiac from European markets in 1994. The same firm announced in 2002 that it was joining in a WHO-based public–private development partnership in Africa. In 2004, newly-minted batches of the aphrodisiac were still found on sale in a Cairo street market. On enquiry it was found that, at the time of withdrawal in Europe, M had licensed the product to its subsidiary in Cyprus so that production could continue for non-European markets. (Personal notes)

It is clearly necessary that if a corporation accepts a global obligation it should be both willing to ensure and capable of ensuring that its intention is carried through at all the levels at which the firm exercises authority. Having made various efforts to raise or restore its reputation in the Third World, the industry cannot now afford to engender the suspicion that its good works are no more than a facade behind which misbehaviour continues.

8.4. An Overview of Obligations

Bearing in mind that the industry's obligations to society in developing countries rest on a broad ethical basis rather than on specific legal rules it can be helpful to summarize them in general terms before considering some of them in more detail.

A corporation which wishes to meet its obligations to the developing world, or to some chosen part of it should at least set out to ensure that, whatever the formal legal requirements:

- its products meet international standards for quality, efficacy and safety
- the products are accessible, particularly in terms of price
- its research programmes take account of third world needs
- the information which it provides is adequate and dependable
- its clinical investigations adhere to accepted standards.

Within a given country, many of these matters lie within the national jurisdiction to which the industry will be subject if it is physically present, and there is no question of a company modifying these obligations. It will however often be faced with a national administration that is weak, inexperienced, understaffed and perhaps corrupt, a situation which one might readily be tempted to misuse. Instead, the challenge is to act decently, and to assist others to do the same. As in other matters one must respect the law and the regulations and, where these are deficient, act according to the standards which ideally should be in place (Jayasuriya 1985, WHO 1988). As an effective senior regulator in an East African country put it in 2003:

Please look on the absence of an effective regulatory regime in some of the countries around us as no more than a temporary blemish on the road to development; no individual and no institution with an ethical sense should use it as an excuse for persisting in commercial or other practices which have clearly had their day. (Interview 3)

One recurrent difficulty is that presented by corruption. Corrupt practices in the administration, the trade and the professions are entirely illegal everywhere, yet in very many parts of the world virtually universal. An experienced country manager in the pharmaceutical industry offered a practical view:

> It is really no use you people telling us not to give bribes. It's a way of life anywhere south of Milan and you can't ignore it unless you want to find yourself out of a job. Yes, I have bribed doctors to prescribe and regulators to sign pieces of paper that were just lying on their desks and I gave Ministers an incentive to change their minds. In some instances I knew I was simply helping them to get a living wage. What I have not done is to bribe them to do anything improper. If I get someone to use a recent and well-documented drug that way, then I have nothing on my conscience. If I didn't do it people would simply get a similar drug from the competition, probably much less reliable. Provided I do this with a conscience I think I'm doing some good in this devious way . . . (Interview 24, translated and abridged).

8.5.   Quality, Safety and Efficacy

Since the bulk of drugs required for use in the developing world are not manufactured there, foreign firms exporting to these countries clearly have a marked influence on the nature and acceptability of supplies. As noted in Chapter 3, the regulatory authorities in industrialized countries have in recent decades to a large extent assumed much of the *de facto* responsibility for ensuring that the medicines available to their populations attain satisfactory standards as regards their quality and the suitability for the purpose for which they are to be sold. Their role is however essentially to verify the manufacturer's attainments in this regard; the legal *(de jure)* and moral responsibility in these matters remains firmly with the manufacturer or the national licensee (see Section 3.5). This distinction, all too easily overlooked in a fully regulated system, is of crucial importance when one considers those many developing countries where a fully effective system of national regulation has not been attained. Public facilities for quality control are commonly deficient or lacking entirely, and with limited human and other resources it is commonly impossible to evaluate regulatory files relating to efficacy, safety or to other matters; even frontier inspections of imports are as a rule far from comprehensive. Only exceptionally can a bilateral donor or an international agency financing and organising supplies be in a position to provide all the necessary assurances.

Under such circumstances a developing country may remain very much at the mercy of foreign industry and trade and the latter's willingness and ability to provide reliable warranties in these matters. Once again: the ethical standard which a firm needs to adopt is clear; irrespective of whether or not an importing developing country is itself able to impose standards or exercise controls, the firm is morally bound to ensure that products attain and maintain in every batch the standards which would be demanded (and in most cases already have been imposed) by a reputable agency elsewhere.

For the bulk of international producers with their own facilities for evaluation, production and quality assurance and control, this norm is readily attainable, the goods commonly being produced in the same plant and under the same conditions as when they are supplied to other parts of the world. Shortcomings can however occur where such a manufacturer has licensed a factory elsewhere to produce the quantities required for certain markets, without himself ensuring sufficient standards:

> A European manufacturer X franchised to an Indian subcontractor B the production and quality control of certain items intended for export to East Africa. No provision was made for inspection by the franchiser X, but samples taken from certain batches, selected at random, were to be forwarded periodically to X for rechecking in Europe. Illegally and unbeknown to X, the Indian firm entrusted the manufacture of one product, a dextran-based blood substitute, to another Indian firm Z, making no provision for batch control. During its use in hospitals in the African country D, the product proved to be contaminated and fatalities resulted. X acknowledged only moral responsibility, but provided some financial compensation to the victims' families and ensured that future supplies would be shipped directly from the European plant. (Interview 126)

8.6.   Access, Prices and Affordability

The serious problem of lack of access to drugs in developing countries was examined by a Working Group of the United Nations Millennium Project in 2003–2005. (Millennium 2005) Although many of the causes of impaired access lie within these countries, one major impediment has been and remains, as noted earlier, that of price. The problem is a longstanding one, which for a time appeared insoluble; the background needs to be understood.

By the eighties of the twentieth century, the west's science-based industry had settled into a stable pattern of business and financing. The income of the multinational corporations, with ample margins for profit and research, was being very largely derived from the western economy, where prices were high and sometimes very high indeed. Whatever was earned from sales to the poorer markets, comprising what had long been "the colonial world", was a secondary bonus which hardly featured in planning and accounting. For simplicity of operation, many a major firm established for each of its products a single global "export price" for such markets; because of the need to cover administration costs, insurance costs, freight charges and import duties as well as the agent's fees the C.I.F. charge was commonly higher than in the firm's domestic price.

> We were running a commodities import house in Lagos in the sixties, dealing in all sorts of packaged items including medicines, for which we had contacts with various drug houses in England, America and sometimes France and Denmark. To keep it simple we generally used their home catalogues and added on thirty per cent or so for charges. That put the medicines even further out of reach of most people around Lagos, but we supplied the Ministers and the Ambassadors and some businessmen and suchlike, and it paid off. (Interview 24)

In this situation there was clearly no serious intention of dealing with most major public health problems. Some examples briefly illustrate the situation that pertained, and that in many parts of the world still exists:

a. *Treating HIV/AIDS in the Ivory Coast and Uganda: 2000* (UNAIDS 2000). By the end of the century, HIV/AIDS affected more than 36 million people, while a further 21.8 million were estimated to have died since the epidemic began. (CDC 2001) Of all AIDS deaths since the epidemic began, 83 per cent had been in Sub-Saharan Africa. (Adu-Bonna 2001) The only reasonably effective treatment capable at the time of containing the disease and saving life involved lifelong administration of three different retroviral drugs, one of these being didanosine. In the Ivory Coast, the costs of using didanosine alone amounted to $3.48 daily. However, the GNP per head of population was only $1.94 daily, and the public health services could provide only some $0.03 per capita daily ($10.95 annually) in drug funding, which by African standards was relatively high. Obtaining the drug at current prices would therefore have involved spending twice the average patient's total income and a hundred times as much as the country had to date been able to afford. To give three drugs would vastly multiply the problem; Efavirenz was 80 per cent more expensive than didanosine and idinavir 160 per cent more expensive.

   The situation in Uganda, where by 2000 some 5 per cent of the population were suffering from HIV infection, was even more serious. Didanosine was on sale at a price equivalent to $5.26 daily, while the GNP per head was only $0.87 daily, and public drug funding amounted on average to only $0.01 daily.

b. *Treating resistant malaria in Indonesia* (EDM 2001). In Indonesia, malaria is commonly due to the highly resistant falciparium parasite. Life-saving treatment was available using malarone. However, a curative course of treatment, if the drug was purchased at the usual global price, cost some $42. This had to be set against the fact that the Gross National Product per head towards the end of the century was only $1.60 daily, and that total annual drug expenditure per head in 1990 was only US$5.80.

c. *Treating cryptococcal meningitis in Thailand* (EDM 2001). *Cryptococcal meningitis* is likely to demand lifelong treatment with fluconazole. The original product as supplied by the company holding the patent was in 2001 sold at a price equivalent to US$14.00 per treatment day. However, the Thai per capita GDP was only $5.47 per treatment day.

The prohibitive influence of price in such situations is evident. While some spokesmen for the pharmaceutical industry advanced arguments to the effect that the non-availability of treatment primarily reflected other obstacles, ranging from failure of distribution to incompetent diagnosis or prescribing, activists were quick to suggest that such explanations only reflected the lack of experience of the pharmaceutical industry in the African situation. It was exchanges such as these which, around the turn of the century, began to result in negotiated measures to alleviate selected problems. Even though progress was to be punctuated by such dramas as the AIDS debacle in Africa, advances were booked:

> By 2001 some initial agreements had been concluded between independent bodies and individual firms to supply specified drugs to particular markets at exceptionally low ("equity") prices. The International Planned Parenthood Federation, UNFPA and the Rockefeller Foundation were among those who signed early supply agreements, one of which provided for the delivery of hormonal (and other) contraceptives at prices as little as 1% of those being charged for the same products in the United States. Even some advanced biotechnical products were incidentally covered; in January 2004 Médécins sans Frontières concluded negotiations for supplies to Sudan of injectable liposoal amphotericin B (AmBisone), is a life-saving treatment for visceral liposomiasis (kala azar) which kills some 50,000 patients yearly. The original price was $3750 for a complete course of treatment; with a 90% discount this was reduced to $350, a reduction sufficient to make the drug accessible at least to severely ill patients who would be unable to tolerate an older and more toxic drug. (Healy 2004)

Agreement by manufacturers to price reductions of this extent may be welcomed enthusiastically or greeted with a degree of suspicion, particularly since they sometimes raise questions regarding the calculation of the original price level. MSF now periodically issues overviews of the offers agreed to date and the terms to which they are subject (MSF 2002). In some cases the conditions set for a developing country are devious, and it can be difficult for an outsider to determine whether such a price reduction represents a genuine attempt to provide assistance or a symbolic public relations gesture having limited practical value or perhaps even masking a commercial ploy. It is at least obvious that if a relief programme is publicly announced it should be regarded as a commitment and implemented:

> In July 2004, an AIDS coalition reported that, when the Pfizer Corporation introduced its donation programme for fluconazole in South Africa, it had under prolonged activist pressure agreed to introduce a similar programme in Latin America and had publicized the fact. In fact, according to the coalition, no such programme had been introduced and sufferers from severe fungal infections accompanying AIDS continued to die as a result. (ACT-UP 2004)

The effect of reducing prices to affordable levels has often been dramatic both in terms of drug usage and public health:

> In Brazil, for example, where a Presidential Decree declared that compulsory licenses on drugs could be issued in the event of a national emergency, the AIDS epidemic was declared to constitute such an emergency. Generic AIDS drugs were then made by government laboratories and given free of charge to all HIV-positive persons. The effect of this policy was to almost halve the number of AIDS deaths between 1996 and 1999, as well as to reduce the incidence of opportunistic infection by between 60 to 80 per cent over the same time period. (Teixeira 2001)

> Conversely, one can quantify the degree of deprivation resulting from high prices in particular situations. In Brazil, as a consequence of the above-mentioned generic initiative, 1000 people with HIV/AIDS can for a given sum of money be treated with the triple combination AZT/3TC + NVP (excluding the cost of diagnostics and other expenses), while with the same amount of money in Thailand, where the same combination of medicines are not available as generic products, it is possible to treat only 350 people, leaving 650 to die. (Perez-Casas 2000)

It could very well be that the pharmaceutical industry is moving towards an altogether broader policy of "equity pricing" in much of the Third World, thereby providing far broader access for the poor to much-needed medicines and opening a door to what in the future may become more lucrative markets. What level of pricing will be sustainable in the long run is still uncertain. Figures reviewed above and in Chapter 6 show that for older drugs which are out of patent the cost reductions achieved can be little short of sensational. For newer medicines still under patent it is unclear how much can be achieved, but the statistics suggest that in many situations the income obtainable by selling to a larger patient population at a lower price can equal or exceed that earned from very limited sales at world prices. All current thinking as regards the future of pricing may however need to be revised as the provisions of TRIPS (see Section 2.2.4) come into force worldwide, with the possibility that generic supplies will be less readily available than hitherto.

The principal legal obstacle arising during negotiations for differential prices has been the desire to find firm guarantees that a medicine supplied to a developing country at a sharply reduced price will not be diverted illegally to a high-priced market. (GSK 2004, Ghana 2003, EC 2002) This has on occasion occurred, though well-designed contracts of supply generally prevent any significant loss; it is currently recommended that goods supplied under such agreements be provided with distinctive packaging so that they are much less likely to be accepted in normal trade channels (DFID 2005).

8.7. Research and Development

As noted in Chapter 5 and above, the possibilities for drug treatment of many diseases existing in the developing world are gravely limited by the fact that they have hardly been the subject of drug innovation. The remote prospects of an adequate financial return from poor countries mean that science-based companies see little temptation to enter these areas with well-financed and viable research projects, even where the patient population is large and sometimes massive. Western governments too for a long period saw little reason to induce the industry to move further in this direction, having a greater interest in the profitable growth of exports to markets where world prices could be demanded (MSF 2005a). MSF has contrasted the stagnation in this field with the massive and immediate effort which was unleashed in the United States to tackle the supposed anthrax threat in 2003 or the international effort which in that same year produced within weeks a diagnostic kit for SARS (Severe Acute Respiratory Syndrome) (MSF 2005a).

Chapter 7 considered possible future changes in the process of funding and stimulating research in order to achieve a greater degree of innovation, and several of the approaches considered there could benefit developing countries. Some of the approaches most widely discussed in recent publications are summarized in Table 8.A; they are not mutually exclusive.

Table 8.A
Possible Approaches to Expanded Drug Innovation for Developing Countries

---

Better definition of therapeutic research priorities both by governments and in international fora.

Reallotment of resources in research-based industry, with reduction in marketing expenditure and in "me-too" research, but greater emphasis on fully innovative programmes for developing countries

Selective pricing policies in all countries to reward innovative products

Prioritized registration policies in all countries to reward innovative products

Government-funded or EU-supported academic programmes in donor countries, attuned to specific Third World goals

Government-subsidized or EU-supported industrial research programmes in donor countries, attuned to specific Third World goals

International Public/Private Partnerships for drug development e.g.
  (1) Medicines for Malaria Venture (MMV)
  (2) Global Alliance for TB Drug Development
  (3) International Aids Vaccine Initiative (IAVI)

Development of an EU Technology Platform for the Pharmaceutical Industry

Creation of independent non-commercial drug research organizations based on philanthropic funding (Model: Oneworld Health)

Non-profit research in a collaborating network of institutions, both academic and commercial, with firm central management. (Model: Drugs for Neglected Diseases Initiative)

Sources: WHO (2004b), Millennium (2005), GSK (2005), DFID (2005), MSF (2001), MSF (2005) and Perlman (2002)

A possible approach in an alternative direction would be for science-based companies to create links with selected centres working in the field of traditional medicines. The use of entirely traditional remedies in Africa and Asia is vast, and is based very largely on native plants. Traditional medicine of this type is as a rule practised independently of western medicine, and many of its remedies have not been systematically examined. Bearing in mind however the extent to which pharmaceuticals used in modern medicine are still those based on (or derived indirectly from) plant sources similar to those used by traditional healers it is indeed likely that, in some instances where synthetic chemistry fails to provide an approach, inspiration will be found in this direction.

Emphatic recommendations for specific projects frequently emerge from the Traditional Medicine Programme of the World Health Programme. For a firm willing both to expand its research in novel directions and to provide direct development assistance, a relatively modest investment in a search for agents derived from traditional tropical medicine could prove both rewarding and prestigious.

8.8. Information and Education

The principles that should govern the provision of information by the pharmaceutical industry in any country have been considered in Chapter 5, and they apply fully in developing countries; information must be adequate, balanced, objective and verifiable. These duties are especially stringent in the developing world where the audience is to such a great extent at the purveyor's mercy. Lack of education and limited access to literature may render the prescriber and others unusually dependent on the information that the industry provides. Marketing and Advertising Codes which have proved effective in western countries should be carefully respected and promotional material should be in keeping with the Data Sheets or Summaries of Product Characteristics produced by recognized authorities. National authorities in developing countries rarely have the capacity to inspect the flow of promotional material or to maintain standards; in such conditions a mutual system of self-regulation of advertising (Chapter 3), which has proven its value in western countries, could be helpful.

In Chapter 5 of this volume, reasons were adduced for the pharmaceutical industry to abstain from direct involvement in education. It could be argued that this standard, conceived in countries where public and other impartial educational systems are fully in operation, applies with even greater force in developing countries where health and professional teaching systems may be deficient and one therefore needs to be doubly cautious as regards any "educational" process that could carry a commercial message. In situations of underdevelopment however one may need to adapt one's approach if there is to be any progress at all. The ideal of impartial teaching must be maintained if education is not to be tainted, but there should always be fair opportunities to allow an industry to make its name known. In a number of countries the pharmaceutical industry has found it possible to assist schools and colleges to obtain well-recognized educational materials from abroad, which would otherwise have been inaccessible because of foreign currency restrictions.

8.9. Clinical Investigation in Developing Countries

The question of clinical investigations in developing countries has sometimes led to acrimonious debate, largely because two different issues have been confused. Criticism in principle of such studies dates largely from a time when it was found that clinical studies of an ethically unacceptable type were being conducted by multinational companies in the developing world in a deliberate attempt to evade the ethical and legal standards that apply to such investigations in the industrialized west. There were similar reports of tainted investigations performed in countries which were at the time behind the so-called "iron curtain":

> In the decade following the thalidomide tragedy in 1960–1, a number of firms were known to have made arrangements for safety investigations of new drugs in human pregnancy using Hungarian women who were on the waiting list for abortion. Such studies could as a rule be carried out rapidly and at low cost, and although the standard was often low the results were used for preliminary in-house screening reviews and on occasion submitted to various authorities in order to obtain early regulatory approval. This type of activity appears to have ceased as international contacts have developed and worldwide norms for clinical work have been established in the literature and in regulation.

The unfavourable publicity likely to be accorded today to such practices by the world media, the consumer movement and other independent monitoring groups could well be sufficient to dissuade any firm from engaging in them.

In much of the developing world, specific legislation and regulation to govern clinical research is still lacking, though the sponsor is often required to notify such studies to the Minister of Health. Whatever the formalities, the standards demanded if trials in human subjects are to be ethically defensible as well as reliable are well defined in the literature and they lay considerable demands on both the sponsor and the investigator (Sections 4.5 and 9.2). Experience (and in some instances specific training and certification) are required. The adoption of these standards in European, American, Commonwealth and Japanese systems of regulation, backed by the Helsinki Declaration of the World Medical Association and by WHO recommendations, has in effect rendered them universally binding, at least in an ethical sense and often in a legal sense as well. The practical problem in many parts of the developing world is that the experience or facilities are lacking to perform these studies in accordance with these standards and thus in a manner providing adequate protection to the trial subject.

Where however clinical work can be performed adequately there is sometimes good reason to do it, principally when one needs to determine the efficacy of drugs under tropical conditions or in disorders that are rare or unknown in western countries. In addition it can be necessary to perform studies of drug metabolism in differing populations because of racial variations. There is, for example, evidence that Asians may require smaller doses of neuroleptic drugs and suffer adverse effects at lower doses than Caucasians even after adjustments for body weight (Wood and Zhou 1991). For various other drugs it has been found that there are significant differences in metabolism and therefore in safe dosage levels as between Chinese/Japanese populations and Europeans (Balant and Bechtel 1994). Less justifiable, but unfortunately on occasion unavoidable, is repetitious work which has to be carried out in a particular country merely to satisfy regulatory demands or accommodate a local situation; in such a situation the formal requirements of the law may go well beyond what ethical considerations would demand – and indeed create situations which are themselves ethically questionable:

> Right up to the mid-nineties we were having to set up formal clinical trials just to please the local people in some countries, especially in Latin America, though it did happen in Africa and elsewhere. We would turn up with a thousand pages of sound clinical material which had passed the regulators in Washington or Berlin with flying colours, only to be told with a smile that we had to provide a number of local studies in some designated hospital round the corner. Here and there one also met a genuine belief that you couldn't believe evidence from over the border, but as a rule there was an element of prestige or money in it – I recall one case where we knew that the regulator was splitting the proceeds with the hospital director. Naturally it was a waste of time, particularly because you often had to deal with people who had really no idea how to do a trial or didn't have enough patients to carry it out properly. The embarrassing thing was when they wanted our help to publish their results in an international medical journal, and our people knew that the findings wouldn't stand up to critical examination. (Interview 4)

Standards established for use in industrialized countries may not always be adequate in Third World situations. Various attempts have been made to define the risks which are or might be associated with drug trials in developing countries and to suggest supplementary precautions. The WHO has suggested standards (Hubscher 1993) and several major pharmaceutical companies have developed internal guidelines of their own (GSK 2002). In part one is dealing with real problems which need to be accommodated, in part one needs to be prepared to rebuff unjustified criticism. From the point of view of a sponsoring company there is an obvious risk that the performance of studies in a developing country's population by a western industry, especially if the subjects are relatively uneducated, will be viewed as highly suspect in the light of current thinking on equity and human rights.

In the local situation it may prove wise to secure clearance of the trial design not only from the national drug authorities and medical association

but also from international experts familiar with the design and performance of studies in the specialism concerned, for example a clinical phar-
macologist attached to a school of tropical medicine. The ethics of the
study need to be discussed with whatever local body is likely to be considered most appropriate – if there is no ethics committee, the opinion of community leaders and religious bodies may prove most helpful. Particular care
must be taken to inform the trial subjects in a manner which they will
understand, given the confines of language and education, and to obtain
their fully informed consent; in some parts of the world it is also the custom that consensus be obtained from the extended family or a community
group. Whatever payments are made to an investigator or a trial subject
should be modest and in keeping with local standards; as in any clinical
study it is important to avoid exposing any person to financial temptation
to act against his better judgement. Finally, when working in a developing
country it may be advisable for the sponsoring company to place its trial
monitor close to where the work is to be carried out so that the study can
be kept under surveillance and standards maintained.

8.10. Partnerships and Organizational Links

For a long period, the public and private drug sectors in developing
countries – and for that matter at the international policy level as well –
worked largely in isolation from one another. Within countries, public and
non-profit drug supply systems had come into being mainly because of the
failure of the private sector to provide nationwide supplies of affordable
medicines. Internationally (see Sections 3.5.10 and 8.12), the research-
based industry had remained suspicious of government intentions.
Relatively recent attempts to develop a measure of collaboration are proceeding cautiously and in particular through a number of public–private
partnerships. As noted in Section 2.9 these are best still regarded as experimental, but at their best they could provide a useful way ahead with the
two sectors playing complementary roles to serve developing countries'
needs. Promising work is emerging in collaboration with (or under the auspices of) the United Nations and its specialized agencies, notably the WHO.
That is entirely logical: western pharmaceutical industries are often not
well placed to select and implement themselves the various forms of activity which they could undertake and which the developing world needs.
Working however in collaboration with international organizations or bilateral donors which can establish meaningful and well-coordinated programmes of assistance in the pharmaceuticals field for particular countries

or in special diseases areas they can achieve a great deal. For the firm, its involvement in such a programme may at the outset appear to comprise little more than humanitarian or charitable aid but, quite apart from the issue of duty, such activities could well serve as a transitional step to closer business involvement with these countries in the future.

Various initiatives taken to date (ABPI 2002, APG 2005, MSF 2005a) suggest that, given appropriate safeguards, collaboration of this type can be productive. Examples relating to drug development and supply include:

> The *Accelerating Access Initiative* in which Merck Inc and other firms have cooperated since 2001 with UNAIDS, the WHO, UNICEF, UNFPA and the World Bank as well as with other bodies to broaden access, affordability and appropriate use of medicines in HIV infections and AIDS-related conditions (UNAIDS 2003).
> *The Global Alliance for TB Drug Development*, formed to accelerate discovery and development of effective and affordable tuberculostatics for TB-endemic. A broad alliance works with commercial R&D pharmaceutical companies to identify promising substances and move them along the development pipeline.

> The *Global Alliance for Vaccines and Immunization* (GAVI), seeking to improve the delivery of Hepatitis B, *Haemophilus influenzae* and Yellow Fever vaccines at a low level of development. GAVI involves international organizations, recipient governments, the vaccine industry, research institutions and service delivery NGOs.

> The *International AIDS Vaccine Initiative* (IAVI), designed to support early discovery and development of an effective HIV vaccine. IAVI receives major financial support from a number of major philanthropic foundations, the World Bank and nine national governments.

> The *Medicines for Malaria Venture* (MMV), intended to select, guide, fund and further research undertaken done by others to discover new antimalarials and ensure their availability. MMV works in partnership with research institutions, ministries of health, disease control programmes, the R&D pharmaceutical industry, academia and non-governmental institutions to improve the availability of safe, effective and affordable antimalarials.

> The *Drugs for Neglected Diseases Initiative (DfND)*, sponsored by Médecins sans Frontieres and others; the Initiative deserves

special mention since it has created what is still a unique form of collaboration between organizations of differing nature and offers a remarkable opportunity for the pharmaceutical industry to participate at very little expense to itself in health development (Pécoul 2004). In these various ways it distinguishes itself from other partnerships, where the effort is directed primarily to disorders such as malaria and tuberculosis which are prevalent both at higher and lower levels of development, and where success would thus provide a reasonable basis for future earnings. DfND is by contrast directed purely to the needs of the poorest countries concentrating its efforts on conditions such as the kinetoplastid diseases (leishmaniasis, trypanothione, and Chagas disease) where lack of purchasing power has formed a serious deterrent to commercially orientated drug research. Designed to profit from the fact that so many pharmacological compounds which could bear promise in rare diseases are, as noted earlier, lying unused on laboratory shelves, DfND aims to secure non-commercial rights to these and examine them further through the participation of a chain of participating state-funded laboratories in different countries. The corporations making these compounds available will be invited and entitled to participate in the final stages of development so that eligible compounds can be put into production and made available rapidly for medical use. Using these and other approaches, DfND currently bears substantial promise. One measure of the pharmaceutical industry's social commitment in the coming years could well be the extent to which it provides practical assistance to DfND and whatever like-minded ventures may coming into being.

Finally, one may note that the larger pharmaceutical companies have in recent years all established their own Foundations or collaborative agreements, involved in various forms of philanthropic or development work.

Examples include *Abbott Global Care Initiatives, the BMS Foundation* and the *Lilly MDB-TB Partnership* (dealing with multiple drug-resistant tuberculosis). (APG 2005)

Without a full insight into the activities and financing of these bodies it is however in some instances not possible to measure the extent of their philanthropic involvement as contrasted with their role in image-building for the parent company.

8.11. Donations

It has become customary for major pharmaceutical companies to make donations, generally of drugs but also in kind, to developing countries, while similar donations may also be provided as part of the relief effort in states of emergency occurring in any part of the world. The total global extent of such donations is not known with any certainty, particularly since many are not quantified or listed with any recognized aid agency. In 2004 the UN Millennium Commission's Working Group on Access to Drugs was informed by industry participants that since 1998 10 major companies in the "Partnership for Quality Medical Donations" had donated products worth $2.7 billion to developing countries, this figure being exclusive of all other donations to the Third World. In principle, aid in kind can be of particular value since the drugs can be put to use at once, the source is usually unimpeachable and because the goods are obtained at low cost from source the extent of the aid is likely to be larger than if financial support were be provided.

> By 2003 Merck Inc. had through its ivermectin project for river blindness (see above) made treatment available to more than 40 million patients yearly in 34 countries, and the programme had been expanded to other conditions. (IFPMA 2004)

The principal problems which have been experienced with donations arise when they are inappropriate to their purpose (Autier 2002); the choice may well have been made to suit the convenience of the donor rather than the recipient. At worst the donation may have served a purpose other than that of providing assistance:

> A U.S. company donated a large supply of a vaccine to a Western African country, the supply being handed over to the Ministry of Health at a ceremony attended by representatives of the U.S. Embassy. Quality control tests shortly afterwards found the entire supply to be life-expired and it was necessary to discard it. An internal investigation revealed that the firm had become entitled to obtain a substantial tax rebate by donating surplus stock to charity before its expiry date was attained. The donation had been publicised by the corporation's public relations department as a demonstration of its humanitarian activities. (Interview 11)

> In Uganda in 1993 two full-size containers were found to be full of donated drugs which were unusable because of inadequate quality, life expiry or their unsuitability for existing needs; destruction would involve major expense for which no funds were available.

In 1996 the WHO, having examined the various abuses of the donation system, whether involving commercial or other donors, drew up a set of guidelines for its member states, which are now widely respected and have in some countries been adopted into law (DAP 1996). A basic principle was that donations of medicines and medical supplies would henceforth be accepted and their importation permitted only if there had been adequate prior consultation with the health authorities. A licence would be granted only if the product met an existing need, was formulated in accordance with scientific principles and held recognized national licences, and would have a sufficient period of validity to allow for import and distribution. A number of national regulations have added a requirement regarding appropriate labelling or accompanying leaflets. There seems no doubt that any company proposing or undertaking donations in kind should respect the rules in force nationally or, should these be lacking, the principles laid down by the WHO.

A particular problem to be solved is that of *language*:

> In 1996, during a consultancy inspection of national drug storage facilities in Ulan Bator, Mongolia, a large batch of antibiotics was encountered which had been supplied for emergency relief by a major European drug supplier and was intended for immediate distribution throughout the country. Both the packaging texts, inserts and background materials were found to be in German, which is not an accessible language in Mongolia. (Interview 42)

A practical solution would be to ensure that supplied or donated medicines are always accompanied by information materials in sufficient quantities to meet the needs of most users, printed in one or more widely accessible languages; in the case of emergency supplies, where there is no opportunity for repackaging in the correct language, translated material in sufficient quantities might be supplied separately.

Unique preparations. On occasion a reasonable demand arises for a drug or drug combination which is not (or is no longer) regarded acceptable by most regulatory agencies in industrialized countries.

> Documented examples relate *inter alia* to:
>
> a. An obsolescent drug for tuberculosis possessing relatively high toxicity, but available at a price within the reach of large populations who would otherwise have no access to treatment. (Interview 88)
>
> b. A fixed combination of antibiotics, to be used in emergency situations or where facilities for bacteriological typing are not available; the manufacturing country proposed to refuse an export licence on the grounds that treatment without laboratory testing would irresponsible. (Interview 88)
>
> c. A request for commercial supplies of a still experimental drug which appeared promising in the treatment of a hitherto resistant and commonly fatal parasitic infection involving children. (Interview 9)

No procedural and ethically sound solution appears to exist for such situations. What would seem advisable is that a pharmaceutical company avoids taking decisions itself in such problematical matters but instead seeks and accepts authoritative advice from an impartial source, for example, that of the relevant technical programme or regional office of the WHO. Whatever solution is adopted it is likely to prove controversial, and no suspicion should be allowed to arise that it has been taken primarily on commercial grounds.

8.12. Essential Drugs

The "Essential Drugs" initiative of the WHO, developed from 1977 onwards, was (and remains) a strikingly successful initiative to improve the situation of medicines in the third world, and one in which the research-based pharmaceutical industry could have played a major role from the start. That it did not do so can only be attributed to an initial lack of foresight in some quarters:

> The initiative was built around a simple concept: the setting of strict priorities in drug selection so as to ensure good use of the funds which could be mobilized to provide drugs for developing countries. In the first instance a group of experts brought together by WHO developed a model list of Essential Drugs – initially 230 items defined as "those which satisfy the health care needs of the majority of the population"; all were well established and available at low cost. Member states were encouraged to develop their own lists according to local needs. Initiatives in later years included training courses for prescribers, based on the use of such a basic list, regular revision of the model list, programmes to promote efficient procurement and in 2002/3 publication of a WHO Model Formulary providing reliable prescribing information (WHO 2003b). In the early phases there was hope within WHO that the International Federation of Pharmaceutical Manufacturers' Associations (IFPMA) would collaborate, encouraging its associated firms to provide massive supplies of drugs to the third world at low cost. In 1977 however the Federation viewed the programme as one which would destroy innovation and seek to limit the range of drugs available, perhaps worldwide:
>
> > An industry spokesman described the WHO initiative as "ill-advised and counter-productive" . . . the industry was "strongly opposed to the concept" – According to IFPMA, if essential drug lists were taken up by governments they would "result in substandard rather than improved medical care and might well reduce health standards already attained." (Cited by Melrose 1982 at p. 180)
>
> The programme therefore sought the bulk of its supplies elsewhere, stimulating rapid growth in the generic industry.

In the 40 years since the Essential Drugs Programme came into being, support to drug supplies has been provided largely through public aid programmes. Bilateral and international support from much of the world has created national chains to deal with the procurement, storage and distribution of medicines; assistance has been given in writing laws and regulations, staffing regulatory agencies, building warehouse and transport systems and publishing drug compendia and bulletins to guide prescribers. In the meantime, the sale of branded "specialities" from multinationals remained very much on a secondary plane, with limited urban distribution to the affluent and sale through private pharmacies. The realization within "big pharma" after the initially negative reaction from IFPMA that the developing world could provide an important entry into an extremely large future market that merited cultivation led major manufacturers to revise their views, and many multinational firms have in later years supplied medicines at negotiated prices to procurement centres working according to Essential Drugs principles.

8.13. Counterfeit and Substandard Drugs

The issue of counterfeiting has been considered above primarily in connection with trademark protection (Section 2.2.4). The practice is extensive in many developing countries and often involves international trading between them; it is only likely to be countered effectively by close international collaboration and inspection, coupled with firm controls in the recipient countries. The latter is a further example of a situation in which there can be valuable collaboration between industry and the health authorities in the developing world.

8.14. Perspectives

Development is a long process, with its ups and downs at every stage; so long as it is still in progress, which is likely to be a question of many decades, one population will continue to enjoy a much higher degree of wealth and health than another. Fortunately, it is also a characteristic of the world of the early twenty-first century that societies work together and that one society provides aid to another; to that end, money, goods, finance and knowledge constantly pass across frontiers for purposes other than that of seeking direct financial reward. By coming to recognize that it has certain duties to the developing world, the pharmaceutical industry has already engaged to some extent in that process.

To return to the issue raised at the beginning of this chapter: it should be clear today that practical and constructive reactions such as the above to the needs of developing countries are rather more than purely voluntary or charitable acts. All rights create obligations; the existence of the right to health (like all human rights) can be regarded as imposing a series of obligations on all parties engaging in the sector. Those rights, meriting respect by the industry just as by all other parties have been summarized as comprising:

- The right to *respect*, and to *freedom from unwarranted interference*; this has been interpreted to mean that those who are in the business of providing preventive, curative or palliative care must ensure that that it is indeed provided when needed. Services once provided, whether commercial or professional, must be continued or further developed.
- The right to *protection;* this goes along with an obligation to the providers to ensure that the weak as well as the strong find their way, all having equal access to health, and that sudden emergent needs are promptly met.
- The right to *fulfilment* brings with it an obligation on others ". . . to facilitate, provide and promote processes ensuring the preservation of the right."

To those more accustomed to the exact technological terms in which drug law and regulation are usually phrased, such standards may seem amorphous and vague, but they represent a roof under which more is constantly growing. Under any of these headings one can find a reflection of the principles of common decency and loyalty, as well as those of honesty and social awareness. Above all, when one has over a long period assumed a task which is supposed to serve society well, has carried it out in the past with some success and proclaimed loudly that one can safely be entrusted with it in the future, one will thereby have made a promise and assumed a duty. That is the essence of the obligations which are now progressively being accepted by the pharmaceutical industry in the developing world.

Chapter 9

Special Situations

9.1. Ethics of Animal Studies

For well over a century, the development of medicines has relied heavily on the performance of animal experiments on a large scale. In the year 2000 in the United Kingdom alone some 2.71 million animal procedures were carried out, 94 per cent of these for safety testing in medicine, with most of these involving drugs. Some 80 per cent of the animals used were rats or mice (Home Office 2001).

Those involved in the performance of these studies argue that they are indispensable, both for initial screening and for later toxicity testing. Of the many thousands of compounds which may be synthesized or newly identified in a laboratory in the course of a few years, only a handful are likely to show promising biological activity; others may be merely toxic and many others inactive. At the moment when these substances first become available there is often little beyond hypotheses to suggest what type of activity might be present unless they are closely similar in structure to existing compounds of known usefulness. The first tests are likely to be carried out in small rodents under full anaesthesia, with a range of measures in place ready to detect any effect on the main organ systems. Should a potentially valuable effect be detected, further tests on larger numbers of animals will examine and quantify it in greater detail. Toxicity studies will begin with administration of high doses to detect the level at which toxicity occurs. Selected substances will then proceed to testing in a range of species, perhaps including rabbits, dogs, cats and primates. The tests likely to be of greatest relevance to man will be those in the higher animals. Should serious work in human subjects be proposed, extensive toxicity studies over long periods will then be performed in animals.

The groups which on ethical and humanitarian grounds oppose animal experiments point to the many occasions on which the evidence from such studies proves to be only partly relevant to man, and sometimes misleading. They stress the need for more effort to find non-animal test systems, while acknowledging the difficulties involved. They insist particularly on the need to avoid animal work when the product at which the research is aimed is not of vital health importance – work to develop cosmetics has been particularly condemned.

The scientists working in this field point emphatically to the failure to date of most attempts to find substitutes for animal studies; investigations using biochemical systems or isolated animal tissues have provided relatively little information. Some promise is borne by the use of transgenic animals which, because of their greater biological resemblance to human subjects may provide reliable evidence in work performed on a much smaller scale than hitherto. To date, however, the prospects for developing comprehensive test systems without involving animals do not appear good, though some biochemical and *in vitro* models are in use. Means of avoiding severe suffering have been developed, and situations in which animal experiments can be avoided have been delineated. All in all, it would seem that policies are developing towards a temporary compromise which can be revised as progress is made towards a further reduction in the need for this type of testing. Manufacturers have sometimes been the subject of violent protests and demonstrations by groups seeking to eliminate animal testing, and both from the point of view of ethics and for the sake of their reputation they must be seen to be making genuine efforts to progress on the issue.

One compromise model is that presented in recent legislation in a number of countries, of which the Netherlands "Experiments on Animals Act", in force since 1997 may be taken as an example (Netherlands 1997). Like similar legislation elsewhere it creates a licensing system. Animal experiments may be conducted only by a qualified licensee and only when they can be considered important in health research:

> A licence shall permit experiments . . . only insofar as the experiments are intended to benefit, either directly or indirectly, the health or nutrition of human beings or animals.
>
> No animal experiment shall be conducted for a purpose:
>
> - which, by expert consensus, may also be achieved by means other than an animal experiment, or by means of an experiment using fewer animals or entailing less distress than the experiment in question;
>
> - the importance of which does not justify the distress caused to the animal.
>
> No animal experiment shall be conducted for the purpose of developing new or testing existing cosmetics covered by rules based on the Commodities Act. Each individual experiment has to be approved by an authorized ethics committee

No animal experiment may be conducted unless . . . a recommendation has been made by an ethics review committee recognised . . . (under this Act) Efforts to prevent excessive suffering are mandatory . . . A licence holder shall be obliged to ensure that the animal suffers as little distress as possible without defeating the object of the experiment.

A licence holder shall ensure that, if the experimental animal could experience distress as a result of acts carried out without anaesthetic, a general or local anaesthetic is administered to the animal to prevent such pain. This obligation shall not apply in cases where the anaesthetic would defeat the object of the experiment. Categories of treatment may be specified by Order in Council which, regardless of the provisions contained in the previous sentence, must always be carried out under anaesthetic.

An animal may not be used more than once for an experiment that entails severe distress. (Netherlands 1997)

This and similar pieces of legislation may be considered good examples of laws built purely on the basis of ethical considerations, though in this case making what was considered to be a necessary compromise with reality. There are minor variations in the rules; several of these pieces of legislation provide for example that ". . . if an animal is in severe distress which cannot be relieved it must . . . be humanely killed immediately regardless of whether the purpose of the research has been achieved." (ABPI 2001) and most systems provide for both regular and unannounced inspection of the premises and of the work in progress.

While opponents of animal studies have claimed that those conducting such work may through sheer exposure to it become callous and inhumane, interviews with those concerned seem to show that the staff involved are fully convinced of the necessary spirit and purpose of the law and will go beyond its mere literal provisions where necessary to ensure that its ethical basis is respected. There also appears be a progressive decline in the extent of animal testing (ABPI 2001, 2002), though the figures are difficult to interpret because of the growth of research programmes; harmonization of the testing requirements set by different national regulatory agencies promises to eliminate duplication of work.

An issue which has from time to time caused concern has been the emergence of evidence that some unwelcome findings emerging from animal experiments have, like some human experimental evidence, been concealed. Although the destruction of animals and records would probably be prevented at the present day by the legislative provisions on record-keeping, the fact that such incidents can occur provides a further reason for seeking to eliminate animal testing of pharmaceuticals wherever one can find an alternative:

> The instance which I have in mind was in the sixties when the company which you name was working on post-marketing safety tests with our principal oral contraceptive and we were testing it on female beagle dogs. After some time several of the dogs developed breast tumours. Management got very concerned, because that could have destroyed the drug, killing it with the regulators if they heard about it. After an internal conference – and they kept no records of it, you understand – the Research Manager ordered the dogs to be destroyed and the records taken out of the files, with everyone told to remain silent. Actually one other oral contraceptive, coming from a different firm which was a bit more honest about it, was taken off the market because of the beagle dog problem. It turned out in the end that all these gestagens used in the pill had this problem in beagle dogs, which throws some doubt on the whole experiment. (Interview 8)

A similar instance of concealment of unfavourable animal findings was cited in Chapter 2 (Section 2.2.5) in connection with employment law, and others are informally known to have taken place.

Destruction of animal evidence will constitute a double offence under current legislation on animal experimentation (since the records will be incomplete and the experiment will no longer have served a purpose in human medicine). If the file from which unfavourable evidence has been deleted is subsequently presented to the drug regulatory agency this will constitute a further offence under drug law (i.e. submission of incomplete evidence).

9.2. Ethics of Human Studies[1]

9.2.1. *General principles of human experimentation*

The conduct of clinical experiments in human subjects will never be free of controversy but the only entirely reliable means of obtaining information on the properties of a pharmaceutical in man is to test it in human subjects; studies in animals or carried out *in vitro* can be no more than complementary. It is also widely agreed that these studies can be rendered very safe, though they may not be made entirely free of risk, by applying

---

[1] For a broader review of ethics, fraud and liability issues in clinical studies see Dukes *et al.* (1998): *Responsibility for Drug Induced Injury* (Second Edition), Chapter 16. IOS Press, Amsterdam, Berlin, Oxford.

a series of standards and rules which have been developed through long experience. The most fundamental series of standards was that issued in 1964 by the World Medical Association as the Declaration of Helsinki and which continued to be revised at intervals thereafter (WMA 1996, ongoing); it is reprinted in Table 9.A. For purposes of regulation it has been supplemented by other and more detailed materials but not amended. The United States Food and Drug Administration has long recognized four basic stages in which a programme of clinical trials should be conducted so that the work proceeds in a logical manner and without undue exposure or risk (see Chapter 4, Figure 4.B). Other regulatory agencies and the International Conference on Harmonization have developed further supplementary rules, primarily with a view to establishing the material that must be gathered to gain drug approval. Ethically acceptable means of conducting clinical trials in children when these are needed are currently being examined by the European Union (ABPI 2005).

Most regulatory agencies, insofar as they are concerned with the approval of clinical trials, require that patients in these trials be covered by the Declaration of Helsinki; a current controversy relates to the fact that the United States FDA does not require this standard for patients taking part abroad in a trial with an Investigational New Drug.

Many parties are involved in ensuring the quality and acceptability of experiments in humans; the present section will be concerned only with those rules – legal or ethical – that bear directly on industry.

9.2.2. *Sponsor and investigator*

It is today virtually unknown for a pharmaceutical company to carry out a clinical study without the involvement of other parties. In the past – and indeed until about 1975 – companies did conduct experiments on their own staff (see Section 2.2.5), maintain their own internal laboratories for human studies or establish laboratories entirely under their own control in hospitals or (in some countries) prisons (Silverman 1985, Braithwaite 1984 at pp. 89–90). Professional, public and political debate led to the realization that under such conditions there was a risk of abuse, with the interests of the company overriding those of the trial participant.

Under present-day conditions there is a clear distinction between the role of the company (the "sponsor" of the trial) and that of the investigator (who should be in an independent position). In theory, the distinction is a simple one. The company's interest is that the trial be performed and that it be reliable; it will therefore contract with a suitable investigator or his

Table 9.A
Declaration of Helsinki (Revision 1996)

I. Basic Principles

1. Biomedical research involving human subjects must conform to generally accepted scientific principles and should be based on adequately performed laboratory and animal experimentation and on a thorough knowledge of the scientific literature.

2. The design and performance of each experimental procedure involving human subjects should be clearly formulated in an experimental protocol that should be transmitted for consideration, comment and guidance to a specially appointed committee is in conformity with the laws and regulations of the country in which the research experiment is performed.

3. Biomedical research involving human subjects should be conducted only by scientifically qualified persons and under the supervision of a clinically competent medical person. The responsibility for the human subject must always rest with a medically qualified person and never rest on the subject of the research, even though the subject has given his or her consent.

4. Biomedical research involving human subjects cannot legitimately be carried out unless the importance of the objective is in proportion to the inherent risk to the subject.

5. Every biomedical research project involving human subjects should be preceded by careful assessment of predictable risks in comparison with the foreseeable benefits to the subjects or to others. Concern for the interests of the subject must always prevail over the interests of science and society.

6. The right of the research subject to safeguard his or her integrity must always be respected. Every precaution should be taken to respect the privacy of the subject and to minimise the impact of the study on the personality of the subject.

7. Physicians should abstain from engaging in research projects involving human subjects unless they are satisfied that the hazards involved are believed to be predictable. Physicians should cease any investigation if the hazards are found to outweigh the potential benefits.

8. In publication of the results of his or her research, the physician is obliged to preserve the accuracy of the results. Reports of experimentation not in accordance with the principles laid down in this Declaration should not be accepted for publication.

9. In any research on human beings, each potential subject must be adequately informed of the aims, methods, anticipated benefits and potential hazards of the study and the discomfort it may entail. He or she should be informed that he or she is at liberty to abstain from participation in the study and that he or she is free to withdraw his or her consent to participation at any time.
    The Physician should then obtain the subject's freely given informed consent, preferably in writing.

10. When obtaining informed consent for the research project the physician should be particularly cautious if the subject is in a dependent relationship to him or her or may consent under duress. In that case the informed consent should be obtained by a physician who is not engaged in the investigation and who is completely independent of this official relationship.

11. In case of legal incompetence, informed consent should be obtained from the legal guardian in accordance with national legislation. Where physical or mental incapacity makes it impossible to obtain informed consent, or when the subject is a minor, permission from the responsible relative replaces that of the subject in accordance with national legislation.

    Whenever the minor child is in fact able to give a consent, the minor's consent must be obtained in addition to the consent of the minor's legal guardian.

12. The research protocol should always contain a statement of the ethical considerations involved and should indicate that the principles enunciated in the present Declaration are complied with.

II. Medical Research Combined with Medical Care (Clinical Research)

1. In the treatment of the sick person, the physician must be free to use a new diagnostic and therapeutic measure, if in his or her judgement it offers hope of saving life, re-establishing health or alleviating suffering.

2. The potential benefits, hazards and discomfort of a new method should be weighed against the advantages of the best current diagnostic and therapeutic methods.

3. In any medical study, every patient – including those of a control group, if any – should be assured of the best proven diagnostic and therapeutic method.

4. The refusal of the patient to participate in a study must never interfere with the physician–patient relationship.

5. If the physician considers it essential not to obtain informed consent, the specific reasons for this proposal should be stated in the experimental protocol for transmission to the independent committee (1, 2).

6. The physician can combine medical research with professional care, the objective being the acquisition of new medical knowledge, only to the extent that medical research is justified by its potential diagnostic or therapeutic value for the patient.

III. Non-therapeutic Biomedical Research Involving Human Subjects (Non-clinical Biomedical Research)

1. In the purely scientific application of medical research carried out on a human being, it is the duty of the physician to remain the protector of the life and health of that person on whom biomedical research is being carried out.

2. The subjects should be volunteers – either healthy persons or patients for whom the experimental design is not related to the patient's illness.

3. The investigator or the investigating team should discontinue the research if in his/her or their judgement it may, if continued, be harmful to the individual.

4. In research on man, the interest of science and society should never take precedence over considerations related to the well-being of the subject.

---

institution; it will define the purpose of the study, draft the investigational protocol (including criteria for the selection of trial subjects), supply the drug in a suitable form, provide practical support as needed (including finance and if necessary analytical assistance) and help the investigator as necessary with the recording and publishing of the findings. The investigator will provide the trial subjects and ensure that they give informed consent to participate; he will ensure that he has the agreement of his hospital ethics committee or a corresponding body to perform the experiment; then he will carry out the trial and report on his findings; throughout he will ensure the welfare of the participants, regarding this as his primary and absolute duty; if at any stage there is a conflict between the need to complete the trial and the welfare of the trial subjects, the latter must take priority.

The reality of a company-sponsored trial is rather more complex. The fact is that the trial would not have been performed at all had it not been for the company and its need to carry out the experiment; the company is therefore bound to be responsible to some degree for the consequences. In carrying out his own obligations, the investigator is also likely to be heavily dependent on the sponsor at each stage, for reliable information and advice as much as for practical support. That will be the case when he agrees to conduct the trial, when he proposes the trial design to his ethics committee,[2] when he encounters unexpected effects and needs to interpret them, and when he produces his report. If at any stage a fault is made or a patient is injured it is therefore unlikely that an arbiter or court will find it to be a failing of the investigator alone; the liability is likely to lie, in whole or in part, with the commercial sponsor.

9.2.3. *The responsibilities of the sponsor*

The law – in part general medical law and in part drug law or other legislation relating specifically to clinical experimentation in human subjects – lays down a series of legal rules with respect to this field, alongside the ethical rules inherent in the Declaration of Helsinki. Some of those duties clearly lie with the sponsor by virtue of his practical working relationship with the investigator and these he cannot abrogate by seeking to pass them on to any other party. When problems arise the sponsor may find himself liable in civil law to a trial subject, to the investigator or his institution, or faced by charges brought by the drug regulatory authorities or even under the criminal law. Depending on circumstances, fault or liability may lie with the corporation or with members of its staff, e.g. a monitor appointed as contact person for the trial, or the head of the clinical investigation department.

---

[2] Ethics Committees in European countries report to a national Ethics Committee Authority established under the law. See, for example, for the United Kingdom SI 2004 No. 1031.

The sponsor's principal duties may be defined under these headings:

a. A duty of care in undertaking, reporting and evaluating *adequate pre-clinical work of high quality* which will form the basis for the decision to undertake work in human subjects.

> The investigator, however competent a clinician he may be, is unlikely to be an expert at interpreting animal or other laboratory data, nor even preliminary clinical work performed by others. He may be quite unable to judge whether the work already performed with the drug is appropriate or of adequate quality or scope to justify his administering it to his patients or volunteers, or sufficient to indicate the most appropriate dose or form of administration during the trial.

b. A duty to *select a competent and reliable investigator.*
   This should be simple, but rarely is so. Unless the new drug seems uniquely promising, many investigators will rarely be prepared to accord it priority, and it is all too tempting to have recourse to a lesser investigator whose scientific standards may be lower than one would wish:

> Our clinical group had several times used Dr X in Austria – he was not brilliant but he worked quickly and to schedule. It was only after three trials with him that an Austrian colleague tipped us off that he worked with a factor 5 – that is to say he would investigate 5 patients and then submit a report on 25 – and get paid for them. (Interview 9)

   Fraud in clinical trials is a recurrent problem of which a firm may be entirely unaware and specialized detective work may be required to find evidence of it. (CERES 2005)

c. A duty to *inform the investigator fully and impartially* of all facts which could be relevant in his agreeing to undertake a trial and in accepting the proposed protocol of study. The sponsor must give no "unjustifiable assurances . . . inadvertently or otherwise, concerning risks or inconvenience." (CIOMS 1982) The data should as noted above include adequate information on all pre-clinical work and on the experience, if any, so far gained with the drug in human subjects; when necessary it should however also extend to data from other sources, such as information on risks seen with related substances. As noted earlier, the form and presentation of these data must be appropriate to the investigator's situation and needs, so that he can take his own decisions and provide appropriate information to the trial subjects.

As under (a), the investigator must receive all the data in a readily understandable form; many firms consider it prudent to attach a commentary and interpretation from an outside expert having no links to the company.

d. A duty to *propose a study protocol which is in accordance with the best current standards of science and ethics and with prevailing laws and regulations.*

Again the investigator, however competent a physician he may be, may have little understanding of protocol design. Here too, many manufacturers have the healthy custom, irrespective of any legal obligation, of consulting one or more independent outside experts before finalizing their proposal for any human study, particularly if it is the first one with a new drug.

e. During the conduct of a study, a duty to *continue to provide the clinicians concerned with all information* becoming available on the drug and its properties, including reports of suspected toxicity, adverse effects and interactions noted elsewhere, and advice on any matters which the investigator may raise.

The trial protocol should encourage the investigator to contact the sponsor if he suspects an unexpected effect or interaction during the study; the sponsor's knowledge of the field may well aid in interpreting it and deciding whether it is sufficient reason to modify or even suspend the trial.

f. Following the study, a duty to *ensure publication at least of the principal results,* irrespective of whether these are favourable to the product or not.

As noted in other sections, registers of clinical studies are now being instituted in various countries (see Chapter 4, Deangelis et al. 2005, Lesney 2005) an important reason being the fact that on too many occasions unfavourable findings have been omitted from regulatory files or unfavourable studies suspended in their entirety. Any firm undertaking trials should ensure that they are promptly entered in an appropriate register.

The firm may find it wise to provide assistance beyond its normal scope, provided it does not risk interfering with the task of the investigator. In particular there may be reason for it to provide information or assistance to an ethics committee which requires a more detailed orientation regarding a proposed trial.

It has long been considered that there is a moral obligation to compensate any participant in a study who suffers injury (Childress 1976). There is also a broader belief that a sponsor should provide insurance to cover loss or injury on the part of the investigator, the institution and the participants, where such loss or injury is a consequence of their involvement in the trial. The Association of the British Pharmaceutical Industry has long recommended compensation in such cases (ABPI 1994) and within the European Union, national legislation now makes such insurance compulsory for patients or volunteers.

> Sponsors and their insurers have on occasion seen fit to pay claims relating to a non-drug related injury, e.g. to a healthy volunteer patient who was injured when his bed collapsed, and another who incurred a nosocomial infection while in hospital for the study.

Finally, it is commonly considered that wherever a fee is provided to the investigator or the trial subjects, over and above the actual costs incurred, it should be reasonable but not excessive. An over-generous payment could be a reason for an individual to agree to take risks against his better judgement.

The sponsor may find himself concerned with many types of ethical issues raised by clinical trials, e.g. the use of placebos, the conduct of clinical trials in developing countries, and the issue of testing drugs in children, women of fertile age, the mentally incompetent and the elderly. When any such issue could arise it is important for the sponsor to be aware of all existing rules and recommendations on the matter, both in order to ensure compliance with authoritative standards and to provide statements and explanations on request.

Other aspects of clinical trials are considered in Chapters 3 (confidentiality of data; reporting of results), 4 (methodology; pregnancy and lactation) 5 ("promotional trials") and 8 (trials in developing countries).

9.3.   Self Medication

9.3.1.   *The nature of self-medication*

Any attempt to define the ethical rules applicable to self-medication is frustrated by the fact that the view of society generally – and of the professions – as to the self-diagnosis and self-treatment of illness has changed several times and continues to change. Attitudes here are determined only in part by what is technically desirable or wise; they also reflect views on the empowerment of the lay person and the proper role of the health professions.

The term self-medication is as a rule not clearly defined in national law or regulation, nor is it used consistently. In its narrowest and most exact sense it refers to the role of "over-the-counter" (OTC) medicines, which have been formulated and manufactured explicitly for purchase and use by the lay patient himself, without the need to consult a physician. These medicines will be sold in pharmacies (or in some countries much more widely) and as a rule they can be advertised directly to the public.

There are however several grey areas in the periphery which need to be excluded from the present review. One comprises the use of a small group of prescription medicines that are highly unlikely to be abused yet which will be required so frequently over a long period by the chronically ill that it would seem unnecessarily burdensome to demand frequent prescriptions; pharmacies may be authorized to issue these without prescription at their discretion to known clients; insulin is an example usually cited. There is also the situation pertaining in much of the world where, irrespective of laws and edicts, many pharmacists or drug retailers sell without prescription a wide range of drugs many of which could better be used under medical supervision. As a rule this practice is in fact illegal in the countries concerned but nevertheless so widespread that it seems unlikely to change in the near future. It may reflect simple failure to implement the law (as in parts of Southern Europe), or the fact that in many areas of the world professional medical care is not available locally or is for many patients entirely unaffordable.

Even in the industrialized world only a century has passed since medical care was only readily available and affordable to a privileged minority. At that time, self-medication was almost universal but also largely discreditable (BMA 1908). Three decades later, with almost universal provision of health services in western society, the view began to develop in some quarters that self-medication was obsolescent. It soon became clear however that there was not always a good reason to trouble the doctor for a minor symptom; there was a reasonable place for a number of simple but genuine remedies that could be used by the lay public to relieve everyday symptoms without the need for medical diagnosis or supervision. By 1970, positive policies based on that view were coming to the fore and a vigorous self-medication industry was responding to them by supplying well-formulated products that were advertised in a responsible manner. Regulatory agencies were classifying products which could be regarded as suitable for home use and which could be advertised directly to the public. The positive view was well developed in a 1975 survey by the Council of Europe which suggested that a logical self-medication policy could be based on a joint consideration of eligible diagnoses, symptoms and medicines. (COE 1975). Self-medication, in the Council's view, was defensible where:

(i) *The medicines used were appropriate.* In particular
   a. They should be harmless and efficacious in the conditions for which they were recommended, and at least harmless in all common, superficially similar condition.
   b. They were harmless and effective within a wide range of dosage.
   c. They were stable, even under unfavourable storage conditions and for long period.
   d. They acted in a clear-cut fashion, demonstrably and quickly.
   e. Their physical attributes should correspond with the layman's concept of an effective medicament, but should not be deliberately misleading.
(ii) *The symptoms or ailments to be treated were not such as to demand expert diagnosis or treatment.*
   The Council listed several categories of such conditions, including major infectious diseases, psychiatric disorders, chronic illnesses of any type and symptoms which could indicate a serious underlying disease.

In a follow-up by the World Health Organization at a later date it was noted that, for self-medication to be defensible:

> . . . indications should be conditions the choice of therapy for which is simple and the prognosis for which, when untreated, is in most cases favourable. Aggravation of the condition should be unlikely, but readily recognizable when it occurs. (WHO/EURO 1986)

In the light of its general rules the Council listed some 30 categories of medicines which, in its view, were justifiably sold for self-medication purposes. It also specifically excluded some types of product ranging from stimulants and hypnotics to aphrodisiacs and abortifacients and as a general principle it considered that a new drug should not be released for the purpose of self-medication until considerable experience had been gained with its use on prescription.

By and large the Council of Europe's norms were those which were emerging at the same time in regulatory practice and which were to be applied for the ensuing three decades; they were also adopted by the World Health Organization. (WHO/EURO 1986, DAP 1995) In the industrialized world, standards such as these are now generally required by law; elsewhere, a company will do well to respect the same standards as a matter of ethics.

9.3.2.   Emergent concepts in self-medication

By 1990, it nevertheless seemed clear that there was a move towards a broader scope for self-diagnosis and self-treatment of illness. Those recommendations of the Council of Europe which were soundly based on technical arguments remained largely unquestioned. The Council had, for example, taken a firm stand against the free promotion and sale of antibiotics because of the risk of a rapid spread of microbial resistance; when a proposal was made to release oxytetracycline for "earache, sore throat, cough with spit, yellow discharge from the nose or painful redness of the skin" (Cargill 1967) it met with no response. Similarly, the Council's view that drugs should remain on prescription if they presented a risk of dependence, accumulated in the body or were likely to produce tolerance or idiosyncrasy remained essentially unchallenged.

The challenge to the Council's standards related primarily to the view, emanating largely from medical practice, that some medicines might in lay hands give a degree of symptomatic relief sufficient to mask serious conditions that would therefore remain undiagnosed and untreated. Public health physicians had, for example, long taken the view that diarrhoea should be allowed to run its course; lay use of drugs to suppress peristalsis could lead to the retention of toxins in the system, and could mask the presence of salmonella infection requiring medical diagnosis and specific treatment. With the growth of mass travel that was not a practical approach to the widespread problem of "tourist diarrhoea"; in consequence antiperistaltic drugs such as imodium, appropriately labelled with warnings against long-term use, were released in many countries by 1985. A very similar shift in thinking led by 1990 to the release of H-2 blockers for gastric distress, followed in some countries by omeprazole. Traditionally, only the antacids had been available on the grounds that anything more potent could mask the presence of peptic ulcer or gastric carcinoma; it was now considered that, provided adequate warnings against prolonged use were provided, more effective remedies could be released for home use. Bland creams for irritative conditions of the skin were, for example, supplemented by corticosteroid creams in low concentration.

There were however controversies on many issues and occasional changes of view:

> In 1995 ketoprofen which had been on over-the-counter sale was redesignated as a prescription item because of the occurrence of adverse effects. (Anon. 1995)

On some occasions, the authorities were more anxious to liberalize than were the manufacturers:

> In March 1989 the Danish Ministry of Health decided that the post-coital hormonal contraceptive Tetragynon ("the morning-after pill") should be made available without prescription. The manufacturer, Schering A.G., immediately discontinued the marketing of the product in Denmark, regarding its use without prescription as excessively controversial. In its view, the use of a post-coital contraceptive required medical advice and supervision including a follow-up examination to ensure that a woman was not pregnant (Anon.1989). This view has since shifted in many countries and a range of identical or similar drugs are now freely sold in many parts of Europe.

It is not clear how far and how fast this trend to a greater liberalization of self-medication will proceed. A very recent development is the OTC release in Britain in 2004 of the first statin (simvastatin 10 mg) for the normalization of blood lipids. The objection has been raised that this will lead to much over-medication, but this has been answered by the provision in certain pharmacies of self-diagnostic equipment so that the customer can measure his own lipid levels. The self-diagnosis and self-treatment of hypertension is moving in the same direction. Debate on all these issues continues. Worldwide overviews of agents released for self-medication have been provided at intervals by the international trade association representing firms working in this field (WSMI 2005).

In Europe, designation of a drug as being eligible for use in self-medication is undertaken by the regulatory authorities according to principles laid down by the European Union Directive 92/26/EEC of 1992. Entirely new chemical entities will not be so released. Their status can however be reassessed at a later date when a request to this effect is made by the holder of the market authorization, and once sufficient field experience with them has been gained to pass definitive judgement on the drugs' value, risks and manner of use. Designation of a drug for OTC use can according to the European Union's rules also be withdrawn after 5 years in the light of experience but it is in fact likely that if any problem were to arise an agency would not hesitate to withdraw the designation at an earlier date.

Many agencies have refused to release preparations for self medication which were excessively attractive for children. e.g. sugar tablets with cartoon faces and bright colours which could readily be mistaken for candies. Some European agencies now prove unwilling to release liquid products containing excessive concentrations of alcohol. Medicinal cough syrups and so-called sedatives advertised for their herbal content have on occasion been found to contain levels of alcohol as high as 74% and cases of addiction both to these and to "tonic wines" have been reported.

9.3.3.   *Promotion and labelling*

The principles according to which information should be provided on self-medication products – and the ethical norms to be respected in advertising these preparations to the public – have been increasingly well-defined over a long period. If self-medication is to be sufficiently safe, both the *general* and *specific* information about it which is provided to the public must be appropriate and reliable, and no improper or exaggerated *claims* must be made. Health professions, the authorities and to some extent the specialized industry working in the field have developed standards for teaching the public to self-medicate in a responsible manner. The "Code of Advertising Practices" of the Proprietary Association in the US similarly urges member companies to promote the responsible use of these remedies (PA 1984) as does the corresponding code in Australia.

Although, as pointed out in Chapter 5 in connection with prescription drugs, the distinction between information and promotion is sometimes artificial, it is reasonable to make this distinction where medicines for self-medication are concerned. The package insert and the labelling are intended to provide the basic information needed by the user; existing codes and standards make it clear that this information must be complete and must not be promotional in character:

> The Code of the Proprietary Medicines Association of Australia notes specifically that the "Consumer Product Information" (i.e. package and insert) ". . . is not an advertising or promotional tool and as such should be confined to factual information . . ." (PMAA 1995)

Media advertising for products for self-medication is by contrast regarded as a different type of activity having primarily promotional purposes. Industry Codes are directed primarily towards the reliability of the claims advanced and do not specify any minimum level of information to be provided (e.g. on safety matters), but they stress that an advertisement should be "simple and uncluttered" by detailed information.

A number of well-recognized principles summarized in industry codes and elsewhere are, insofar as they relate to safety, as follows:

a. Public advertising for medicines should be informative and clear, and not give the impression that the product is capable of doing more than it actually can.
b. It should not advocate the habitual taking of medicine, and there should be advice to consult a doctor if a problem persists.
c. It should be precise about the therapeutic merit of the preparation and not speak simply of a general enhancement of well-being.
d. It should warn against excessive use of the product and point out its possibilities for harmful effects.
e. It must avoid creating a real or imagined need.

The question as to whether safety information should be included in an *advertisement* to the general public is not entirely settled. Some countries have required such information to be included others have not. The WHO. "Ethical Criteria for Medicinal Drug Promotion", which covered both professional and public advertising, did specify the need for such information (WHO 1988), but does not appear to have addressed specifically the issue of promotion for self-medication. Some confusion was introduced when the European Communities sought to deal with the issue:

EC Directive 92/28/EC requires that an advertisement to the general public be set out in such a way that the message is clearly an advertisement. (EC 1992/28) Other than the name of the product, however, the Directive does not specify exactly which information is to be provided, yet it requires that it include "the information necessary for correct use of the medicinal product" a well as "an express, legible invitation to read carefully the instructions on the package leaflet or on the outer packaging …"

The term "information necessary for correct use of the medicinal product" is not defined and is not identical to that used in Directive 92/27/EEC relating to the labelling and package insert. It could be interpreted either to mean that all categories of information, including safety information, must be included in an advertisement (other than a brief "reminder" announcement) or that the obligatory cross-reference to the packaging texts will suffice.

The former interpretation was adopted by the authors of a study of advertising in 11 countries prepared for the International Organization of Consumers Unions in 1994, though they also applied the less clear WHO criteria of 1988. Assuming that safety information was required in advertising they found that of 183 public advertisements examined 153 omitted contra-indications, 159 omitted side effects and 143 omitted warnings (Kaldeway *et al.* 1994). The study has been challenged by the proprietary medicine industry which considers that the European Directive was here wrongly interpreted; the industry has also pointed to research indicating that inclusion of safety information in public advertising is ineffective. It seems likely that the lack of clarity in Directive 92/28/EEC will persist until it is resolved either by the Community itself or judicially in cases of injury attributed to lack of safety information.

An issue currently being tackled both by regulatory agencies and industry is the provision of package inserts in secondary languages, e.g. for minority populations and migrant workers, who may otherwise be exposed to risk through lack of information and guidance, particularly if purchasing drugs in a culture to which they are not fully accustomed (Maciejewski 1994). Some firms (and professional pharmacy associations) have to their credit on occasion produced multilingual instructions for use which can be provided to the purchaser when necessary.

In particular, the fact needs to be stressed that self-medication must only be used briefly and the physician consulted if the symptoms are not promptly relieved. Claims, whether as regards efficacy or safety, cannot be judged by the principle of *"caveat emptor"* since a patient anxious to find a remedy for his illness may be more inclined to accept even preposterous claims than he would be in other situations.

Should a manufacturer find himself facing charges that he has failed to provide adequate warnings it will be important for him to be able to demonstrate that his warnings were not only present but were also obvious and clearly formulated. An interesting set of complementary Guidelines from the Proprietary Association (now the Consumer Healthcare Products Association) in the US recognizes the need to stress to the consumer any change which may have been introduced in product labelling, relating, for example, to safety or dosage, since this may otherwise go unnoticed (PA 1994). As with prescription medicines, the risk of over-information must be avoided:

> In 1994 the U.S. FDA announced measures to simplify and shorten packaging texts for O.T.C. drugs in order to reduce confusion. It was pointed out that the current label for aspirin contained more than 500 words including some, relative to risk prevention, which certain consumers would not understand. (Marketletter 1994)

There are also some matters on which the lay person may have inadequate background knowledge, for example, the extreme sensitivity of the very young and very old to certain drugs; texts need to be explicit on such matters where they apply. (Australia 1992)

> Detailed standards for the advertising of self-medication products include those laid down by the Council of Europe in its 1975 report on Abuse of Medicines (COE 1975), the European Proprietary Association (AESGP 1977 and revisions) and some of its national member associations of manufacturers, the Proprietary Association (now CHPA) in the U.S.A. (PA 1994) as well as the unique multi-party Board of Control (Keuringsraad) established in 1926 by the media in The Netherlands (SRC 1993). At the European level, the general standard dating from 1984 that no advertisement in any field shall be "misleading"(EC 1984/450) has been supplemented by Directives from 1992 specific to pharmaceutical packaging texts and pharmaceutical advertising. (EC 1992/27) Similar but more detailed provisions are to be found in the various national and industrial codes of practice, though it is not always clear whether they apply to advertising or to packaging materials.

Once again, however, the difference in standards internationally must be stressed; what is today regarded as reprehensible in the US or Western Europe is still common practice in some other parts of the western world, and a court dealing with an individual case will be unlikely to acknowledge standards of behaviour which have not been recognized in the community in which it is administering justice.

9.3.4.   Liability for self-medication products

There is no doubt that a manufacturer can still be held liable for failure to warn a user of risks of a self-medication product, perhaps even on matters which might be considered to be well-known to the public:

> In a U.S. case brought against the manufacturer of the paracetamol-based analgesic Tylenol in 1994 the plaintiff claimed that as a result of his drinking wine daily his liver had been sensitized to the hepatotoxic effects of paracetamol. After taking the drug for several days for influenza he experienced acute liver toxicity demanding hospitalization. It was alleged that defendant knew of the danger of using Tylenol if alcohol was regularly taken, but had not warned users of the risk. Instead the advertising had implied that the drug was "doctor recommended" and entirely safe. A Federal court awarded some $8 million in damages.[3]

It is notable that in this case the fact that the directions folder had been approved by the FDA did not constitute a valid defence.

---

[3] Benedi v. McNeil Consumer Products Inc. (1994): Case as cited by Moch J.W. and Borja A. Moch J.W., Borja A. and O'Donnell J. (Eds.) (1995): *Pharmacy Law*. Lawyers and Judges Publishing Co., Tucson, AZ at pp. 42–43.

9.3.5.   Future developments

In this situation, it is hardly possible to determine the ethical principles to which a manufacturer should adhere during the coming years. In industrialized countries with readily accessible medical services, regulatory authorities seem likely to change their principles only slowly, and in the ongoing debate between the authorities and the self-medication industry much will have to depend on the experience already gained. Certainly, there is to date little or no real evidence of harm having resulted from the liberalized use of antiperistaltic drugs or H-2 blockers. On some other fronts – such as the need to maintain strict control over dependence-producing drugs and prevent the frivolous use of antibiotics – public health considerations are likely to demand a cautious approach. In the present regulatory climate, further developments are likely to run in parallel in Europe, the USA and Japan with other industrialized countries following suit; consultation with the organized self-medication industry has proved fruitful. In the meantime, as in other parts of the world, there will be a need for a responsible approach both to labelling and advertising so that the public itself learns to appreciate that, in its own interest, self-medication needs to be kept within limits.

9.4.   Manufacturing and Supply of Vaccines

The production and supply of vaccines is governed by many of the same legal and ethical principles which hold for medicines in general. Some exceptional technical issues relating to vaccines are touched on incidentally in other chapters. One may also note a number of operational differences; vaccines are often governed by legislation separate from that concerned with drugs, and the bodies responsible for their assessment and approval are as a rule separate from the drug regulatory agencies though their mode of operation is similar. It is also the case that in some major vaccine-producing countries the manufacture of these products is wholly or in part in the hands of a state-controlled public health laboratory rather than a private firm.

Differences from drugs as regards issues of the manufacturer's responsibility and his liability for injury can arise for various reasons where vaccines are concerned. In particular

    a. These products are often administered to healthy individuals. Such administration is often required (or emphatically recommended) by the state as a means of protecting the community against epidemic disease, i.e. the interests of the community as a whole may override the interest of a particular individual who has had no positive desire to be vaccinated or to take the accompanying risks.[4] If the recipient is injured, the question arises as to where he may submit a claim for damages, particularly in view of the fact that in much of the world it is difficult or impossible to bring legal proceedings against the state.

b. Although vaccines are used as part of a state programme, the products are often administered without the intervention of a physician; semi-skilled staff may administer them, while oral vaccines may be taken by the individual without assistance. Again the problem of seeking compensation for injury from the state, e.g. if a state employee makes an error in the course of injection or the patient receives inadequate information, may arise.

c. Vaccination involves administering potentially infectious material which can cause injury to a third party. Contact with a smallpox vaccination subject can result in infection to an infant with eczema, resulting in eczema vaccinatum; similar complications have occurred following poliomyelitis vaccination. The injured party will be in a particularly difficult situation as regards the identification of a defendant from whom he can claim compensation where this is justified.

In Britain, the United States and elsewhere, persons injured by vaccination have because of these formal complexities often sought compensation from the vaccine manufacturer for want of any other means of securing a remedy. For a long period this created an extremely difficult situation for manufacturers, especially in the USA. Where there had been a manufacturing defect in the batch concerned this was, as in the case of drugs, entirely just, but in the majority of cases a court found itself obliged to postulate some hypothetical fault on the manufacturer's part in order to ensure that the victim could be compensated. In many instances, a court would hold that there had been neglect of a postulated duty to warn the user of the risk involved. In some cases the reasoning on this score was extraordinarily artificial:

> In *Reyes v. Wyeth Laboratories* in 1974, a U.S. Federal Court upheld a jury verdict in favour of a young girl who contracted polio as a result of receiving the vaccine because the Wyeth company had not warned the parents of the remote risk that the

---

[4] Jacobson v. Massachusetts (1905): 197, U.S. 11.

vaccine might cause the disease, even though it was unlikely that a proper warning would have deterred the parents from having the child vaccinated. Since the vaccine was to be administered by the local country health clinic, it was not clear from the opinion how the manufacturer was supposed to give these warnings.[5]

In some (though not all) instances, claims against the manufacturer by third parties also succeeded despite a reasonable effort by the firm to provide a warning:

> In *Givens v. Lederle* (1977), again in the U.S., a Court applied the *Reyes* reasoning to an instance where the mother of a child vaccinated with the Sabin oral vaccine in a pediatrician's office contracted poliomyelitis. The doctor had not given the mother notification of the possibility that she could catch polio from her child. The manufacturer argued that he had fulfilled his duty by providing a package insert which explained this risk. The firm also attempted to distinguish this case from *Reyes*. Unlike the former case, where the patient was participating in a mass immunization campaign and the vaccine was administered by a public health nurse, the child's own doctor had here made the decision as to whether the child should be vaccinated. The manufacturer based part of his case on a line of precedent which held that, in instances where there is an established doctor-patient relationship, the duty to warn in the case of prescribed medication rests with the doctor (the "learned intermediary" concept) The court nevertheless decided in favour of the plaintiff.[6]

With a long series of such cases decided in the favour of plaintiffs, a number of manufacturers decided very reasonably that they could hardly continue to supply vaccines to government programmes if they were to be held liable for injuries that were in no sense their fault. The issue came to a head when in 1976 the swine fever virus was discovered in humans in the US, and a national immunization programme was recommended. Manufacturers were willing, as a public service, to supply the vaccine at close to cost price, but refused to provide it at all unless they were protected from liability. Under a temporary emergency order, the US assumed liability for injury, other than that attributable to manufacturing errors. Ultimately, in 1986 the Congress passed the National Childhood Vaccine Injury Act which essentially created a no-fault compensation scheme.[7]

> Cases are regularly reported where large sums are paid from the Compensation Programme to children who have suffered permanent injury. "A New Jersey girl

---

[5] Reyes v. Wyeth Laboratories (1974): 498 F 2d 1264 (5th Cir.).

[6] Givens v. Lederle (1977): 556 F 2d 1341 (5th Cir.).

[7] Pub. L. No. 99-660, 100 Stat. 3755 (codified as amended at 42 U.S.C. $300aa-1 to -34 (West 1991, Suppl. 1992).

whose mental development stopped at 2 months old after a routine immunization has received a $4.7 million settlement from a national trust fund. More than $3 million of the award will go to an annuity that will pay for the child's care as long as she lives. Its payout could exceed $61 million if she lives to 71." (Washburn, 2002)

A more recent measure in the US is the Homeland Security Act of 2002, dealing with terrorism and the possibility of terrorist use of small-pox virus; the Act provides general protection for persons and institutions assisting the government during a bioterrorism incident and specific pro-tections for smallpox vaccination programmes, ensuring that the govern-ment will deal with claims for any injury that may occur. It may therefore be assumed that in this special situation again the manufacturer will be protected against any claims that may arise.

In Britain, where vaccination injury claims against manufacturers in the absence of fault had similarly proved problematical, the Vaccine Damage Payments Act of 1979[8] covers damage caused to a person by vac-cination (including vaccination of his/her mother while pregnant with him/her) against a series of designated diseases, including whooping cough, tetanus, smallpox, tuberculosis, measles, rubella, poliomyelitis and diphtheria. The Act also covers persons disabled by close contact with a person who has been vaccinated against one of the qualifying diseases. Similar vaccine damage legislation now exists elsewhere in the European Union as well as in Japan and Switzerland.

Manufacturers may still be faced with claims for vaccine damage where there is no provision for compensation through other channels, but in such cases the defendant should always examine the possibility that some older legislation provides an alternative remedy. In Germany, for example, a law of 18 July 1961,[9] modified to some extent in 1971,[10] exploited a principle inherent in the laws of German states for many years providing for the state to compensate injury suffered by individuals as a consequence of official acts; this principle had already been employed prior to 1961 to provide compensation in cases injured by compulsory smallpox vaccination and even by the "recommended" vaccination against tuberculosis.

---

[8] Vaccine Damage Payments Act, 1979, C.17.

[9] Bundesgesetzblatt (1961) at p. 1012.

[10] Bundesgesetzblatt (1971) at p. 1401.

9.5.   Blood and Blood Products

The problems relating to blood products intended for transfusion are closely analogous to those arising with medicines. For a great many years the most common injuries that were reported resulted from hospital errors (such as administration of incompatible blood). More recently, these complications have been dwarfed by those resulting from the supply and use of infected blood, especially material carrying the HIV virus and thus potentially capable of transmitting AIDS.

The logistics of blood supply tend however to be different to those of drug supply. Whole blood and labile products derived from it (e.g. packed erythrocytes) are not in most countries outside the American continent considered as commercial products; they are often obtained, supplied and processed by Government or voluntary non-profit agencies (such as the Red Cross) and/or supplied free of charge, and thus fall outside provisions of commercial law; there may however be specific statute law relating to blood products which in some countries sets very specific requirements as regards such matters as quality, manufacturing defects and injury.

In some countries, the problem of HIV contamination of blood products (such as Factor VII and Factor IX) proved to be primarily a consequence of fractionation of commercially procured blood donations obtained by the main US commercial enterprises in this field (Armour, Alpha, Baxter and Cutter), some of the donated blood being contaminated with viruses. The numbers of cases are vast since a single contaminated blood sample may, as a result of mixing blood from multiple donors into a single batch, result in infection of many patients. In France alone between 1992 and 1994 a special fund established for this purpose granted compensation to 4,000 infected patients.

Special funds have now been operative in many countries for some years, providing compensation without proof of fault. Where fault has been demonstrated, cases have been brought successfully against the health authorities, the blood transfusion service or the manufacturers. The blood supplier may be liable in negligence if infected blood has not been screened out.

In a 1992 American case, a non-profit blood bank (UBS) was sued for failing to screen a blood donor properly for potential infection with the AIDS virus, as a result of which the recipient of a transfusion had been infected. The court held that there was a presumption in favour of the defendant UBS if they had adhered to the industry standard of care. However, in such a case the plaintiff is permitted to rebut that presumption by presenting expert testimony to indicate that the standard of care maintained by the school of practice to which the defendant adhered was unreasonably defective as compared with others as regards its ability to protect against the type of harm experienced by the plaintiff.[11] This can be more problematical in the field of blood than where drugs are concerned since there have been various schools of practice and it may be difficult to prove which of these are entirely adequate.

As of May 1997, a number of producers of blood derivatives in the USA agreed on pacts both with the federal government and with 20 of the states, laying the basis for a multi-million lawsuit settlement over Factor VIII and IX products which had transferred AIDS or the AIDS virus to haemiphiliacs.[12]

A practical problem where blood products are concerned is that it may be difficult to determine the defendant since the labelling and hospital records may not indicate the original source of the blood from which a derivative was prepared. In Japan, the Government agreed with the five main manufacturers of concentrate used in haemophilia care to join with it in making substantial payments into a settlement fund from which compensation could be paid. Also in Japan the new Product Liability Law that came into effect in 1995 may be applied; however, by virtue of a parliamentary amendment, liability is excluded for "complications of blood transfusion such as those caused by contamination by viruses the complete removal of which by existing technology is impossible."[13] This is of course analogous to the "State of the Art Defence" allowed under European Product Liability legislation.

European Community:[14] By virtue of Directive 89/381/EEC stable industrially prepared blood products intended for a large number of patients, namely albumin, coagulation factors and immunoglobulins, now fall under the Community's pharmaceuticals legislation; these products are therefore subject to the same rules on manufacturing and marketing as pharmaceuticals. The same Directive gives binding force to the measures recommended by the Council of Europe and the World Health Organization on the selection and control of blood donors, and supplements them with quality procedures specific to blood derivatives.

---

[11] United Blood Services, Div. of Blood Systems Inc. v. Quintana (1992): 827 P 2d 509.

[12] Anon. (1997): Medical firms reach pacts clearing way for AIDS settlements. *Wall Str. J.,* May 1st, *B8*.

[13] Yawata M. (1994): Transfusion and Japan's product liability law. *Lancet, 344, 120.*

[14] Brunko P. (1994): Les exigences communautaires relatives aux médicaments dérivés du sang et du plasma humains. *Ann. Pharmaceut. Franc., 52, 89–98 (In French).*

A final point of relevance to a manufacturer who is sued for liability on this score is that he might in theory be able to lodge a claim himself against an individual blood donor who proves to have been the source of contaminated blood. Learned authors have stressed the fact that the donor bears an important part of the responsibility for the safety of transfusion practice. As early as 1977 the League of Red Cross Societies defined it as the duty of the donor towards the recipient to provide safe blood.[15] This duty involves taking note of the information given to him on "safe donor behaviour" and informing the transfusion service accordingly on any aspect of his health or behaviour which could be in conflict with this standard. A donor who gave blood after knowingly exposing himself to the risk of AIDS infection would certainly transgress this norm.

9.6.   Controlled Substances

9.6.1.   *Legal instruments governing controlled substances*

The control of narcotics, dangerous drugs and psychotropic substances throughout the world is based primarily on a series of multilateral treaties concluded from 1912 onwards, which were intended to ensure that substances with dependence potential and abuse liability were used only for valid medical and scientific purposes. The Single Convention on Narcotic Drugs of 1961,[16] with its subsequent amendments, incorporates all earlier agreements. It provides for strict controls on the cultivation of the opium poppy, the coca bush and the cannabis plant and controls their products and close analogues of the latter, through the stages of trading and processing down to the level of final distribution and use. The "manufacturer" is thus an essential link in this chain and is accorded specific duties.

The Convention on Psychotropic Substances of 1971[17] extended the international system for control to other dependence-producing drugs. Among the most dangerous of the substances with which it deals are the hallucinogen LSD (lysergic acid diethylamide) and the stimulant amphetamines.

---

[15] Hantchef Z.S. (1977): The development of blood transfusion and its legislative and economic impact (Editorial). *Transfusion-Noter, 11 and 12.* League of Red Cross Societies, Geneva.

[16] *Single Convention on Narcotic Drugs* (1961): United Nations, New York.

[17] *Convention on Psychotropic Substances* (1971): United Nations, New York.

More controversial additions to controls under the Convention were made later and involve drugs (such as hypnotics and tranquillizers), which are not free of risk but were considered to present less of a threat to society.

In practice, the two Conventions complement each other, and appropriate mechanisms exist for bringing new substances under the control of the Conventions as necessary, or altering the level of control set for existing compounds. Substances listed in either of the various conventions are graded into one of four "schedules", to indicate the extent of the controls needed on each. However, the four schedules of the Single Convention on Narcotic Drugs and those of the Psychotropic Convention do not run entirely in parallel. The classifications are summarized in Tables 9.B and 9.C.

9.6.2.   Duties of the manufacturer

All the provisions of the Conventions have been assimilated into national law, where necessary with some adaptation, and both the applicable rules and the sanctions prescribed for offences under the legislation are those of national law. The United States Controlled Substances Act of 1970, for example, embodies the provisions of both Conventions though it uses its own five-level classification (see Table 9.D). In the United Kingdom, the Misuse of Drugs Act of 1971 provides separate

Table 9.B
Schedules Under the Single Convention on Narcotic Drugs

I	Dangerous substances in the opiate, cocaine and cannabis groups as well as the raw plant materials and extracts used for manufacture
II	Weaker narcotics more commonly used for medical purposes
III	Preparations containing Schedule II drugs in low concentrations
IV	Dangerous drugs of little therapeutic use which can be forbidden completely by state authorities

Table 9.C
Schedules Under the Convention on Psychotropic Substances

I	Highly dangerous substances of little or no therapeutic use
II	Dangerous substances, hardly needed in therapy
III	Short- and medium-acting barbiturates which are useful but which have been and easily can be abused
IV	Hypnotic, tranquillizing and analgesic drugs which are widely used therapeutically but have addictive properties

Table 9.D
Schedules of Control in the United States

I   Drugs having no safe and acceptable use in the US; may be used only in govern-
    ment-approved research
II Psychoactive drugs with a high potential for abuse. Subject to production and
    import quotas and licences. Special security measures apply (e.g. vault storage).
    New written prescription required for each sale. Maximum criminal penalties for
    unauthorized trafficking
III Drugs with lesser potential for misuse. Written or oral prescription required. Up to
    5 prescription refills allowed within 6 months
IV (Similar to III but with lesser penalties for offences)
V   Drugs with slight potential for misuse. No prescription required, but product may
    only be sold to adults and for valid medicinal purposes

classifications for degrees of risk, for the various levels of duty incumbent on parties and for occurrence of addiction. In almost all cases the substance in question will be intended as a medicine and subject to the provisions of the national medicines legislation as well as to those concerning controlled substances.

A national administration conforms to the Conventions essentially by a strict registration system, involving a chain of licensees, to trace the origins, whereabouts and usage of all controlled substancees. Criminal penalties are prescribed for unregistered possession or use. The outline provided below, setting out the consequences for the manufacturer, represents a typical system:[18]

The national legislation under the Conventions creates a closed system of distribution at all stages for those authorized to handle controlled substances in any way. Each such individual or firm is registered under a unique number and each (whether as importer, exporter, manufacturer, distributor, hospital, pharmacy, practitioner or researcher) is required to maintain complete and accurate inventories and records of all transactions involving controlled substances, and to ensure their secure storage (e.g. with secure housing, guards and alarm systems).

A controlled substance may only be sold or transferred if the buyer provides his unique number in advance to the seller. All international transactions must be reported to the government authorities. Complete records must be kept of all quantities of controlled substances manufactured,

---

[18] Adapted and abbreviated from the provisions of the US Controlled Substances Act, 1970.

purchased and sold. Each substance must be inventoried every 2 years. This provision is designed to detect and discourage many forms of diversion including internal diversion, such as pilferage by employees. Records for Schedules I and II drugs must be kept separate from all other records of the handler; records for Schedule III–V substances must be kept in a "readily retrievable" form. The former method allows for more expeditious investigations involving the highly abusable substances in Schedules I and II.

The keeping of records is required for distribution of a controlled substance from one manufacturer to another, from manufacturer to distributor (and from distributor to dispenser). In the case of Schedule I and II drugs, the supplier must receive from the prospective purchaser a special order form made available by the authorities only to persons who are properly registered to handle drugs in Schedules I and II; the form is preprinted with the name and address of the customer, and the drugs must be shipped to this name and address. The form is issued in triplicate: the customer keeps one copy; two copies go to the supplier who, after filling the order, keeps a copy and forwards the third copy to the nearest drug control office. For drugs in the lower schedules (III–V) the supplier is under an obligation to verify the authenticity of the customer, and will be held fully accountable for any drugs that are shipped to a purchaser not having a valid registration. Manufacturers must submit periodic reports of the Schedules I and II controlled substances that they produce in bulk and in dosage forms. They also report the manufactured quantity and form of each narcotic substance listed in Schedules III–V, as well as the quantities of psychotropic substances listed in Schedules I–IV which have been synthesized. Both manufacturers and distributors are required to provide reports of their annual inventories of these controlled substances. These data are entered into a system maintained by the authorities for purposes of monitoring the distribution of controlled substances throughout the country, and identifying retail level registrants who receive unusual quantities of controlled substances.

9.6.3. *Ethics and controlled substances*

In view of the rigorous controls applicable to controlled substances one might well ask what place is left for ethics. In fact there is much opportunity to behave ethically or otherwise, namely as regards the substances classified in the lower schedules, such as the benzodiazepines. The regimen under the conventions is essentially concerned with possession, storage and distribution and imposes no controls on the advertising and promotion which, as considered in Chapters 4 and 5 play, have played a prominent role in the use and abuse of substances of this type. One is bound to wonder whether, had the evidence of benzodiazepine dependence become public knowledge at an earlier phase, they would have been classified so lightly:

> In 1964, the World Health Organization's Expert Committee on Dependence Producing Drugs had identified the newly introduced chlordiazepoxide as a substance which could produce "dependence of the barbiturate type"; diazepam was at the time too new for the Committee to assess its dependence-producing potential. None of the benzodiazepines were at the time scheduled; only in 1984, in the face of opposition from the pharmaceutical industry, were 33 benzodiazepines placed in the lowest schedule (IV) of the International Convention on Psychotropic Substances, with the barbiturates in schedule III, despite the emergent evidence which confirmed the extent of benzodiazepine dependence. In Britain's three-level classification, the barbiturates are similar placed in class B, the benzodiazepines in class C. In America, on the other hand, both the benzodiazepines and the barbiturates are to be found in Class 4 of its five-level classification.

One cannot assess the likelihood of a reclassification, now or in the future, but in view of current knowledge and the caution now universally applied to controlled substances, it might in retrospect have been desirable to handle the benzodiazepines with a greater degree of commercial restraint throughout their career than was in fact in evidence.

9.7. Alternative and Miscellaneous Medicines

9.7.1. *Products on the borderline*

There are numerous products which lie on the borderline of pharmacy. Depending on the exact definitions in national law and the manner in which these are interpreted they may or may not be brought within the scope of drug control. Some are borderline products in the sense that their therapeutic reputation is based on popular belief rather than on science, others in the sense that they are useful and effective but not entirely what the lawmaker had in mind. Some find their way into pharmacies; many more are sold in the "health stores" or similar outlets which in many countries retail a wide range of goods that are popularly regarded as useful in promoting or restoring health.

The most curious case is surely that of what in the United States have since 1995 been known officially as "nutrition supplements"; it merits consideration if one is to form an idea as to where duty and responsibility lie in these borderline areas. Other borderline groups can thereafter be considered more briefly.

9.7.2. "Nutritional Supplements" in the US

The prospect of increasing the sales of certain medicine-like products by reclassifying them has sometimes proved financially attractive to producers. From the point of view of business, reclassification as non-drugs will enable them to escape the costs and complications of drug regulation and may enable them to be distributed through a wider range of outlets.

In 1994, after substantial pressure from the trade, the US Congress passed the Dietary Supplement Health and Education Act; in consequence of the Act, a wide range of items which had hitherto been subject to the full rigour of the Food and Drug Administration's drug regime were reclassified as "dietary" (i.e. nutritional) supplements. (Avorn 2004 at pp. 64–66, Noah 2005) The term appears to have been chosen for the sake of convenience since many of the items were neither nutritional items nor supplements in any true sense. Some were herbal products having a popular reputation for their medicinal value. Heavily advertised and sold through health stores their sales expanded rapidly.

> One example may be taken, namely that of a range of products based on extracts from the various Asiatic species of *ephedra* plants. Since ephedrine and related substances were known to have an appetite depressant and fat mobilizing effect they were heavily promoted as slimming remedies and were reported to have grown into a "billion dollar industry." After a period, a considerable number of adverse reactions were attributed to these products, including multiple cases of heart disorders, hypertension and cerebral haemorrhage, including some 10–20 known fatalities. The FDA attempted to use its residual powers to place restrictions on the *ephedra*-based products, but was in part restrained by the House Science Committee which placed doubt on the reliability of the adverse reaction reporting system. The FDA was unable to tap into other sources of adverse reaction data because of the limitations imposed by the 1994 Act, and the House was advised that the trade would strongly oppose any revision of the Act. In the meantime, independent studies of the products in question pointed to the variability of the source material, the occurrence of an 18-fold variation in the ephedrine content among the products and the presence of other ephedrine-like substances in the extracts; all this would point to the fact that gross overdosage with these substances, which are known to raise blood pressure, could on occasion occur. The complications and fatalities in the US had international repercussions; in Denmark, in particular, a registered and standardized ephedrine-based product had to be withdrawn from the market because of extensive litigation and official

concern following prominent but inexact reports of certain American cases, ephedrine being confused with *ephedra*. In 2004 it was reported in the pharmaceutical press that the FDA had taken steps to prohibit the *ephedra*-based products but according to a further report in April 2005 the ban had been overturned by a Federal Court. (Scrip 2005 at p.16)

While in the given circumstances no final scientific judgement on this case is possible, there is reason to conclude that in this situation a series of potentially dangerous or ineffective products were, for purely commercial reasons and through political pressure, released for use as "nutritional supplements" without proper evaluation of their efficacy/risk ratio. Particularly bearing in mind the popular belief that "health products" sold outside the health chain are natural, beneficial and harmless, they are likely to be used without hesitation. In such a situation the liability for injury must lie with the manufacturer.

9.7.3.   *Miscellaneous products*

(i) Alternative and complementary medicines   This miscellaneous group comprises products claimed on the basis of "alternative teachings" to have curative or prophylactic effects. They have in common the fact that they do not carry the approbation of scientific medicine and have not sought or obtained the approval of a recognized regulatory authority. Some have been tested scientifically and found to be ineffective. They include products based on the teachings of Hahnemann (Homoeopathy), Rudolf Steiner (Anthroposophy) and various religious groups, as well as numerous traditional medicines based on European or foreign herbal usage. Many have been the subject of adverse reaction reports, though because they are not as a rule used professionally there is considerable underreporting; health authorities have, on many occasions removed "alternative" products from the market because of adverse reactions, either due to their inherent problems or to manufacturing defects. There are some comprehensive overviews of adverse effects to this class of products. (Ernst 2000) It is common for the authorities to insist on some form of declaration of their status on the label, e.g. "This product is formulated according to the principles of the . . . school, and has not been formally evaluated to confirm its efficacy or safety." Quality evaluation, where it is performed, lies with the general inspectorate system for consumer products and relates primarily to absence of contaminants.

Viewed from the point of view of a *bona fide* pharmaceutical firm, it has as a rule proven judicious to remain at a distance from these classes of products, which lack the scientific backing required to ensure that they are effective, safe and of sufficient quality. Many clearly do not achieve these standards and some are sufficiently dangerous to raise issues of liability. Where there is reason to consider that a product might have latent merit – and many scientific products have throughout time been developed from traditional or undocumented practices, it can always be accessed for critical examination and – in the event of a positive finding – developed further as a medicine.

   (ii) Foods with medical claims   For very sound reasons, foods and medicines are allocated to separate groups both in formal legislation and in the public consciousness. They serve different purposes, are supplied through different channels and demand a different type of care and supervision. As a rule the distinction has been respected; occasionally, however, in order to serve commercial purposes, products have been reclassified to some degree in what could well be termed a misleading manner; the consequences can be confusing and sometimes undesirable:

> Particularly from 1990 onwards a concerted effort was made to develop packaged foods which would not merely supply nutrition but also promise better health. Two courses appear to have been followed.

> *(a) "Fortified foods:"* Although the average European diet provides for all dietary needs with no need for supplementation, manufacturers introduced into their ranges of packaged foods new variants at premium prices, "fortified" with supposedly health-giving supplements, primarily vitamins and minerals. Both the latter have over a long period been sold separately to the public in the form of tablets and capsules by the pharmaceutical industry. It has been argued that both these and the fortification now added to foods are entirely wasteful and superfluous to need and are the subject of misleading information to the public. It was earlier imagined that these practices were unlikely to be harmful except when substances are added in unusually high doses or poorly documented additives are used. However concern has now arisen as to the safety of "functional foods"; the safe upper level of intake of calcium can, for example, easily be exceeded in a well-nourished population. Studies are now under way to examine the impact of these practices and the possible risks attached to them. (Meltzer et al., 2003)

> (b) *"Functional foods:"* This is a promotional term having no medical or nutritional connotational, although some advertising has carried the suggestion that bodily function will be enhanced. The term has been applied to fortified foods, to premium foods of an existing type having no particular health-giving characteristics, to modified foods in which, for example, a saturated fatty acid has been replaced by an unsaturated equivalent etc. Others consist of biological substances (e.g. enzymes) which have been described in the literature but the function of which is not known. It could be useful if the law were to set certain criteria for the use of such terms.

(iii) Cosmetics as medical products   Efforts to enhance the effect (or attractiveness) of cosmetics have sometimes involved the addition of pharmacologically active ingredients.

Like foods, cosmetics are in a class of their own, and are viewed in that light by the public. Bearing in mind the precautions attaching to the use and disposition of medicines in the home the distinction is a meaningful one.

A cosmetic is essentially designed simply to maintain the good external condition and attractiveness of the skin using bland ingredients; disorders of the skin require specific diagnosis and medical treatment. Among the "medicinal cosmetics" unadvisedly marketed at various times are creams containing antibiotics (intended to counter infections but capable of promoting bacterial resistance when used cosmetically in low doses) and others containing oestrogenic hormones (intended to rejuvenate the skin but in fact capable of deranging the menstrual cycle or inducing cancers). Some having only a local effect (e.g. acne creams based on sulphur and resorcinol) have been regarded as acceptable.

(iv) Contraceptives as medicinal products   While hormonal contraceptives, based as a rule on a combination of two pharmacologically active substances given either orally or by injection, have since their introduction been dealt with under pharmaceutical law ("products modifying physiological function"), older types of contraceptives have not. Chemical contraceptives, since they are placed in a body cavity and have spermicidal components with a mild degree of toxicity, could well be considered to fall under the same definition though generally they have continued to be handled as in the past under general legislation on "wares"; adverse reactions are unusual and generally reflect no more than a degree of hypersensitivity to the active substance. Condoms, except for some special products impregnated with spermicides, cannot reasonably be considered to fall under drugs legislation and have generally been dealt with under laws relating medical devices.

(v) Medical devices with pharmacological components   A number of medical devices in effect are simple systems for releasing an active substance into the body; they can be studied clinically in a manner analogous to other release systems such as slow release tablets. Generally, as in the case of transdermal release systems, the device itself does not enter the body but when it does complications can ensue.

The Norplant contraceptive system uses small rods impregnated with a progestagenic substance; the rods are inserted subdermally and release the active substance over a period of time. In a number of users the rods migrated within the body and were difficult to recover, especially where they had become fragmented; litigation has ensued.

Plastic intrauterine contraceptive devices were originally designed to provide purely mechanical or irritative interference to nidation of the zygote, thereby preventing pregnancy. Alternative versions of the system have been introduced in which copper is added to enhance the irritant effect or which release a progestagenic substance. Both the purely mechanical devices and the later versions have on occasion penetrated the uterine wall and have been found either in the pelvic cavity or elsewhere in the body.

The findings in the above cases show the need for thorough testing of any carrier material entering the body, to determine its tolerance at the intended site and its resistance, both physical and chemical, to physiological conditions. It may be difficult or impossible to study the long-term acceptability of these systems adequately in animal models, and prolonged studies in human subjects are likely to be called for. The manufacturer of Norplant trained a large number of practising physicians in the insertion and removal of the device and in any analogous situation this would be a wise course to follow.

(vi) "Recreational Substances"   Although various types of medicinal drugs, particularly the amphetamines and other stimulants, have commonly been misused for "recreational" purposes, there has generally been no attempt to bring within the scope of pharmaceutical law those wares which are used purely for social purposes, even though they have pharmacological activity. Alcohol and tobacco have long been subject to their own specific legislation, while marihuana, khat and other social drugs have as a rule remained entirely unregulated, the preparation and trade generally being informal.

Alcohol, as noted above has frequently been used as a flavourant or solvent in medicines. Some of the products concerned have contained high concentrations of alcohol and misuse and dependence have been reported. In countries where alcohol is prohibited for religious reasons one encounters a certain number of alcohol-based medicines, which are sold as tonics or cough mixtures but are apparently used to a large extent as social drugs.

Classification of *tobacco products* as medicines has on occasion been proposed in the United States as a means of containing both use and publicity, but no definitive steps have been taken.

Marihuana, widely tolerated as a social drug, has found some medical uses, notably in suppressing nausea and vomiting in patients on cytostatic treatment. It currently appears likely that some standardized preparations will be formulated specifically for this purpose, rendering them eligible for approval as drugs.

9.8. Orphan Drugs

The term "orphan drug" has been used widely for a product that is no longer manufactured because of lack of demand (see Chapter 8) or that has for similar reasons never been developed by its originator to the point of marketing (ibid). "Orphan diseases" are those, primarily existing in poor populations, for which the potential drug market is insufficiently attractive to a research-based manufacturer to justify his undertaking research. As noted in other chapters, a series of solutions to these problems are emergent, involving government financing, non-profit research, and public–private partnerships.

> In 1983 the United States Congress passed the Orphan Drug Act to encourage pharmaceutical companies to manufacture drugs for rare diseases by granting tax credits and exclusive marketing rights over a period of seven years. An early volunteer was Merck Inc. which undertook to manufacture a known drug for Wilson's disease. Merck also undertook the free supply of Mectizan for the treatment of river blindness (see Chapter 8), a notable example of an orphan disease.

> In 1999 the Multidisciplinary Association for Psychedelic Studies (MAPS) succeeded in obtaining an Orphan Drug Designation for marihuana for development as a treatment for the AIDS wasting syndrome.

> Extensive use has been made of the provisions of the Act both by large and small firms: 7 orphan drugs have been designated for support during 2004 alone.

> Similar legislation on orphan drugs has been passed in Japan (1993). Australia (1998) and the European Union (2000). Each sets a ceiling on the number of eligible patients where orphan drug support is requested (e.g. in Europe 5 patients per 10,000 inhabitants, equivalent to a total of 185,000 patients yearly).

Any pharmaceutical company might find it ethically attractive to engage in such work on a larger or smaller scale when the opportunity presents itself.

There have been contested allegations of misuse of America's Orphan Drug Act in that a US company finding a profitable alternative market use for a drug developed under these provisions can nevertheless continue to enjoy the tax breaks and monopoly and can charge high prices for the use of the drug for the designated purpose. If these charges are correct, it is regrettable that a legal instrument conceived with an idealistic purpose should have been abused in this way.

9.9. Veterinary Drugs

Veterinary medicines are by and large identical with medicines for human use, differing only and in part in their dosage forms and emanating from the same companies that produce medicines for man. The legislation that has been created to deal with them is largely identical to that applicable to the latter though with its own adapted rules and administrative bodies (see, for example, EC 2001/82). The only substantial differences relate to *pricing*, the permitted *channels of sale*, the question of *environmental contamination* and the issue of *residues*. Manufacturers may also be involved in certain issues of *distribution*.

Veterinary medicines are most likely to enter the direct environment of man when they are used in animals bred as a source of food. Residues may remain in meat of slaughter animals or in fish exposed to pharmaca (such as antibiotics used on a large scale in the course of fish farming), and similarly can be present in eggs, milk, honey or products derived therefrom. The concentrations found are rarely sufficient to cause toxic effects but sensitization can occur, eliciting allergic reactions either when the same food with the same contaminant is consumed again or when the individual is subsequently treated medically with the same drug. It would be reasonable to require that these issues are covered in information material supplied by the manufacturer to the user.

As in the case of human medicines the manufacturer (or his agent) is responsible for providing the national regulatory authority – which usually maintains close links with the regulatory body for human drugs – with evidence of quality, safety and efficacy. In the case of veterinary medicines this will necessarily include adequate evidence of the permissible indications, dosage and relevant precautions in the species in which the drug is to be used. Recommendations on the maximum residue limits will have to be provided. For older drugs these will generally correspond to those published in the literature or in official guidelines and directives (e.g. FDA/VET 2005, EC 1990/2377); for newer drugs the manufacturer will be required to conduct studies to determine these limits, as well as scientifically based advice to the user on "withdrawal times" following treatment before material from the animal can be made available for human consumption.

Complementary to these requirements are those on residue limits in processed foods, such as cheese or compounded products. Here, the relevant duties are defined in food law rather than pharmaceutical law. The relevant legislation is maintained by the UN Food and Agricultural Organization of the United Nations.

The most usual mode of distribution of veterinary drugs has been analogous to that prevailing in human medicine, i.e. through veterinary wholesalers and pharmacies, with prescription by veterinary practitioners. However, in some countries there has also been a considerable sale of these products by manufacturers direct to farmers for non-prescription use, analogous to the tradition of self-medication in human medicine. Practice in this respect has varied strongly from one country to another; concern has concentrated on the possibility of residues and of excessive use of antibiotics which readily enter the milk. Future legislation seems unlikely to eliminate non-prescription sale but will be directed towards avoidance of excessive use. The manufacturer's duties will primarily relate to the provision of reliable information. It may be noted that in the European Union and certain other countries the administration of certain hormonal and other substances to animals, e.g. as growth-promoting agents, is now forbidden (EC 1996/22).

Chapter 10

The Duties of the Generic Manufacturer

10.1. The Nature of the Generic Drug Industry

As noted in Chapter 1, the pharmaceutical industry is today largely spilt into two classes. The research-based (or "science-based") companies concentrate on the manufacture and sale of branded and patented medicines, many of them developed in their own laboratories, while the generic manufacturers produce (largely under non-proprietary names) medicines developed by others, on which there are no current patents or on which they have obtained licences from the respective patent holders. The two types of business are not rigidly separated and many firms engage in both forms of activity, but the "science-based" and "generic" manufacturers do tend to have distinct characteristics and are in part subject to special legal and regulatory provisions.

The end-result, in terms of the products actually reaching the patient, is intended to be similar to the extent that both branded and generic products are required by law and regulation to attain the same high standards of quality, safety and efficacy, and that where information is provided to the prescriber or user it must be dependable. The principal practical difference between the two is that the "generic" product is as a rule available at a much lower price than the speciality, rendering it attractive both to individual purchasers and to health systems or insurers. As indicated in earlier chapters, generic companies are in a position to offer their products at low prices in part because they have no need to undertake full research and development; in principle a generic equivalent can be registered if the applicant provides evidence that in medical use it is fully capable of replacing the speciality; provided the active substance is the same and the preparation as a whole is shown to be bioequivalent to the original product and of sound quality, neither animal studies nor full clinical trials to demonstrate efficacy and safety will be demanded. There are however other reasons for the low prices that generic manufacturers can offer. Many of them work with low-profit margins; they expend less on publicity and public relations than do science-based firms; and some conduct a part of their manufacturing in low-cost countries, either in their own facilities or under contract.

Over a period of some 15 years the generic drug manufacturing industry has undergone a marked evolution not only with regard to its size but also with its status in the health scene. In its early days it was commonly seen as a somewhat marginal area of business, as has commonly been the case where firms concentrate their efforts on copying the work of others; the suspicion lurked in many quarters that generic producers were likely to deliver second-rate goods to purchasers looking for bargains. In legal terms, the industry sometimes appeared to be exploring the borders of legality, both as regards the licensing regulations and the patent regime. That situation has changed radically, though some of the earlier prejudices remain; the generic pharmaceutical industry is now well recognized as an entirely legitimate major player in the world of drug supply, benefiting from its own legal provisions and in a position to make a major contribution to the accessibility of medicines in many different situations.

10.2.   The Significance of the Generic Industry

The generic pharmaceutical industry has become the dominant supplier of the developing world (Chapter 8), and has developed a firm hold on the markets of industrialized countries as well. Estimates of its market share are surprisingly variable, but in the United States, generics currently account for about half of all prescribed medicines while in Europe there have been considerable differences between north and south. In those European countries where speciality drug prices are generally low and regarded as affordable (France, Italy, Spain and Portugal), generics held only a small proportion of the market for a long time, though the figures are disputed and the proportion is rising. The generic share of prescriptions reaches 12 per cent in the Netherlands, 22 per cent in Britain, 39 per cent in Sweden and 41 per cent in Germany; in the latter countries, health insurers and systems have been faced with high speciality prices and financial limitations, and they have therefore turned to generics in order to work within their budgets. Since the patents on many original drugs are due to expire in the next decade, corresponding to a market of some $45 billion in western countries (Datamonitor 2004, Barrett 2005), much further expansion of generic supply is to be expected.

Some impression of the extent to which prices of specialities and generics differed in Europe by the mid-1990s is given in Table 10.A (Tafuri 1994), showing the unit prices for the H-2 blocker ranitidine in 1993.

The public relationship between the science-based industry and the generic manufacturers cannot be described as an easy one, even though

Table 10.A
Unit Prices for Branded and Unbranded Ranitidine (Price per defined daily dose in Euros)

Country	Branded	Generic
Italy	1.26	1.15
United Kingdom	1.04	0.43
France	1.50	1.09
Germany	1.43	0.93
Poland	0.27	0.15
Russia	0.65	0.10

behind the scenes there are mutual supply agreements; on the market, competition is fierce with the science-based manufacturers sometimes hinting to health professionals and to the public that generic products are likely to be no more than cheap copies of dubious quality, benefiting improperly from the innovative achievements of others:

> Research based pharmaceutical companies have unique advantages in manufacturing medicines according to high standards of quality and safety, since they alone have mastered the tasks of assuring quality control, designing and implementing manufacturing processes and plants, and constructing and commissioning primary and secondary manufacturing plants. (Industry submission to HOC 2005)

The competition between the two groups, each exerting its own influence on governments and international agencies, is reflected in the complexity of the agreements and legal rules which have grown up in attempts to ensure that generic competition does not threaten the innovative contribution made by the science-based industry but that populations also retain access to affordable medicines.

The present review will consider only the *bona fide* generic industry; the entirely different issue of spurious and counterfeit drugs has been discussed in Chapter 2.

10.3. Governments, Laws and Generics

The attitude of any government towards the generic pharmaceutical industry is inevitably the product of the evolutionary process sketched above but also of the interplay of divergent interests. The legislator finds himself under intensive pressure from the research-based industry to bear in mind its own interests and the need to finance innovation by maintaining adequate prices; the health services and health insurance agencies stress on the other hand the massive economies that they can achieve by using generic equivalents; in the meantime the trade authorities cite the obligation to conform to the patent provisions of TRIPS and Doha; and the agency providing development aid insists on the need to provide poor populations in the third world with advanced drugs at low cost. The legislative approach which emerges from any attempt to balance out all these and other competing priorities is bound to differ from one country to another. The situation as it has evolved in the United States, Europe and India is reviewed in the sections which follow. Other countries seem likely to base their own TRIPS-inspired legislation on variants of these three models.

10.4. Generic Drugs in US Law

From the time that the 1938 Food, Drugs and Cosmetics Act introduced a full drug assessment and approval system, and for the following 46 years, low-cost generic drugs were relatively insignificant in the United States. Under Food and Drug Law a generic substitute could in principle be manufactured as soon as the patent on the original drug expired. To be brought to market, however, it would have to be the subject of a full New Drug Application, including costly studies in animals and man, essentially repeating what the originator company had done in the past. Only a third of original drugs were therefore in fact copied when their patents lapsed; the rest could retain their monopoly for as long as they survived.

Change came only with the passage through Congress of the Drug Price Competition & Patent Term Restoration Act (better known as the Hatch-Waxman Act) of 1984:

> By creating the so-called Abbreviated New Drug Application (ANDA), the new Act allowed FDA approval of generic products through a shorter and less costly route than that prescribed for innovator drugs, the only requirement now being that the new version of the product must be shown to be "bioequivalent" to the original. The Act also allowed technical development of the generic to start even while the originator drug was still protected by patents. ANDA offers four alternative routes for marketing of generic drugs. Three routes – called Paragraph I, Paragraph II, and Paragraph III certifications – apply to ANDA filings that do not involve challenges to patents still protecting brand-name products. Through these routes, more than one generic version is able to reach the market at the same time, creating a very competitive situation. The fourth route, called Paragraph IV certification, applies when patent protection has not yet expired but the generic producer claims either that the patent is invalid or that his product does not infringe it. Paragraph IV certification has from the start provided an additional stimulus to

the generic industry to act quickly; a firm that chooses to file under this Paragraph will be eligible for a 180-day period of generic exclusivity with no other generic being approved during that time. During the exclusivity period, too, a generic drug company is permitted to innovate around patents for brand-name drug products.

While the Hatch-Waxman Act also included provisions favouring originator companies, such as the possibility of extending patents, its effect on the use of generics was dramatic. So long as a speciality had only one generic equivalent, the latter was likely to be priced just sufficiently below the original to attract a proportion of buyers; as soon as several generic equivalents of a drug began to compete with one another, however, prices could fall dramatically and the face of the market would change. Since pharmacists were in principle permitted to dispense the generic version of a drug even where the prescriber had selected the original, physicians had little influence on the course of events. By 2002, generics accounted for some 50 per cent of prescriptions, though because of their ever lower prices they commanded only 10 per cent of the American market (Jaeger 2002).

Despite this dramatic effect, the Act soon proved to have its shortcomings as far as generic medicines are concerned. One provision of the Act, vigorously exploited by patent owners from an early phase onwards, was that when a Paragraph IV ANDA was filed, the innovator company would almost always sue the generic company for patent infringement, an action that according to the Act would automatically trigger a 30-month stay, during which the FDA was not permitted to act on the NDA. Patent owners then realized that if they were to take out supplementary patents on a drug during this period, and to list these publicly in the FDA's so-called Orange Book, these new patents could then according to the Act provide the basis for seeking further 30-month stays on the generic firm's abbreviated application. If the supplementary patents were carefully timed, the ultimate effect could be to delay the introduction of the generic equivalent by a matter of years.

Typical was the effort made by GSK's US subsidiary to protect its antidepressant Paxil (paroxetine hydrochloride) from generic competition. The Canadian firm Apotex filed a Paragraph IV ANDA for a generic version of Paxil in March 1998. GSK sued Apotex for infringement, triggering an initial 30-month stay, which expired in November 2000. However, GSK subsequently listed additional patents in the Orange Book and on the basis of these proceeded to bring further successive infringement suits against Apotex, creating an automatic stay on FDA assessment of more than five years.

The generic industry firmly condemned such practices which it regarded as an abuse of the system, particularly because later patents, which could be entered in the Orange Book without any assessment of their relevance, appeared in some cases to have little or no bearing on the issues of efficacy or safety with which the FDA was concerned. Following a study by the Federal Trade Commission of these and other practices and possible abuses, the Congress passed in 2002 the Greater Access to Affordable Pharmaceuticals Act which limited the number of automatic stays to one (Rouhi 2002). The innovative industry in turn protested but has continued to litigate wherever possible, and generic firms too have continued to bring cases denying the validity of particular patents.

On a series of other issues attempts have been made to adjust – or bend – the rules in favour of one party or the other; in particular, the FDA has defined more exactly the types of supplementary patents which are valid for inclusion in the Orange Book. However, attempts to counter the growth of generics continue, even to the extent of illegal "anti competitive agreements" to dissuade generic manufacturers from entering a market. One recent development in the US is that, in view of the evident popularity of low-cost alternatives, a number of innovator companies are now introducing "authorized generic" versions of their own products, apparently attempting to suggest thereby that these are in some way superior to the generics produced by others. It is clear that, with the ongoing conflict of interests, this will not be the last development in the market, and that both law and regulation will continue to adapt to a changing situation for a long time to come.

10.5.   Generic Drugs in the European Union

As far as patent law is concerned, the passage of TRIPS and the subsequent Doha Declaration led to a review and revision of some parts of Europe's harmonized pharmaceutical legislation which was completed in 2004 (De Stasio and McClay 2004). Compromise provisions were introduced in an attempt to enhance the protection accorded to originator companies across the European Union while at the same time improving access within Europe to low-priced generics. These seemingly contradictory objectives have in the view of both sections of industry been reasonably well served, though there will still be a need for interpretation and adjustment, with both parties seeking to strengthen their position further.

Within member states of the European Union, the special exceptions to patents provided for in TRIPS and at Doha will hardly be applicable;

acute national health emergencies are, for example, rare in this part of the world. For supply to markets within Europe, an originator firm will therefore essentially retain its monopoly on a new drug as long as the patent holds good or some form of supplementary protection (e.g. based on data exclusivity, see Section 2.2.4) can be secured. Generic suppliers who already have an extensive hold on the market by concentrating on the supply of drugs having no patent protection (or on which voluntary licenses can be obtained) are however likely to see their turnover expand further as ever more drug patents expire and as health financing agencies, especially in Mediterranean countries, turn increasingly to low-cost supplies. Many member states have adopted – or are proposing to adopt – general "generic substitution" – permitting a dispensing pharmacist to issue a generic equivalent even where the physician has prescribed the specialty (see Section 10.8). Finally, the revised law makes provision for the supply of generics from European member states where a foreign country at a low level of development or having no manufacturing facilities of its own issues a compulsory licence to a European generic manufacturer.

> The new "Regulation on compulsory licensing of patents for export of pharmaceutical products to certain countries with public health problems" is designed to create the legal framework to implement the WTO Decision into the law of EU Member States. It specifies that a compulsory license can only be issued by a least developed country or a country with no manufacturing capacity. Such a country will then be allowed to issue a compulsory licence under which a generic manufacture can produce the product and supply it exclusively to the country issuing the licence; the licence will specify which medicines are to be manufactured and in what amounts, and provided exclusively to the country issuing the licence and a fee will be payable to the originator company and patent holder. Safeguards will be provided against re-importation into the EU.

One issue on which the generic sector is less than content with the new arrangements is the fact that within Europe, unlike America, there is still no "Bolar provision" under which, prior to the expiry of a patent, a generic producer can undertake preliminary scientific work on its manufacture and quality control, so as to ensure its prompt introduction once the patent lapses.

10.6. Generic Drugs in India

Following the passage of the TRIPS agreement of 1994 there was particular debate as to the future legal situation in India because of the country's role as a major supplier to developing countries of low-priced generic medicines, including copies of drugs still enjoying patent protection elsewhere. In March 2005, the Indian parliament indeed amended the country's patent laws to bring them into line with TRIPS.

India's Patent Act of 1970 in essence set aside substance patents and built a new system built around the patenting of manufacturing processes. In force down to 2005, it allowed Indian companies to copy inventions patented by others so long as the manufacturing process was sufficiently different. The provision was widely used, and a very large numbers of drug manufacturing and exporting firms were established, using reverse engineering to synthesize products which elsewhere were protected against imitation. The legislation encountered severe opposition from foreign businesses and patent holders; it was this opposition, backed by heavy lobbying on the part of the international pharmaceutical industry and sometimes sparking boycotts of Indian trade and interests, that led the Government following heavy lobbying by the international pharmaceutical industry to seek membership of the World Trade Organization and to adhere to TRIPS. A temporary ordinance to amend the law within the deadline set by TRIPS was issued in 2004 and formed much of the basis for the law which passed the Parliament in March 2005 subject only to approval by the President. The new legislation is something of a compromise to ease the transition to a new situation and enable the Indian generic industry to adapt to it. Essentially:

a. Existing generic copies of drugs discovered and patented before 1995 will remain legally in production.
b. Innovator companies which have discovered particular drugs after 1995 but before 1 January 2005, and which have submitted patent applications for these substances prior to the latter date can still be issued with substance patents under the new law.
c. Innovator companies can patent new formulations of old drugs (including co-formulations of more than one drug), provided the new formulation is "demonstrably superior" to the old.
d. Any new drug developed after 1 January 2005 will be eligible for a 20 year patent.

The new provisions mean that Indian generic companies will henceforth have little chance of engaging in the production of new drugs discovered and patented from 2005 onwards unless they succeed in obtaining either voluntary licences from the originator companies or compulsory licences issued by other countries to meet emergencies. They will however be protected in some measure from patents now to be granted on existing drugs (under "b" above) since under a special transitional arrangement, any generic copies which are already in production can continue to be supplied until the new patents are actually issued, a process which may take 2 years or more. Once such a new patent comes into effect, generic production can only continue provided agreement is reached with the patent holder in a voluntary licence against a "reasonable" fee. To date, there is no certainty that the two parties will have similar ideas as to what constitutes a fair fee; patent attorneys have quoted a figure of 5 per cent but elsewhere in the world much higher figures have been demanded by originator firms. Under the law, local generic companies have a right to contest patent applications for a variety of reasons before a patent is granted, but it is uncertain how effective this mechanism will be.

The new Indian Law contains "compulsory licensing" provisions in line with the DOHA provisions, under which the government could allow patents to be broken if generic drugs were required for a health emergency. However, some AIDS advocate fear that India may not grant compulsory licenses for AIDS drugs since in this country AIDS is not considered a national health emergency. Some experts have suggested that the bill's language is broad enough for the Indian government to issue a national compulsory licence on a drug if it is considered that the originator company is charging an excessive price, but it is not clear how this will be determined.

Time will show how effective this new legislation will be in practice in sustaining Indian generic supplies, especially since strong legal challenges from the originator companies are to be expected. There is bound to be national litigation and there may be challenges under the TRIPS regime, especially since the Law is in some places ambiguous. One unexpected effect of the new law could be an upgrading of Indian industry. With low-cost generic exports in the long run becoming less simple to develop, firms could consolidate into a smaller number of high-quality units and aim for the very large generic markets which, as patents expire, are opening up in Europe and North America, finding it more attractive to serve these than the developing world.

10.7. Generics and Data Exclusivity

In Section 2.2.4, the rules now applicable within the European Union as regards data exclusivity for regulatory files were outlined. By virtue of Directive 2001/83/EC, generic applicants for a market authorization in Europe may rely on data filed for the original product provided the latter has already been authorized for a certain period; that period will comprise

6 or 10 years depending on the law of the country holding the files in question. With a large number of generic applications now being lodged in Europe various points of interpretation arise and are reaching the Courts. They included cases where more than one country is involved and instances where an application for a drug relies on the file of a second similar version of the drug but where the second version has relied in its market application on a yet earlier version. The entire procedure has not yet been in operation long enough to see clearly how it will develop, but clearly some unanticipated complications may occur. An example is provided by a preliminary ruling of the European Court, delivered late in 2004:

> The case concerned related to a series of closely similar products based on the antidepressant fluoxetine (Prozac) Eli Lilly obtained authorization in the United Kingdom for its original Prozac capsules (Product A") on November 25th 1988. The firm went on to obtain an independent authorization for Prozac liquid (Product B) in Denmark in October 1992. Two weeks later, at the end of October 1992, Lilly successfully submitted an abridged application for Product B in Britain, taking the earlier British authorization for Product A as its point of reference; it admitted that the capsules and the liquid were not identical but provided evidence that they were bioequivalent, i.e. the liquid was a "line extension" of the capsules. Seven years later in 1999, after expiry of the fluoxetine patent, the independent firm APS submitted in Britain an abridged application for its own liquid version of fluoxetine (Product C) claiming that it was "essentially similar" to Lilly's Product B. This, it was claimed in turn, in fact dated back to 1988 when the original capsules were authorized. This would mean that it has been authorized in the Community for more than ten years prior to the APS application,. The British authorities took the view that APS could not use Product B as its point of reference since that product itself had been registered in the Community for less than 10 years. APS brought an application for judicial review to the High Court, which in turn sought a primary ruling from the ECJ at Luxemburg. The latter concluded that the APS's application was validly conceived since it referred to B which was merely a new pharmaceutical form of A, and A itself had been authorised for marketing in the Community for at least the six or ten year period stimulated in Directive 2001.[1]

If this line of reasoning is carried through one might expect even longer chains of multiple cross-referral to emerge.

10.8.   Generic Substitution

As noted above, the European Union is now, primarily for economic reasons, in favour of "generic substitution", a practice already in use in

---

[1] Judgement of the European Court of Justice, 9 December 2004 (C-36/03).

many of its member states. Britain has been a partial exception, having substituted generic products for prescribed specialities only under strict hospital conditions or in emergencies. It is clear that the extent to which substitution is practised will have a marked effect on the balance between speciality and generic sales. The science-based industry is critical of the principle, arguing that the prescriber may have valid reasons for ensuring the use of the original product, for example where the patient is likely to have less faith in the treatment if the substitution is made. To the public, the science-based industry has continued to drop cautious hints that constitution of a generic may not be precisely the same as that of the original product, a statement which could unnecessarily undermine trust in the generic version (ABPI 1999). Particularly in the United States some concern has been expressed as to whether the original and the generic versions are indeed mutually replaceable in all situations; the case of drugs with a narrow therapeutic margin is cited, and numerous examples have been provided. According to the medical literature there are indeed a range of situations in which generic substitution is inadvisable but there are many others where the original can be replaced with impunity by the generic equivalent. The most logical rule would appear to be to permit and encourage generic substitution as a principle, while maintaining a carefully formulated list of exceptions covering those cases in which it should not be applied; it does not seem that the public interest would be served if generic substitution were to be regarded as an exception.

From its early days, European Law has followed America's Hatch-Waxman example in permitting the generic manufacturer to obtain marketing approval for his product on the basis of an "abridged application", the essential evidence being that the medicine is truly medically equivalent to the original. This can however mean (and frequently does) that the primary and the secondary manufacturer use different excipients, colourings, flavours and finishing processes; provided however that the two products are fully bioequivalent as regards their rate and degree of release into the body and any other characteristic which could affect either their use in treatment or their tolerability, these differences will be of no significance. It is just possible, as noted above, that for certain drugs with a narrow therapeutic index such differences could matter, as could the inclusion or exclusion of an excipient to which some users are allergic. All these are elements which the generic manufacturer should be able to take into account in developing his product and providing evidence to regulatory agencies; where there is even slight doubt as to equivalence, the secondary manufacturer will be well advised to use a formulation which is as close as possible to that of the original product.

10.9.   Generic Biologicals, Biogenerics and Biosimilars

In considering the laws and regulations affecting the pharmaceutical industry there has up to this point been no reason to draw any distinction between drugs synthesized or extracted as pure substances in the laboratory (such as an antihistamine) and those complex biological products having similar uses in prophylaxis or therapy but which are derived from living organisms. The latter are a very heterogenous group, including vaccines, sera, natural insulin, blood derivatives, or extracts of bacteria or plants; at the present day very many biologicals are biotechnology-derived products, produced by means of recombinant DNA technology. Although the means of preparation and assay differ, and these "biologicals" often fall under different regulatory procedures, most of the general principles of law and regulation applied to chemical drugs apply similarly to these products.

One essential difference between medicinal drugs and biologicals arises however when, following long-term approval and field use of a biological, a "generic" copy from another source is submitted for licensing to the relevant regulatory authority. In the case of chemical drugs, the "copy" will have to demonstrate bioequivalence, and the active component of the copy will have to be chemically identical in both products. These principles are not easy to apply where generic copies of biologicals are concerned. As Karst puts it:

> Typical biological product characteristics include a complex three-dimensional structure essential to the product's function, chains of several hundred or thousand amino acids and specific glycosylation patterns. These characteristics are difficult to measure with current science, and significantly complicate a determination that two products are "the same". (Karst 2004)

A further but related dilemma lies in the fact that for biotechnology products one can rarely refer to any authoritative and neutral specification, such as is likely to be accessible for a chemical drug in the national pharmacopoeia.

All this could mean that, rather than submitting an "abbreviated application" under America's FDC Act or an "abridged application" under European law, providing only proof of equivalence, a generic producer of a biological might find himself required to submit a complete file. This would be at least as wasteful and undesirable as would the repetition of experiments and trials with a chemical drug. "Generic biologicals", especially when developed using recombinant DNA technology, could prove considerably cheaper to make and sell than more traditionally prepared products of the same type but this advantage might evaporate if extensive studies of efficacy and safety were to be called for.

Although an ideal procedure for the registration of biogenerics does not seem to have been developed and tested under any regulatory system to date, practical solutions, adapted to the individual case, appear to be emerging.

> In the USA in 1989 the FDA approved a generic equivalent version of a botulinium toxin type A for the treatment of strabismus and blepharospasm purely on the basis of published clinical material on earlier preparations. In 1996 the FDA issued a guideline on the subject in 1996 declaring that it would require only proof that the new preparation was "comparable" to its predecessor, and that "comparability" could be demonstrated in various ways appropriate to the case such as the physical and other characteristics of the material. In the following year the agency refused to licence a generic version of conjugated oestrogens from pregnant mare's urine because it could not confirm that there was physical comparability; in that sane year however it accepted a generic version of human menopausal gonadotrophin even though the principal active component had a different isoform from that in the original product. In yet other cases the agency has appeared willing to accept evidence that the originator and generic products have been extracted or processed in a closely similar manner; this seems to have been the case when in 2002 the FDA accepted the reintroduction of human urokinase, apparently because it was prepared in a manner similar to that employed when the product was approved and marketed earlier. The principles are to be further worked out by the FDA itself but it would seem that a flexible approach to the problem will be sought.

In the European Union a Commission Directive on what were termed "similar biological medicinal products" was issued in 2003. The term "biosimilar", adopted during the preliminary studies, acknowledged in effect that the original and the generic versions might not be entirely identical or even in all respects equivalent and it could well imply that European agencies will apply the same flexibility in this matter that the FDA is attaining.

Problems seem most likely to arise where a product of recombinant DNA technology is submitted as a replacement or successor to a preparation originally extracted from natural materials. It would seem very probable that in such a case the equivalence will need to be demonstrated by at least some clinical testing. In addition, an examination of possible immunogenicity is likely to be mandated.[2]

---

[2] It may be noted that on 20 December 2004 the US Food and Drug Administration released a draft guideline for industry entitled "ANDA's: Pharmaceutical Solid Polymorphism. Chemistry, Manufacturing and Controls Information." The text is intended to assist applicants submitting Abbreviated New Drug Applications where the substance concerned exists in polymorphic forms. The draft guideline provides recommendations as to "sameness" where there is possible polymorphism.

10.10.   The Future Status of the Generic Pharmaceutical Industry

As was stressed above, the generic industry is no longer in any sense a secondary player in the pharmaceutical field. As patents expire and health services seek to economize, its growth seems set to continue, at least until the coming wave of patent expiries has run its course (Class 2005). Regulations and policies with respect to it are increasingly specific and clear. Inevitably, however, there will be two ongoing debates regarding the borderline which separates it from the science-based sector. The one will concern the conditions which must be met if a generic drug is to be acknowledged as fully equivalent to its patented congener. In that respect one must expect new methods of analysis to be developed, but also new challenges to arise, such as those already coming with biosimilars. The other debate will continue to tackle patent issues, with generic manufacturers exploring possible opportunities as vigorously as the originator companies strive to put them out of reach. Events show that many opportunities still do present themselves; the terms laid down by Doha leave multiple doors open, as do the national laws now emerging in member states. The fact that many originator firms do not trouble to take out patents in some secondary markets and may be open to voluntary licensing in others creates openings that are sometimes overlooked.

On the other hand, there is little to be gained from seeking to live on the uncertain fringes of the law. It still happens on occasion, and especially when the patent situation regarding product or process is in any sense unclear, that a generic pharmaceutical company takes a risk in this connection, assuming that the patent owner will not succeed in obtaining legal redress or that the court system in the country concerned will be insufficiently efficient to handle the case or to give judgement for a number of years, during which the generic can thrive unmolested. As experience with such litigation grows in a range of countries, however, judges are seeking to define the rules of play in ever clearer terms; Courts can act rapidly and decisively if a complaint is brought in good time and a wise judge will not hesitate to pass down rebukes to one party or the other where they are deserved:

Various cases in England have involved the Glaxo Smith Kline drug paroxetine (the antidepressant Seroxat). Protection of the basic substance expired in 1999 but GSK has a number of secondary patents which several generic firms have either overlooked or defied. GSK's own Seroxate is based on paroxetine hemihydrate and to evade this some generics firms therefore used the anhydrous form. The latter however has its own UK Patent Nr, GB 2,297,550. In October 2002 GSK brought an interim injunction against Generics (UK) Ltd for breach of this patent, and in November 2002 it similarly sought an injunction on these grounds against Apotex Europe and others. Both injunctions, requiring the defendants to desist with immediate effect, were promptly granted and the decision was upheld on appeal. In both cases, Mr Justice Jacob commented that the defendant had been well aware of the patent for a long time and could at an earlier phase have applied for a declaration of non-infringement, launched a petition to revoke or invited the claimant to sue.

An interim injunction, in various legal systems, is a severe and almost immediate remedy which a Court can grant when the circumstances warrant rapid action. In these cases it was considered to be warranted *inter alia* by the fact that by introducing the generic product the damage to the claimant would be immediate, and by the fact that the generic firms had failed to take earlier action to "clear the way" legally when faced with a patent of which they were aware.

In one or the other way the science-based industry and the generic industry now complement each other efficiently; as the rules of play become better understood one may hope that they will also do so harmoniously. One possible development is a greater measure of control over the generic industry by major science-based firms, and the consequences of this may need to be examined should it lead to an impairment of competition.

The British parliament's Select Committee, reporting in April 2005, noted that "Over the past decade, there have been significant changes in the pattern of UK generic manufacturing ownership, leading to increasing domination by large international generic manufacturers. In general, these manufacturers operate independently of, and in competition with, the major brand name companies. However, the £4.4 billion acquisition of two major generic producers by the Swiss firm, Novartis, in February 2005, may presage a major change. Novartis, the world's sixth-largest producer of branded drugs, is now the world's largest manufacturer of generics." (HOC 2005, para 28)

A final comment must be that the generic industry is as bound to the rules of honest commerce as any other. The fact that in America some generic manufacturers have refrained from launching generics after signing anti-competitive agreements with brand-name firms is not a welcome sign. During the period 1999–2000 there was considerable turbulence in the generic drug market in Great Britain, with substantial price increases and evidence of price-fixing; as a result the maximum prices of a series of top-selling generic drug products, which had hitherto been uncontrolled, had to be brought within the ambit of the government's Pharmaceutical Price Regulatory Scheme (PPRS) (HOC 2005, para 120). Having acquired a well-deserved reputation for the modesty of its prices, the industry now needs to be particularly wary of betraying it.

Chapter 11

The Pharmaceutical Industry and Social Controversy

Some of the activities of the pharmaceutical industry which have given rise to controversy – such as matters relating to advertising, to animal studies or so-called disease mongering – have been considered in previous chapters. It is however also the case that, by the very nature of some of the products which it delivers, the industry can find itself embroiled in wider controversies to which it is not in fact a direct party. These tend to involve conflicts with an ethical background, commonly associated with a particular religious belief; if these beliefs are widely held among the population they may however be reflected in provisions of law or regulation.

During recent decades this has been most prominently the case with respect to products related to sex and reproduction, particularly the oral contraceptives, the "morning after pill" and the abortifacients. An entirely different social controversy has grown with respect to gene patents.

11.1. The Ethics of Contraception

Few general pharmaceutical firms have been involved in the production of mechanical or chemical contraceptives, but from 1960 onwards a number of major firms developed or licenced oral contraceptives based on hormonal components. They thereby became to some extent involved in public debate regarding the acceptability of these products. During the early years of production more than one of these firms had to come to terms with the attitude of members of their staff or workforce who, because of firm rejection of contraception by the Church to which they belonged, did not find it possible to become involved in the production, handling or sale of these products.

That particular company had a problem because a lot of its employees were Catholics and at the time wouldn't have dreamt have touching a contraceptive. Eventually, they told us, the management consulted a particular monastic order which had fairly liberal ideas. Their view literally was that the workers could handle the "pill" as a purely contractual task without getting involved in it, undertaking not

to perform the work "with heart and soul." Coming from the monastery that seemed
to satisfy most people and production went ahead, but some still had a bad conscience and they asked to be transferred to other work (Interview 16)

A further problem arose in those countries where, because of prevailing ethical views, contraception was not regarded as an acceptable
indication which could serve as a basis for drug approval. This obstacle
was generally overcome by demonstrating clinically the value of the product in gynaecological indications such as menorrhagia, dysmenorrhoea or
irregularity of the menstrual periods. The contraceptive effect was then
mentioned secondarily, e.g. in the form of a warning to the effect that during use of the product conception could not occur.

Although there has in recent years been much litigation relating to
oral contraceptives this has related to issues which could arise with any
drug (e.g. ineffectiveness or injury) and not to social issues.

A current controversy with ethical overtones relates to the increasingly wide practice of making oral contraceptives available "OTC" without prescription but the formal arguments raised in this connection
generally relate rather more to possible risks (e.g. due to use without prior
medical examination) than to ethical matters.

11.2.   The "Morning after Pill"

The "morning after pill" has approximately the same composition as
an oral contraceptive but with the components present in higher doses.
Taken within a period of some hours after coitus it is considered to prevent implantation of the zygote and hence the onset of pregnancy (SPUC
2003). Opposition to such products, largely from the same activist groups
as those dealing with abortifacients (Section 1.2.3), is based on the view
that life must be considered to begin at the time of insemination, and that
suppression of pregnancy after coitus amounts to abortion. Again the controversy is largely social, involving either attempts to prevent registration
for what is considered an illegal indication or campaigns to limit public
sale or require prescription; there have however been some doubts regarding safety, should the pregnancy continue and be exposed to the influence
of the hormones. In Britain, debates centred around Government decisions
in 2000 to release the product for sale in community pharmacies and to
allow for some distribution free of charge through schools and other channels, leading to charges that the authorities were "promoting promiscuity".
Public advertising was permitted but was heavily criticised by pro-life

groups; the company concerned declared that it had sought to avoid caus-ing offence (Telegraph 2002). In Italy, the Vatican's Pontifical Academy for Life issued in 2000 a formal confirmation of an earlier church view that the product must be considered as an abortifacient and could therefore not be tolerated. As of 2005 the authorities in the USA were still consid-ering release of the "morning after pill" for OTC-sale.

The various social protest movements seem unlikely to have conse-quences for manufacturers as far as registration is concerned, since when problems are anticipated it is generally possible to obtain approval for a medical indication. However in the Philippines in 2002, a government decision made any form of trading in the morning-after pill illegal on the grounds that it must be considered as an abortifacient.

11.3. Abortifacients

The principal debate regarding abortifacients is that which has taken place regarding the Roussel product RU-486 (mifeprostone); the case illustrates several of the legal and ethical problems which can confront the manufacturer of such a product (FMF 2000, SPUC 2003, NYSRLC 2004).

RU-486, a prostaglandin, was first marketed as an abortifacient in France in September 1988 by the French Company Roussel-Uclaf. The sale was sus-pended a month later by the Chairman of the Company, reportedly after activists had threatened the firm and its employees, the threats including a consumer boy-cott of all the firm's products. Two days later the French Government, which had a 36% share in the firm, ordered it to re-introduce the product. In Britain the product was licensed for sale in 1991 and by 2002 it was being used by some 24,000 women yearly in England and Wales. In the USA, anti-abortion activists again threatened reprisals if the drug were introduced there, but other groups urged the firm to make it available. In 1994 Roussel assigned the US patent rights for the drug to the Population Council which submitted a new application to the FDA; the drug was approved in September 2000. (Kreeger 1994) The anti-abortion movement had in the meantime called for a consumer boycott of all products owned by Roussel or its German parent company Hoechst unless the allocation of the licence to the Population Council were withdrawn. (NRLC 2005) Roussel originally claimed to have ended all involvement with RU 486 in 1994 with allocation of the licence to the Council but in fact continued to man-ufacture it until 1997 when it transferred all remaining rights in the drug to a former staff member trading as Exelgyn, who in turn arranged for manufacture by a third party. The drug is currently registered in the European Union though not in fact marketed in a number of countries where there is likely to be activist opposition to its use.

11.4. Patenting of Biological Materials

An entirely new type of socially sensitive field in which some parts of the pharmaceutical industry are becoming heavily involved relates to the patenting and exploitation of biological materials, processes or genetic structures. The entire principle of patents in this field and the licensing of such fundamental biological knowledge for commercial use has been criticised from many sides, sometimes because of misunderstandings, but there is also genuine concern (Scotland 2005, HGA 2000, Paradise 2005).

As carried out between 1990 and its completion in 2003, the Human Genome Project was coordinated by the US Department of Energy and the National Institutes of Health with commercial partners; in its early years the Wellcome Trust in Britain become a major partner, and further entrants joined from other countries (Doesgenomes 2005). Primary goals of the Project were to identify all the more than 20,000 genes in human DNA as well as the sequences of the three billion constituent chemical base pairs. It was from the start the intention to transfer related technologies to the private sector, the expectation being that the basic knowledge acquired through the project would render possible a better understanding of disease and the development of new types of highly specific therapy, including drugs created with a tailor-made structure for predesigned purposes. It was evident that this could comprise a potentially important new opening for research in the pharmaceutical industry. As early as 1999, 10 pharmaceutical companies and the UK Wellcome Trust announced the establishment of a non-profit foundation to find and map common single-nucleotide polymorphisms (SNPs). Their goal was to generate a widely accepted, high-quality, extensive, publicly available map using SNPs as markers evenly distributed throughout the human genome. The consortium planned to patent all the SNPs found but to enforce the patents only in order to prevent others from patenting the same information. Information found by the consortium was to be freely available. While many SNPs apparently have no effect on cell function, others are thought to predispose the individual to disease or influence the response to a drug.

Within a short period of time a very large number of patents had been filed on the basis of this and associated work, and it become clear that genetic patients could become the basis for many future developments in the field of medicine. At an early stage, however, the active involvement of the pharmaceutical industry in what was conceived as a form of "patenting nature" raised protest, since it was considered that in this way even academic research in the field could be blocked. As a normal rule, plain "products of nature" cannot be patented. Under standard patent law in most industrialised nations, the patent applicant must show that his/her invention is novel, non-obvious and useful. According to the practice which has evolved in very recent years, DNA products can become patentable but only when they have been isolated, purified or modified to produce a unique form not found in nature (CSTS 2005). Proponents of gene patenting argue that where a new therapeutic agent has been developed by such processing of a natural product it thus acquires a patent situation closely analogous to that of a new synthetic chemical molecule resembling that of the natural substance that inspired it. This has not stilled the controversy; very large numbers of patents are now being filed in this area and the complexity of the material obviously raises the fear that a drug company might be found to have acquired rights to exploit a fundamental piece of nature (e.g. a vital gene fragment), the functions and uses of which they had not yet adequately specified yet which gives them a monopoly on a route to further knowledge.

A report to the International Bioethics Committee of UNESCO considered the issue of gene patents but set it alongside other areas in which the protection of intellectual properly has been criticised, including drugs themselves. Drawing a comparison with the risks associated with the patenting of other forms of entirely new knowledge, as illustrated by the attempt in 2001 to exclude generic AIDS drugs from South Africa, the report argued that the 20-year duration of patent protection as a universal rule was "arguably excessive" as regards genomic sequences which composed the human genome thread and the rapid advance of knowledge about them. Patents already granted and applied for would add greatly, and for many years, to national health budgets. Specifically with respect to human genome patents the report concluded that:

> Unless the rise in patents in relation to the human genome is soon curtailed, "the cost of future therapies and genetic tests will become prohibitive for most human beings and nations . . . . .

> Ultimately . . . . . . there is a conflict or tension between ethical principles – those that uphold the right to protection of the creative inventions of the human mind – and those that uphold the right to life, the right to health protection and promotion and the solidarity of the entire human family. In the context of intellectual property law it is necessary to resolve this conflict in a just way. The present intellectual property law, municipal, regional and international, falls short of doing this.

The Council of Europe's Committee on Legal Affairs and Human Rights has similarly taken the view, supported by many researchers, patient groups and medical professional organizations, that genes are "the common heritage of mankind" and that one must be very hesistant to recognized patents filed with respect to them.

The issue still goes well beyond the scope of the present study and the debate is likely to continue as useful products of this type of this research emerge and the question arises whether one step on the road to exploitation indeed could not block a subsequent one. To cite Paradise and Sherwin, writing from the US in 2005:

> A growing body of research suggests that gene barriers create barriers to research and development of technologies and impede healthcare by hindering access and increasing costs. Gene patent holders can use their exclusive control over genetic material to present other researchers from using the specific genetic sequence for further research . . . . . . Scientific collaboration is stifled because some researchers refuse to share patent tissue samples or preliminary findings because they each want to be the first one to discover the profitable gene . . . (Paradise 2005).

In view of the protests which have already come to the fore, and the manner in which governments have already immersed themselves in the issue, it seems likely that society will now remain very watchful as industry makes use of genome knowledge and will find compromises on the issue of intellectual projection in this matter. There would appear to be every likelihood that society will find itself obliged to find a middle road, ensuring that specific aspects or applications of genetic knowledge developed by a company specifically for a therapeutic or diagnostic purpose could enjoy protection for a sufficient period to exploit that discovery, but without forming an obstacle to the conduct of other scientific work, whether commercial or not, that could provide either further new treatments or develop fundamental knowledge of broad usefulness.

11.5. Future Involvement in Social Controversy

As a rule, pharmaceutical companies have carefully sought to avoid involvement in social controversy relating to the purposes for which their products are used. For a product with an uncontested medical indication the firm will as a rule seek approval based on that indication only and leave the debate regarding its more controversial use to be carried on in other circles. However the example of the morning-after pill in the Philippines provides a reminder that a government could render any form of trading in such a product illegal. In the case of RU-486, Roussel's hesitation to disseminate the drug widely was due in part to opposition in principle from its German parent company and in part to consumer boycotts of all the company's products organized by activist groups. A major problem could however arise if society should adopt new moral concepts involving the use of pharmacological agents exclusively intended and suited for a contested purpose, e.g. the rapid and painless induction of euthanasia. If such a situation should develop, any company supplying the product might do best to follow the Roussel example and transfer it to others, e.g. a public health agency, both for production and distribution.

Chapter 12

Postscript: The Way Ahead

12.1. Medicines in the Mist

Any impartial analysis of the pharmaceutical industry's evolving place in the community since the Second World War inevitably ends up painting a bewildering picture of ups and downs, achievements and disasters, pride and prejudice. The predictions made by the futurologists of the 1950s went wrong as events ranging from therapeutic breakthroughs to toxic tragedies to the drastic liberalization of society intervened and alternated. The pharmaceutical industry grew triumphantly but sometimes recklessly. The community through its policy makers tried to react adequately, first in one way and then in another; it did not always understand what was going on and it was buffeted variously by a dread of risk, a fervent desire for better medicines and dreams of greater prosperity for society as a whole.

The lawmakers have over the years provided a million rules which are supposed to guide and govern the situation. Much has been achieved in securing adherence to them. In a large part of the world the drug scene of 2005 is incomparably better than that of 1945. Yet today one expert observer after another warns that we are on a dangerous course and they come with predictions of doom. Marcia Angell, Richard Sykes, Jerry Avorn, David Henry, Patrice Trouiller, Richard Horton and others like them are hardly ragged-trousered rabble rousers, yet Charles Medawar's phrase "Medicines out of control?" – complete with question mark – sums up their common concern. A tenth of the world is over-medicated, nine-tenths are neglected; all along the line, irrespective of whether we look at research, prices, advertising, prescribing, patents, counterfeiting or just plain trading, things are somehow out of joint.

12.2. The Trouble with Law

We have talked for 60 years about policy, law and regulation in this field. Have they failed us? To a degree, yes; in a sense, they were bound to do so, because it was assumed that they could act in isolation. The Law has its limitations. One can regulate technicalities in this field, and we have done so massively. But it is much more difficult, acting on behalf of the community, to mould through processes of law the evolution of a broad process such as this, that cuts across the interests of health, science and medicine. It can be hard to serve Hippocrates and Mammon at the same time. Even when one contrives to devise rules and policies, they have to evolve through trial and error, they have to grow with society, and society in turn has to accept them both in letter and spirit. The law is also on occasion slow-moving, and it is less than perfect because of political compromises which were necessary to assure its passage; and when passed it may not be implemented as it should be – whether because of indolence, inefficiency or ignorance.

The internationalization of both drug control and communications creates opportunities but also new problems. Is it at all sure how proceedings could be instituted against an international authority taking a dangerously incorrect decision or engaging in corruption? How will one ensure that in the global economy transnational corporations are made (and remain) accountable to society? (Paul and Garrect 2000; Richter 2001) How can control on advertising be properly applied to material disseminated across borders on the internet? One has some ideas (ABPI 2005b) but no certainties.

A notion has arisen that litigation, brought, for example, by injured parties, can back up and strengthen the statute law in a field such as this. That is only to a certain extent true. Litigation can establish principles which become widely accepted and ultimately find their way into the statutes, but some critics consider that this erodes respect for the court system and, ultimately the rule of law (Lytton 2004). It is in any case only likely to happen in a society where litigation is both massive and efficient and the damages heavy, as is the case in the United States (Vernick 2004). Litigation brought against a defendant with almost bottomless resources can be a ruinous proceeding (Social Audit 2005), and even intensive litigation may not do much to drive an injurious medicine from the market. In the American situation, a manufacturer with a highly profitable but noxious drug may find it more profitable to settle cases quietly for many millions of dollars until the patent expires, rather than take more appropriate corrective action.

Above all, if law is to work, notions of what constitutes decent and ethical behaviour have to evolve in parallel with it. Law and regulation, created by the community, can complement and buttress good behaviour within the industry but can never impose it. And ethical governance within the industry has, unhappily, failed repeatedly, in the circle where it is most needed; we shall return to that problem in a moment.

12.3.   The Trouble with Governments

Governments and their legal experts are fond of grand gestures. A broad problem is identified; an apparent cause is found and headlined, and a straightforward solution is identified. Where drugs were concerned, that happened in several stages, considered in Section 3.4.1. Two centuries and more ago, there was a concern that drugs were not pure, so rules were made to render them so, and pharmacopoeias and inspectorates were set up. A hundred years later there was the issue of safety; Salvarsan, Elixir of Sulfonilamide, Stalinon and thalidomide in turn raised their ugly heads, and each was dealt with by making or expanding legal rules to ensure that drugs would be rendered safe, and setting up machinery to ensure that the rules were applied. The supervision of all that was entrusted to Ministries of Health – who in due course found themselves obliged to expand the rules much further when they were found not to work to everyone's satisfaction. When society became concerned about over-prescribing and wastage, it became the task of national health services or insurance agencies and educators, working with the blessing of the law, to look for solutions; they are still struggling. Then again there was the concern that drugs were too expensive, running in parallel with another concern that they might not be expensive enough to pay for proper research; departments of health, finance and social affairs found themselves battling with these issues. All the time, a hundred other problems have been descending upon governments, and one by one they have been provided with supposed regulatory solutions and sometimes (but not always) with regulatory godfathers to apply them. And in the background there is the horrifying plight of the developing world and its lack of therapeutic care, with no single authority in place to ensure that it receives proper attention and finance; since it is not a domestic concern, there is the constant temptation to pass it up to international agencies and hope that it will then in one way or another be relieved. Meanwhile, in the international arena, there are things happening with the industry and its involvement in TRIPS and the so-called TRIPS-plus which do not bode at all well for the third world (Jorge 2004).

This division of responsibility can be bewildering when dealing with the day-to-day problems of the drug sector. As noted above, the pharmaceutical sector cuts across the fields of health, science and medicine, but the compartmentalization of law and government means that the pharmaceutical industry is bound to find itself involved with many more than three ministries, departments or institutes and with multiple laws. In a single week in a single country, a company may have dealings with a Ministry of Health, an autonomous Drug Regulatory Institute and Departments of Industry, Trade, Labour, Agriculture, Environment and Education as well as with a series of Universities – to name only the most frequent contacts. It is not uncommon for multi-sectoral issues to be considered in an interdepartmental meeting, in which the representative of each department of agency handles his facet of the matter but in which the industrial participant may well be in the strongest position to ensure that action is taken since he has a uniquely broad overview. Unfortunately, he also has a strong partial interest in the form that such action should take. Working from day to day in this way can be complicated enough for all parties, but when an issue is also the business of a regional or international agency, taking decisions may be fearfully complex.

A simple but thorny example of all this was presented during the deliberations of the British House of Commons Select Committee in 2004–2005 (HOC 2005, para 392). Confronted with the fact that the Department of Health was not ideally equipped to deal with economic and financial matters affecting industry, the Committee inclined to the view that these should be transferred to the Department of Trade and Industry. It is understandable, yet in a sense it is a move in the wrong direction, further fragmenting the face which government presents to a strong industrial sector. Is the question of what constitutes a fair price for a medicine a matter of health or of business policy? Obviously it is both, and a government needs to be capable of looking at it from both points of view and finding a just solution. What is lacking not only in Britain but in many other countries is a clearly formulated overall National Drug Policy, such as has been recommended and defined by WHO for many years (WHO 1988c, 2001). Some developing countries, having arrived on the scene later, have been guided by international consultants and organizations into tackling matters in that way. Tiny East Timor managed it in 1998 ("The National Drug Policy is intended to ensure that effective and safe drugs of good quality are available and affordable to the entire population and are appropriately used") and countries ranging from Afghanistan to Australia have done it in a more elaborate but very clear manner. Just those two words "appropriately used" puts the business of ensuring rational use of drugs firmly onto the government agenda, where in much of the world it is still lacking. Only in April 2005 was such a broad policy proposed by Britain's Select Committee (HOC 2005 at para 390). Even more valuable would be a National Therapeutics Policy, balancing the merits of drug treatment against the alternatives, hence avoiding an exaggerated dependence on medicines as opposed, for example to physiotherapy or psychotherapy; the approach would meet the Committee's call to balance out these various approaches to patient care ((HOC 2005 at paras 388 and 391). Unfortunately, since there is neither a well-funded body to ensure that non-drug treatments are studied and assessed as thoroughly as medicines, nor a united team of impartial propagandists to assist doctors in choosing between them, it is unlikely that this will happen to any appreciable extent in the near future.

Pull together all the significant aspects of national drug policy, and you may be well on the way to improving things, seeing the wood again instead of the trees, realizing that you need balance and fairness on many different fronts. The false notion that "drug regulation" with its licences and its million rules is the essence of drug policy needs to be consigned to the realm of the fairies; it is just one tree, albeit it an impressive one. Where regulation proves disappointing is where it is not well adapted to current needs, or where it is out of touch with commercial thinking. Although there has been criticism of the extent to which regulators move into industrial appointments and industrial experts into regulation, such moves sometimes do a power of good for mutual understanding. No one is likely to have a more realistic view as to what is admissible or inadmissible in an advertisement or a proposed clinical protocol than the individual who until recently has been creating these things himself; and the regulator who moves into a corporate post usually takes much community-oriented thinking with him.

Public policy towards a large industry such as this must be endowed with the proper tone and authority to lead industry firmly in the right direction where specific drug issues are concerned; at times, regulators have been unreasonably severe, while at other moments they have been too brotherly to the firms with which they deal. To cite the Select Committee once more:

> . . . the industry may be seen as a scapegoat for failings elsewhere. For many years it has been left to its own devices. The regulatory system, the medical profession and Government have all failed to ensure that industry's activities are more clearly allied to the interests of patients and the NHS (HOC 2005 at para. 339)

> . . . for want of critical scrutiny by, and lack of deference and accountability to, the public and public bodies, the industry lacks the discipline and quality control that it needs but cannot itself provide. The industry's complaints of excessive regulation are understandable but self regulation is not at present effective. (HOC 2005 at para. 340)

The closeness that has developed between regulators and companies has deprived the industry of rigorous quality control and audit (ibid)

The Committee also considered how other bodies – academic, scientific and professional – might seek to be more effective than in the past at providing industry with feedback and quality control. They have been hindered to date by "lack of transparency, limited resources, significant dependency on industry funding, and some conflicts of interest" (HOC 2005 at para. 340). Here too there is an opportunity for change.

12.4. The Trouble with Corporations

12.4.1. The discrepancy

There is no need to decry the technical abilities of the pharmaceutical industry. It has attained higher standards of quality than were ever achieved before; it is capable of efficiently taking promising discoveries from the academic world, from military and research institutions and making them ripe for use in medical care. It has great skills in the study of toxicology, in mass production and distribution and in the processing of information. Even where it chooses to live from the scientific achievements of others rather than engaging in discovery itself, it manages the process well. Society could well do without its massive armies of travelling propagandists, but even they have abilities which could be put to much better use. These qualities of a vast and capable industry could serve society very well provided that the fundamental ethic is honed anew that its ongoing role is indeed to serve society well, honestly and economically, while providing an attractive reward to its investors. Yet at that point there is a paradoxical discrepancy in its way of behaving.

Take any major pharmaceutical corporation and you will find some resounding declarations of corporate ethics or social responsibility which have been made on its behalf. Follow then the acts of that same corporation as they are reflected in the journals, the business bulletins and the law reports and you will find that same corporation behaving despicably every day somewhere in the field. If this volume had set out to chronic the industry's unfortunate brushes with the law it would have been ten times the size. That is not its intention, but those things must be its concern. Angell, Medawar and the rest are right about what is wrong. It is as if, in its breathless evolution, the pharmaceutical industry has grown apart from the society that it is supposed to serve, ranking its own needs and ambitions where convenient above those of the community. All too often it has ranked the creation of an image above the earning of an honest reputation (Lawton 2004). Even when respecting the broad lines laid down by law and regulation, it has too often from day to day skirted the boundaries of what is socially and even legally permissible. To adapt Lord Atkin's phrase in the case of *Donoghue v. Stevenson* (1933), the pharmaceutical industry has forgotten to be a good neighbour. Whatever wonders are performed from year to year in the scientific sector to which it belongs, the industry has in the wide world somehow lost the knack and name of decent behaviour. As the British Parliament's Select Committee put it in 2005:

> We do not doubt the legitimacy of commercial objectives, the contributions of the pharmaceutical industry to health and the overlap of commercial and health interests, but this inquiry left us in no doubt that the scope for conflict between health and trade interests is huge (HOC 2005 at para. 341)

The move from a social-democratic to an aggressively liberal society is still too young for anyone to know with certainty how things should function in the future; there is no functioning model that one would unhesitatingly wish to emulate. America in particular has its own problems and the critics of the pharmaceutical situation in that country are especially firm in their calls for change. (Angell 2004, Goldstein 2004, PCAF 2004, Spitzer 2004 and many others)

12.4.2. The perils of success

The problems which the pharmaceutical industry currently faces are not primarily issues of law, but they are in many respects ethical issues born of critical reflection on a long period of self-seeking behaviour. A generation of astute business leaders have discovered the extent to which, in those parts of the world which have experienced a long economic boom, the available wealth can, given the necessary skills, be skimmed off; much of that wealth has accrued over the years to what has become known, sometimes with a touch of derision, as "big pharma". Where real breakthroughs fail to emerge from the laboratories, it has proved possible to seduce clients to plump for products which have little more novelty to offer than their name and image. And where one's own laboratories fail for a time to deliver, there is the promise of the biotechnology industry in the side streets with uncertain but tempting promises of great innovations to come.

12.4.3. *The sense of impregnability*

Whatever the current concerns around it, the industry has learned to trust its own opinions and practices so implicitly that on the surface it still seems to exude confidence. Its salesmen and detailmen retain their firm grip on the practising physician, still capable of securing a firm market foothold; the bulk of the world's medical journals continue to float on a massive income from drug advertising. While exciting new drugs are few and far between, any western market somehow finds itself treated each year to numerous new products, variants or combinations. Poorly founded estimates of the costs of drug development are accepted, adopted and quoted uncritically as a basis for policy and negotiation; politicians still side largely with an industry which provides high-class employment and healthy exports. Industrial pressure in the right political circles has bolstered the protection afforded by data exclusivity and patents, to the peril of the low-cost generic imitations needed to save lives in the third world. And, nurtured by propaganda, a patient faced with a choice of medicines will readily turn to the most expensive item, in the often mistaken belief that it offers a better hope of a return to health than anything at a lower price. Thriving national economies can afford luxury and a degree of waste, but many economies across the world are not thriving; some struggle to pay and many more have no hope of paying at all until or unless there is change; all are increasingly vociferous in their demands that the industry makes a more genuine effort to meet their needs.

If anything boosts a sense of impregnability in a large industry such as this it is that remarkable process known as public relations. It is good that positive achievements are publicized. It is less good that an industry which has lost much of its reputation through shameful behaviour should be able to regain it by setting aside vast sums for image building; yet it is possible, it happens, and it appears to have become a knee-jerk reaction to any adverse development.

12.4.4. *Attitude to the law*

In the most basic sense this is generally a law-abiding sector of society; the industry pays its taxes, it is a good and enlightened employer, and it adheres to the bewilderingly comprehensive network of technical regulations and edicts to which it is subject. Viewed economically, it has for many years rewarded its shareholders well and dependably, contributing in that way a remarkable sum to pension funds in the western world and thus to the sustenance of a fair proportion of the population; as an exporter it has greatly enriched the countries in which it is primarily based. Viewed technically it has attained – and often pioneered – the highest standards. It is also an industry that has repeatedly stressed its commitment to the people and their health, more particularly through the achievements which it claims as a creator of new and ever better medicines. Yet despite all these proofs of good citizenship, one might suggest that it is high time for the pharmaceutical industry to regard the statute law as an expression of duties to be fulfilled proudly than an inventory of industrial rights to be claimed aggressively. One too often finds that pharmaceutical companies, rather than acting according to the spirit of health law, interpret it minimally and with an ill grace, while surrounding themselves with an army of lawyers ready to face any challenge to their interests. Animal and clinical studies of new drugs may be performed strictly according to the relevant regulations and directives, yet in too many instances vital but inconvenient findings have been concealed or rendered difficult of access – only one aspect of the trend within the industry to regard truth as a flexible commodity. That would be a serious enough accusation if one were dealing with the manufacturers of lawnmowers; it is appalling that it can be advanced with good reason where matters of life and death are concerned. It is as if the industry has developed a serious degree of over-confidence in its ability to select, manipulate and embroider facts, covering its behaviour with whatever veneer of idealism is likely to satisfy the audience that presents itself. This is not the true voice of the industry, its scientists and stockholders; it is all too obviously the product of a public relations apparatus.

One is not generalizing here from isolated examples or misdeeds from the distant past. Just one example of current malpractice where information is concerned is the extent to which pharmaceutical companies now engage in ghost-writing both to bolster their corporate images and to adjust in their favour the scientific material reaching the medical journals. Elliot, discussing the technique, saw it as part of a process of "buying off the entire apparatus of academic medicine" (Elliot 2004). One can easily object that no health professional need allow his publications to be composed by a ghost-writer with a slanted view, or agree to being cultured as a puppet in the form of a "key opinion leader". But it may be demanding much of human nature to expect that all those involved will succeed in fully retaining their objectivity once a wealthy pharmaceutical house has taken them under its wing.

12.4.5. Contempt

Both success and impregnability as defined above bring with them the risk that one will at a given moment become contemptuous of the remainder of society and its interests. Every drug regulator has experienced the moment when a corporate delegation arrives displaying impatience with the foolish and petty bureaucratic procedure to which it is now being obliged to submit. It is not tactful to display such feelings, but on occasion they flicker through, both here and in public debate. Halfdan Mahler's brilliant introduction in the World Health Assembly of the 1970s of the concept of Essential Drugs, designed to spend limited resources wisely, was dismissed with audible contempt as a means of ruining the industry; 30 years later that same industry did its name much harm by a massive attack in the South African courts on the Government's measures to provide low-cost drugs for AIDS victims. On some fronts, over-confidence has bred naivety; if one does not listen to the views of another party one does not learn from them. As Richard Laing and his colleagues have pointed out:

> The drug industry's view that Essential Medicines Lists are only for the public sector of the poorest nations has not changed much in 25 years. The current IFPMA paper about essential medicines repeats that view and says that policies extending restrictive drug policies to industrialized countries pose a serious threat to the delivery of effective health care and to investment in drug research (Laing *et al*. 2003).

At times the sector seems to be doing its best to lose its reputation, perhaps because it has become so accustomed to manipulating governments, entire professions and the public with success that it has come to believe that it can build a future that way. It is a technique at which certain bodies claiming to speak on the industry's behalf excel: it may be time for organizations such as IFPMA and PhRMA to be put quietly out to pasture and the lobbyists sent home, so that society can deal directly at last with those honest businessfolk and men of science who are really capable of serving the best interests both of society and industry and who appear, when one meets them behind closed doors, to be impatient to do so.

12.5.   Time for Change

12.5.1.   Is change essential?

The questions which arise as to the industry's present and future course – and in recent years there have been many of them – relate almost entirely to its behaviour in society and its compliance with the spirit of public policy, law and regulation. Until very recently, fundamental calls for reform of the industry came largely from activists, voices crying in the wilderness. That is no longer the case. Repeatedly, as this century gets into its stride, one encounters criticism of the pharmaceutical industry in circles where it would earlier have been unthinkable. Reactions to the industry's acts or omissions range from insistence by individual writers that companies show a greater degree of social responsibility to concerns in the major medical journals regarding the suppression of information, the uncertain safety of new drugs or the prices demanded for them. Governments strive in their various ways to control not only the content of drug advertising but also the disproportionate expense which it involves. As to the public, long insulated by the health services from the industry but now alerted to it by alarming headlines, opinion polls suggest that only a minority of the informed public today believe that pharmaceutical factories are serving the community as they should (NZZ; Hunt 2004).

The still limited but growing involvement of some investors, both individual and corporate, in calls for corporate ethics in the pharmaceutical companies whose finance they provide, could well grow to a source of influence which managements will need to respect. When in March 2005 the Oxford University Staff Campaign took the lead in compiling an *Investor Statement on pharmaceutical companies and the health crisis in emerging markets* it was supported by 12 large investment groups managing funds exceeding £600 billion, much of the investment being in multinational corporations (US $2005). Only weeks later the Select Committee of Britain's Parliament published its extensively documented report on the pharmaceuticals field, replete with calls for change:

> . . . the industry's influence has expanded and a number of practices have developed which act against the public interest. (HOC 2005, Summary)

> There is reason to fear that the industry has positively nurtured anxieties about ill-health. (HOC 2005 at para. 6)

> . . . The fundamental problem, it is alleged, is that the industry is increasingly dominated by pressure from its investors and the influence of its marketing force and advertising agencies rather than its scientists. (HOC 2005 at para. 6)

Sir Richard Sykes, himself a prominent figure in British industry, appeared as a witness before the Committee and was forthright in his statements:

> Today the industry has got a very bad name. That is very unfortunate for an industry that we should look up to and believe in, and that we should be supporting. I think there have to be some big changes. (HOC 2005, Summary)

It was not always so. Old Eli Lilly, Henry Wellcome and Saal van Zwanenberg,[1] all born in the nineteenth century, were sound businessmen but they were also idealists who saved lives by making the best medicines they could; they paid their stockholders and themselves a fair reward without flouting the law, pushing the prescriber aside or mongering mythical diseases. The greater part of the pharmaceutical industry has long born the title "ethical" which dates from the day of these pioneers, but it has not always merited it; these men created a tradition that deserves to be restored.

In 2000, in her first analysis of the place of the pharmaceutical industry, Marcia Angell defined the industry's duty to society at large and called for reform (Angell 2000). During the five ensuing years there has been ample debate, but there has also been an ample demonstration of the need to act as she proposed. The South African debacle, the misery of the cox-2 inhibitors, the Baycol story, the revelation of the marketing history of the benzodiazepines and the SSSI inhibitors, a series of battles over prices and patents and the worsening situation of the third world leave one in no doubt. Certainly, from some of the Boardrooms there have been expressions of willingness to reform:

> Unless the pharmaceutical industry achieves its objective of being an accepted and valued player in society, we will be at a disadvantage in every new law and regulation that comes up. (Vasella 2000)

And yet, in the light of past experience, one wonders. Does this mean that the industry must earn this reputation with the community or merely ensure that it is created by yet more image manipulation?

One is not looking for a revolution. The pharmaceutical industry, in one form or another, is obviously indispensable. It has shown how much good it can do when it tries. Calls to nationalize it (or "internationalize" it, whatever that may mean) are not realistic. It is dangerously easy to condemn an entire industrial sector, as some have done, for political reasons or because of its malpractice in a particular field. Precisely because we need the industry one needs to examine, objectively but with sympathy, the question as to whether the pharmaceutical industry as it currently functions can be said to be serving the world community as well as it might, as assessed by the extent to which it performs its basic duties and meets reasonable expectations.

Much of what has been said above points to numerous areas in which industry could genuinely serve the community better than it does. Some of the questions that arise in that connection deserve a final mention here.

---

[1] Founders of Eli Lilly, Burroughs Wellcome and Organon respectively.

12.5.2. Is change possible?

Looking globally at this industry one is bound to be impressed by what it can do, and how much more it could do given a proper sense of priorities and social responsibility. Technically, if one listens to the experts, there is no doubt about it. If any large corporation with experience in the antibiotic field were convinced that it needed to provide a breakthrough cure for malaria or tuberculosis within 5 years, and that its corporate life depended upon it, it could probably manage to do it. Scientifically it could be achieved but, during those 5 years there might be such a dip in the profits that its financial backers would not permit the company to continue with the venture. There would be a call for more pot-boilers to keep the marketing people happy.

Ethically, one could see a possibility for change, with part of the impulse coming from outside pressures and part from within. A vast number of people within the industry are scientists or health professionals with their own professional idealism, as discussed in Chapter 3; others are perfectly honest businessmen, recognizing at least the desirability of restraining unbridled competition and excessively aggressive promotion, quite apart from the need to respect the public health dimension. There is a readiness among these people to take the declarations of intent and codes of conduct seriously. Research scientists who may have tended to regard their marketing colleagues as innocent rascals (a not uncommon view) may realize that they themselves now urgently need to engage in the debate on ethics and decency.

At the global level one could well anticipate in the long run the emergence of a universal code of sound ethics for the industry, with real possibilities for enforcement. It remains an ideal, and one which in a market fought over by thousands of firms with wildly differing philosophies of business may still be far away; the ethical conviction must develop first, but in the meantime the ideal is worth cherishing.

12.5.3. The flow of money

If anything is to be achieved, there surely needs to be an adjustment in the flow of money in and around the pharmaceutical sector. It is the community that pays for drugs, and is often required to pay for them heavily; it has long done so willingly, assured that it is necessary if drug discovery is to be maintained. Yet whatever one's social beliefs it is surely no less than fair to conclude that this same community deserves a full insight as to where its money goes, and that it has a right to demand change when it emerges that a great deal of that money goes to wasteful propaganda and litigation and a much smaller sum to research, some of which is not even designed to be truly innovative. Equally strong is the argument on behalf of the developing world which has profited so little from recent advances in treatment. Large sums of money are wasted through over-prescribing and inappropriate prescribing. When one sets the sums needed for third world innovation against the degree of wastage known to occur it is very apparent how much better society's resources could be used. The world has 6000 million people, and at a modest estimate a quarter of them are really ill. Surely that is sufficient to merit reallocation of funds to a more serious programme of drug development than they are offered at the present day?

12.5.4.   *Bigger, better and broader?*

In the new economy, "growth" is a mantra; what was once praised as stability is now condemned as stagnation. The question nevertheless arises whether the pharmaceutical mega-corporations which have grown up ever faster in the last decade are truly best placed to develop and maintain the ethic of scientific business which the health sector has a right to demand. Their remoteness from social reality is becoming alarming. It is alleged, by those who know, that smaller breweries produce much better beer than large ones; in an age of biotechnology might the small drug company not prove very soon to be closer to its patrons and assess their needs more con-scientiously than the large one? It is hard to take seriously one particular corporation which, after gobbling up so many others that it had acquired an unequalled capacity for scientific discovery, proceeded to close down research units left and right, bolster its earnings, and devote itself in all seriousness to promoting penile erection and propagating the fictitious belief that depression is a deficiency disorder. Can one take such a firm at face value except as a machine to produce wealth? Does the world of patients not deserve something rather better?

Dr Angell, to quote her one last time, has characterized the mega-industry as one which was formerly famed for its research, yet now lives largely from licensing and marketing. That may not matter very much pro-vided the end-result is sound; collaboration with small productive biotechnology units, public health institutions and the academic world might actually restore the flow of innovation, with Big Pharma essentially managing the process – but one still lacks the proof that it can happen, and there are plenty of ethical problems to be solved as regards the interaction between industry and the universities (ESN 2002).

12.5.5.   Trends to change?

As ever, in a world where facts are manipulated to suit the convenience of the provider, it remains excruciatingly difficult to know to what extent the pharmaceutical industry is truly about to turn the corner and to head in the direction which the policy makers and lawmakers always intended. One has been seduced by fine words a little too often to take them seriously. Some wealthy corporations have yet to learn that, when called to account over an unethical practice, they will serve their image better by terminating the practice, and admitting that they have sinned, than by seeking to defend what has happened. Drug donations to poor populations provide excellent publicity for industry as a benefactor; yet too many donations have been inappropriate, and sometimes even primarily of benefit to the donor. Again it was good, very recently, to see that how one multinational has called into being and funded a Foundation to debate and tackle health issues in the developing world; it provided excellent prestige material for the Journals. Yet one is inevitably reminded of that same multinational's current involvement in promoting in other parts of the world, at apparently comparable expense, the use of one of its drugs for the treatment of what can only be regarded as a disorder of its own creation.

12.5.6.   Forwards

There are many steps to be taken if the ethical basis of the pharmaceutical industry is to be firmly laid and subsequently maintained in good repair into the future (HAI 2004). One must not waste too much time on perfecting the methodology, but every step needs to be well-founded. Paul Hunt, the United Nations Special Rapporteur on the right to health, has stressed that the degree of social responsibility of a firm can and must be measured and made known: as he put it in 2004:

> I am struck by the absence of accessible, effective, transparent and independent accountability mechanisms in relation to corporate social responsibility (Hunt 2004).

The individual observer may be concerned about profits and prices, advertising techniques, or adverse reactions. Yet again and again it is the frightening image of illness in the developing world that primarily fires the call for reform. Looking retrospectively at the growth and development of the research-based fraction of the pharmaceutical industry over several decades one can see trends to increasingly high-cost high-profit operation, providing economic benefits to part of the world yet insufficiently counterbalanced by the promised universal health benefits for which one might hope. The world's poor are by far the most numerous and least resilient victims of the current imbalance in effort and investment. No integral programme of reform is yet at hand; yet one can now define the need for a broad and objective social re-evaluation of this industry and its performance, aiming to identify ways to adjust its development to the needs of the new century. In the past the pharmaceutical industry has shown itself sufficiently flexible and adaptable to take in its stride many changes in the environment in which it works. There can be no real doubt that it is similarly capable of facing the current call for reform and responding to it positively and adequately, in a manner which will benefit not only the world community but also industry itself.

List of Selected References

Many of the authors and institutions whose publications are cited in the text have also produced much more material on the same themes. A number of these additional publications from the same sources have been added here as "further reading".

Abbott F.M. (2002): *Compulsory licensing for public health needs. The trips agenda at the WTO after the Doha Declaration on Public Health.* Occasional Paper Nr. 9: Friends World Committee for Consultation: Quaker United Nations Office, Geneva.

Abbott F. M. (2004): *The Doha Declaration on the TRIPS Agreement and Public Health and the Contradictory Trend in Bilateral and Regional Free Trade Agreements.* Occasional Paper: Quaker United Nations Office, 14 April.

ABPI (1992): *ABPI Code of Practice for the Pharmaceutical Industry.* Association of the British Pharmaceutical Industry, London, January 1991 (in revision as of 2005).

ABPI (1994): *Clinical Trials Compensation Guidelines.* Association of the British Pharmaceutical Industry, London.

ABPI (1999): *Generic Medicines.* Association of the British Pharmaceutical Industry, London.

ABPI (2001a): *The Cost of Medicines – Good Value for Patients.* Association of the British Pharmaceutical Industry, London.

ABPI (2001b): *Animal Research for Human Medicines.* Association of the British Pharmaceutical Industry, London.

ABPI (2002a): *Providing Developing World Medicines.* Association of the British Pharmaceutical Industry, London.

ABPI (2002b): *House of Lords Select Committee: The Use of Animals in Discovering Medicines.* Association of the British Pharmaceutical Industry, London.

ABPI (2005a): *Clinical Trials and Children's Medicines.* Association of the British Pharmaceutical Industry, London.

ABPI (2005b): *The UK Blue Guide on the Advertising and Promotion of Medicines.* Association of the British Pharmaceutical Industry, London.

Achilladelis B. and Antonakis N. (2001): The dynamics of technological innovation; the case of the pharmaceutical industry. *Res. Policy*, 30, 535–538.

ACT-UP (2004): Pfizer Zap. (July 2004) http://www.actupny.org/reports/Bangkok/pfizer-zap.html.

Adnan K. (2000): *Taking up the Challenge: Business and the Global Compact.* Adnan Kassar; text distributed during the UN Millennium summit, 6–8 September.

Adu-Bonna K. (2001): *AIDS in Africa website,* Chapter 4, data published as of May 5th 2001, citing UNAIDS and WHO statistics.

AESGP (1977): *A.E.S.G.P. (European Proprietary Association): The European Code of Standards for the Advertising of Medicines.* (1977 and later revisions) A.E.S.G.P., Paris.

Ahmad S.R. (1990): *Bitter Facts about Drugs.* HAI Pakistan, Karachi.

Allbutt T.C. (1921): *Greek Medicine in Rome.* Macmillan, London.

Allen F.K. (1994): *Secret Formula – How Brilliant Marketing and Relentless Salesmanship made Coca-Cola the Best-known Product in the World.* Harper Business, New York.

Alsop R.J. (2004): *The 18 Immutable Laws of Corporate Reputation.* Kogan Page, London.

Amsterdam (1994): *Declaration on the promotion of patients' rights in Europe.* Proceedings of a consultation at Amsterdam, 28–30 March 1994 under the auspices of the WHO Regional Office for Europe. WHO, Copenhagen.

Amsterdam (1999): *Amsterdam statement on access to medicines* (issued by a meeting organized by HAI, MSF and CPT; Amsterdam 25–26 November, 1999). Text cited in WHO Drug Information (1999): 23, 223. World Health Organization, Geneva.

Andrew M., Jøldal B. and Tomson G. (1995): Norway's National Drug Policy. *Dev. Dialogue, 1,* 25–53.

Angell M. (2000): The pharmaceutical industry – to whom is it accountable? *N. Engl. J. Med., 342 (25),* 1902–1904.

Angell M. (2004a): *The Truth About the Drug Companies; How they Deceive us and What to do about it.* Random House, New York, NY.

Angell M. (2004b): *The Truth About the Drug Companies.* New York Review of Books.

Annan K. (2001): UN General Assembly. Follow-up to the outcome of the Millennium Summit. *Report of the Secretary-General.* UND. No. A/56/326. UNGA, New York.

Anon (1984): Aleotti on "death" of Italian industry. *Scrip, 905,* 1.

Anon (1989): Post-coital contraceptive removed from Danish market. *Outlook,* June 10, 1989.

Anon (1995): Ketoprofen switched to Rx in Italy. *Scrip,* 21.

Anon (2003): *Litigation Discussion Forum: Hidden Toll of DES, a Generation Later.* Posted 24 June 2003. Lawtomation.net, Lawrence E. Feldman and Associates.

APG (2005): American Pharmaceutical Group Welcomes Framework for Industry Action on Access to Medicines. London.

APMA (2000): *Australian Pharmaceutical Manufacturers Association. Code of Conduct of the Australian Pharmaceutical Manufacturers Association.* (13th Edition). Australian Pharmaceutical Manufacturers Association Inc. Sydney.

Appelbe G.E. and Wingfield J. (1993): *Dale and Appelbe's Pharmacy Law and Ethics* (Fifth Edition). The Pharmaceutical Press, London.

Archibugi D., Held D. and Koehler M. (1998): *Re-imagining Political Community: Studies in Cosmopolitan Democracy.* Stanford University Press, Stanford, CA.

Arnold J.D. (1980): Incidence of injury during clinical pharmacology research and indemnification of injured research subjects at the Quincy Research Center. *Report to the President's Commission for the Study of Ethical Problems in Medicine and Biomedical and Behavioral Research* (unpublished stencil).

Aronson J.K. (1996): Positive inotropic drugs and drug used in dysrrhythmias. In: Dukes M.N.G. (Ed.): *Meyler's Side Effects of Drugs* (Thirteenth Edition). Elsevier, Amsterdam, Lausanne and New York at p. 445.

Arras J. and Rhoden N. (1989): *Ethical Issues in Modern Medicine.* Mayfield Publishing, Mountain View.

Art. 355(d): Food Drug and Cosmetic Act, 21 U.S.Congress, Art.355(d).

Attaran A. (2003): *Malaria drug treatment: prescriptions for curing policy.* Paper presented to the UN Millennium Task Force, on Access to Medicines.

Attaran A. and Sachs J. (2001). Defining and redefining international donor support for combating the AIDS pandemic. *Lancet, 357,* 57–61.

Australia (1992): House of Representatives Standing Committee on Community Affairs. *Prescribed Health (Part 1): Regulation and the Pharmaceutical Industry.* Parliament of the Commonwealth of Australia, Canberra at pp. 19–20.

Autier P., Govindaraj R., Gray R., Lakshminarayanan R., Nassery H.G., and Schmets G. (2002): *World Bank Study: Drug Donations in Post-Emergency Situations*. World Bank, Washington, DC, 2002.

Avorn J. (2004): *Powerful Medicines*. Knopf, New York.

Balant L.P. and Bechtel P. (1994): Inter-ethnic differences in dose–response studies. In: Walker S. (Ed.): *The Relevance of Ethnic Factors in the Clinical Evaluation of Medicines*. Kluwer Academic Publishers, Dordrecht, Boston and London.

Bale H. (2005): *The Pharmaceutical Industry and Corporate Social Responsibility*. IFPMA, Geneva. http://www.responsiblepractice.com/enlish/insight/ifpma. Consulted 19 March 2005.

Ballance R., Pogany J. and Forstner H. (1992): *The World's Pharmaceutical Industries*. Published for UNIDO by Edward Elgar Publishing, Aldershot.

Bannenberg W. (2000): *Action on essential drugs*. Presentation on behalf of WHO South Africa Drug Action Programme to the 13th International AIDS Conference, Durban.

Banta H.D. (2001): Worldwide interest in global access to drugs. *JAMA*, *285*, 2844.

Barrett A. (2005): More bitter pills for big pharma. *Business Week Online*, 10th January.

Biscarini L. (1992): Anti-inflammatory analgesics and drugs used in gout. In: Dukes M.N.G. (Ed.): *Meyler's Side Effects of Drugs* (12th Edition). Elsevier, Amsterdam, London, New York and Tokyo at p. 195.

Black D. (1976): *The Behaviour of Law*. Academic Press, Orlando, San Diego and New York.

BMA (1908): *Secret Remedies (1908) and More Secret Remedies (1912)*. British Medical Association, London.

BNF (2001): *British National Formulary* Nr. 42, September 2001. British Medical Association and Royal Pharmaceutical Society, London.

Bok D. (2003): *Universities in the Marketplace; The Commercialization of Higher Education Commercialization of Higher Education*. Princeton University Press, Princeton, NJ.

Boseley S. (2004): Drug giant ignored Vioxx heart risk. *The Guardian*, 5th November.

Botros S. (1992): Ethics in medical research: uncovering the conflicting approaches. In: Foster C. (Ed.): *Manual for Research Ethics Committees*. King's College, London.

Bowie N. (1982): *Business Ethics*. Prentice-Hall, Englewood Cliffs, NJ.

Boyer N. (1986): *U.S. State Department*, as quoted by Chetley (1990) (q.v.) at p. 92.

Bradford H.A. (1960): *Controlled Clinical Trials*. Blackwell, Oxford.

Brahams D. (1990): Safety in overdose and drug licensing. *The Lancet*, *335*, 343–344.

Braithwaite J. (1984): *Corporate Crime in the Pharmaceutical Industry*. Routledge and Kegan Paul, London, Boston and Henley.

Breggin P.R. (1998): *Talking Back to Ritalin*. Common Courage Press, Monre, ME.

Breggin P.R. (2001a): *Ritalin Class Action Suits*. http://www.breggin.com/congress.html(2001).

Breggin P.R. (2001b): *Talking Back to Ritalin* (Second Edition). Perseus Publishing, Cambridge, MA.

Broder S., Bolognesi Dm Yarchoan R., Weinhold K. and Mitsura H. (1989): Credit government scientists with developing anti-AIDS drug. *New York Times*, 28 September.

Bryan J. (1980): Morning sickness drugs – good news? *General Practitioner*, *11*.

Buitendijk S. (1984): DES – The time bomb drug. In: *Report of the 13th European Symposium on Clinical Pharmacological Evaluation in Drug Control*. World Health Organization, Regional Office for Europe, Copenhagen.

Buse K. and Walt G. (2000): Global public–private partnerships for health, parts I and II. *Bull. World Health Org.*, *78*, 549–61 and 699–709.

BVG (1963): Besluit Verpakte Geneesmiddelen (Netherlands Decree on Packaged Medicines).

Byström, M. and Einarsson, P. (2001): *TRIPS: Consequences for Developing Countries: Implications for Swedish Development Cooperation*. SIDA, Stockholm.

Cambanis T. (2002): Cancer drug pitched in support groups – effort highlights an ethical debate. *Boston Globe*, 12 November 2002, p. A1.

Canada (1997): Drugs Directorate. *Canadian Foundation and Drugs Programme: Roles and Consultation Related to Advertising Review and Complaint Adjudication*. Policy Issues. February 18, 1997.

Cargill D. (1967): Self-treatment as an alternative to rationing medical care. *Lancet, 1*, 1377–1378.

Carter (2003): Investigation by the Carter Foundation into the manufacturing costs of generic companies. Data cited at SEAM 2003 (q.v.).

CC (1101): Civil Code of France. Art. 1101.

CDC (2001): National Center for HIV, STD and TB Prevention; figures available on the Centre's website as of May 5th 2001.

CDER (2001): *2001 Report to the Nation: Improving Public Health Through Human Drugs*. Centre for Drug Evaluation and Research (CDER), Rockville MD.

CDER (2005): *CDER Report to the Nation: 2000*. http://www.fda.gov/cder/reports/RTN2000/RTN2000-3.HTM. Consulted December 21st 2004.

CEO (2000): *Campaign for a Corporate-Free U.N.* Corporate European Observatory, Amsterdam.

CERES (2005): Jay P. Medicolegal investigations. *Ceres News, 27*. Consulted: 4 April 2005.

Cervello V. (1884): Recherches cliniques et physiologiques sur la paraldéhyde. *Arch. Ital. Biol., 6*, 113–34.

Chadwick R. (Editor): *Encyclopaedia of Applied Ethics*. Academic Press, San Diego, London, Boston, 1998.

Chernavsky A. (2005): Homepage: The Pharmaceutical Industry. Consulted 16 May.

Chetley A. (1990): *A Healthy Business? World Health and the Pharmaceutical Industry*. Zed Books, London.

Childress (1976): Compensating injured research subjects: The moral argument. *Hastings Centre Report, 6*, 21–27.

China (2000): *China Gets Tough on Counterfeit Medicine Makers*. Applesforhealth.com, 2(Nr 28), December 8th 2000.

CIA (2000): *National Intelligence Estimate: The Global Infectious Disease Threat and its Implications for the United States*. Central Intelligence Agency, Washington, DC.

CIOMS (1982): *Guidelines for Biomedical Research involving Human Subjects*. Council for International Organizations of Medical Sciences, Geneva.

CIPR (2002): *Report of the UK Commission on Intellectual Property Rights*, September 2002. Her Majesty's Stationery Office, London.

Class S. (2005): Whither generics? Why major restructuring lies ahead. *J. Gener. Med., 2(3)*, 232–239.

CMH (2001): Commission on Macroeconomics and Health, 2001.

CNN (2005): Documents: Prozac use reports more likely to list suicide. *CNN News*, January 4th 2004, posted 1906 GMT.

Cockburn R., Newton P.N., Kyeremateng A., Akunyili D. and White N.J. (2005): The global threat of counterfeit drugs. *PloS Medicine (Public Library of Science), 2(4)*, e100.

COE (1975): *Abuse of Medicaments: Report by a Working Party, 1972–1973*. Council of Europe, Strasbourg.

Collier J. (2002): Regulating the regulators. *Lancet, 360 (9427)*, 2199.

Collier J. and Iheanacho I. (2002): The pharmaceutical industry as an informant. *Lancet, 360 (9343)*, 1405–1409.

Companies Act (1985): *United Kingdom: Companies Act*. HMSO, London.

Congress (1906): U.S.Congress: (1906) An Act for preventing the manufacture, sale or transportation of adulterated or misbranded or poisonous or deleterious foods, drugs, medicines and liquors. 59th Congress, 1st Session, 34 US Statutes 768.

Copeman W.S.C. (1967): *The Worshipful Society of Apothecaries of London; A History 1617–1967*. Pergamon Press, Oxford.

Correa C. (2002a): *Implication of the Doha Declaration on the TRIPS Agreement and Public Health. Health Economics and Drugs: EDM Series Nr. 12*. World Health Organization, Geneva.

Correa C. (2002b): *Protection of Data Submitted for the Registration of Pharmaceuticals*. South Centre.

CPA (2005): Prescription medicines code of practice authority. *Monthly Reports* issued by the Association of the British Pharmaceutical Industry, 1993–2005 (continuing).

CPBC (2005): *Code of Ethics*. College of Pharmacists of British Columbia. http://www.bcpharmacists.org/standards/ethicslong. Consulted 3 February 2005.

CRA (2004): *Innovation in the Pharmaceutical Sector: A Study Undertaken for the European Commission*. Charles River Associates, London.

CS (2004): Colloidal Silver, CS Pro and the FDA http://www.csprosystems.com/CSInfoPg.html. Consulted 23.04.2005.

CS (2005): Colloidal Silver Home Page. http://educate-yourself.org/cs/. Consulted 18 April.

CSTS (2005): *Special Focus: Genome Patents*. Center for the Study of Technology and Society. http://www.tecsoc.org/biotech/focuspatents.htm

Daemmerich A. (2003): Regulatory laws and political culture in the United States and Germany. In: Abraham J. and Lawton S.H. (Eds.): *Regulation of the Pharmaceutical Industry*. Palgrave/ Macmillan, London at pp. 11–41.

DAP (1995): Action programme on essential drugs. *Report of the Expert Committee on National Drug Policies*. (WHO/DAP/95.9). World Health Organization, Geneva.

DAP (1996): *Drug Action Programme: Guidelines for Drug Donations*. DAP 96/2. World Health Organization, Geneva.

Datamonitor (2004): Impact of patent expiry on the top five pharmaceutical companies. *J. Gener. Med., 1(4)*, 381–384.

Davidoff F., DeAngelis C.D., Drazen J.M., Hoey J., Høygaard L., Horton R., Kotzin S., Nicholls G., Nylenna M., Overbeke J.P.M., Sox H.C., Van der Weyden M.B. and Wilkes M.S. (2001): *Sponsorship*, Authorship and Accountability. *Lancet, 358*, 854–856. *(Also published in other medical journals)*.

De Stasio S. and McClay N. (2004): Review of the European pharmaceutical legislation. *J. Gener. Med., 1(4)*, 295–304.

De Vries T.P.G.M., Henning R.H., Hogerzeil H.V. and Fresle D.A. (1994): *Guide to Good Prescribing (1993)*. WHO/DAP/93.1. WHO, Geneva.

Deangelis C.D., Drazen J.M., Frizelle F.A., Haug C., Hoey J., Horton R., Kotzin S., Laine C., Marusic A., Overbeke J.P.M., Schroeder T.V., Sox H.C., and Van der Weyden M.B. (2005): Is this clinical trial fully registered? *JAMA*. (Early Release, posted May 23rd, 2005).

Defoe D. (1722): *A Journal of the Plague Year*. London.

DFID (2003): *Access to Medicines: DFID Policy Division Plans 2003/2004*. DFID, London.

DFID (2004): *Increasing Access to Essential Medicines in the Developing World: UK Government Policy and Plans*. DFID, London.

DFID (2005): *Increasing Access to Essential Medicines in the Developing World*. DFID, London.

DiMasi J.A., Hansen R.W., Grabowski H.G., and Lasagna L. (1991): Cost of Innovation in the Pharmaceutical Industry. *J. Health Econom.*, *10*, 107–142.

DMFA (1995): Danish Ministry of Foreign Affairs. *Review and Appraisal Report*, Essential Drugs Management Programme, Uganda. Euro Health Group A/S and Uganda Essential Drugs Programme.

Doesgenomes (2005): *Human Genome Project Information: The Human Genome Program of the U.S.* Department of Energy Office of Science. http://www.ornl.gov/sci/techresources/ Human_Genome/home.shtml. Consulted 30 April 2005.

Dollery C.T. (1972): Mercurial diuretics. In: Meyler L. and Herxheimer A. (Eds.): *Side Effects of Drugs*, Vol. VII. Excerpta Medica, Amsterdam.

Douglas J.D. (1984): Liability for medical injuries caused by ADR – An industrialist's viewpoint. In: Byström H. and Ljungstedt N. (Eds.): *Detection and Prevention of Adverse Drug Reactions*. Almqvist and Wiksell International, Stockholm.

Drahos P. and Braithwaite J. (2002): Intellectual property, corporate strategy, globalisation: TRIPs in context. *Wisc. Int. Law J.*, *20*, 451–480.

Drahos P. (2004): *The Free Trade Agreement and the Pharmaceutical Benefits Scheme*. Evatt Foundation, University of Sydney.

Drugintel (2001): Raplon (rapacuronium). DrugIntel Website. Consulted February 2nd 2005.

DTB (2003): Yasmin advert withdrawn – why and how. *Drugs Therap. Bull.*, *41(3)*, 1–2.

DTI (1987): Department of Trade and Industry: *Guide to the Consumer Protection Act 1987*. London.

Dukes M.N.G. (1963): *Patent Medicines and Autotherapy in Society*. Drukkerij Pasmans, The Hague.

Dukes M.N.G. (1981): The paradox of clioquinol and SMON. In: D'Arcy P.F. and Griffin J.P. (Eds.): *Iatrogenic Diseases* (Second Edition, Update). Oxford University Press, Oxford, New York and Toronto.

Dukes M.N.G. (1984): The epidemiology of adverse reactions. In: Byström H. and Ljungstedt N. (Eds.): *Detection and Prevention of Adverse Drug Reactions*. Almqvist and Wiksell International, Stockholm.

Dukes M.N.G. (1985): *The Effects of Drug Regulation: A Survey Based on the European Studies of Drug Regulation*. For the World Health Organizaion's Regional Office for Europe. MTP Press, Boston.

Dukes M.N.G. (1987): *The true history of vaccination*. Paper presented at the World Health Organization's Regional Office for Europe, 1987.

Dukes M.N.G. (2001): *Report to the World Bank on the Drugs Inspectorate in Uttar Pradesh*.

Dukes M.N.G. (2002): Accountability of the pharmaceutical industry. *Lancet*, *360*, 1682–1684.

Dukes M.N.G. (2004): Hormone replacement therapy (2004). In: Aronsen J.K. (Ed.): *Side Effects of Drugs Annual 27*. Elsevier Science Publishers, Amsterdam, Boston etc. at pp. 423–426.

Dukes M.N.G. and Lunde I. (1981): The regulatory control of non-steroidal anti-inflammatory agents. *Eur. J. Clin. Pharmacol.*, *19*, 3–10.

Dukes M.N.G., Vernengo M. and Watt R.L. (1997): Pharmaceutical regulation and legislation. In: Quick J. et al. (Eds.): *Managing Drug Supply* (Second Edition). Management Sciences for Health, Boston, MA.

Dukes G., Mildred M. and Swartz B. (1998): *Responsibility for Drug-Induced Injury* (Second Edition). IOS Press, Amsterdam, Berlin and Oxford.

Dunne J.F. (1993): Personal communication.

Dworkin R. (1977): *Taking Rights Seriously*. Gerard Duckworth, London.

Dye C., Williams B. et al. (2002): Erasing the world's slow stain: Strategies to beat multidrug-resistant tuberculosis. *Science*, *295*, 2042–2046, www.tballiance.org/2_1_2_MDR_TB.asp.

Dyer C. (1991): Halcion banned in U.K. *Br. Med. J.*, *303*, 877.

Dyer C. (2004): New 20 year patents threaten to end AIDS drugs for developing countries. *Brit. Med. J.*, *329*, 1308.

EC (2002): EC Commission: Tiered Pricing for Medicines exported to Developing Countries, measures to prevent their reimportations, and tariffs in developing countries. EC Brussels.

EC (2003): EC Commission Directive 2003/94/EC of 8 October 2003, laying down the principles and guidelines for good manufacturing practice in respect of medicinal products for human use and investigational medicinal products.

EC (2005): Commission of the European Communities: Proposal for a Regulation of the European Parliament and of the Council on compulsory licensing of patents relating to the manufacture of pharmaceutical products for export to countries with public health problems. Brussels.

EC 1984/450 (1984): *E.C.: Council Directive 84/450/EEC of 10 September 1984 relating to the approximation of the laws, regulations and administrative provisions of the Member States concerning misleading advertising.* Commission of the European Communities, Brussels.

EC 1985/374 (1985): *European Community. Directive on liability for defective products.* (85) 374 Commission of the European Communities, Brussels.

EC 1990/2377 (1990): Council Regulation (EEC) Nr. 2377/90 of 26 June 1990 laying down a Community Procedure for the establishment of maximum residue limits of veterinary medicinal products in foodstuffs of animal origin.

EC 1992/27 (1992): Council Directive Nr. 92/27/EEC of 1992 on the packaging of medicinal products for human use.

EC 1992/28 (1992): Council Directive 92/28/EEC of 31 March 1992 on the advertising of medicinal products for human use. *Off. J. Eur. Commun. L 113(13–18)*, Art 4(1).

EC 1996/22 (1996): Council Directive 96/22/EC of 29 April 1996 concerning the prohibition on the use in stockfarming of certain substances having a hormonal or thyrostatic action and of beta-agonists, and repealing Directives 81/602EEC, 88/146/EEC and 88/299/EERC.

EC 2001/82 (2001): Directive 2001/82/EC of the European Parliament and of the Council of 6 November 2001 on the Community code relating to veterinary medicinal products.

ECC (2001): EC Commission, *Compulsory Licensing and Data Protection*.

ECJ 36/03 (2003): Marketing Authorisation for Generics: Judgement of the European Court of Justice, December 9th 2004 (C-367/03).

Editorial (1997): BMJ editorial: Regulating the pharmaceutical industry. *Br. Med. J.*, *315*, 200–201.

EDM (2001): Data provided by WHO/EDM staff, March 2001.

E-drug-digest (2002): *E-drug website: ARV parallel export from Africa to Europe.* Report from W. Bannenberg, 7 October.

Edwards I.R. (2005): (Editor): *Regulation of Vioxx: Success or Failure?* (Summary of a discussion between experts). Uppsala Reports, April, 11–13.

Edwards N. (2003): *Molecule of the Month – Taxol.* www.bris.ac.uk./Depts/Chemistry/MOTM/taxol.htm (Accessed 21 November 2002).

EGA (2003): European Generic Association: Statements on line (http://www.egagenerics.com), October 2003; also statements to the EGA Annual Conference, Rome, 10–11 November. European Generics Association, Brussels.

Ehrlich P. and Hata S. (1910): Die Experimentelle Chemotherapie der Spirillosen (Syphilis, Rückfallfeber, Hühnersprillose, Frambösie). J Springer, Berlin.

EIGP (2005): *Code of Practice for Qualified Persons*. EIGP, Sweden, 2005.

Elliott C. (2001): Pharma Buys a Conscience. *The American Prospect*, *12*(*17*), 24 September 2001.

Elliot C. (2004): *How the Drug Industry is Branding itself with Bioethics*. Medical Examiner website; posted December 15th 2003; consulted 15th February.

Enstad M. (1995): *Comparison of Drug approval Norway – The Netherlands: 1985–1994*. Department of Pharmacoepidemiology and Pharmacotherapy, University of Utrecht.

Ernst E. (2000): Risks associated with complementary therapies. In: Dukes M.N.G., Aronson J.K. (Eds.): *Meyler's Side Effects of Drugs* (Fourteenth Edition). Elsevier, Amsterdam, Lausanne, New York and Oxford.

ESC (2000): *Economic and Social Council: Substantive issues arising in the application of the International Covenant on Economic, Social and Cultural Rights*. General Comment Nr. 14 (2000): The right to the highest attainable standard of health. 11 August 2000.

ESN 2002: Anon (2002). Ethics Corner – "point". *Endocrine Soc. News*, *27*(1), 1–5.

EUDRA (2004): *EU: Rules Governing Medicinal Products in the European Union*, Vol. 9: Pharmacovigilance. European Commission, June 2004.

European Commission (1996): *Scientific Conference on Growth Promoters and Meat Production – Proceedings*. Office for Official Publications of the EU Communities, Luxemburg.

Everard M. (2003): *The AIDS medicines and diagnostics facility*. Presentation to the SEAM/Rockefeller Symposium, New York, 10–11 November.

FDA (1992): *Environmental inspection report* dated December 9th 1991 and March 3–4, for Upjohn Co., Kalamazoo, Mich. (authors: Erspamer D.M. and Young R.S.K.). Food and Drug Administration, Rockville, MD.

FDA (2004): *FDA Consumer Education: Counterfeit Medicines – Filled with Empty Promises*. U.S. Food and Drug Administration. September 17th 2004.

FDA/VET (2005): http://www.fda.gov/ora/inspect_ref/iom/ChapterText/580.htm.

Felleskatalog (1999): *Felleskatalog over Farmacøytiske Spesialpreparater markedsført I Norge (Joint Compendium of Pharmaceutical Specialities marketed in Norway)*. Felleskatalogen A.S., Oslo.

Filehne W. (1884): Über das Pyramidon, ein antipyrinederivat. *Berl. Klin. Wschr.*, *7*, 641–642.

Fleming A. (1929): On the antibacterial action of cultures of a penicillium, with special reference to their use in the isolation of B. influenzae. *Br. J. Exp. Pathol.*, *10*, 226–236.

FMF (2000): Feminist Majority Foundation (FMF): FDA considers restrictions on Mifepristone. *Fem. Maj. 12,* 1.

Folb P.I. and Dukes M.N.G. (1990): *Drug Safety in Pregnancy*. Elsevier, Amsterdam, New York and Oxford.

Fontanarosa P.B., Rennie D. and DeAngelis C.D. (2004): Postmarketing surveillance – lack of vigilance, lack of trust. *JAMA*, *292*(21), 2647–2650.

Foster C. (2003): What are ethics, and can they be regulated?" In: Abraham J. and Lawton S.H (Eds.): *Regulation of the Pharmaceutical Industry*. Palgrave Macmillan, London.

Frost R. (2005): *Corporate Social Responsibility and Globalization: A Reassessment*. http://www.aworldconnected.org/article.php/524.html Consulted 19 March 2005.

Gandhi I. (1981): *Address to WHO Geneva*, May 1981; cited by Xavier N.V. (q.v.).

GAO (1999): General Accounting Office: NIH clinical trials: various factors affect patient participation. *Report to Congressional Requesters*. September.

Garratt C. (2005): *Data presented to the MSF Working Group on Intellectual Property Rights, Paris, 4–5 April 2005* (unpublished).

Ghana (2003): *Increasing Access to Medicines: An Assessment and Policy Options for Ghana*. Ministry of Health, Accra, Ghana, and DFID Health Systems Resource Centre, London.

Giles H.Mc. (1965): Encephalopathy and the fatty degeneration of the liver. *Lancet, I*, 1075.

Gillespie-White L. (2001): *What did Doha Accomplish?* International Intellectual Property Institute. November 19th, 2001.

GNN (2005): *Guerilla News Network: Fighting Big Pharma in Little Digwall*. Http://gnn.tv/articles. Consulted 26 March 2005.

Goldstein R. (2004): *Drug Industry Scandal a "Crisis"*. Global Policy Forum, New York.

Goodman L.S. and Gilman A. (1941): (Editors.) *The Pharmacological Basis of Therapeutics*. Macmillan, New York.

Goozner M. (2004): *The $800 million Pill; the Truth Behind the Cost of New Drugs*. University of California Press, Berkeley and Los Angeles, California.

Gorlin J. (1999): *An Analysis of the Pharmaceutical-Related Provisions of the WTO TRIPs (Intellectual Property) Agreement*. IP Institute.

Gorlin J. (2000): *Encouragement of New Clinical Drug Development: The Role of Data Exclusivity*. IFPMA, Geneva.

Greider K. (2003): *The Big Fix: How the Pharmaceutical Industry Rips off American Consumers*. Perseus Books, Cambridge, MA.

Griffin J.P. (1977): The seven deadly sins: a U.K. view. In: Paget G.E. (Ed.): *Quality Control in Toxicology*. MTP Press, Lancaster at pp. 29 and 31.

GSK (2001): *The GlaxoSmithKline Code of Conduct 2001*. Quoted from Society and Environmental Review, GSK London.

GSK (2002): *Clinical Trials in the Developing World*. GlaxoSmithKline, London.

GSK (2004): *Developing World Challenges: Access to Health Care – GSK's Approach*. GSK.

Guilloux A. and Moon S. (2000): *Hidden Price Tags: Disease-Specific Drug Donations: Costs and Alternatives*. Médécins sans Frontières, Geneva.

GUSTO (1993): An international randomized trial comparing four thrombolytic strategies for acute myocardial infarction. The GUSTO investigators. *N. Engl. J. Med., 329(10)*, 673–682.

't Hoen E. (2002): TRIPS, pharmaceutical patents and access to essential medicines: A long way from Seattle to Doha. *Chic. J. Int. Law, 3(1)*, 27–46.

HAI (1996): Health Action International. *Drug policy at the 49th World Health Assembly*. [Briefing paper]. Amsterdam.

HAI (2004): *Attending to a Sick Industry*. Health Action International, Amsterdam.

H.P. (1958): "Stalinon": A therapeutic disaster. *B.M.J., 515*; see also *Sem. Thérap., 34(1)*.

H.P. (1958): Stalinon: A therapeutic disaster. *B.M.J.* March 1st; 515.

Harvey K. (2001): *The Pharmaceutical Benefits Scheme: History, Current Status and Post-Election Prognosis*. http://www.econ.usyd.edu.au/drawingboard/digest/0111/harvey.html

Hawthorn F. (2003): *The Merck Druggernaut; The Inside Story of a Pharmaceutical Giant*. Wiley, Hoboken, NJ.

Healy D. (2004): *Let Them Eat Prozac: The Unhealthy Relationship between the Pharmaceutical Industry and Depression*. New York University Press, NY.

Healy S. (2004): AmBisome price reduction benefits patients. *MSF Access News*, July 2004, 1.

Held D. (1998): Democracy and globalisation. In: Archibugi D. (Ed.): (q.v.) at pp. 11–27.

Henderson D. (2004): The role of business in the modern world (Institute of Economic Affairs). Cited by Brittan S. The not so obvious corporate task. *Financial Times*, 27 August.

Henry D. and Lexchin D. (2002): The pharmaceutical industry as a medicines provider. *Lancet*, 360, 1590–1595 (16 November).

Henry D. and Lexchin D. (2002): The pharmaceutical industry as a medicines provider. *Lancet, 360 (9345)*, 1590–1595.

Herxheimer A. (2003): Relationships between the pharmaceutical industry and patients' organizations. *Br. Med. J., 326*, 1208–1210.

HGA (2000): *HGA: The Human Genome Gold Rush*. Human Genetics Alert, press briefing.

HOC (2005): *House of Commons: Select Committee on Health (Fourth Report)*. London, April.

Hofmann-LaRoche (1970): *Advertisement: "The Sixties"*, quoted by Medawar C., Power and Dependence, Social Audit, London 1991.

Hogerzeil H. V. (undated): *Evidence presented to the Working Group on Access to Drugs*. United Nations Millennium Project, 2003–5.

Hogerzeil H.V. and Casanovas J. (2003): (undated): *Access to Essential Medicines as part of the Fulfilment of the Right to Health*. Unpublished paper made available to the author, 2003.

Hogerzeil H.V., Bimo, Ross-Degnan D., Laing R.O., Ofori-Adjei D., Santoso B., Chowdhury A.K.A., Das A.M., Kafle K.K., Mabadeje A.F.B., and Massele A.Y. (1993): Field tests for rational drug use in twelve developing countries. *Lancet, 342*, 1408–110.

Holm S. (2005): *Forgetting to be Nice – The National Institute for Clinical Excellence's Preliminary Recommendations Concerning Drugs for the Treatment of Alzheimer's Disease*. Cardiff Centre for Ethics Law and Society, March.

Holmer A.F. (2002): Innovation is key mission. *USA Today*, May 31st.

Home Office (2001): *Data on Animal Experiments in the United Kingdom during the year 2000*; as cited by ABPI 2001 (q.v.).

Horton R. (2004): Comment: Vioxx, the implosion of Merck, and aftershocks at the FDA. *Lancet, 364 (9446)*, 1995–1996.

HRG (2004): *Health Research Group: Letter to FDA Calling for Criminal Investigation of AstraZeneca*. HRG Publication Nr. 1703, August 3rd, 2004.

HRREC (2004): *Human Rights Research and Education Centre: Interdisciplinary studies in law: globalization, justice and law*. University of Ottawa, 14 September 2004.

Hubscher O. (1993): Ethics of drug trials in developing countries. *World Health Forum, 14*, 25–27.

Hunt P. (2004): *UN pricks pharma's conscience*. Address to the Novartis Foundation for Sustainable Development (NFSD), Basel. NZZ Online, December 24th, 2004.

Huttin C. (2002): Experiences with reference pricing. *Int. J. Risk Safety Med., 15(2)*, 85–91.

IAPCG (2000): *Interagency Pharmaceutical Coordination Group: Report on Activities in 1996–1999*, WHO/UNICEF/UNFPA/World Bank.

ICESCR (1966): International Covenant on Economic, Social and Cultural Rights. Office of the High Commissioner for Human Rights, United Nations, Geneva.

ICESCR (1976): International Covenant on Economic, Social and Cultural Rights, adopted by the UN General Assembly, 1966.

IFPMA (1994): *International Federation of Pharmaceutical Manufacturers' Associations, Code of Pharmaceutical Marketing Practices*. Geneva.

IFPMA (2004): *Merck Mectizan Donation Program*. IFPMA, Geneva.

IMS (2004): http://open.imshealth.com/webshop2/IMSinclude/i_article_20040518b.asp.

INRUD (2002): INRUD update: in INRUD news. *Newslett. Int. Network Rational Use of Drugs, 11*, 1–2.

IRENE (2000): *Controlling Corporate Wrongs: the Liability of Multinational Corporations*. Report of a seminar held at the University of Warwick, 20–21 March.

Jaeger K. (2002): As cited by Meadows M: Greater Access to Generic Drugs. Statement by the Food and Drug Administration.

James A. (2002): Medicines, society and industry. *Lancet, 360*, 1346.

Jarrett S. (2003): *UNICEF bulk procurement of vaccines and pharmaceuticals.* Presentation to the SEAM/Rockefeller Symposium, New York, 10–11 November.

Jayasuriya D.C. (1985 and revisions): *Regulation of Pharmaceuticals in Developing Countries.* World Health Organization, Geneva.

Jennings M.M. (1997): *Business: Its Legal, Ethical and Global Environment* (Fourth Edition). South-Western College Publishing, Cincinnati, OH.

Jolleys J.V. and Oleson F. (1996): A comparative study of prescribing hormone replacement therapy in USA and Europe. *Maturitas, 23,* 47–53.

Jorge M.F. (2004): TRIPS-plus provisions in trade agreements and their potential adverse effects on public health. *J. Gener. Med., 1(3),* 199–211.

Joseph, K. (1972): *Hansard* (*House of Commons Debates*). 847, Nr. 22, Cols. 440–441.

Jüni P., Nartey L., Reichenbach S., Sterchi R., Dieppe P.A. and Egger M. (2004): Risk of cardiovascular events and rofecoxib: cumulative meta-analysis. *Lancet, 364(9446),* 2021–2029.

Kaldeway H., Wieringa N., Herxheimer A. et al. (1994): *A searching look at advertisements.* University of Groningen and International Organization of Consumers Unions.

Kalish S., Gurwitz J.H., Krumholz H. et al. (1995): A cost-effectiveness model of thrombolytic therapy for acute myocardial infarction. *J. Gen. Int. Med., 10,* 321–330.

Kanavos P. (2003): *The Economic Impact of Pharmaceutical Parallel Trade.* London School of Economics and Political Science; study undertaken with support from Johnson and Johnson, November.

Kaplan W.A., Laing R.D., Waning B. and Levison L. (2002): *Pharmaceutical regulation and quality assurance.* Unpublished paper by the Boston University School of Public Health for the RPMPlus Project.

Kaplan W.A., Laing R.D., Waning B. and Levison L. (2003): *The impact of regulatory interventions on pharmaceutical access and quality: what is the evidence and where are the gaps in our knowledge?* Unpublished paper by the Boston University School of Public Health, 1 February.

Karst K. (2004): Presages to the coming war over generic biologics. *J. Gen. Med. 1(2),* 155–163.

Kast A. (1888): Sulfonal, ein neues Schlafmittel. *Berl. Klin. Wschr., 25,* 309–314.

Kaul I. (2000): *Global public goods: a new way to balance the world's trade.* Le Monde Diplomatique, June.

Kawasaki, E. and Patten, J. (2002): *Drug supply systems of missionary organizations: identifying factors affecting expansion and efficiency.* Case Studies from Uganda and Kenya, Boston, WHO/EDM.

Kent (2005): *Chicago-Kent College of Law: Papers and Commentaries on Gene Patents.*

Kew S.T. (2004): Industry gifts and hospitality – what are the acceptable limits? *Berita Akademi, 23(1),* also citing Fitzpatrick C:No more free launches. *BMJ* 2003;327:342.

Kim J., Millen J., Irwin A. and Gershman J. (2000): *Dying for Growth: Global Inequality and the Health of the Poor.* 2000. Common Courage Press, Monroe, ME.

Kinney E.R. (2001): The international human right to health. *Indiana Law Rev., 34,* 1465.

Korchagina V. (2001): Ministry forming agency to fight fake pills. *Moscow Times,* 10th. October

Kreeger K.T. (1994): Some researchers are pleased, others indifferent, as RU 4876 moves towards ready availability in US. *The Scientist, 8(16),* 1.

Laing R., Waning B., Gray A., Ford N. and 't Hoen E. (2003): 25 years of the WHO essential medicines lists: progress and challenges. *Lancet, 361,* 1723–1729.

Laing R.D. (2001a): *Health and pharmacy systems in developing countries*. Paper delivered to the WHO/WTO Workshop on Differential Pricing and Financing of Essential Drugs, Høsbjør, Norway, 8–11 April.

Laing R.D., Hogerzeil H.V. and Ross-Degnan D. (2001b): Ten recommendations to improve use of medicines in developing countries. *Health Pol. Plan.*, *16*, 13–20.

Laurence D.R. and Carpenter J.R. (1998): *A Dictionary of Pharmacology and Allied Topics*. Elsevier, Amsterdam.

Lawton V. (2004): Evidence presented to the House of Commons Select Committee. Cited in: "We'll fix pharma's image" industry tells UK MP's. *Scrip*, *3021*, 2, January 19th, 2005.

Leon, D.A. and Walt G. (2001): (Editors). *Poverty, Inequality, and Health: An International Perspective*. Oxford University Press, New York.

Lesney M.S. (2005): Pharmaceutical industry issues its plan for voluntary clinical trials registry. *OB/GYN News*, February 1st.

Leufkens H.G.M. (Editor) (1994): *The Future of Medicines in Health Care: Scenario Report for the Netherlands Group on Future Scenarios for Health Care*. Bohn Stafleu van Loghem, Houten, The Netherlands.

Levi M. and Shapiro S. (1987): Metamizol; een honderjarige treurnis. (Metamizol: a century of misery). *Ned. Tijdschr. Geneesk*, *131*, 1680.

Lewis T. (1933): Clinical science. *Br. Med. J.*, *ii*, 717.

Lexchin J. (1997) : What information do physicians receive from pharmaceutical representatives? *Can. Fam. Phys.*, 43, 941–945.

Lexchin J., Bero L.A., Djulbegovic B. and Clark O. (2003): Pharmaceutical industry sponsorship and research outcome and quality: systematic review. *Br. Med. J.*, *326*, 1167–1170.

Light D.W. and Lexchin J. (2004): Will lower drug prices jeopardize drug research? *Am. J. Bioeth.*, *4*(1), W3–W6.

Lilly (2003): *Building Healthier Societies Through Partnership – May 2004 Update*, www.lillyMDR-TB.com).

Lohmann L. (1990): Whose common future? *The Ecologist*, *20(3)*, 82–83.

López R. (1997): Personal communication to Barbara Mintzes (see Mintzes B).

Los A.B.M. and Smit Sibinga C.T. (1989): De persoonlijke verantwoordelijkheid van de bloed-donor voor de veiligheid van de bloedtransfusiepraktijk (The personal responsibility of the blood donor for the safety of transfusion practice). *Ned. Tijdschr. Geneesk.*, *133*, 1157–1158.

Loucks M. (2003): Statements cited byAngell M. (op. cit 2004) at pp. 232–233.

Love J. (2000): Frequently asked questions about compulsory licensing. *Int. J. Risk Safety Med.*, *13*, 2.

Lunde P.K.M. (1984): WHO's programme on essential dugs: background, implementation, present state and perspectives. *Dan. Med. J.*, *31*, 1ff.

Lynch H.T., Quinn T. and Severin M.J. (1990): Diethylstilbestrol, teratogenesis and carcinogenesis: medico/legal implications of its long-term sequelae, including third generation effects. *Int. J. Risk Safety Med.*, *1(3)*, 171–194.

Lytton T.D. (2004) (Editor): *Suing the Gun Industry: A Battle at the Crossroads and Mass Torts*. University of Michigan Press, Ann Arbor, MI.

MacDonald R. (2005): Prioritising neglected diseases related to poverty. *BMJ*, *331,* 12.

Maciejewski C.S. (1994): The dilemma over foreign-language labeling of over-the-counter drugs. *J. Leg. Med.*, *15(1)*, 129–154.

Magendie F. (1822): Formulaire pour la préeparation et l'emploi de plusieurs noveaux méedica-ments, comme tels que la noix vomique, la morphine, etc. Mequignon-Marvis, Paris.

Mamdani M. (1992): Early initiatives in essential drugs policy. In: Kanji N., Hardon A., Harnmeijer J.M., Mamdani M. and Walt G. (Eds.): *Drugs Policy in Developing Countries.* Zed Books, London.

Mann J., Gostin L., Gruskin S. and Brennan T. et al. (1994): Health and human rights. *Health and Human Rights, 1(1),* 6–23.

Mann R.D. (1984): *Modern Drug Use: An Enquiry on Historical Principles.* MTP Press Ltd., Lancaster, Boston and The Hague.

Mansfield P.R. (1992): Organon, the IFPMA code and the WHO ethical criteria. *MaLAM Newsletter,* December 1992, 1.

MAPS (1999): Designation of marihuana as Orphan Drug. *Bull. Multidisciplinary Assoc. Psychedel. Stud., 9(3),* 19.

Marketletter (1994): FDA simplifies OTC labels. *Marketletter,* 19 September.

Marks J. (1978): *The Benzodiazepines – Use, Overuse, Misuse, Abuse.* MTP Press, Lancaster.

Martindale (1977): *The Extra Pharmacopoeia.* (27th Edition). Pharmaceutical Press, London.

Mathiason N. (2002): Company ethics? They're not our business. Mathiason N, *The Observer.* November 17th.

Matthews M. (2005): Institute for policy innovation: Senate to make world safe and profitable for drug counterfeiters and terrorists. Statement cited in *US Newswire* April 19th.

McGarity T.O. and Shapiro S.A. (1980): The trade secret status of health and safety testing information: reforming agency disclosure policies. *Harvard Law Rev., 93(5),* 837–888.

Medawar C. (1979): *Insult or Injury? An Enquiry into the Promotion of British Food and Drug Products in the Third World.* Social Audit, London.

Medawar C. (1992): *Power and Dependence.* Social Audit, London.

Medawar C. and Hardon A. (2004): *Medicines out of control? Antidepressants and the Conspiracy of Goodwill.* Aksant Academic Publishers, The Netherlands.

Medawar C. and Hardon A. (2004): *Medicines out of Control?* Askant Academic Publishers, The Netherlands.

Meltzer H.M., Aro A., Andersen N.L., Koch B. and Alexander J. (2003): Risk analysis applied to food fortification. *Public Health Nutrition, 6(3),* 281–290.

Merrills J. and Fisher J. (2001): *Pharmacy Law and Practice* (third edition). Blackwell Science, Oxford.

Meyler L (1960): *Side Effects of Drugs, 1958–1960.* Excerpta Medica Foundation. Amsterdam, London and New York.

Meyler L. (1964): *Schadelijke Nevenwerkingen van Geneesmiddelen.* (*Side Effects of Drugs*) Van Gorcum & Comp., Assen.

Millennium (2000): *United Nations Millennium Declaration, UN 2000: General Assembly Resolution 55/2* (September 8th).

Millennium (2004): *Access to Essential Medicines: Draft Final Report from Task Force 5 of the United Nations Millennium Development Goals Project: Infectious Diseases and Access to Essential Medicines: Working Group on Access to Medicines.* UN Millennium Project, United Nations, New York.

Millennium (2005): *Investing in Development: Millennium Project Report to the Secretary General.* UNDP and Earthscan, London and Sterling VA.

Mintzes B. (1998): *Blurring the Boundaries – New Trends in Drug Promotion.* Health Action International, Amsterdam.

Mnyika K.S. (1991): Irrational drug use in Tanzania. *Health Policy & Plan., 6,* 180–184.

MOH Brazil (2001): *National AIDS Drug Policy.* Ministry of Health of Brazil, Brazil at p. 21.

Moncrieff J., Hopker S. and Thomas P. (2005): Psychiatry and the pharmaceutical industry. *Psychiatric Bull.*, *29*, 84–85.

Moran M. (2004): *Priority medicines for Europe and the world: Tuberculosis.* Background Paper provided to the UN Millennium Working Group, June.

Moses Z. (2002): The pharmaceutical industry paradox. *Reuters Business Insight*.

Mossialos E. and Dukes G. (2001): Affordably priced new drug for poor populations: approaches for a global solution. *Int. J. Risk Safety Med.*, *14*, 1–29.

Moynihan R. (2003): Who pays for the pizza? Redefining the relationships between doctors and drug companies. *Br. Med. J.*, *326*, 1189–1192 and 1193–1196.

MRC (1922): Reports of the Salvarsan Committee (1922); II – *Toxic Effects Following the Employment of Arsenobenzol Preparations.* Medical Research Council. His Majesty's Stationery Office, London.

MSF (2001): *Fatal Imbalance – The Crisis in Research and Development for Drugs for Neglected Diseases.* Médécins sans Frontières, Geneva.

MSF (2002 and revisions to 2005): *Untangling the Web of Price Reductions: A Pricing Guide for the Purchase of ARVS for Developing Countries.* Médécins sans Frontières, Geneva.

MSF (2002a): Figures cited in a circular letter from the MSF-sponsored Campaign for Access to Essential Medicines, July 24th, 2002. Médécins sans Frontières, Geneva.

MSF (2002b): *Untangling the Web of Price Reductions: A Pricing Guide for the Purchase of ARV's for Developing Countries* (Second Edition). Médécins sans Frontières, Geneva.

MSF (2003a): *New Tricks to Limit Access to Affordable Medicines.* Access no. 9. Médécins sans Frontières, Geneva.

MSF (2003b): *Trading Away Health.* Access no. 9 at p. 2. Médécins sans Frontières, Geneva.

MSF (2003c): *Surmounting Challenges: Procurement of Antiretroviral Medicines in Low- and Middle-Income Countries – the experience of Médécins sans Frontières.* Published for the Campaign for Access to Essential Medicines, WHO and UNAIDS, Médécins sans Frontières, Geneva.

MSF (2003d): *Fatal Imbalance*; *Is The Bar Being Raised too High?* Médécins sans Frontières, Geneva.

MSF (2004): *Website: R&D System is Failing to Meet Health Needs in Developing Countries.* Briefing note as presented to the Ministerial Summit on Health Research, Mexico City, 16–20, November 2004.

MSF (2004a): *TB Care in the 21st Century.* Medecins sans Frontieres, Geneva.

MSF (2004b): *Access to Medicines at Risk Across the Globe. What to Watch out for in Free Trade Agreements with the United States.* Medecins sans Frontieres, Paris.

MSF (2005a): *R&D System is Failing to Meet Health Needs in Developing Countries.* Medecins sans Frontieres.

MSF (2005b): *Now That the Dust has Settled: the Consequences of the New Indian Patents Act.* Médécins sans Frontières, Paris.

MSF/AEM (2002): *MSF Campaign for Access to Essential Medicines: From Durban to Barcelona – Overcoming the Treatment Deficit.* Médécins sans Frontières, Geneva.

MSH (2005): MSH: *Managing Drug Supply* (2004 edition). Published in collaboration with the World Health Organization. Management Sciences for Health, Boston, MA.

MSH/WHO (2000): *International Drug Price Indicator Guide*: 2002 Edition. Management Sciences for Health, Boston, MA and World Health Organization, Geneva.

Mukherjee J. (2004): Basing treatment on rights rather than ability to pay: 335. *Lancet, 363*, 10971–11072.

Naik G. (2002): GlaxoSmithKline actively pursues drug licenses. *Wall Street Journal*, 13 February at p. B2.

Nairobi (1985): *Nairobi Conference on Rational Use of Medicines*, 1985. Published by WHO 1987.

Nature (1983): Editorial: Who says what drugs to license? *Nature*, *303*, 559.

NDMA See P.A.

Netherlands (1997): The Dutch experiments on animals act; entry into force February 5th.

Newton P.N., White N.J., Rosendaal J.A. and Green M.D. (2002): Murder by fake drugs. *Br. Med. J., 324(7341)*, 800–801.

Nielsen J.R. (1986): *Handbook of Federal Drug Law*. Lea & Febiger, Philadelphia, PA, p. 3.

NIHCM (2000): *NIHCM Foundation: Prescription Drugs and Intellectual Property Protection*. NIHCM Foundation Issue Brief: August 2000. National Institute for Health Care Management, Washington DC.

NIHCM (2002): National Institute for Health Care Management Research and Education Foundation: Changing Patterns of Pharmaceutical Innovation. May.

Noah B.A. *et al.* (2005): Symposium: The Dietary Supplement Health and Education Act: Regulation at a Crossroads." *Amer, J. Law & Med, 31(2&3)*, 141–163.

Noller K.L. (Editor) (1992): DES Update. In: *Clinical Practice of Gynecology*. New York: Elsevier Science Publ. Co.

Norso (2000): *Natural Feeling: Norso Biomagnetics*. 1999/2000. http://naturalfeeling.com/howit-works.html. Consulted 3.6.2004.

Notes (1998): Notes taken in Court during proceedings realleged injury due to the drug B.M; Atlanta, GA.

NRLC (2005): National Right to Life Committee: RU 486. httpp://www.powerweb.net/dcwrl/ru486.htm (Consulted 15.1.2005).

NYSRLC (2004): New York State Right to Life Commission: RU486 (2004).

NYTimes (2004): Lan C: Drug companies try to improve public image. *New York Times*, 8 July.

OCA (2004): *Organic Consumers Association (California): Debate Over Possible GE Crop Ban in California Rice Growing County*. Little Marais, MN.

OCA (2004): Organic Consumers Association: *Pressure mounts for ban on GE pharm rice and other crops in US*. http//www.organicconsumers.org/ge/rice072604.cfm Posted July 26th.

OECD (1969): Organization for European Economic Collaboration and Development: *Gaps in Technology – Pharmaceuticals*. (Rapporteur: Dukes M.N.G.). OECD, Paris.

OECD (2000): *OECD Health Data 2000*. Organization for Economic Cooperation and Development, Paris.

Offerhaus L. (1987): Metamizol; een honderjarige treurnis. (Metamizol, a century of misery) *Ned. Tijdsch. Geneesk., 131, 479* and *1681*.

Okie S. (2001): *AMA criticized for letting drug firms pay for ethics campaign*. http://www.mercola.com/2001/sep/8/ama_ethics-htm.

Oslo (2003): *A theoretical model of a National Drug Policy*. University of Oslo: International Master's Course in Public Health (Drug Policy Course).

Osmond B. (2002). *A brief description of the revolving drug fund of the Khartoum comprehensive child care programme*. Discussion paper for the Save the Children Fund (UK).

Oxfam (2001): *Dare to Lead: an Oxfam Briefing Paper on GlaxoSmithKline*. Oxfam, Oxford.

Oxfam (2002): *Beyond Philanthropy*: *The Pharmaceutical Industry, Corporate Social Responsibility and the Developing World* . Report from Oxfam, VSO and Save the Children. July 2002.

P.A. (Proprietary Association) (1984): *Voluntary Codes and Guidelines of the O.T.C. Medicines Industry*. Proprietary Association, Washington, DC, Arts. 2-10. (The Association is now known as the Nonprescription Drug Manufacturers Association (NDMA)).

PAA (1995): P.A.A. Code of Practice, April 1995, Art. 3.

PAGB (2004): Figures supplied by the Proprietary Association of Great Britain to House of Commons Select Committee, 2004.

Palmlund I. (1997): The marketing of estrogens for menopausal and post-menopausal women. *J. Psychosom. Obstet. Gynecol., 18(2)*, 158–164.

Panyarachun H.E.A. (1998): *Human rights and business ethics*. Keynote address: International Symposium on Human Rights and Business Ethics. 24 October, Bangkok.

Paradise J. and Sherwin B. (1995): *Gene Patents*. Issued by the Institute on Biotechnology and the Human Future. Chicago-Kent College of Law, Chicago IL.

Paul J.A., Garred J. (2000): *Making Corporations Accountable*. Global Policy Forum, New York.

Pavin M., Nurgozhin T., Hafner G., Yusufy F. and Laing R. (2003): Prescribing practices of rural primary health care physicians in Uzbekistan. *Trop. Med. Int. Health, 8*, 182–190.

PCAF (2004): *Buying a Law: Big Pharma's Big Money and the Bush Medicare Plan*. Public Campaign Action, 15 January.

PCGA (2001): Productivity Commission, Government of Australia. Paper Nr. 16: Research Report: International Pharmaceutical Price Differences. July.

PD (2003): Anon: HK Company offers compensation to guarantee anti-SARS drug. *People's Daily* (Beijeng), May 13th.

Pear R. (2003): Drug companies increase spending on efforts to lobby congress and governments. *New York Times*, 1st June, A1, 33.

Pécoul B. (2004): New drugs for neglected diseases: From pipeline to patients. *PLoS Med., 1*, 19–22.

Pécoul B., Chirac P., Trouiller P. and Pinel J. (1999): Access to essential drugs in poor countries – A Lost Battle? *JAMA, 281*, 361–367.

Pekkanen (1973): *The American Connection*. Follett Publishing, Chicago, 1973, as cited by Medawar 2004 at p. 32.

Pelman A.S. and Angell M. (2002): How the drug industry distorts medicine and politics: America's other drug problem. *New Republic*, 16 December, 27–41.

Peninsula (2005): IANS Report: Every fourth drug sold is a fake, say medicos. *The Peninsula* (*Qatar*), 25 April.

Peretz (1981): Statement by Michael Peretz, executive vice-president of the International Pharmaceutical Manufacturers Association (1981) as cited by Chetley 1990 (q.v.) at p. 70.

Perez-Casas C. (2000): HIV/AIDS Medicines Pricing Report – Setting objectives: is there a political will? Update: December 2000. Campaign for Access to Essential Medicines. Médecins Sans Frontières.

Perlman D. (2002): *Drug firm seeks cures over cash*. San Francisco Chronicle, August 19th.

Pharmaceutical Industry Profile (2002): *Pharmaceutical Research and Manufacturers of America*, Washington, DC.

Picariello (2005): Standards for the pharmaceutical application of PAT. www.iptonline.com/articles/piblic/ASTMInternational.pdf.

PICTF (2001): *Report of The Pharmaceutical Industry Competitiveness Task Force*. PICTF London, 2001, as cited by HOC 2005.

Pinel J., Varaine F., Fermon F. et al. (1997): Des faux vaccins anti-meningocoque lors d'une epidemie de meningite au Niger. *Med. Maladies Infect., 27*, 1–5.

Pjonline (2004): Second counterfeit medicine discovered in UK. *Pharm. J., 273*, 334. www.pjonline.com

PMAA (1995): *Code of Practice, Art. 7.3*. Proprietary Medicines Association of Australia, North Sydney.

Prasad S. (2003): Insights of a paediatrician entering the pharmaceutical industry. *Pharmaceut. Phys.*, *12(4)*, 18–21.

Proprietary Association of America (1994): *Voluntary Codes and Guidelines of the O.T.C. Medicines Industry.* Proprietary Association, Washington, DC.

PSA (1998): *Code of Professional Conduct.* Pharmaceutical Society of Australia.

Psaty B.M., Furberg C.D., Ray W.A. and Weiss N.S. (2004): Potential for conflict of interest in the evaluation of suspected adverse drug reactions: use of cerivastatin and risk of rhabdomyolysis. *JAMA*, *292*, 2622–2631.

Public Citizen (2001): *Rx R&D Myths: The case against the Drug Industry's "Scare Card".* Public Citizen Congress Watch.

Public Citizen (2003): *Drug Companies Deploy an Army of 675 Lobbyists to Protect Profits.* www.citizen.org: Public Citizen Congress Watch: The Other Drug War 2003. Consulted August 2003.

QSM (2003): Quality assurance and safety of medicines: Prequalification Project of the World Health Organization. http://mednet3.who.int/prequal/about.shtml. Consulted 9 December 2003.

Quick J.D. (2003): Ensuring access to essential medicines in the developing countries: A framework for action. *Clin. Pharm. Ther.*, *73*, 1–6.

RCPE (2005): *RCPE Response to draft document on The Duties and Responsibilities of Pharmaceutical Physicians.* Royal College of Physicians of Edinburgh, Edinburgh, January 2005.

Revill (2004): Sleeping pills can kill, drug firm warns. *Observer* (London), December 5th.

Reye R.D.K., Moran G., Baral J. (1963): Encephalopathy and fatty degeneration of the viscera: a disease entity in childhood. *Lancet*, *2*, 749.

RFSTE (2001): *An Activist's Handbook on Intellectual Property Rights and Patents.* Research Foundation for Science, Technology and Ecology, New Delhi, 2001.

Rice T.M. (1999): Statement in the U.S. Senate: Competitive problems in the pharmaceutical industry. 10, 4233.

Richter J. (2001): *Holding Corporations Accountable: Corporate Conduct, International Codes and Citizen Action.* Zedbooks, London and New York.

Richter J. (2004): *Public–Private Partnerships and International Health Policy-Making.* How can Public interests be Safeguarded? Ministry of Foreign Affairs, Helsinki, Finland.

Rietveld A.H. and Haaijer-Ruskamp F.M. (2002): Policy options for cost containment of pharmaceuticals. *Int. J. Risk Safety Med.*, *15*, 29–54.

Robin E.D. (1984): *Matters of Life and Death: Risks vs. Benefits of Medical Care.* W.H.Freeman and Company, New York at p. 81.

Robinson J. (2001): *Prescription Games.* Simon & Schuster, UK, London.

Rost P. (2004): cited in: Big Pharma given a right Rost-ing. Pharmi-Web: http://www.pharmi-web.com/pwToday/default.asp?row_id=352.

Rouhi A.M. (2002): *Beyond Hatch–Waxman: Legislative Action Seeks to Close Loopholes in US Law that Delay Entry of Generics into the Market.* C&EN, Washington, DC.

Safemedicines (2005): Recent Counterfeit Alerts. Partnership for Safe Medicines. USA. http://www.safemedicines.org/safety/counterfeit.html.

Salvarsan (1922): *Reports of the Salvarsan Committee (1922): II – Toxic effects following the employment of arsenobenzol preparations.* Medical Research Council, London. His Majesty's Stationery Office.

Sanders J.C. (1982): De patienteninformatie in het kader van de produktenaansprakelijkheid. (Patient information as an aspect of product liability) *Pharm. Weekbl.*, *117*, 142–144.

Sannerstedt R., Berglund F., Flodh H., Lundberg P., and Prame B. (1980): Medication during pregnancy and breast-feeding. *Int. J. Clin. Pharmacol.*, *18*, 45ff.

Sasisch L. (1997): Cited by Mintzes B 1998, q.v.

Schlosser E. (2001): *Fast Food Nation – The Dark Side of the All-American Meal*. Houghton Mifflin, Boston and New York.

Schutz T.P. (1989): *Returns to women's education*. PHRWD Background Paper 98/001. World Bank, Washington, DC.

Scotland (2005): *Patenting Life? – An Introduction to the Issues*. Society, Religion and Technology Project. Church of Scotland. Consulted 20/04/2005.

Scrip (1977): *Scrip World Pharmaceutical News* (*259*), 9, PJB Publications, Richmond.

Scrip (2000): Scrip's Yearbook, PJB Publications, Richmond.

Scrip (2004a): Scrip Nr. 2923, February 4th.

Scrip (2004b): Scrip Nr. 2930 , February 27th.

Scrip (2004c): Scrip Nr. 2943/44, April 14th/16th.

Scrip (2004d): Scrip Nr. 2947, April 28th.

Scrip (2005): Scrip Nr. 3048, April 22nd.

SEAM (2003): *Presentations made at the SEAM/Rockefeller Foundation Symposium on Pooled Procurement*. 10–11 November 2003. New York.

Shepherd M. (1972): The benzodiazepines. *Prescrib.* J. *12*, 144–147.

SI 2004/1031 (2004): *The Medicines for Human Use (Clinical Trials) Regulations 2004*. Statutory Instrument 2004 No. 1031.

SIF (2004): Social Investment Forum; Media Overview.

SIF (2005): *UK Social Investment Forum: Research Reveals Increasing Burden of Corporate Responsibility Reporting*. London Stock Exchange, 2004/04/05.

Sigelman D.W. (2002): *Dangerous Medicine. The American Prospect* (on line), 13(17).

Silverman M. and Lee P.R. (1974): *Pills, Profits and Politics*. University of California Press, Berkeley, CA.

Silverman M., Lee P.R., and Lydecker M. (1982): *Prescriptions for Death: The Drugging of the Third World*. University of California Press, Berkeley.

Silverman W.A. (1985): *Human Experimentation*. Oxford University Press, Oxford, New York and Tokyo.

Simpson S. (2002): The benefits of formal training in pharmaceutical medicine – a medical director's view. *Pharmaceut. Phys.*, *13(1)*, 10–11.

Sjöström H. and Nilsson R. (1972): *Thalidomide and the Power of the Drug Companies*. Penguin Books, Harmondsworth, Middx.

Social Audit (2005): A suitable case for litigation? *Social Audit*. London.

Soda T. (1980) (Editor): Drug-induced sufferings – medical, pharmaceutical and legal aspects. Excerpta Medica, Amsterdam, Oxford and Princeton.

Spitzer E. (2004): *Higher standards*. Paper presented to the Chautauqua Institution, July 12th.

SPUC (2003): *Society for the Protection of Unborn Children: RU486/prostaglandin briefing*.

SRC (1993): *Informatie betreffende de werkwijze van de Reclame Code Commissie*. (*Information on the procedures of the Netherlands Advertising Code Commission*) Stichting Reclame Code, Amsterdam at p. 19; see also: Anon. (1995): Een stempel krijg je niet zomaar (You don't get a stamp of approval so easily). Zelfzorg, March, 4–6.

Statistics (2004): Prescriptions dispensed in the community. *Statistics for 1993–2003*: England. http://www.publications.doh.gov.uk/prescriptionstatistics/index.htm.

Steinhardt R.G. (2003): *Corporate Responsibility for Human Rights*: *International and Comparative Perspectives*: *The new Lex Mercatoria*. Institute for Public and International Law, University of Oslo.

Stiglitz J. (2004): The social costs of globalisation. *Financial Times*, February 25th. at p. 13.

Stockley I. (1996): *Drug Interactions* (Fourth Edition). Pharmaceutical Press, London.

Stricker B.H.Ch. (1992): In: Stricker B.H.Ch. (Ed.): *Drug-Induced Hepatic Injury* (Second Edition). Elsevier, Amsterdam, London and New York at pp. 100–103.

Submission (2004): Submission to the UN Millennium Commission (Working Group on Access to Medicines) by members of the Group representing the science-based industry.

Sunartono D. (1995): From research to action: the Gunungkidul experience. *Ess. Drugs Monitor*, *20*, 21–22.

Swoboda (1999): *The ethics of pharma-economics*. An examination of the limit of corporate responsibility in the Pharmaceutical Industry. Lecture, 2 April 1999. Web.gsia.cmu.edu/ethics/ swoboda-1999.pdf.

Tafuri G., Creese A. and Reggi V. (1994): National and international differences in the prices of branded and unbranded medicines . *J. Gen. Med. 1(2)*, 120–127.

Teather D., Tomlinson H. (2004): Drug firms accused of spending more on own shares than R&D. *Guardian*, October 12th at p. 20.

Teff H. and Munro C. (1976): *Thalidomide, the Legal Aftermath*. Saxon House, Farnborough.

Teixeira P.R. (2001): *The Brazilian experience in universal Access to Drugs.* Paper delivered to the WHO/WTO Workshop on Differential Pricing and Financing of Essential Drugs, Høsbjør, 8–11April.

Telegraph (2002): Anon. Morning-after pill advert sparks criticism. *The Daily Telegraph*, 24 January 2002.

The Cardiac Arrhythmia Suppression Trial (CAST) Investigators (1989): Preliminary report: effect of encainide and flecainide on mortality in a randomized trial of arrhythmias suppression after myocardial infarction. *N. Engl. J. Med.*, *321*, 406–412.

Tickell S. (2005): *The Antibiotic Innovation Study: Expert Voices on a Critical Need. Report on interviews conducted for the Dag Hammarskjold Foundation*, Upsala, September 2005.

Times (2004): Anon: Drug firm "kept quiet about lethal side-effect." *The Times*, November23rd.

TPC (1992): Government of Australia (1992): Trade Practices Commission; *Final Report on the self-regulation of promotion and advertising of therapeutic goods*. Canberra, ACT at p. 7.

Trap B. and Lessing C. (1995): *ZEDAP Survey 1995*. Ministry of Health and Welfare, Harare.

Trap B., Holme H.E. and Hogerzeil H.V. (2002): Prescription habits of dispensing and non-dispensing doctors in Zimbabwe. *Hlth Pol Plan.*, *17*, 268–296.

TRIPS (1994): *The TRIPS Agreement: Appendix to the Final Act of the Uruguay Round of Trade Negotiations of 1994*. See also: UNCTAD (1996): *The TRIPs Agreement and Developing Countries*. UNCTAD/ITE/1. UN Publications, New York and Geneva.

Troullier P., Olliaro P., Torreele E., Orbinski J., Laing R. and Ford N. (2002): Drug development for neglected diseases: a deficient market and a public policy failure. *Lancet*, *359*, 2188– 2194.

TRS (1977): *WHO Technical Report Series*, No.615.

Tuffs A. (2001): Bayer faces potential fine over cholesterol lowering drug. *Br. Med. J.*, *323*, 415.

Tufts (2001): Tufts Center for the Study of Drug Development (Press Release): *Tufts Center for the Study of Drug Development Pegs Cost of New Prescription Medicine at $802 Million*. November 30th.

Türmen T. (1999): Making globalisation work for better health. *Development: Special issue on Responses to Globalisation – Rethinking Health and Equity*, *43(4)*, 8–11.

TWN (2001): High Time for UN to break "Partnership" with the ICC.

UDHR (1948): Universal Declaration of Human Rights. United Nations General Assembly, resolution 217 A (III) of 10 December.

UN (1948): *Universal Declaration of Human Rights.* Art 25(1). U.N. Resolution 217 A (III), United Nations, New York.

UN (2003): *Norms of Responsibility of Transnational Corporations and Other Business Enterprises with Regard to Human Rights.* UN Doc. E/CN.4/Sub.2/2003/XX, E/CN.4/Sub.2/2003/WG.2/WP.1 United Nations, New York.

UN (2005): UN Economic and Social Council: (15 February 2005) Commission on Human Rights: *Report of the United Nations High Commissioner on Human Rights on the responsibilities of transnational corporations and related business enterprises with regard to human rights.*

UNAIDS (2000): UNAIDS: *Report on the global HIV/AIDS epidemic,* June 2000.

UNAIDS (2003): *The Accelerating Access Initiative.* UNAIDS, Geneva.

UNCHR (2000): UN Commission on Human Rights. *Proposed Draft Human Rights Code for Companies,* Geneva, 25 May 2000.

UNCTAD (2005): http/globstat.unctad.org/html/lg_tncw0_data.html. Consulted April 2005.

USS (2005): *Ethics for USS Online: ISS Promotes Access to Medicine.* Ethics for USS, Oxford.

UT (1998): *College of Pharmacy: Students' Handbook – Code of Ethics.* University of Texas, Austin, TX.

Van Hall E. (1997): The menopausal misnomer. *J. Psychosom. Obstet. Gynecol., 18(2),* 59–74.

Vasella (2000): Cited by Pilling D. *Drugs industry must show heart. Financial Times,* November 24th.

Velasquez G., Madrid Y. and Quick J.D. (1998): *Health Reform and Drug Financing: Selected Topics.* WHO, Geneva.

Vernick J.S., Mair J.S., Teret S.P. and Sapsin J.W. (2003): Role of litigation in preventing product-related injuries. *Epidemiol. Rev., 25,* 90–98.

Von Liebig J. (1832): Über die Verbindungen, welche durch die Einwirkung des Chlors und Alkohol, Aether, ölbildenes Gas und Essiggeist entstehen. *Ann Pharmacol (Heidelberg),* l, 182–230.

Wagstaff G. (2001): as cited in Bhushan I. et al: *Human Capital of the Poor in Vietnam.* Asian Development Bank.

Walsh A. (1975): Personal communication.

Warner S. (2004): High-priced biotech drugs: Are they worth it? *The Scientist,* December 6th 2004 at pp. 42–43.

Washburn L. (2002): *Girl gets $4.7M for Vaccine Injuries.* hhttp://www.whale.to/a/girl.html. Consulted 26 January 2005.

Watal J. (2000): *Intellectual Property Rights in the WTO and Developing Countries.* Kluwer Law International.

Wax P.M. (1995): Elixirs, diluents, and the passage of the 1938 Federal Food, Drug and Cosmetic Act. *Ann. Intern. Med. 122(6),* 456–461.

Weissbrodt D. (2000): *Proposed draft human rights code of conduct for companies.* Working Paper prepared for the Commission on Human Rights, Sub-Commission on the Protection and Promotion of Human Rights. 52nd Session, Item 4 of the Provisional Agenda, Working Group on the Methods and Activities of Transnational Corporations, 18 May.

White N.J. (1999): Antimalarial drug resistance and mortality in falciparum malaria. *Trop. Med. Intl. Health, 4,* 469–470.

WHO (1946): *Constitution of the World Health Organization.* WHO, Geneva.

WHO (1988): *Ethical Criteria for Medicinal Drug Promotion.* WHO, Geneva.

WHO (1988): WHO: *Ethical Criteria for Medicinal Drug Promotion.* WHO, Geneva, paras 14–16.

WHO (1990): The Role of the Pharmacist in the Health Care System. Document WHO/PHARM/DAP/90.1. WHO, Geneva.

WHO (1995): *Report of the WHO Expert Committee on National Drug Policies*, June. (WHO(/DAP/95.9).

WHO (1997): *WHO: Public–Private Roles in the Pharmaceutical Sector.* WHO/DAP/97.12. WHO, Geneva.

WHO (1998a): WHO/DAP: *Estimating Drug Requirements – a Practical Manual.* WHO, Copenhagen.

WHO (1998b): World Health Organization, Drug Action Programme: *Health Reform and Drug Financing.* Document WHO/DAP/98.3 at p. 4.

WHO (1999): WHO and collaborating bodies: *Guidelines for Drug Donations.* Revised edition, 1999. WHO/EDM/PAR/99.4. WHO, Geneva.

WHO (2000a): *WHO Medicines – Strategy: Framework for Action in Essential Drugs and Medicines Policy – 2000–2003.* WHO, Geneva. See also draft of *Framework for Action in Essential Drugs and Medicines Policy 2004–2007* (WHO 2003). WHO, Geneva.

WHO (2000b): WHO/essential drugs and medicines policy: global comparative pharmaceutical expenditures with related reference information. *Health Economics and Drugs.* EDM Series no. 3. EDM/PAR/2000.2) 56.

WHO (2000c): WHO/EDM 2000.1 (2000): *The Essential Drugs Strategy.* WHO, Geneva.

WHO (2000d): WHO: Major progress, yet huge inequities remain. *WHO Policy Perspectives on Medicines*, 2, *1*. WHO, Geneva.

WHO (2000e): *WHO Policy Perspectives on Medicines*, 2, WHO, Geneva.

WHO (2000f): WHO: Country progress indicators for components of WHO Medicines Strategy 2000–2003. *Policy Perspectives on Medicines*, *1*, Table 2. WHO, Geneva.

WHO (2001): Resolution WHO 55.14 of the 54th World Health Assembly on *Accessibility of Essential Medicines.*

WHO (2002a): 25 questions and answers on health and human rights. *Health and Human Rights Publication Series*, *1*, 10, WHO, Geneva.

WHO (2002b): WHO: *Global Strategy for Traditional and Complementary Alternative Medicine 2002–2005.* WHO, Geneva.

WHO (2002c): Promoting rational use of medicines: core components. *WHO Policy Perspectives on Medicines*, 5. WHO, Geneva.

WHO (2002d): *WHO: How to Develop and Implement a National Drug Policy* (Second Edition). WHO, Geneva.

WHO (2002e): *WHO: Core Indicators for Monitoring National Drug Policies.* WHO, eneva.

WHO (2002f): WHO: Access to essential medicines is fundamental to human rights. *Policy Perspectives on Medicines*, *4*. WHO, Geneva.

WHO (2003): Effective medicines regulation: Ensuring safety, efficacy and quality. *WHO Policy Perspectives on Medicines*, *Nr. 7.* WHO, Geneva.

WHO (2003): Resolution WHO 56.27 of the 56th World Health Assembly on *Intellectual Property Rights, Innovation and Public Health.*

WHO (2003): *World Health Report 2003: Shaping the Future.* World Health Organization, Geneva.

WHO (2003a): *Substandard and Counterfeit Medicines*. WHO Fact sheet no. 275 November 2003. WHO, Geneva.

WHO (2003b): *WHO Model List of Essential Medicines*. WHO, Geneva.

WHO (2003c): The quality of antimalarials – a study in selected African countries. Maponga C. and Ondari C. (Eds.): WHO, Geneva.

WHO (2003d): How to develop and implement a national drug policy. *WHO Policy Perspectives on Medicines*, *6*. WHO, Geneva.

WHO (2003e): *WHO Model Formulary*. ISBN 92 4 254559 3. WHO, Geneva.

WHO (2003g): WHO Fact Sheet no. 274 (3 by 5 programme for HIV/AIDS) September 2003. WHO, Geneva.

WHO (2004): WHO Medicines Strategy: Countries at the Core 2004–2007. WHO/EDM/2004.5, WHO, Geneva.

WHO (2004): *The World Medicines Situation*. World Health Organization, Geneva.

WHO (2004): *WHO: Priority Medicines for Europe and the World*. WHO/EDM/PAR/2004, WHO, Geneva.

WHO/Bhutan (2002): *WHO: Bhutan Essential Drugs Programme: A Case History*. WHO/EDM/DAP/2000.2. WHO, Geneva.

WHO/EURO (1986): *Guidelines for the Assessment of Medicinal Products for Use in Self-Medication*. WHO, Regional Office for Europe, Copenhagen.

WHO/EURO (1988): *Clinical Consensus Document: The Clinical Investigation of Drugs Used in the Treatment of Rheumatic Diseases*. WHO. Regional Office for Europe, Copenhagen.

WHO/EURO (1993): *Clinical Pharmacological Evaluation in Drug Control*. EUR/ICP/DSE 173. World Health Organization, Regional Office for Europe, Copenhagen.

WHO/EURO (1993a): WHO Regional Office for Europe: *Drug Utilization Studies: Methods and Uses* (Dukes M.N.G. Editor). WHO Regional Publications: European Series No. 45. WHO, Regional Office for Europe, Copenhagen.

WHO/EURO (1993b): World Health Organization. *Clinical Pharmacological Evaluation in Drug Control*. EUR/ICP/DSE 173, WHO, Copenhagen.

WHO/EURO (2003a): Dukes M.N.G., Haaijer-Ruskamp F.M., de Joncheere C.P. and Rietveld A.H. (Editors): Drugs and Money. (Seventh Edition). WHO Regional Office for Europe, Copenhagen and IOS Press, Amsterdam.

WHO/HAI (2003b): *Medicine Prices – a New Approach to Measurement*. (2003 Edition). WHO and Health Action International, Geneva.

WHO/IFPMA (2000): *Improving Access to Essential Drugs Through Innovative Partnerships*, WHO, Geneva.

Willis S.H. and Ruger J.R. (1994): Pharmacoepidemiology: a view from the US courtroom. In: Strom B. (Ed.): *Pharmacoepidemiology* (Second Edition). Wiley, Chichester, New York and Baltimore.

Wilson R.A. (1966): *Feminine Forever*. M. Evans, New York.

Wilson R.A. and Wilson T. (1963): The fate of non-treated postmenopausal women: a plea for the maintenance of adequate estrogen from puberty to the grave. *J. Am. Geriatr. Soc.*, *11*, 347–361.

WMA (1996): *Declaration of Helsinki. 1964, 1975, 1983, 1989, 1996 and ongoing*. World Medical Association, Helsinki.

WOG (1958): *Wet op de Geneesmiddelenvoorziening* (Netherlands Medicines Act).

Wood A.J.J. and Zhou H.H. (1991): Ethnic differences in drug disposition and responsiveness. *Clin. Pharmacokinet.*, *20*, 350–373.

World Bank (1993): *Guidelines for the Development of Drug Policy in Developing Countries*. (Stencil)

World Bank (1993a): World Development Report 1993: *Investing in Health*. World Bank, Washington DC, 1993.

World Bank (1993b): Broun D. and Dukes G. *National Drug Policies and Use of Resources: A Briefing Paper*. World Bank, Washington, DC.

WSMI (2005): Prescription to non-prescription switch. *World Self-Medication Industry*.

WTO (2001): WTO Council for Trade-Related Aspects of Intellectual Property Rights, Special Discussion on *Intellectual Property and Access to Medicines*, *4*, WTO Doc No IP/C/M/31 (Restricted) (July 10, 2001).

Xavier N.B. (2001): *Patents for Future*. Vakils, Feffer and Simons, Mumbai.

Yamey G. (2002): Public sector must develop drugs for neglected diseases. *Br. Med. J.*, *324*, 698.

Yellowcard (2005): *MHRA: Essential Information about Drug Analysis Prints*. Medicines and Healthcare Products Regulatory Agency, London.

Yemen (1996): Government of Yemen: *Statistical Report of the Supreme Board of Drugs and edical Appliances*. Sanaa.

Yuan L. (2004): *Towards systematic analysis and policy recommendations for ATEM*. Presentation to U.N. Millennium Task Force Nr 5.

Zaveri N.B. (2001): *Patents for future for mankind, future for inventor & owner, future for science and technology*. Vakils, Feffer & Simons, Mumbai.

Index

Note: Legal cases and the titles of publications are listed in Italics.